Alternative Histories of English

Most histories of English in use at undergraduate and graduate levels in universities tell the same story. Many of these books are sociolinguistically inadequate, anglocentric and focus on standard English. This leads to a tunnel vision version of the history of the standard dialect after the Middle English period.

This ground-breaking collection explores the beliefs and approaches to the history of English which do not make it into standard textbooks. A range of leading international scholars show how the focus on standard English dialect is to the detriment of those which are non-standard or from other areas of the world. Exploring texts from a largely non-anglocentric perspective, they reveal the range of possible 'narratives' about how different varieties of English may have emerged.

Alternative Histories of English includes histories other than the standard varieties of the language and areas of the world other than Britain and the USA. Emphasis is placed on pragmatic, sociolinguistic and discourse-oriented aspects of English rather than the classical ones of phonology, grammar and lexis. Contributors consider diverse topics which include South African Indian English, southern hemisphere Englishes, early modern English women's writing, and 'politeness'.

Presenting a fuller and richer picture of the complexity of the history of English, the contributors to *Alternative Histories of English* explain why English is the diverse world language it is today.

Richard Watts is Professor of English Linguistics at the University of Berne, Switzerland. **Peter Trudgill** is Professor of English Linguistics at the University of Fribourg in Switzerland.

Alternative Histories
of English

**Edited by
Richard Watts and
Peter Trudgill**

London and New York

First published 2002
by Routledge
11 New Fetter Lane, London EC4P 4EE

Simultaneously published in the USA and Canada
by Routledge
29 West 35th Street, New York, NY 10001

Routledge is an imprint of the Taylor & Francis Group

© 2002 Richard Watts and Peter Trudgill

Typeset in Baskerville by
Prepress Projects Ltd, Perth, Scotland
Printed and bound in Great Britain by
The Cromwell Press, Trowbridge, Wiltshire

British Library Cataloguing in Publication Data
A catalogue record for this book is available
from the British Library

Library of Congress Cataloging in Publication Data

ISBN 0–415–23356–9 (hbk)
ISBN 0–415–23357–7 (pbk)

Contents

Figures

Tables

Contributors

David Crystal is honorary professor of linguistics at the University of Wales, Bangor. His authored works are mainly in the field of language, and include *The Cambridge Encyclopedia of the English Language* and *The Cambridge Encyclopedia of Language*. The founding editor of *Linguistics Abstracts, Journal of Child Language* and *Child Language Teaching and Therapy*, he is currently editor-in-chief of a series of general reference encyclopaedias.

Elizabeth Gordon is a fourth-generation New Zealander, born and educated in Christchurch, New Zealand. She studied at the University of Canterbury (Christchurch) and University College London. Since 1967 she has been teaching at the University of Canterbury, where she is an associate professor in the Department of Linguistics. For the past 20 years she has specialised in sociolinguistics, and her research is mainly into aspects of New Zealand English. She is co-leader of the Origins of New Zealand English project (ONZE) at the University of Canterbury.

Dawn Harvie is working on her doctorate in linguistics at the University of Ottawa. She is the editorial assistant for *Language Variation and Change* and has both written and edited works on African-American English.

Andreas H. Jucker is Professor of English Linguistics at the Justus Liebig University Giessen. His current research interests focus on the history of English, historical pragmatics and cognitive pragmatics. Publications include *Social Stylistics, Historical Pragmatics* (edited), *Discourse Markers* (co-edited), *Current Issues in Relevance Theory* (co-edited), *Historical Dialogue Analysis* (co-edited) and *History of English and English Historical Linguistics*. He is the series editor of *Pragmatics & Beyond New Series* (Amsterdam: Benjamins) and the co-editor of the *Journal of Historical Pragmatics*.

Rajend Mesthrie is Professor of Linguistics at the University of Cape Town and currently President of the Linguistics Society of Southern Africa. His research interests are in sociolinguistics generally, with an emphasis on lanuage contact and variation in the South African context. He is the editor of the forthcoming *Concise Encyclopedia of Sociolinguistics* (Elsevier, 2001).

Sharon Millar is associate professor at the Institute of Language and Communication, University of Southern Denmark, Odense, where she teaches English language and linguistics. Her research interests include language prescription and norms, rhetoric, language acquisition and comprehension. She is particularly interested in the interface between sociolinguistics and psycholinguistics, that is the interrelationship between social/cultural factors and cognition. Ongoing projects range from the nature of metalinguistic awareness among Danish children to the rhetorical analysis of letters-to-the-editor in the Danish press.

Jim Milroy is Professor Emeritus of Linguistics, University of Sheffield. He formerly lectured in English language at the Queen's University of Belfast and is now working in the Department of Linguistics at the University of Michigan. He is author of *The Language of Gerard Manley Hopkins* (Andre Deutsch, 1977), *Linguistic Variation and Change* (Blackwell, 1992) and (with Lesley Milroy) *Authority in Language*, 3rd edn (Routledge, 1999).

Terttu Nevalainen is Professor of English Philology and the Director of the Research Unit for Variation and Change in English at the University of Helsinki, Finland. Her research project 'Sociolinguistics and Language History' has produced the *Corpus of Early English Correspondence* and a number of studies on English historical sociolinguistics. Her other research interests include phonetics and historical lexicology.

Shana Poplack is Professor and Canada Research Chair in Linguistics and Director of the Sociolinguistics Laboratory at the University of Ottawa. An expert in linguistic variation theory and its application to diverse areas of language contact, she has published widely on code-switching, Hispanic linguistics, Canadian French and numerous aspects of African-American English.

Dennis R. Preston would have been a professional basketball player if it hadn't been for his height (5'10") and some small lack of speed. Instead, he is a sociolinguist and dialectologist, at present the President of the American Dialect Society and Director of the 2003 LSA Summer Institute. His main interests are dialect acquisition, language attitudes, folk linguistics (including perceptual dialectology) and general questions of variation and change, including variationist approaches to second language acquisition, He lives quietly with his wife Carol and mother Roena at the end of a cul-de-sac in Okemos, Michigan, USA, where he is in charge of the cooking.

Andrea Sudbury is a post-doctoral fellow at the University of Canterbury, Christchurch. She has research interests in sociolinguistics, particularly dialect contact in the southern hemisphere.

Peter Trudgill is the monolingual Professor of English Linguistics at the bilingual University of Freiburg/Fribourg in Switzerland. He is a Fellow of the British Academy and of the two major Norwegian Academies. His main publications are in the fields of sociolinguistics and dialectology. He is proud to be the Honorary President of the Friends of Norfolk Dialect society.

Gerard Van Herk has recently completed a doctorate in linguistics from the University of Ottawa. He has collected primary data and published articles on African-American and Barbadian Englishes.

Katie Wales is Professor of English Language in the School of English, University of Leeds, UK, and Dean of Learning and Teaching in the Faculty of Arts. She is a Fellow of the Royal Society of Arts (FRSA) and a Fellow of the English Aassociation (FEA). She is editor of the journal *Language and Literature* and ex-Chair of the Poetics and Linguistics Association (PALA). She is a member of the editorial board of the journal *English Today*. Her publications include *Dictionary of Stylistics*, 2nd edn (Pearson Education, 2001), *Personal Pronouns in Present-day English* (Cambridge, 1996) and *The Language of James Joyce* (Macmillan, 1992).

Richard Watts is yet another monolingual Professor of English Linguistics at the University of Berne in multilingual Switzerland. His work has been in the fields of linguistic politeness, pragmatics and the sociolinguistics of English. His previous publications include *Power in Family Discourse* (Mouton de Gruyter, 1991), *Politeness in Language* (with Sachiko Ide and Konrad Ehlich, Mouton de Gruyter, 1992) and *Standard English: The Widening Debate* (with Tony Bex, Routledge). He is currently involved, together with Peter Trudgill and David Allerton, in a research project on the development of a new endo-normative variety of English emerging within Switzerland.

Introduction

In the year 2525[1]

Peter Trudgill and Richard Watts

Imagine for the moment that we are historical linguists of the 'English'(?) language in the year 2525 looking back at the year 2000. It is likely that what we would see would be a richness in terms of dialects – some currently more visible, such as the forms of Standard English, throughout the world, most others more regional and submerged – on a par with the richness that Old and Middle English present to us now, and possibly more so. Unfortunately, however, histories of English as they are typically written most often ignore this richness. Such histories have hitherto tended to tell very much the same story. In spite of obvious differences between them, most textbooks in the field have for the most part presented a system of self-perpetuating orthodox beliefs and approaches which is passed down from one generation of readers to the next. It is difficult, for example, for the modern reader to avoid the impression that the focus of any history of English is necessarily the history of the present-day standard variety. It is true that the histories of Old and Middle English are inevitably histories which involve a recognition of at least regional diversity. But after the Middle English period the focus has traditionally been on the history of the standard dialect. (This then raises the question of which standard variety is being referred to and how a 'standard' variety should be defined.) Generally, histories of English have concentrated, as far as the modern period is concerned, on Standard English in England, with an occasional nod in the direction of the USA and with no acknowledgement of the simple fact that during roughly the last 200 years English has also been spoken, and written in a standard form, by sizeable communities of native speakers in Australia, New Zealand and South Africa, to name only the three most populous areas. Worse, there has been perhaps even less recognition that English has been written and spoken in Scotland for as long as it has been in England.

If the whole point of a history of English were, as it sometimes appears, to glorify the achievement of (standard) English in the present, then what will speakers in the year 2525 have to say about our current textbooks? We would like to suggest that orthodox histories of English have presented a kind of tunnel vision version of how and why the language achieved its present form with no consideration of the rich diversity and variety of the language or any appreciation of what might happen in the future. Just as we look back at the multivariate nature of Old English, which also included a written, somewhat standardised form, so too might the observer 525 years hence look back and see twentieth century Standard English English as being a variety of peculiarly little importance, just as we can now see that the English of King Alfred was a standard form that was in no way the forerunner of what we choose to call Standard English today.

There is no reason why we should not, in writing histories of English, begin to take this perspective now rather than wait until 2525. Indeed, we argue that most histories of English have not added at all to the sum of our knowledge about the history of non-standard varieties of English – i.e. the majority – since the late Middle English period. It is one of our intentions that this book should help to begin to put that balance right.

Our other major intention is the following. In the majority of orthodox histories, most emphasis has been placed on the traditional linguistic foci of phonology, grammar and lexis. We would like to argue for greater coverage of sociolinguistic, pragmatic and discourse-oriented aspects of the language also. Since Labov, it has been clear to all that a complete account of linguistic change must include a sociolinguistic component. Many of the lessons that have been learned from sociolinguistics, however, do not seem to have been taken up by writers of orthodox histories of English. Some of the contributions to this volume attempt to rectify this neglect by discussing the language of women and ethnic minorities, which have been shown to have been of at least equal importance to that of men and majorities when it comes to understanding language change. After all, there have been ethnic minorities in the anglophone world for most of its history and women for all of it. In addition, there has been little recognition that language change is also carried out, albeit unconsciously, by speakers as they use their language in various forms of discourse. Indeed, we are not even at all well informed about how discoursal and pragmatic aspects of the English language have changed during its history. This is particularly the case at the intersection of these two categories – women's discourse and the discourse of minorities – something which some of the authors in this volume also address.

So it is perhaps not too far-fetched to say that many of the orthodox histories of the English language have been sociolinguistically inadequate, anglocentric and based on Standard English. In order to counter this traditional approach, we have chosen in this book to focus attention on:

1   the history of a selection of important non-standard varieties of English;
2   the history of varieties of English beyond England and the USA;
3   the history of communicative and pragmatic aspects of the language;
4   the history of styles and registers other than formal written English;
5   the history of the language as it has been used by speakers and writers other than White males.

Since these five foci largely concern developments in the English language after 1600, we have restricted our attention to the time span between roughly 1600 and the present. The book has been divided into two parts: the first dealing with points 1 and 2, the second with points 3–5.

It is not our intention here to detract from the value of previous, more orthodox histories of English. We fully recognise the enormous value of the research embodied in these volumes, particularly insofar as the history of the first thousand years of the language is concerned. As variations on a theme, the authors of those histories have often used unorthodox methods of looking at the history of English, e.g. going backwards through time, or focusing more on topics than on periods. Our purpose in this book is not to challenge the validity of other histories, but to suggest that the time has come to open up the field to include histories of varieties other than the standard varieties of the language, other areas of the world than Britain and the USA, and other levels of linguistic description than the classical ones of phonology, grammar and lexis. We stand to gain by a fuller and richer picture of the fascinating complexity of the history of English, a picture which attempts to explain why English is the very varied world language that it has become today. If this book is still in print in 2525, something which we hope for and indeed expect, it would be good to feel that we are at least providing readers – if they are still able to understand twenty-first century English – with some sense of that variety.

Note

1 For all readers who are a little less long in the tooth than the editors of this volume or whose musical interests belie other tastes, 'In the year 2525' was a pop song which reached the top of the hit parade in the late 1960s.

Prologue

1   The legitimate language

Giving a history to English

Jim Milroy

Introduction: language histories as codifications

The word 'history' is often understood simplistically to mean an accurate account of what happened in the past; yet, the writing of history can depend on differing underlying assumptions and can lead to differing interpretations. There can therefore be *alternative* histories of the same thing, including alternative histories of language. This chapter is about what may be called the *conventional* history of the English language, as it appears in many accounts, e.g. Jespersen (1962) and Brook (1958). This is seen as a particular *version* of history, which is one of a number of potential versions, and it is assumed that this version has reasonably clear and recurrent characteristics. The most prominent of these are: (1) strong emphasis on the early history of English and its descent from Germanic and Indo-European, and (2) from 1500 onward, an almost exclusive focus on standard English. Thus, the functions of this history are primarily to provide a lineage for English and a history for the standard language (in effect, the recent history of English is defined as the history of this one variety). Plainly, if we chose to focus on varieties other than the standard and if we did not accept the validity of the *Stammbaum* model of language descent, the version of history that we would produce would be substantially different.

This conventional history, as it appears in written histories of English for the last century or more, can be viewed as a *codification* – a codification of the *diachrony* of the standard language rather than its synchrony. It has the same relationship to this diachrony as handbooks of correctness have to the synchronic standard language. It embodies the received wisdom on what the language was like in the past and how it came to have the form that it has now, and it is regarded as, broadly, definitive.

The clearest examples of codifications are histories of grammar and taxonomic accounts of successive sound changes. More discursive accounts, however, also have characteristics of codifications: they classify English as Germanic; they stipulate the dates of Old, Middle, and Modern English; they define the influence of French on English; they codify the Great Vowel Shift; and so on. As manuals of usage are believed to carry authority, so histories of language (including historical dictionaries) are also believed to carry authority. They can give time-depth to the everyday forms of the current language and thereby seem to justify these forms and even sanctify them. They are, however, selective. They foreground and legitimise certain parts of the attested evidence from the past and give justifications for rejecting other parts of the evidence. By sifting through the evidence, they establish a *canon* for the orthodox history of English.

Virtually all popular histories before 1980 subscribed broadly to much the same model of language history – the descent from Germanic and the history of the standard – with disputes about methods and about specific points, such as the pronunciation of Early Modern English *a*, but not usually about principles. As the imposition of authority and the definition of a retrospective canon require acceptance and belief, it is at this point that we need to look more closely at how *the ideology of the standard language* (Milroy and Milroy 1999) affects historical accounts. This ideology has language-internal and language-external aspects. The language-internal aspect is a drive toward uniformity and intolerance of variability, but the characteristic that we are primarily interested in here is not language-internal: it is, broadly, social in its effects. I will consider this ideology here in so far as it affects the manner in which historical developments have been presented. The important term here is *legitimisation*.

The selection of one variety as the standard variety and the diffusion of this variety through codification and prescription establish it as the canonical variety. This leads to a sense of legitimacy of this variety. The manuals of usage are effectively law codes, and using non-standard forms is analogous to disobeying the statutes enshrined in law codes. With certain exceptions, as we shall see below, non-standard varieties are seen as illegitimate, and the standard language comes to be looked upon as representative of the English language as a whole. Thus, when the term 'correct' is used in reference to a linguistic form, it has legalistic – and frequently moral – overtones.

Aside from the synchronic imposition of prescriptive grammars and social sanctions against those who do not conform (see Lippi-Green 1997; Milroy and Milroy 1999), there is, however, another aspect of legitimisation, which has the effect of giving even higher status to a language, chiefly in its standard variety. This is what we have called *historicisation*, and historicisation is what this chapter is chiefly about. The histories themselves become from this point of view part of the process of legitimisation. Historicity is an important contribution to the legitimisation of a language, because the possession of a known history strengthens the sense of lawfulness (and recall that many of the world's languages do not have written histories). Speakers can feel assured that it has not simply sprung up overnight like a mushroom (as some 'inferior' languages may be thought to have done): it has an ancestry, a lineage, even a pedigree, and it has stood the test of time. As Lodge (1993: 8) puts it:

> ... standard languages acquire what can be termed 'retrospective historicity', that is they are given, after the event, a glorious past which helps set them apart from less prestigious varieties ...

The more ancient the language can be shown to be, the better, and it is also desirable that, *whatever signs there may be to the contrary*, the language should be shown to be as *pure* as possible. It should not be of mixed ancestry, and it should not have been 'contaminated' – its intrinsic nature should not have been altered – by whatever influences other languages may have had on it. However, it has not been easy for scholars to legitimise English in some of these ways, because this particular language is more than averagely resistant to being forced into the desired mould. But, as we shall see, they have tried very hard to create for English the longest and the purest history possible.

Legitimisation: giving the language a history

Leith (1996: 95–135) and Lass (1997) have described histories of languages as 'stories', and Lass (1997: 5) has further identified history with myth: 'the histories of languages ... are, like all histories, myths'. Although this may be overstated, language histories can certainly acquire mythic aspects – myths of origin, myths of decline and fall, and myths of progress or decay. The Indo-European hypothesis, for example, although rationally arrived at, can be used as a myth of origin and as a support for ideological positions, and, at various times in the last few centuries, many people have been convinced that the English language is in terminal decline because of serious misuse by speakers or writers (see Milroy and Milroy 1999). This view is sustained by an apocalyptic myth, which holds that evil forces are eternally conspiring to destroy the language. Mythic beliefs can be very powerful: believers know that they are simply 'true'. As the *Shorter Oxford English Dictionary* definition of *ideology* puts it, these 'ideas and ways of thinking' are, especially, 'maintained irrespective of events'. Ideologies, of course, can slide seamlessly into myths.

Although myth and legend can certainly affect our beliefs about what happened to the language in the past (some legends are uncritically repeated in history after history), it is extremely desirable in the tradition that the historical investigations themselves should be carried out by legitimate and accountable methods of internal linguistic analysis. Many learned investigations have been carried out, and they have been most highly valued when they have analysed the internal structural properties of the language – its phonology, grammar and lexicon – rather than the sociopolitical embedding of the language. The main features of the lineage and historical development of English, as established in the nineteenth century and early twentieth century, were supported by mainly internal linguistic analysis and argumentation. It is important to emphasise this because, if the analysis is language internal, it is felt that social value judgements are not involved, and the analysis can therefore be viewed as objective, non-ideological, and reliable. This evaluation was crystallised by Saussure, but was believed in by many who had no knowledge of Saussure: 'My definition of language presupposes the exclusion of everything that is outside its organisation or system – in a word of everything known as external linguistics' (Saussure 1983: 20).

Although this internal analysis is in principle non-evaluative, it is in practice virtually impossible in a history to avoid evaluative judgements. Some of the ideologies involved are very obvious. Others are more subtle, and they often concern principles of selection from the data available. The choice of the standard variety as the lawful variety, with the sidelining of other varieties, is driven by considerations that are not internal to language, but are plainly affected by belief systems. Similarly, the cleansing of the data by expunging 'vulgar', 'provincial' or 'dialectal' forms from the analysis has been very common, and similarly motivated. It is inconvenient if too many variants are recognised, invariance is felt to be desirable, and certain attested forms are excluded from the historical account as they are thought not to be valid for various reasons. The desire to establish invariant states of language in the past provides an excuse for biased selectivity. In reality, of course, these language states were not invariant.

The Saussurean internal/external dichotomy is relevant here, as it requires the exclusion of social and geographical variation and sociopolitical information of all kinds. This leads to a focus on an invariant standard form of languages such as English, and this, paradoxically, smuggles into the enterprise a host of judgements of a sociopolitical kind, as the standard form is always defined by mainly language-external argumentation. There is no objective language-internal reason why we should believe that the focus on standard and uniform states will give us better insights into the history of English or the nature of language change than will the study of non-standard or variable states. However, it is difficult to prevent ideological factors from intruding into our 'objective' analysis.

Sometimes, these ideological intrusions are openly admitted. Many scholars have been influenced by ideologies of race, class and nationhood, and notions of linguistic prestige. Very influential scholars have explicitly stated that the history of standard English *is* the legitimate history of English, and the authority of these scholars has ensured that their views have survived into succeeding generations. At the same time these scholars have usually believed that internal analysis is primary and that it is carried out objectively. Among those who have explicitly stated that historical description of English must be based on standard English are historians of very high prestige, including Henry Sweet, H. C. Wyld, Otto Jespersen and, later in the twentieth century, E. J. Dobson – and since much of what I say about these scholars may seem rather negative, I should perhaps add that their writings are still among the indispensable classics of the subject. I have discussed this matter quite fully elsewhere (J. Milroy 1999), and I will confine my comments here to the underlying distinction that drives much of this work: the alleged difference between *legitimate* linguistic changes and *corruptions*.

Legitimate and illegitimate change

Writing in 1899, Sweet stated that traditional dialects were subject to 'disintegrating influences' and were 'less conservative than' the standard 'dialect'. The historical development of English should therefore be accessed through 'literary documents' and evidence from 'educated colloquial speech' (Sweet 1971: 12). A generation later, Wyld (1927: 16–17) and Jespersen (1922: 68) uttered very similar views. We need to appreciate how strong was the literary influence on these scholars. For Wyld, 'the main objects of our solicitude' must be 'the Language of Literature and Received Standard Spoken English'. Jespersen stated that the importance of dialects had been 'greatly exaggerated', and that they are 'further developed' than standard languages 'with their stronger tradition and literary reminiscences'. These scholars were reacting against the Victorian enthusiasm for investigating rural dialects and, at the same time, they were attaching the canon of language history to the canon of literary history, of which it was (for them) a branch. This had the effect of conferring high status and respectability on English, for it is, after all, the language of Shakespeare. But Wyld also had a great deal to say about 'vulgar' and 'provincial' forms of language (e.g. Wyld 1927: 56).

In Wyld's very influential model of the distribution of language varieties, rural dialects are viewed as lawful varieties, and the forms found in them are 'provincial', not 'vulgar'. Although they are not of much importance (as they contribute little to literary history), they, with the standard, are regarded as possessing histories, and it is this historicity that legitimises them. But there is a third type: the 'Modified Standard', and this type (effectively urban English) is liable to be 'vulgar'. Many of its features are seen as uneducated and incorrect attempts to imitate the 'Received Standard', not as legitimate forms. Wyld's classification clearly implies that, unlike rural dialects, modified standards *do not possess historicity*: their forms are illegitimate forms of *standard* English; therefore, they cannot contribute to valid synchronic or diachronic descriptions of the language. By implication, differences that might be detected in these varieties would not represent legitimate linguistic changes, but illegitimate 'vulgarisms' or 'corruptions'. In the next generation, this selectivity and rejection of non-standard forms is particularly clear in E. J. Dobson's account of English pronunciation from 1500 to 1700.

Dobson (1968) argued strongly that there was such a thing as early modern standard English, but at virtually every point in his work, it is plain that what he was describing is an elite variety – defined by social status of *speakers* rather than standardness of language, i.e. despite his focus on internal structure, his criterion was speaker-based and external to language. Evidence for early pronunciation that can be described as 'vulgar' or 'dialectal' was simply rejected. For example, Dobson (1968 II: 151) noted that one source (Pery) 'shows the vulgar raising of M[iddle] E[nglish] *a* to [e]'. This, according to Dobson, is not surprising because Pery's speech 'was clearly Cockney ... The evidence of such a writer does not relate to educated St[andard] E[nglish]'. So into the wastebasket it goes, along with many other 'vulgarisms', even though it attests to early raising of /a/ – a feature that subsequently affected mainstream varieties of English. It is as though uneducated speakers are not allowed to be involved in language history.

This narrowness seems to arise from a single-minded search to discover and describe the *single* variety that can be authoritatively stated to be the direct ancestor of present-day standard English. It must have single parentage and direct descent: these will make it legitimate, theoretically invariant, and largely pure. The idea of single parentage is itself derived from comparative reconstruction methodology and so appears to be non-ideological, but ideological factors do enter in. Dobson's search is, apparently, driven much more by an ideology of social prestige than by internal linguistic reasoning. I will not speculate here as to whether the genetic model of language descent is itself inherently ideological.

Aside from their concern to historicise the standard language, these scholars had inherited from the past the idea that some changes are legitimate whereas other apparent changes are merely 'corruptions'. The clearest statement of the distinction – a generation before Sweet – is in the work of a distinguished American scholar, George Perkins Marsh:

> In studying the history of successive changes in a language, it is by no means easy to discriminate ... between positive corruptions, which tend to the deterioration of a tongue ... and changes which belong to the character of speech, as a living semi-organism connatural with man or constitutive of him, and so participating in his mutations ... Mere corruptions ... which arise from extraneous or accidental causes, may be detected ... and prevented from spreading beyond their source and affecting a whole nation. To pillory such offences ... to detect the moral obliquity which too often lurks beneath them, is the sacred duty of every scholar.
>
> (Marsh 1865: 458)

Some of the Victorian 'corruptions' (including 'Americanisms') complained of by Marsh and others have long since become linguistic changes, and there is no known way in which an incipient 'lawful' change in progress can be objectively distinguished from a 'corruption'. However, the belief that some forms of language (such as urban dialects) are not valid forms, and that changes observed in them are not legitimate changes, has persisted until very recently and may still be current in some quarters. Some people, it seems, should not be allowed to participate in language change.

The intrusion of social, and even moral, judgements into a subject that is alleged to possess a scientific and objective methodology could not be clearer than it is here. In interpreting the past, this conviction has often blinded scholars to facts that are staring them in the face. For example, although there is ample evidence in Middle English spellings that initial [h]-dropping was variably present in the thirteenth century, this evidence could not be taken seriously by them, as [h]-dropping is a modern 'vulgarism'. It was inconceivable to them that some sturdy Anglo-Saxon yeoman could have dropped his [h]s; even if he had, this could not be a valid part of the history of the language anyway. It was preferable to explain it away purely speculatively as invalid evidence arising from Anglo-Norman unfamiliarity with written English (Skeat 1897), and to exclude it from the canonical history (see Milroy 1983), even though it is a completed sound change in many dialects.

The recent history of English as it has been handed down to us is, almost exclusively, the history of what is claimed to be *standard* English. Yet, as I have implied above, what has been described as sixteenth century standard pronunciation would be more correctly labelled: *the pronunciation of gentlemen and persons of rank including members of the Royal Court.* 'Standard' in this use is identified with 'high status', but it is the high status of *speakers* that is involved, not of language, since language in its internal properties is indifferent to status. Thus, when these scholars refer to standard English they do not mean 'the most uniform variety' – defined by its internal properties. They mean 'English as used by high-ranking persons'. This implies that the language does not belong to all its speakers – only to a select few.

Elite pronunciation, however, is not necessarily standard pronunciation. It is quite unlikely that there was a general consciousness of a *standard* pronunciation in 1600: what people did know about were socially marked pronunciations that were indexical of social status, regional origin and belongingness. A particular standard pronunciation may also happen to be a high-status pronunciation, but it is not the status of speakers that defines a variety as a standard. It is internal uniformity, wide acceptance in society, and wide adaptability in different functions that are the important factors in standardisation. If the prestige of speakers and writers becomes involved, this is secondary. These scholars seem to have created between them something amounting to a myth, which is that *the history of English pronunciation since 1500 is a unilinear and exclusive history of 'polite' or 'elite' English.* Other varieties did not exist, or were unacceptable English, or were not important. Unsurprisingly, there have been discernible effects of their views on scholars of later generations, who have been influential in their turn. I have space here for one example.

According to Gimson (1970), the 'Received Pronunciation' ('RP') that developed, probably in the 'public' boarding school system, in the nineteenth century is a direct descendant of the language of the Elizabethan Court (approximately what Dobson described) three centuries before, and Honey (1997) seems to have a similar view. This gives an ancestry to RP that makes it respectable, but it assumes rigid unilinearity and smuggles class distinction into a description that is supposed to be objective and language internal. It is apparently unthinkable that RP could have had more humble origins or that socially inferior varieties could have contributed to it; therefore, it is a history of one elite accent developing in a straight line without regard for the massive variability that necessarily existed in successive speech communities in the course of three centuries. RP in this account has a single parent, just as the modern standard language in general is believed to have single parentage: the elite accent of the Elizabethan Court is projected forward to the nineteenth century in a sociolinguistic vacuum in which the upper classes are totally insulated from the effects of other orders of society. The fact that this is all intrinsically unlikely is, it seems, irrelevant. The speech of the Court could even have been recessive, as upper-class language often seems to be, and might well have had little effect on the future. Furthermore, it is arguable that Victorian RP was strongly influenced by *middle* class speech, as the Victorian expansion of the public school system affected chiefly the middle class. However this may be, the main generalisation here is that RP is given an approved history and a respectable, legitimate ancestry which is narrowly unilinear and pure. But language change does not proceed in straight lines: speech communities are complex networks of relationships, and language is always variable. These general facts about language in society are largely neglected in conventional historical accounts of English.

Legitimisation: dialects and Germanic purism

It is well known that a strong interest in English rural dialects developed in the nineteenth century, its great monument being Alexander Ellis's five-volume *Early English Pronunciation* (1869–89). In some ways, this research interest was felt to be in opposition to the interests of historical linguists (Wyld disapproved of it and considered it to be irrelevant after the medieval period), but in other ways it was complementary, and it could potentially support certain ideological claims – about the richness and diversity of English, for example. It was strongly antiquarian and continued thus into the late twentieth century. The effect was to historicise the rural dialects of English – to give them histories side by side with the standard language and, in some cases, to codify them. That is to say that they became in the later nineteenth century *academically* legitimate: if this had not been so, it would not have been necessary for Sweet, Jespersen and Wyld to play down their importance. In that century, following the Industrial Revolution, the population of urban areas was rising rapidly: to the antiquarian mind it was important to describe the rural dialects before they died out, much as scholars now hurry to describe endangered languages. They were treasure troves to be plundered for the precious information that they preserved about the past states of the English language, and the language of the peasantry was often thought to be purer – i.e. more Anglo-Saxon – than the standard language. The early volumes of the *Transactions of the Philological Society* contain articles on English rural speech, many of which are purist in tone and hostile to French and classical influences on English (see J. Milroy 1977).

The strong Germanic purist movement that developed in the later nineteenth century was bound up with dialectological interests. There was a prominent train of thought that we can describe as 'anti-standard', which held that as rural dialects were 'purer' than the standard language they were of greater value in historical researches. If there was evidence that a rural dialect had been influenced by the standard, this was described as *contamination* or some similar term. An important ideological aim behind this movement was to support the view that English has a legitimate Germanic ancestry (mainly Anglo-Saxon, but also Norse), and the French element was quite often considered to be illegitimate. The most extreme Anglo-Saxon purist, the Rev. William Barnes, not only wrote poetry and translated the Song of Solomon into his native Dorset dialect (1859), he also wrote a grammar of the English language (1878) using a pure Germanic vocabulary. 'Grammar' was *speechcraft;* 'consonant' was *breathpenning;* 'degrees of comparison' were *pitches of suchness.* What is important here is that, by these means, rural dialects were legitimised and the Germanic ancestry of English further validated. Urban dialects, as we have noticed, were emphatically *not* believed to be of antiquarian value and were *not* legitimised. Until the late 1960s, no British scholar who hoped for career advancement would have undertaken a study of an urban variety.

The nineteenth century, however, was also a century of empire, and the standard variety had become an important world language. The rise of dialect studies is, paradoxically, related to this, in that it is the whole glorious language that now has to be given a history, and this happens when the language, primarily in what is believed to be its standard, literary variety, is felt to be important enough for this to be appropriate – typically when it has achieved the status of the chief language of a nation-state, and in some cases a great empire. As the status of the standard variety is at this point rather secure, it becomes acceptable, in certain cultural and intellectual climates of opinion (notably those that followed the Romantic movement), to inquire into the histories of other varieties (such as rural dialects) and give them histories also. These thus become legitimate parts of the history of the language as a whole, and, although they are given a subsidiary place, they can be seen as enriching that history.

There is probably an additional ideological reason why rural, but not urban, dialects were acceptable. As rural dialects are known to be recessive, spoken only by peasants in remote places, they are unthreatening to the status of the standard. Thus, it is ideologically safe to view them as legitimate forms. Those aspects of the history that are not inquired into do not, however, become legitimate parts of the canon, and, as it happens, the widely used urban varieties that have been traditionally excluded from study are the ones that actually pose the greater potential threat to the continuation of the standard. They have an unfortunate habit of intruding themselves into it: the urban 'vulgarisms' of one period can become the mainstream forms of another, and this cycle has probably been in operation for centuries. Urban varieties, from medieval London English onward, are a vital constituent part of the real history of English. In a purely scientific world of objective language scholarship, these developing varieties would have been valued as crucially important in the study of language change, but this ideal world is one that has never existed.

Historicity: the ancient language

All languages must have histories in so far as all languages have had some form of existence through time, but only a few languages have attested histories. When a language has no recorded history, the main way in which some information about its history can be recovered is by the comparative method, and this is in principle free of social evaluations. Languages with recorded histories are also subject to comparative method, but these also necessarily have social histories, as records of them were all produced in some form of sociopolitical context, and more information about the past states of such languages is accessible. The problem of determining the true 'history' of these historically attested languages becomes one of how the accidentally preserved records of the past are to be interpreted and expounded for those periods of time in which such records are available. English is one of these languages.

It is in this interpretative activity that ideological positions intrude. English as the language, first of one powerful nation-state and subsequently of others (pre-eminently the USA), and also the language of a great empire, must be given a glorious history, which, as we have noticed, should be a very long history, preferably unbroken and continuous and – as far as possible – pure. Change within the language should preferably be endogenous, and not triggered by external influences such as language contact. But the problem with English as a language – one that makes ideological positions almost impossible to avoid – is that at first sight *it does not fit very easily into the desired pattern*. As a Germanic language, it is in many respects the 'odd man out': it has characteristics that look more like Romance than Germanic; Old English ('Anglo-Saxon', up to AD1100) is very different from Middle and Modern English. Modern German is more similar to Old High German and Italian is arguably more similar to Classical Latin than English is to Anglo-Saxon. Middle English (1100–1500) seems, on the surface, to have appeared quite suddenly as a language rather distinct from the Old English that preceded it. It is therefore quite possible to argue plausibly that the development of English has *not* been continuous, but has been interrupted at some points, and that it is *not* pure: this is, broadly, the position of C.-J. N. Bailey (1996). The efforts of language historians over the past 150 years, however, have been rather single-mindedly devoted to demonstrating that *despite appearances to the contrary*:

1   English is a very ancient language;
2   English is *directly descended from the Germanic branch of the Indo-European family of languages*;
3   English dates *from the fifth century settlement of Germanic tribes in the island of Britain*;
4   English has an unbroken and continuous history since that time and *is the same language now as it was then*;

5   English *is not a mixed language*: changes in its structure have come about
    for mainly language-internal reasons and have not been sufficient to alter
    its essential character.

The fact that these propositions do not all appear to be self-evidently correct
has made it particularly desirable that they should be strongly affirmed,
ingeniously argued for, and stoutly defended. The ideology requires that
English should be ancient and pure with a continuous history.

The answers we are able to give to the above propositions, however, are
largely ideological. In the historical dimension, we cannot define what is
'English' and what is not 'English' by internal analysis *alone*. We cannot
demonstrate by internal analysis alone when 'English' began, or when one
stage of English gave way to another. Nor can we demonstrate by internal
analysis alone that Anglo-Saxon is the same language as modern English, or
a different language which is its direct ancestor, or a related language which
is not a direct ancestor. To answer these questions, we have to appeal to
ideological positions.

Some commentators have given English a very long history, and its ancient
lineage has been seen as a matter of great pride. In this vein, one writer
(Claiborne 1983, cited by Bailey 1991) claims that English is 8,000 years old.
Competent historians of English have wisely contented themselves with rather
lesser claims, but they are tendentious nonetheless, and they have been
expressed in this way since the later nineteenth century. Here is Walter Skeat
– a very distinguished medievalist:

> … eyes should be opened to the Unity of English, that in English literature
> there is an unbroken succession of authors, from the reign of Alfred to
> that of Victoria, and that the English which we speak now is absolutely
> one in its essence, with the language that was spoken in the days when
> the English first invaded the island and defeated and overwhelmed its
> British inhabitants.
>
> (Skeat 1873: xii, cited in Crowley 1990)

This is a common Victorian theme, and it is often expressed as being about
nationhood and race as well as language. More immediately, it is associated
with literary and cultural history, and it remained a familiar claim well into
the later twentieth century. If the fifth century is when the English language
began, it becomes possible to assert (more or less as a 'fact') that 'English'
has one of the oldest literatures in Europe. If it is asserted that Anglo-Saxon
literature is actually English literature, it can also be argued that this
literature must be included in any university English literature syllabus. At
the Universities of Oxford and London and others that were influenced by
them, it most certainly was. Yet, we can easily – possibly more easily –
demonstrate on internal linguistic grounds that Anglo-Saxon is *not* English
and that the literature is *not* part of the history of 'English' literature. It is

also an Old Germanic language and an Old Germanic literature, like Old Norse and Old High German. The question cannot be decided by internal analysis alone, because it is not wholly a linguistic (or even a literary) question: it is ideological. Utterances like those of Skeat are statements of sentiment, not of fact.

Statements like this often imply, or assert, the identity of language with nation, and this underlies the traditional view on the origins of English as a distinct language. It is usual to state that 'English' dates from the fifth century settlement in Great Britain of a set of Germanic-speaking peoples – the Angles, Saxons, and Jutes. As the spoken dialects of these peoples had presumably been much the same before they settled in Britain, this date is arbitrary in linguistic terms and is determined by geography and politics rather than by any known linguistic factor. The language during this period was a West Germanic dialect or series of dialects, very similar to Old Frisian, Old Saxon and Old Low Franconian. It differed from Old Frisian chiefly in the fact that it happened to be spoken on the island of Britain, and only negligibly in linguistic form. There are no texts from that period, and there is no reason to suppose that in the fifth century there were substantial differences among these West Germanic dialects. Even written Old Frisian, if we allow for different spelling conventions, looks very similar to some dialect of Old English. The language of the following thirteenth century Frisian extract is similar to the much earlier Old English of the tenth century:

> Thet was thet fiarde bod: Thu skalt erian thinne feder and thine moder, thet tu thaes-to laenger libbe

> [That was the fourth commandment: Thou shalt honour thy father and thy mother, that thou mayest live the longer]
>
> (Robinson 1992: 184)

If it were possible to assemble a set of similar contemporary early texts from Old Frisian and the four major dialects of Old English and we had no further information about these varieties, it would almost certainly be difficult to say on language-internal grounds alone whether they represented one language or more than one, or where to draw the line between them. A Middle English text, on the other hand, would display obvious differences.

From the nineteenth century onwards there has been a huge mass of detailed scholarship on the relations between Germanic languages. Hans Frede Nielsen has reviewed much of this, and for the purpose of tracing ideological influences, certain main features stand out. First, it appears to have been Henry Sweet (an Englishman) who first postulated (1877: 562) the prior existence of a pre-English 'Anglo-Frisian' stage, and later H. M. Chadwick (also British) who commented (1907: 60) that there can be no doubt that Frisian is 'by far the [language] most nearly related to English'. Nielsen's conclusion (1981: 256–7) is that Old English is indeed most similar to Old Frisian. The ideological effect here is that Anglo-Frisian supplies the immediate pre-history of English and extends its pedigree backwards. It becomes possible in principle for someone like Claiborne to state that 'English' was actually spoken on the continent before the invasion of Britain, and, indeed, there is no purely linguistic reason why, if we recognize Old English as 'English', this should not be accepted – in language-internal terms it is a seamless continuum. From this point of view, the English language *as a language* does not have a beginning.

But this is not what most scholars have wanted to believe, as there has also been a strong tendency, again traceable to Sweet, but supported by others, to claim that the Anglo-Saxon dialects (Kentish, West Saxon, Mercian, Northumbrian) were not differentiated at the time of the settlements: they underwent differentiation after the invasion of Britain (Nielsen 1981). As the settlers came from different places and settled at different times, this is hardly plausible: its purpose appears to be ideological. This putative unity suggests a beginning for the English language within Britain, as the undifferentiated variety is then identifiable as the beginning of English as a single separate language. There is no direct empirical evidence to demonstrate this, but there is good reason to believe that, on the contrary, the dialects *were* differentiated. But internal analysis of linguistic forms is not in itself capable of settling this kind of question: it is ideological.

Anglo-Saxon has to be a unity that is distinct from these other languages, but at the same time closely related to them and descended from the same ancestor. In this way, it is given both a distinct beginning and a lawful ancestry. It is legitimised.

Historicity: the continuity and purity of English

The standard view of the transition from Old to Middle English is that, although it appears in the texts to be abrupt, it was actually gradual, and this of course backs up the idea of the ancient language and unbroken transmission. Old English, however, is structurally very unlike Modern English or most of Middle English in a number of ways. To show that it is the 'same' language on purely internal grounds actually requires some ingenuity. It is much easier to show that it is different. There are, for example, several case distinctions, three grammatical genders, a predominantly Germanic vocabulary, many noun declensions and verb conjugations, and word-order conventions which, although variable, resemble other Germanic languages more than they resemble modern English and later Middle English. As C.-J. N. Bailey (1996: 351) points out, although Middle English can be rapidly acquired by the modern reader, 'it takes a long while for the same individual to learn Anglo-Saxon inflections and grammar, and that person cannot read it (even with a lexicon) with any ease after several months of working at it'. Generations of English literature students in Britain have, often reluctantly, been required to read Old English in the original on the grounds that Old

English literature is 'English' literature, and they have frequently opined that it resembles Dutch or German more than it resembles English. It is not self-evident *from its internal form alone* that it is the same language as modern English, or even that it is the direct forebear of modern English.

To conventional historians of English, this difficulty has merely constituted a challenge. English *has* to have ancient origins, it *has* to have a clearly defined lineage, it *has* to be a Germanic language, and the transition from Anglo-Saxon to Middle English *has* to be seamless. Scholars have had to find as many reasons as possible to argue for continuity. For them, this Anglo-Saxon language was definitely English, and to emphasise the point they preferred to call it Old English, rather than Anglo-Saxon. Jespersen (1962: 17–54), writing about Old English (the first edition of this book was published in 1938), repeatedly called the language and the people simply 'English', rather than 'Anglo-Saxon'. Let us look, however, at a brief passage from King Alfred's writings:

> Ælfred kyning hateð gretan Wærfærð biscep his wordum luflice and freondlice; ond ðe cyðan hate ðæt me com swiðe oft on gemynd, hwelce wiotan iu wæron geond Angelcynn ...

> [King Alfred bids to greet his bishop Wærfærth in affectionate and friendly words; and (I) bid to inform you that it came very often into (my) mind, what learned men there used to be throughout the English people (or nation) ...]

If we did not know the provenance of this text and had no other Old English (OE) texts, we would be unlikely to classify it as 'English' or even relate it closely to *Middle* English. It is defined as English because it is known to have been a language related to modern English that was spoken on the soil of England by a famous king who is credited with uniting the country as one nation (*Angelcynn*), and who called the language *englisc*, even though he was a *Saxon*. So it is English for reasons that are historical, political, geographical, and ideological. What is important here is that to define it as the same language as the modern one is to justify the extension of the history of English back to the fifth century.

Strong continuity from OE through Middle English (ME) to Present-day English (PresE) has been generally favoured, and there has been a tendency to explain the many changes in terms of internal developments within the language, rather than, for example, by adducing the possible effects of other languages or the possible structural effects of language contact situations in general. It is common to come across the argument that many of the apparent phonological differences between OE and Early Middle English (EarlyME) are purely scribal (a result of the displacement of the OE writing system by one influenced by Norman French), and it is possible to single out two influential papers in the 1930s that were viewed as further consolidating the continuity of English. The first, by Malone (1930), argues that many of those features that are thought to characterise ME had already made an appearance in OE. The second is a famous essay by Chambers (1932) 'On the continuity of English prose from Ælfred to Thomas More and his school'. This is focused on the Norman Conquest and plays down its importance, attempting to correct the pro-Norman (or anti-Germanic) bias of historians and literary critics. In a careful analysis, the Anglo-Saxon prose-writing tradition is shown to have survived in many of its characteristics throughout the transitional period and well into Early Modern English (EModE). In fact, this essay was aimed at the literary critics who rejected Anglo-Saxon literature as not 'English', and not primarily at linguists. Nonetheless, it was most certainly used as part of the argument for the continuity of the language, in times when the historical study of language was an appendage to the study of literature, and when the vast differences between speech and prose were not well understood. Subsequently, a great deal of industry was expended on backing up the continuity argument. It is clearly stated by, for example, Bennett and Smithers (1966: xlviii–xlix), with reference to ME, that: '... the impact of an alien language spoken by a new ruling class did not substantially affect or modify the structure of English'; the same view has been expressed by many others.

Written documents still appear in a later version of Alfred's dialect (West Saxon) until around 1100. Shortly after this there is a sudden apparent change, and the language begins to look more like PresE, especially in eastern parts of the country (the mid-twelfth century Peterborough Chronicle continuations have lost grammatical gender and many inflectional distinctions); yet, until the mid-thirteenth century, most ME dialects are not particularly easy for the modern reader. The early Victorian scholars who planned the *New (Oxford) English Dictionary* seem to have been quite clear on what constituted the beginning of English. With great precision they dated it at 1258, not the fifth century (Crowley 1989a: 113). This decision was not only practical, but reasonable in terms of internal linguistic structure, and we can look at the language of a well-known thirteenth century lyric to see why it was:

Blow, northerne wynd,
Sent þou me my swetyng!
Blow, norþerne wynd,
Blou, blou, blou!

(Bennett and Smithers 1966: 121)

This is plainly English and is dissimilar to the language of Alfred, and the same applies to other contemporary texts. The scholars who insisted on continuity and identity of OE with PresE (such as Skeat, cited above) also knew this, but they were to varying degrees ideologically committed to proving that what appeared to be so was not actually so. What looks different is – really – similar, and, conversely, what looks similar is – really – different. Varieties that look similar in more modern times (e.g. Shakespeare's English and ours) are often said to have been in reality much more divergent from each other than they appear, whereas OE is argued to be much more similar to later ME than it appears. The vigour with which the argument is pursued is in inverse proportion to the plausibility of the claim. It depends on the obvious fact that OE does not seem to the uninitiated to be 'English', so it has to be proved that it really *is* English.

Although it is known that OE was in some counties in intimate contact with Old Norse and that the language was subsequently strongly influenced by Norman French, this gradualist unilineal view of the history of English is still the preferred view. It has been part of the conventional discourse of English language history for well over a century. Recently, it has been suggested that English has changed as much in the last four centuries (since Shakespeare) as it did in the four centuries between King Alfred and 1300. If this were true, we might have to accept that the development from OE to ME is a seamless continuum and that OE is therefore the same language as modern English. But it is not true.

Roger Lass subscribes to part of this claim – at least with reference to phonetic history. He states (Lass 1997: 205n) that 'the likelihood that Shakespeare ... would have been auditorily intelligible to a modern English speaker is vanishingly small'. It is of course true that there have been many internal changes in English since 1600 (in the conventional history almost nothing happened after 1600), but it is quite likely that Elizabethan English, if it survived today, would sound like a somewhat archaic dialect of English and would be largely intelligible – more intelligible to mainstream speakers than an unadulterated rural dialect of present-day Lowland Scots, for example. There is no method precise enough to calculate probabilities either way, but having listened to and understood the recording of Dobson's rather archaic reconstruction of Shakespeare's pronunciation, I find it strange that this claim can be made so confidently. Shakespeare wrote in a variety of modern English.

In agreement with the conventional history, Lass also advocates a general late dating of changes in the history of English and hence a relatively slow development of the modern language; thus, Shakespeare's pronunciation can be represented as relatively archaic. Whereas Minkova and Stockwell (1990), cited by Lass (1997: 289–90n), argue that the lowering and centralisation of the vowels in *bit, put* took place before 1300, Lass argues for the mid-seventeenth century at the earliest. There is a difference of nearly four centuries. Clearly, alternative chronologies of changes make a great deal of difference to what we think Shakespeare might have sounded like, and it will be clear from my advocacy of an early date for initial [h]-loss that I favour relatively early dating of changes when the evidence permits this (see further Milroy 1992). That is, I favour the view that, since we do not have direct access to these things, we must accept that early changes are possible or probable in variable language states. This differs from the conventional view, and suggests that even Middle English could have had 'advanced' varieties that were quite similar to PresE. But the fact that there can be such wide disagreement demonstrates in itself how difficult it is to find reliable and consistent criteria for interpreting purely internal evidence. Opposing views can be resolutely maintained, although they can usually be neither verified nor falsified; thus, the way is open for ideological positions and special pleading to enter in.

Nowhere is this clearer than in the case study (by Kaufman) in Thomason and Kaufman (1988: 325–7), in support of the view that English is not a mixed language. Using the example of Robert of Gloucester (*c.* 1300), they state (1988: 326): 'We doubt that from Alfred to Robert more change occurred than from Shakespeare to us'. They then list a number of differences among these, some of which (such as 'lexical attrition and simplification') are effectively meaningless in the context, while others, such as some alleged vowel changes, are idiosyncratic. They are in any case highly selective. But, most significantly, they do not print an extract either from Alfred or Robert. This is wise, because if they did they would destroy their case. Although Robert's south-west Midland variety maintained more conservative features than the above extract from the lyric (north-west Midland), it *obviously* does not resemble OE more than it resembles modern English:

> In þis manere the barons began hor vrning:
> A Freinss knigt was at Gloucetre, þe sserrue þoru þe king,
> Sir Maci de Besile, and constable also.
> þe barons it bespeke þat it nas nogt wel ido ...

> [In this manner the barons began their attack (lit: 'running'): a French knight was at Gloucester, the sheriff of (lit: 'through') the king, Sir Maci de Basile – and constable also (of the king). The barons agreed that it was not well done]

To justify the claim that this is very close to Alfred's English would take a great deal more ingenuity than Kaufman shows in his discussion.

The traditional scholars who argued the same case were aware of the strong prima facie difficulties that faced them in pursuing their argument. This case study, however, is full of rash and sweeping generalisations – a specimen is: 'Southmarch has just eight Norsification features' (Thomason and Kaufman 1988: 291) (What?) – and there are some astonishing *ex cathedra* pronouncements about the time-depth of established standard English and its influence on dialects. The impression is given that everything is definitively known as fact. Their account of the Great Vowel Shift (GVS) (Thomason and Kaufman 1988: 327) demonstrates precisely why their main claims cannot be taken seriously. They declare that it started with the diphthongisation of /iː/ and /uː/ in or around 1420; then followed a number of raisings in a definite order – in 1430, 1475, 1500, and 1525. No one, of course, actually knows any *facts* about the implementation of the GVS (everything is inferential), almost everything about the order of the changes is disputed, no specialist would dare to specify such exact dates for each individual change, and some believe that there was no such thing as the GVS anyway. But Kaufman *knows* these things and others as established facts, with no need for argument or demonstration. Furthermore, the few quotations given approvingly from Bennett and Smithers (1966) and other conventional historians do not prove that these scholars were either right or wrong.

As for 'mixed' languages – if English does not fit Thomason and Kaufman's narrow definition of 'mixed', it does not follow that it is not mixed by some other definition or that there cannot be differing degrees of mixing. C.-J. N. Bailey in his response (1996: 341) correctly observes that in their argument 'ideology wins over demonstration'. The picture they paint has a strange air of unreality about it, and the driving force behind it is the same ideology of language that has motivated the conventional historian for well over a century – defence of the pure and ancient language and the continuous, unbroken history. The case has been stated over and over again. This study demonstrates how stubbornly the conventional view on purity and continuity has persisted and how desperately it is still defended.

Conclusion

Nothing I have said in this chapter is intended to imply that conventional scholars have always been wrong, and that I know better than they did how the history of English should be presented. What I have attempted to show is something more modest, which does not determine as fact whether English is pure or impure, ancient or modern. This is that the typical history has been influenced by, and sometimes driven by, certain ideological positions. The first of these implicitly suggests that the language is not the possession of all its native speakers, but only of the elite and the highly literate, and that much of the evidence of history can be argued away as error or corruption. The effect of this is to focus on what is alleged to be the standard language, but this is actually the language of those who have prestige in society, which may not always be a standard in the full sense. Of course, it may often be the same as the standard language, but this elitism can also mislead us into believing that speech communities are far less complex than they actually are and that the history of the language is very narrowly unilinear. We need a more realistic history than this.

The second position can be briefly characterised as an ideology of nationhood and sometimes race. This ideology requires that the language should be ancient, that its development should have been continuous and uninterrupted, that important changes should have arisen internally within this language and not substantially through language contact, and that the language should therefore be a pure or unmixed language. I have tried to show that much of the history of English is traditionally presented within this broad framework of belief. The problem, I have suggested, is that, prima facie, English as a language does not seem to fit in well with these requirements. For that reason, much ingenuity has been expended on proving that what does not seem to be so actually *is* so: Anglo-Saxon is English, the development of English has been uninterrupted and the language is not mixed. The most recent strong defence of this position – by Thomason and Kaufman (1988) – is merely the latest in a long line. It demonstrates that this system of beliefs is – for better or worse – still operative in the historical description of English.

Part I

The history of non-standard varieties of English

The purpose of this section of the book is to focus on aspects of the histories of as many as possible of those varieties of English which have often – or even always – been neglected in histories of the language. These are varieties which have been marginalised by historical linguists because they have been regarded as non-standard, and/or which have been ignored because they have been considered to be socially or geographically peripheral in some way. We would point out, as justification for this, that there are very many more non-standard than standard varieties of English in the world; that they are spoken by many more people than Standard English; and that to ignore them does our understanding of the history of the English language no service at all. Non-standard dialects of English have histories too, and these histories are sometimes especially helpful because, as a result of the absence of standardisation, many of the forces of linguistic change are played out in these varieties in a much more unfettered and revealing way than in the standard dialect. We would also point out that the disregarding of varieties of English simply because the people who speak them are not White Englishmen who have for centuries been established in the southeast of England is also not only totally ethnocentric, anglocentric, 'austrocentric' (as Katie Wales says) and unjustifiable, but is also short-sighted in that it disregards an enormous mass of historical data from some of the most interesting and diachronically revealing varieties of the language in existence.

The chapters in this part of the book by Wales, on northern British English, and by Gordon and Sudbury, on the Englishes of the southern hemisphere, try to redress the geographical balance. This is also the focus of Trudgill's paper – on lesser-known varieties of the language – which looks at the native-speaker Englishes of a surprisingly large number of small and often unknown communities in different parts of the world which are nearly always ignored by linguistics scholars and which remain untreated in most historical linguistic discussions. The bias against non-standard varieties is tackled in the chapter by Poplack, van Herk and Harvie, which takes as its starting point the remarkable Ottawa Grammar Resource on Early Variability in English, with a particular focus on implications for the study of the history of African American Vernacular English, which in turn also does something to rectify the ethnocentrism of many histories. Preston's paper on attitudes to varieties of English in North America also deals with the evaluation of non-standard Englishes; and, since Standard English has its origins in the south of England, the paper by Wales also inevitably confronts this issue of the importance of non-standard varieties. Finally, the chapter by Mesthrie tackles the prejudice against the Englishes spoken by non-White speakers in his fascinating examination of the history of Indian English in South Africa. This chapter also confronts the prejudice against 'new' varieties of English – 'newness' probably also being a factor in the relative lack of discussion in the textbooks of the southern hemisphere varieties generally.

2 The history of the lesser-known varieties of English

Peter Trudgill

Histories of the first thousand years or so of the English language obviously have to have a rather narrow geographical focus. Four hundred years ago, in 1600, English had no very important role as a foreign or second language anywhere, and was spoken as a native language in a very small area of the globe indeed: it was the native language of the indigenous population in most of England, and in the south and east of Scotland. It was, however, absent from much of Cornwall and from Welsh-speaking parts of Shropshire and Herefordshire; most of the population of Ireland was Irish-speaking; nearly all of the population of Wales was still Welsh-speaking; the inhabitants of the Highlands and Hebridean Islands of Scotland spoke Gaelic; those of Orkney and Shetland spoke Scandinavian Norn; the population of the Isle of Man was Manx-speaking; and the inhabitants of the Channel Islands were still French-speaking.

During the course of the 1600s this situation changed dramatically. English arrived as a native language – as a result of colonisation – in Ireland, in what is now the United States, and in Bermuda, Newfoundland, the Bahamas, and the Turks and Caicos Islands. It also spread during this time into many island and mainland areas of the Caribbean: Anguilla, Antigua and Barbuda, Barbados, the Cayman Islands, Jamaica, Montserrat, St Kitts and Nevis, the British Virgin Islands, the American Virgin Islands, and the mainland areas of Guyana and Belize. And it is not widely known that areas other than these (in modern times cricket-playing Commonwealth) countries were also settled by anglophones: eastern coastal and island areas of Honduras, Nicaragua and Colombia remain English-speaking to this day. The Dutch island colonies of Saba, St Maarten and St Eustatius have also been English-speaking since the early 1600s; and the mainly Papiamentu-speaking Dutch colony of Bonaire has a sizeable number of indigenous anglophones too.

During the eighteenth century English began its expansion into Wales and north-western Scotland, and into mainland and maritime Canada.

In the nineteenth century, again as a result of colonisation, English expanded to Hawaii, and into the southern hemisphere – not only to Australia, New Zealand and South Africa, as is well known, but also to the South Atlantic Islands of St Helena, Tristan da Cunha and the Falklands, and in the Pacific to Pitcairn Island and Norfolk Island. There was also expansion from the Caribbean islands to eastern coastal areas of Costa Rica and Panama; and the repatriation of African Americans to Sierra Leone and Liberia, as well as an African-American settlement in the Dominican Republic. During this time also Caribbean Islands which had hitherto been francophone started on a slow process of becoming anglophone to different degrees: Dominica, St Lucia, Trinidad and Tobago, Grenada, and St Vincent and the Grenadines. Other little-known anglophone colonies which still survive today were also established during the nineteenth century in southern Brazil, by American southerners fleeing the aftermath of the Civil War, and in the Bonin islands of Japan, by New England and Hawaiian whalers and seamen, and on one of the Cook Islands in the South Pacific. There are also today long-standing indigenous groups of British-origin native anglophones in Namibia, Botswana, Zimbabwe and Kenya.

It is also worth noting that restructured forms of English, known as creoles, are spoken in many parts of the world: since the seventeenth century in Surinam, and since the early nineteenth century in Papua New Guinea, the Solomon Islands, Vanuatu and northern Australia. The English-based creole Krio has also been spoken in Sierra Leone, West Africa, at least since the early 1800s, although Hancock (1986) has argued for the presence of an anglophone community there since the early 1600s. Creole varieties are, however, not discussed in this chapter. Neither are varieties of English, such as Nigerian English, which are basically second-language varieties of the language.

Of all the areas just mentioned, it is safe to say that only the English of the British Isles, mainland North America, Australasia, South Africa, and, to a lesser extent, the creoles of the Caribbean and the South Pacific, have attracted large amounts of attention from historical linguists. In this chapter I suggest that there is an alternative to this concentration on these major (in demographic terms) varieties. I examine the histories of the other – relatively ignored – native varieties of English in lesser-known areas of the anglophone world, in chronological order of their settlement. (I do not, however, deal here with the diaspora African-American English-speaking communities of Nova Scotia, Liberia, Sierra Leone, and Samana in the Dominican Republic as these are dealt with elsewhere in this volume.) Research into the grammar and phonology of a number of these lesser-known varieties is currently in progress. Linguistic details of these varieties of English, including some rather remarkable similarities between many of them, are discussed, for example, in Trudgill *et al.* (forthcoming). Comments on the linguistic characteristics of these varieties in what follows are based either on my own research in the areas in question – as in the case of Bermuda, the Bahamas, Newfoundland, Cape Breton Island, Prince Edward Island, the Chatham Islands, and Guernsey – and/or on tapes that are either commercially available or have very kindly been made available to me by others (see Acknowledgements).

Newfoundland

The island of Newfoundland has an area of 112,790 km^2. The population is about 550,000. About 95 per cent of these are of British and Irish origin, while fewer than 3 per cent are of French extraction.

Newfoundland was originally settled by Indians and Inuit (Eskimos). Viking ruins dating from about AD1000 show that Norse speakers from Iceland and Greenland were the earliest Europeans to reach the area. The official European 'discoverer' of Newfoundland was the Genoese-Venetian John Cabot, who arrived on the island in 1497 sailing under the English flag, but the Grand Banks had been known to Basque and Breton fishermen much earlier. In the 1500s English, French, Basque, and Portuguese fishermen were in competition for the fishing grounds, and by 1600 England and France were the chief rivals. Attempts made at colonisation during the 1600s were not well received by the English fishermen nor, after 1634, by the English crown. In fact, in 1699 Parliament prohibited settlement of the island except in connexion with cod fishing. During the seventeenth and eighteenth centuries the island's population nevertheless increased, and Britain appointed a governor in 1729 and established a court system in 1792. These remained, however, only during the summer, and a settled colony was not recognised until 1824. Large groups of immigrants were brought in with the peak year of 1814–15 seeing the advent of 11,000 people, mainly Irish Catholics. Most rural areas are inhabited either by people whose ancestors came as early settlers from Dorset and Devon and/or by people with (rather later) origins in south-eastern Ireland.

The history of the settlement of Newfoundland goes a long way to explaining the current linguistic situation there. The phonology of modern Newfoundland English is characterised by considerable social variation by North American standards, and nonstandard grammatical forms, such as present-tense -*s* for all persons, occur very frequently and high up the social scale. It is, too, one of the few places in North America where it can be said with any degree of certainty that traditional dialects, in the sense of Wells (1982), survive. There is also some well-documented regional variation (see Paddock 1975; Wells 1982: 498–501). A first impression for English English speakers is that speakers 'sound Irish', but closer inspection shows that this is not the case. Overall, varieties seem to be the result of a mixture of Southern Irish English and south-western English English varieties, but in different proportions in different places. In communities where immigration from Dorset and Devon played an important role, older speakers may for example still have initial-fricative voicing in *fish*, *thimble*, *seven*, *ship*, and a number of Irish-origin syntactic features can be found in Irish-influenced areas, such as habitual aspect expressed by *do be* as in *They do be full* (see Clarke 1997, 1999).

Bermuda

Bermuda is a self-governing British colony about 900 km east of Cape

Hatteras, North Carolina. Its total land area is 54 km², and the population is about 60,000. It is said to have been discovered by the Spanish navigator Juan Bermudez, probably between 1503 and 1511. The first anglophones to arrive were some Puritans who were shipwrecked in 1609. In 1612, sixty English settlers were sent to colonise the islands. African slaves were transported to Bermuda beginning in 1616, and soon the Black population was larger than the White. In 1684 Bermuda became a crown colony (Zuill 1973). About 60 per cent of the population are of African origin. Whites are mostly of British origin, but descendants of Portuguese labourers from Madeira and the Azores who arrived during the 1800s are also to be found and some Portuguese is still spoken.

Bermudan English has not been extensively studied, although see Ayres (1933), Trudgill (1986), and Cutler *et al.* (forthcoming). There are noticeable differences between the speech of Blacks and that of Whites – the former being more Caribbean in character, the latter more like the English of coastal South Carolina.

The Lesser Antilles

It is well known that the majority of the population of Belize, of Jamaica, and of the eastern Caribbean are of African origin. The English-based creoles, semi-creoles and post-creole continua spoken in many of these former, and in a few cases current, British colonies are rather well known to linguists (see Carrington forthcoming).

It is much less well known, however, that the Lesser Antilles of the eastern Caribbean contain a number of communities of White anglophones. The point about these communities is not of course that they are racially 'White' but that they are in many cases the direct cultural and linguistic descendants of immigrants from the British Isles and as such speakers of English which, while clearly Caribbean in character, may in some respects show differences from that of Black West Indians, especially since residential and social segregation has been maintained in some places for hundreds of years.

Of the islands which have significant White populations today, direct White emigration to Barbados began in 1627, with large numbers of the migrants being unemployed or otherwise impoverished people from England, many of them coming from or via London, Bristol, and Southampton, who took positions as servants in these newly established colonies. (Immigration also began to St Kitts in 1624, but no White community survives there today.) Many of the English who arrived later in the 1650s were prisoners of the English Civil War or transported criminals. Irish immigration was also significant, particularly in the wake of Cromwell's harrying of Ireland in the 1650s, when many of the arrivals were also in fact political prisoners or prisoners of war.

The Dutch (but English-speaking) island of Saba was claimed by the Dutch in 1632 but settled by White anglophones coming, often as escapees from indentured labour, from other islands over a considerable period of time lasting until the 1830s. This isolated White community today forms about half the population of the island. Montserrat had a population of Whites until quite recently who came originally from St Kitts: there was one community of Irish-origin Catholics, and another of Scottish and English-origin Protestants. Anguilla has a community of Whites who arrived from other islands in the late 1600s, later reinforced by other arrivals from other islands who came around 1800. White immigration to St Lucia from Scotland, with some settlers arriving also from England and Ireland, dated from the 1830s, but most if not all of these have subsequently emigrated.

Some White communities descend from people who were relocated from other islands by government policy in the 1860s. This relocation was a response to the perceived poverty and unemployment of poor Whites in a number of the original communities. One community arrived in St Vincent from Barbados, and another in Bequia in the Grenadines, and a third in Grenada itself. For further details on settlement patterns and dating, see Holm (1994).

The English of these communities has been very little studied apart from pioneering work by Williams (1987, 1988), which looks at the very interesting question of verbal aspect in White Caribbean English and the extent to which aspectual systems derive from Irish English, British English, and/or Caribbean creoles.

The Bahamas

The Bahamas form an independent state which is a member of the British Commonwealth. They are an archipelago of about 700 islands to the southeast of Florida, with a population of about 270,000.

The Bahamas were originally inhabited by Lucayan Arawak Indians, originally from the South American continent, who had probably been driven into the Caribbean by the Caribs. In 1492 Columbus first landed in the Bahamas. Although he took formal possession of the islands in the name of Spain, the Spanish did not really make any attempt to settle them. Between 1492 and 1508, they enslaved 40,000 natives to work in the mines on Hispaniola, and by the time the English arrived the Bahamas were uninhabited. Serious English involvement began in 1629 when King Charles I granted Sir Robert Heath, the Attorney General of England, territories in America including the Bahamas. He too made no effort to settle the Bahamas. However, in the 1640s, Bermuda was suffering from religious disputes, and in 1647 Captain William Sayle, a former governor of Bermuda, decided to look for an island where religious dissidents could worship. The 'Company of Eleutherian Adventurers' was set up in London, and in 1648 Sayle sailed with about seventy settlers (Bermudan dissidents and others from England) for the Bahamas. It is not known where they arrived, but it is thought that they settled on the island of Eleuthera. They had planned a plantation colony. This was largely unsuccessful, however, and a number of settlers, including

Sayle himself, returned to Bermuda. Other Bermudan migrants continued to arrive, however, and the island of New Providence was settled from Bermuda in 1656. In 1670 six 'proprietors' were granted the islands by Charles II, and accepted responsibility for government. They were mostly not concerned about the islands, however. Things did not go well, and piracy became prevalent. In 1717, therefore, the King commissioned Captain Woodes Rogers as the Governor, and by 1728 he had managed to exterminate piracy. After the American Revolution, from 1782 onwards, many American loyalists fled, some of them with slaves, to the Bahamas. This had the effect of doubling the White population and trebling the Black. A minority of the population today is thus descended from English pioneer settlers and loyalist refugees. Most of the population is of African descent (Albury 1975).

The English of White Bahamians, then, has two main sources: the Bermudan English of the original settlers, and the North American English of the Loyalists. Some of the Loyalists were from the American South, but Abaco and northern Eleuthera islands in particular were settled by Americans from New England and New York (Holm and Shilling 1982). There was also some White immigration from the Miskito coast (see below) when this area was ceded by Britain to Spain in 1786, and Andros island in particular was settled from there. It is no surprise, then, that their accents are non-rhotic (as indeed are those of Black speakers) (see Shilling 1982; Wells 1982: 588–91; Cutler *et al.* forthcoming).

Black Bahamians too have different origins (see Holm 1980), some being descended from slaves who actually arrived in the Bahamas, others being originally from the American South or the Caribbean. According to Holm and Shilling (1982: vii) Black Bahamian English is probably most like the mainland American creole Gullah. It is certainly 'closer to white English than comparable varieties in the Caribbean proper, but much further from white English than the vernacular Black English of the United States'. The phonology differs from that of White speech in, for example, having monophthongal realisations of /ei/ and /ou/. There are also certainly a number of African American Vernacular English (AAVE) and/or Caribbean creole-like features in the syntax (see Holm and Hackert 1996).

Central America

San Andrés and Providencia are Caribbean islands with a total land area of about 45 km² and a population of about 35,000. They lie about 180 km off the coast of Nicaragua and about 700 km northwest of mainland Colombia. They nevertheless constitute part of Colombia: Colombia controlled what is now Panama until 1903, which helps to explain this geographical anomaly. The islands were settled in 1629 by English Puritans, and subsequently also by Jamaican planters and their Black slaves. The islands were officially decreed to be Spanish in 1786, and they became part of Colombia in 1822, after Colombian independence. The discussion by Washabaugh (1983) makes it clear that these islands, too, speak a typically Caribbean creole form of English.

The Bay Islands are a group of eight small islands off northern Honduras. They have an area of 250 km^2 and are situated about 55 km offshore in the Caribbean. The islands were first sighted by Columbus in 1502 and were settled in 1642 by English buccaneers. Between 1650 and 1850 Spain, Honduras, and England disputed ownership of the islands (see Davidson 1974). The islands were officially annexed to Britain in 1852 but were then ceded to Honduras in 1859. English-speaking Protestants formed the majority of the population until about 1900, when hispanic Hondurans from the mainland began settling, but indigenous anglophones still form about 85 per cent of the population, which also includes non-anglophone Black Caribs (see below). The population is currently about 20,000: Black, White and mixed. At least at the level of acrolectal Whites, the accent is rhotic though obviously Caribbean (see Ryan 1973).

The Miskito coast is the Caribbean coastal area of Nicaragua and Honduras consisting of a strip of lowland about 70 km wide and 350 km long. Columbus visited it in 1502, but there was not much European presence there until the arrival of buccaneers in the 1650s. England established a protectorate over the local Miskito Indians, who the region is named after, and the area was a British dependency from 1740 to 1786.

In Nicaragua, the British founded the principal Miskito coast city of Bluefields. Spain, Nicaragua, and the United States at different times disputed the legitimacy of this dependency. The issue was settled as far as Nicaragua was concerned by the occupation of what is now the Nicaraguan part of the coast by Spain in 1786, and later by a British–American treaty of 1850.

There are about 30,000 native speakers of English in this area of Nicaragua who look to Bluefields as their centre. Most of them are of African origin. Several hundred, however, are Rama Indians, and another several hundred are so-called Black Caribs, who were transported from their native island of St Vincent to this area by the British in the late 1700s. The Miskito Indians number about 70,000. Some of them, too, are native speakers of English and are included in this figure, but, of those who have retained their own language, a large number also speak the local variety of English as a second language. According to Holm (1978, 1983) and O'Neil (1993) it is a typically Caribbean form of English with many creole features.

English is also spoken in many different locations on the Caribbean coast of mainland Honduras where, however, language shift to Spanish seems to be taking place (Warantz 1983). As far as I know, these varieties have not yet been investigated by linguists.

The anglophone Corn Islands of Nicaragua, Great and Little Corn Island, lie in the Caribbean about 80 km offshore from Bluefields. The population is about 2,500. The islands were leased by treaty to the United States by Nicaragua from 1916 to 1971. The English of these islands is also typically Caribbean.

For a general overview of this area, see Lastra (forthcoming). For further details on settlement patterns and dating, see Holm (1994).

Saint Helena

This island is a British colony in the South Atlantic Ocean, 1,950 km west of Africa. It is about 120 km^2, and the population is about 6,000. It was discovered in 1502 by the Portuguese but the English learnt of it in 1588. It then became a port for ships travelling between Europe and the East, and in 1659 the East India Company took possession. By 1673 nearly half the inhabitants were imported slaves. Napoleon was confined on the island from 1815 until his death in 1821. The island's population is largely of mixed British, Asian, and African descent.

The English of St Helena is perhaps best described as a creoloid (see Schreier *et al*. forthcoming). It has, for example, a number of creole features such as copula deletion, but is nevertheless obviously English.

The Cayman Islands

These are a British colony of three major islands in the Caribbean, about 290 km northwest of Jamaica. The population is about 25,000. About a quarter of the Caymanians are European, mostly of British origin; about one-quarter are descendants of African slaves; and the remainder are of mixed ancestry. The Islands were first sighted by Columbus in 1503. They appear to have been uninhabited, but known to Carib and/or Arawak Indians. They were subsequently visited by Spanish, English, and French ships but were not claimed by any nation until they were ceded to England in 1670. Most of the settlers were British mariners, buccaneers, shipwrecked passengers, plus land-grant holders from Jamaica and African slaves (see Holm 1994). The Cayman Islands were a dependency of Jamaica until 1959, when they became a separate dependency.

Washabaugh (1983) shows that the phonology is clearly Caribbean, but variably rhotic.

Turks and Caicos Islands

The Turks and Caicos are a British crown colony consisting of two small groups of islands at the south-eastern end of the Bahamas about 145 km north of the Dominican Republic. The Turks group consists of Grand Turk and Salt Cay. The Caicos group consists of six main islands: South Caicos, East Caicos, Middle Caicos, North Caicos, Providenciales, and West Caicos. The population is about 14,000.

A pre-Columbian Indian – possibly Arawak as on the Bahamas – culture may have existed on the islands, but they seem to have been uninhabited at the time of their 'discovery' by the Spanish explorer Juan Ponce de León in

1512. They were not settled by Europeans until 1678, when Bermudans arrived and set up a salt industry. The Caicos Islands were also settled by loyalist refugees from the USA after the War of Independence. As in the Bahamas, they established cotton plantations employing slaves. In 1799 the islands were annexed by the Bahamas, but in 1848 they were granted a separate charter. After the abolition of slavery in 1843 the plantation owners left the islands, leaving their former slaves in control. The colony was placed under the control of Jamaica from 1874 until 1959, and became a separate crown colony in 1962 when Jamaica became independent. Over 90 per cent of the inhabitants are Blacks.

The speech of the islands is often described as being very close to Bahamian English. It is clearly true that there are many phonological and grammatical similarities, but Cutler (see Cutler *et al.* forthcoming) reports that a number of Bahamian lexical items are not known on Grand Turk. Holm also suggests (1989: 489) that the English may be somewhat different from that of the southern Bahamas. He reports (personal communication) that certain students at the College of the Bahamas in Nassau where he taught in 1978–80 were said by other students to have 'Turks accents'.

Turks Islanders claim that people in the Caicos Islands speak differently. This is possible but awaits investigation. Grand Turk was settled mainly by Black and White Bahamians, while the Caicos Islanders descend from American slaves brought there by American loyalist planters in the 1780s. They have traditionally been more isolated and had less access to education.

India

English first arrived in India as a significant feature as a result of British colonisation and administration especially from about 1750 onwards, although the English had had commercial interests in India much earlier than that. It is well known that a distinctive second-language form of Indian English is today widely used as a lingua franca among educated elites in India, and that English plays an important role in government, education, and the media, although only a very small minority (nevertheless constituting many millions of people) have a good command of the language. The linguistic characteristics of Indian English are also well known (see Trudgill and Hannah 1994). However, it is less well known that a form of Indian English is the native language of the Eurasian or Anglo-Indian community in India, which includes about 100,000 people who are of mixed British and Indian origin. The phonology of this variety is outlined in Wells (1982: 624–6).

The Canadian Maritimes

In the seventeenth and eighteenth centuries Nova Scotia was the site of a struggle for power between England and France. Halifax was founded by the British in 1749 to counteract French influence with a population of about

4,000 British settlers. In the 1750s the French Acadian settlers, who had refused to swear allegiance to the British crown, were expelled, and new immigrants arrived from the British Isles and New England. Gaelic-speaking Scottish Highlanders settled in a number of areas of Cape Breton Island, where some Gaelic is still spoken to this day. Protestant Germans founded the town of Lunenburg in 1750, and Ulster Scots set up farms in the Truro and Onslow districts. After the American War of Independence about 35,000 American loyalists arrived and by 1800 New Englanders formed about half of the population. Later, Irish people arrived via Newfoundland or directly from Ireland and settled in and near Halifax. (There are also Black communities near Halifax and Shelburne – see Chapter 5.)

Prince Edward Island was claimed by France early on but was not colonised until 1720, when 300 settlers from France arrived. Fishermen and trappers from the francophone Acadian mainland colony in New Brunswick established several other small communities on the island. The British occupied the island in 1758, expelling most of the French-speaking settlers, though some francophone families still remain in some areas. The island was formally ceded to Britain in 1763. More than three-quarters of the population are descendants of early settlers from the British Isles: Highland Scots, Ulster Scots, English, and southern Irish, but as in Nova Scotia there are also descendants of American Loyalists who arrived after the American War of Independence. In the 1800s religious tensions between people of Irish Protestant and Catholic origin was not unknown.

The British took over New Brunswick in 1713 and expelled most of the French-speaking Acadian settlers in 1755. Many of them went to Louisiana, and some later returned. The first English-speaking settlers came north from New England and moved into the St John River valley in 1762. There was then a big influx of 14,000 loyalist Americans after the War of Independence, who came mostly from the New York area. The English-speaking majority today – about two-thirds of the population – thus consists largely of descendants of American loyalists, together with the descendants of Scottish, Irish, and English settlers who arrived in the 1700s and 1800s.

Canadian English as it is spoken from Vancouver to Ontario has been very well described. The English of the Maritime Provinces is, however, not so well known to linguists, and while the English of younger educated speakers in urban areas such as Halifax is not radically different from that of the rest of Canada, rural Maritime English is distinctively different, having a number of similarities with the English of Newfoundland, and phonological features which appear to owe much to Irish and/or Scottish and/or American influence (see Emeneau 1935; Wilson 1975; Pratt 1988; Trudgill 2000).

Quebec: the Magdalen Islands

The Canadian Iles de la Madeleine are in the Gulf of St Lawrence between Prince Edward Island and Newfoundland, 240 km southeast of the Gaspé Peninsula. There are nine main islands with a total land area of 230 km^2.

The largest islands are Havre-Aubert (Amherst), Cap aux Meules (Grindstone), Loup (Wolf), and Havre aux Maisons (Alright). The islands were 'discovered' by Jacques Cartier in 1534, although Basque and Breton fishermen had known about them long before that. They acquired a settled population in 1755, when many of the Acadian French colonists of Nova Scotia who were expelled by the British escaped there. The islands were ceded to Britain in 1763 and annexed to Newfoundland, but were made a part of Quebec in 1774. At the end of the 1700s the population was reinforced by further Acadians who had earlier taken refuge on the French-owned islands of St Pierre and Miquelon, but who now preferred the British Monarchy to the French Republicans. The population today is about 14,000. About 90 per cent of these, as this history would lead one to suspect, are French-speaking. However, there is a long-standing community of about 1,500 anglophones who are mainly of Scottish and Irish origin and who today live for the most part on Ile d'Entrée and La Grosse Ile.

Pitcairn Island

This isolated British colony is about 2,200 km southeast of Tahiti in the south Pacific. The main and only inhabited island has an area of about 5 km^2, and the population in 1992 was fifty-two. It was 'discovered' in 1767 by British navigators, but, though uninhabited, showed signs of previous Polynesian habitation or at least visitation. The modern population, as is well known, is descended from the mutineers of the British ship HMS *Bounty* and their Tahitian companions. After a lengthy stay on Tahiti, the crew, led by the first mate, Fletcher Christian, mutinied when their voyage to the West Indies had got only as far as western Polynesia, and set their captain William Bligh and a number of loyal sailors adrift. They headed back to Tahiti, where they collected a number of local women and a few men, and, fearing discovery by the Royal Navy, set off again. They reached Pitcairn in 1790, where, in the interests of secrecy, they burnt their ship. The island community survived undiscovered until found by American whalers in 1808. In 1856, because of overpopulation, some of the islanders were removed to Norfolk Island (see below). The population is currently declining owing to emigration to New Zealand.

A range of varieties of English appear to be open to islanders (see Ross and Moverley 1964; Källgård 1993). The most basilectal of these resembles an English-based creole and has many features of Polynesian origin (Trudgill *et al.*, forthcoming). There has been some considerable controversy about its exact status (see Mühlhäusler 1998), but I have suggested (Trudgill 1996) the term 'dual source creoloid' for this variety.

Tristan da Cunha

This South Atlantic British dependent territory consists of six small islands which are about half-way between southern Africa and South America. The only populated island, Tristan da Cunha, has an area of about 100 km^2 and a population of about 290. It is said to be the most remote permanently inhabited settlement in the world, the nearest habitation being St Helena, which is about 2,000 km distant. The islands were discovered in 1506 by a Portuguese sailor, Tristão da Cunha. A British garrison was stationed on Tristan da Cunha in 1816, as a result of fears that it might be used as a base for an attempt to rescue Napoleon from St Helena (see above) and the islands were formally annexed to Britain. When the garrison left in 1817, three soldiers asked to stay, and during the 1800s they were joined by shipwrecked sailors, a few European settlers, and six women from St Helena. By 1886 the population was ninety-seven. In 1961 a volcanic eruption threatened the settlement, and the inhabitants were evacuated to England. Most of them returned to Tristan in 1963. The English (see Schreier forthcoming a; Trudgill *et al.* forthcoming) is remarkable. It is mainly of English dialect origin but shows some signs of pidginisation, though probably not enough to be considered a creoloid (see Schreier, Sudbury and Wilson forthcoming). It has a number of grammatical features found nowhere else in the anglophone world (see Schreier forthcoming b).

Bonin Islands

Almost certainly the least-known anglophone community in the world, these Japanese-owned islands, known in Japanese as Ogasawara-gunto, are in the central Pacific Ocean, about 800 km southeast of Japan proper. There are three main island groups: the Beechey Group (Anijima and Chichijima); the Parry Group (Mukojima); and the Bailey Group (Hahajima). The population is about 2,000. The islands were discovered by the Spanish navigator Ruy Lopez de Villalobos in 1543. They were then claimed by the USA in 1823 and by Britain in 1825. The islands were formally annexed by Japan in 1876, but, after World War II, they were a placed under US military control. They were returned to Japan in 1968. The English appears to be mainly American in origin (see Long 1998, 2000, forthcoming) and has many similarities to New England varieties. It also has similarities to a number of other island Englishes which are not necessarily very easy to explain (Trudgill *et al.* forthcoming).

Palmerston

Palmerston English is a variety spoken on Palmerston Island, Polynesian *Avarau*, a coral atoll in the Cook Islands about 430 km northwest of Rarotonga, by descendants of Cook Island Maori and English speakers. What we know about the settlement is that William Marsters, a ship's carpenter and cooper from Gloucestershire, England, came to uninhabited Palmerston Atoll in 1862. He had three wives, all from Penrhyn/Tongareva in the Northern Cook Islands. He forced his wives, seventeen children and numerous grandchildren to use

English all the time. Virtually the entire population of the island today descends from the patriarch. Ehrhart-Kneher (1996: 530) considers Palmerston English a dialectal variety of English rather than a contact language. She writes that it appears to be a classic case of mixing and vernacularisation of a type which has 'produced languages which, while new languages, are varieties of English rather than new languages without genetic affiliation in the usual sense' (see Trudgill *et al.* forthcoming).

The Falkland Islands

This British colony in the South Atlantic Ocean lies about 500 km east of the South American mainland. There are two main islands, East Falkland and West Falkland, with a total land area of about 12,200 km^2 and a population, of British descent, of about 2,100. In 1690 the English captain John Strong made the first recorded landing on the islands. The islands' first settlement was established in 1764 by the French under de Bougainville, closely followed by a British settlement in 1765 on West Falkland. The Spanish purchased the French settlement in 1767, and succeeded in temporarily expelling the British from West Falkland between 1770 and 1771. The British withdrew from West Falkland in 1774 for financial reasons but without renouncing their claim to sovereignty. The Spanish settlement on East Falkland was in turn withdrawn in 1811. In 1820 the Argentinean government, which had declared its independence from Spain in 1816, proclaimed its sovereignty over the Falklands, but in 1831 an American warship attacked an Argentinean settlement on East Falkland and in 1833 a British force expelled the few remaining Argentinean officials. In 1841 a British governor was appointed for the Falklands, and by 1885 a British community of about 1,800 people had been established on the two islands. The Falklands became a British colony in 1892. A new focused dialect of English has developed in the capital and only town, Port Stanley, but in rural West Falkland each village apparently shows connections with the particular part of England from which it was settled (see Sudbury 2000; Schreier, Sudbury and Wilson forthcoming).

The Chatham Islands

This island group is about 800 km east of New Zealand. The largest island, Chatham Island, is 900 km^2 in area. Pitt Island is about 21 km to the southeast. The indigenous population was the Polynesian Moriori, who were conquered and exterminated by the New Zealand Maori from 1835 onwards. The islands were annexed by New Zealand in 1842. The current population of about 750 is mainly White with some people of Maori or mixed Maori and Moriori origin. The English is indistinguishable from that of New Zealand, but 'broad' New Zealand accents are found much higher up the social scale than in New Zealand itself.

The Channel Islands

The islands of Jersey, Guernsey, Herm, Sark, and Alderney were until the 1800s Norman French-speaking in spite of the fact that they had been under the English and British crown since 1066, as they still are today, though they are not actually part of the United Kingdom as such but rather autonomous dependencies. The local French patois is now very much in retreat, but the English which has now mostly replaced it has a number of distinctive characteristics which have been little described; but see Ramisch (1989) and Barbé (1995), who discuss features of the local syntax and morphology, which appear to owe something to the influence of French as well as to the dialects of the southwest of England. Ramisch indicates, and I can confirm, that the pronunciation of English at least on Guernsey is basically of a rhotic southwest of England type, though with some second-language features such as *th*-stopping.

Norfolk Island

This is an Australian dependent territory in the south-western Pacific, about 1,600 km northeast of Sydney. The island, with an area of 35 km^2, has a population of about 2,750. Captain Cook discovered the uninhabited island in 1774. It was claimed by New South Wales in 1788 and settled by a small group which included fifteen convicts. This was abandoned in 1814, but a new penal colony was established there from 1825 to 1855, when it was relocated in Tasmania. In 1856 the Pitcairn Islanders, descendants of the mutineers on the Bounty, were resettled on Norfolk Island (see above). Not all of the islanders were happy, however, and eventually two separate groups returned to Pitcairn. Norfolk Island's current population includes about one-third who can claim to be the descendants of mutineers, the remainder being descendants of later settlers, mostly from Australia and New Zealand. A strong Polynesian influence, stemming from the Tahitian input into Pitcairn, is still apparent in the culture and customs of the island. The local English of Norfolk Island, which is spoken by only about 25 per cent of the current population, is still rather like that of Pitcairn (Flint 1964), but less basilectal, and it has been argued that it is really a 'cant' or 'antilanguage' (Laycock 1989).

Brazil

At the end of the American Civil War in 1865, thousands of Americans from the defeated South left the United States for ever. Some went to Mexico and the West Indies, and some even made it as far as Japan and Egypt, but the largest number of those that left went to Brazil, perhaps as many as 40,000 of them, where they founded a number of settlements. The best known of these is called Americana, which is situated about 150 km northwest of Sao Paulo, and which has today about 200,000 inhabitants. The conservative southern English of this community, as described by Montgomery and Melo

(1990, 1995), as well as by Bailey and Smith (1992), is of considerable interest for reconstructing the history of English in the southern United States. The language of the community was for many decades a Southern variety of American English, and there are many hundreds of older people today who still speak a conservative form of English which has its roots in, particularly, Georgia and Alabama. Gradually the community has become bilingual in English and Portuguese, and most younger people are as comfortable in Portuguese as in English, if not more so.

Southern and eastern Africa

English is the official language of Zimbabwe, and much teaching in schools is also carried out in English, except in the case of the youngest Shona- and Ndebele-speaking children. Zimbabwe has had a White, mainly British-origin population since settlers arrived from Botswana in 1890. However, only about a quarter of the White population at independence in 1980 were born in Zimbabwe. About 50 per cent had immigrated from Europe, mainly Britain, and about 25 per cent from South Africa. (Today, about 25 per cent of Whites living in rural areas are Afrikaners.) There are also Zimbabweans of mixed race, called 'coloureds', who are mainly anglophone. The Zimbabwean English of the native anglophone population resembles very closely that of South Africa, but according to Wells (1982) it has never been systematically studied. Native English-speakers make up less than 1 per cent of the total population of 11 million.

Botswana was a British protectorate from 1885 and an independent Commonwealth nation since 1966. White settlement in Botswana, consisting of some Afrikaners and fewer English-speakers, dated from the 1860s and has always been confined to farms in areas bordering South Africa. At its greatest, the White population never totalled more than 3,000. The English of the local population is South African in type.

British interest in Kenya began in the 1880s, and in 1890 Kenya became a British protectorate. Large-scale settlement by Whites began in 1901, many anglophones coming from South Africa as well as from Britain. Modern European Kenyans, mostly British in origin, are the remnant of that farming population. At the time of independence in 1963, most Europeans emigrated to southern Africa, Europe, and elsewhere. Most of those remaining today are to be found in the large urban centres of Nairobi and Mombasa. They now constitute much less than 1 per cent of the 30 million population. The English of the settlers has not been systematically investigated, as far as I know, but it clearly resembles that of South Africa to a perhaps surprising extent.

Namibia, as Southwest Africa, was a German colony from the 1880s. In 1915 it came under South African control, and it achieved independence as a member of the Commonwealth in 1990. About 6 per cent of Namibians are of European ancestry: Afrikaners constitute about 3.5 per cent and Germans about 1.5 per cent of the population. Anglophones of British origin thus constitute only about 0.5 per cent of the total population although English is the national language and is said to be the home language of about 3 per cent of the population. About 10,000 people of European origin have left Namibia since independence. Native Namibian English is, unsurprisingly, of a South African type.

Conclusion

Studies of the history of the English language up to 1600 obviously have to be confined to the British Isles, though it has to be said that the standard histories most often have relatively little to say about Scotland, or about the anglophone enclaves in Ireland. After 1700 there is, however, no real excuse for histories of the language which confine themselves to England, or even to England and the United States. It is true that, increasingly, historical linguists have been looking at the development of English in the other major anglophone nations: Canada, South Africa, Australia, and New Zealand. But, with the honourable exception of Holm (1994), the minor anglophone locations have been widely ignored. In the above I have dealt mostly with the external history of the lesser-known varieties of English. I have referred, however, at a number of points, to other works, including forthcoming works, dealing with the internal, linguistic histories of these varieties. It seems that some of the most important sociolinguistic and linguistic developments involving English have taken place in these other, 'alternative' parts of the world where English is spoken natively, and that much work remains to be done on their internal, linguistic history also.

Acknowledgements

Tapes and other materials have very kindly been made available to me by Jeffrey P. Williams, Danny Long, Daniel Schreier, Karen Lavarello, John Holm, Alison Shilling, and Anders Källgård. I am very grateful to all of them. Also very many thanks for corrections and comments on earlier drafts of this chapter to John Holm and Jeffrey P. Williams.

3   'North of Watford Gap'

A cultural history of Northern English (from 1700)

Katie Wales

Introduction

Tony Crowley (1991: 2) has noted significantly how the 'history' of the English language has generally been seen as a 'seamless narrative'; and one which, we may add, on the evidence of the many textbooks on the subject published, assumes this history to be that of standard English, especially after the Middle English period. Indeed, Burnley's explicit comment, odd though it is, on his own work underlines the traditional orthodoxy: that he 'sustains the consensus view of the development of the language through successive historical periods *to the goal* of present-day standard English' (Burnley 1992: x) (my italics). In this accepted version of history handed down from generation of students to generation, dialects of English, safely subsumed under the catch-all term 'non-standard' varieties (and labelled only in relation to the standard), are marginalised, ceasing to have any significance after the emergence of a written standard in London during the fifteenth century. It is as if they have no existence: yet even though dialect features were indeed submerged by the spread of the standard in formal and literary writings, popular dialect literature continued in both oral and written forms, and dialects flourished in spoken discourse, as today, albeit subject to hegemonic condescension and even ridicule. Of course, the 'silence' of dialects in public spheres means that evidence for their earlier history before an age of technical recording can be hard to retrieve. There is also the problem, which hinders dialect studies even today, that certain aspects of dialect study have been comparatively neglected, namely syntax, pragmatics and prosody (stress and intonation), and, until fairly recently, the study of urban speech.

These and other reasons may account for the fact that focused studies of the history of regional varieties are scarce: as far as I know, there is no detailed or extensive history of Northern English, for example.[1] Not that this history is completely ignored in traditional accounts, especially for the Late Old English and Middle English periods, although, strangely, Skeat (1911: 24) dismisses this period of the dialect's history as 'with a few insignificant exceptions ... a total blank'. For due weight has indeed to be given, for example, to the 'contributions' of Northern English, most probably under the impact of the Scandinavian settlements in the Danelaw area, to the 'development' of the language generally. So, with the loss of inflexions earliest in the North, particularly in the noun phrase, the Germanic system of grammatical gender is weakened then lost; the third person plural pronoun *they* first enters the language in the Northern dialects.

Even granted the general problem of data gathering, especially from earlier periods, and of establishing therefore historical continuities between present-day dialect forms and those of the past (Cheshire and Stein 1997: 5), there is a complex and dynamic 'story' of Northern English to be gleaned from a heterogeneity of discourses, literature, cultural practices and folk-beliefs. In this chapter I have space only to take up the story around the year 1700; but it is a tale overall, I would stress, of dialectics: of shifting boundaries and ideological oppositions, of conflicting cultural and mental landscapes and stereotypes. Much of this story has to do with Northern English's ideological, political and cultural relations with 'standard' English; but it also has to do more particularly with its relations with spoken 'London' English, the English of the metropolis; and more generally still with English spoken 'down South'. It is this latter relationship, based on a semiotic opposition ('the North–South divide') deeply rooted in a thousand years of history, which marks the story of Northern English as being quite different from the story of, for example, East Anglian, or South-west English. Another deeply rooted but ambivalent relationship is that between Northern English and Scottish English. Moreover, as we shall see, flavouring or colouring the narrative from 1700 onwards are culturally determined and conflicting images of the North itself which strongly influenced perceptions of the Northern vernacular. One, under the influence of Romanticism, saw Northern peasants as manifestations of the 'pure' and 'noble savage' surrounded in their solitude by a 'sublime' landscape of mountains and lakes; another, with the impact of the Industrial Revolution, saw the North as a smoke-begrimed industrial landscape, inhabited by the poverty-stricken working-class masses (a stereotype still unfortunately familiar).

The 'boundaries' of Northern English

The question of the definition of 'Northern English' and what it comprises, especially its southern limits, raises interesting and quite significant issues to do with the relations between geographical or political boundaries and linguistics; and also between psycho-geography and public perceptions of dialect areas, an aspect of language study generally that has only recently come to be explored (notably by Preston; e.g. Preston 1989). The phrase 'the North–South divide' is popularly used in the media, by politicians and by estate agents, and although the North comes off the worst in perceived standard of living, wages, etc. the actual boundary is never defined. This *austrocentrism* or discrimination in favour of the South is intensified by *metrocentrism*, discrimination in favour of the capital (see further Wales 2000). For Londoners, the North begins in popular parlance 'North of Potters Bar', or 'North of Watford'. Beyond the northern limits of the former Greater London Council and the last stop on the underground Metropolitan Line is the cultural wilderness; London as England's political capital is the perceived centre of gravity, the deictic anchorage, the *origo* by which everything else is judged inferior and insignificant. An early 'North of Watford' joke is found in 1580: Richard Kereforde thought it 'but a sport to deffraude a northern man, ffor so he termeth all northeron men that be born xxti mylles north from London' (cited in Jewell 1994: 147). For the Romans, the part of the country nearest to Rome with its capital Londinium was certainly *Britannia superior* (lit. 'upper'); and beyond a Mersey–Wash line, with its capital at Eboracum (York), was *Britannia inferior* (lit. 'lower'). Even beyond that, over Hadrian's Wall between the Tyne and the Solway Firth lay *Britannia barbara* ('barbarous') (McArthur 1985: 24).

From the sixteenth century onwards there appears the first of many references to the river Trent as a cultural and also linguistic divide. So George Puttenham in his oft-quoted passage in the *Art of English Poesie* (1589) advises the fashionable poet that he should neither 'take termes of Northernmen, such as they use in daily talk, whether they be noble men or gentlemen ... nor in effect any speech used beyond the river of Trent ... it is not so courtly nor yet so current as our Southern English is ...'. William Harrison's *Description of England* (1577) divides the country into 'south of Thames', 'Thames to Trent' and 'North of Trent'. Remember that Hotspur, son of Henry Percy Earl of Northumberland, in Shakespeare's *I Henry IV* complains about the share of the kingdom proposed for him, 'the remnant northward, lying off from Trent', 'north from Burton here', as being too small: 'See how this river comes me cranking in' (Act 3, i). The river Trent marks the threshold of civilisation well into the eighteenth century: Daniel Defoe in his account of his *Tour through the Whole Island of Great Britain* (1724–26) refers anxiously on more than one occasion to having to make the crossing. Dramatically, his dilemma is confirmed in a striking image:

> Having thus passed the Rubicon [i.e. the Trent] and set my face Northward, I scarce knew which way to set forward, in a country so full of wonders ... and yet to leave nothing behind me to call on as I came back, at least not to lead me out of my way on my return ...
>
> (1927 edn, p. 552)

Unusually for England's rivers, the Trent generally flows on a south–north axis, not east–west/west–east (and so creating Lincolnshire, as it were); but its outflow into the Humber estuary marks another frequently cited boundary. As early as the ninth century, King Alfred, writing from his Winchester capital on the decline of learning, laments that on his ascension there were very few 'on this side of the Humber' (*behionan Humbre*) who could read their mass-books in English, or translate an epistle from Latin; and he thinks that there were not many 'on the other side of the Humber' (*begiondan Humbre*).

Cultural considerations aside, the Humber/Trent, the southern limit of *lops* ('fleas') and *wark* ('ache') is still a significant southern 'border' for many Northerners today, whose political territory did once stretch this far, as Anglo-Saxon naming practices reveal. Northumberland or Northumbria, the northernmost region settled by the Angles, and at one time the most powerful and cultured kingdom in England, stretched from the Firth of Forth well beyond Hadrian's Wall down to the Humber. It comprised the two ancient kingdoms of Bernicia (north of the river Tees, i.e. the present Durham and Northumberland and the Scottish border area) and Deira (twixt Tees and Humber, i.e. North and East Yorkshire). It also straddled the Pennines, and took in Westmorland and part of Lancashire. In the early part of the Anglo-Saxon period Cumberland had been still strongly Celtic, and linked to Wales, but in Edwin of Northumbria's reign in the seventh century this link had been severed, and all of the north-west eventually became part of this Northern kingdom, at least the north-west region to the north of the Ribble.

Indeed, for the Middle English period a 'Ribble–(Calder–Aire)–Humber' line along those rivers was a significant linguistic divide between Northern and (North) West Midland speech, marking the ancient Northumberland–Mercia boundary (see Wakelin 1972); marking the confluence of a significant set of eight phonological isoglosses that clearly distinguished traditional rural Northern speech well into the twentieth century.[2] By the late twentieth century it had receded northwards into rural Northumberland, where, for example, /kʊəl/ 'coal' and /lɪəf/ 'loaf' (cf. general educated Northern /oː/ in both); 'wrang' ('wrong' [ME *a*]); and 'coo' ('cow' [ME *u*]) may still be heard amongst older speakers, and are indeed stereotypical markers of the speech of this part of the North. The long vowel /uː/ for /aʊ/ however, as Beal (2000) notes, has become lexically symbolic amongst urban Geordie football fans, in the word *Toon* ('Town') for Newcastle's football team.[3]

Technically speaking then, the area round present-day Liverpool, Manchester and West Yorkshire would in the Middle English period have been Mercian territory south of the Ribble, and linguistically speaking Midland or Mercian English, not (Old) Northumbrian. For convenience, and also following popular perceptions (especially amongst fellow Northerners), I myself will follow Orton *et al.* (in the 1960s) in distinguishing 'six counties' of Northern England for the twelve-part *Survey of English Dialects* (SED): Northumberland, Durham, Cumberland, Westmorland, Lancashire and Yorkshire (all three traditional 'ridings'), i.e. north of the Humber–Mersey; and so also including the cities of Manchester and Sheffield, alongside Liverpool and Hull.

Orton and his team (and see also Orton and Wright 1974: 3) were not convinced by the idea of dialect boundaries, let alone the notion of a 'North–South' linguistic divide, focusing instead on the meticulous reconstruction of the historical development of individual dialect forms from Middle English. Other linguists, non-dialectologists, have been bolder. Wells (1982) is quite explicit in positing a 'North–South' linguistic divide, though his reasons for its placement, on a NE–SW line running from the Wash right 'down' to the Severn, are not clear. It is actually quite close to John Ray's sectioning of the country in his *Collection of English Words* (1674), as noted by Ihalainen (1994: 201). Trudgill's (1990) North–South linguistic boundary is similar, except that it 'rises' in the SW Midlands, to the middle of the Welsh border: a Wash–Shropshire line perhaps. His sixteen dialect areas, and a broad distinction between a linguistic North and South, are based on a set of pronunciation variables including initial *h/h*-dropping; silent or present *g* in *-ing* forms; final or absent *r*, and what Wells would term the FOOT–STRUT distinction. As a result, much of his Midlands ('East Central' and 'West Central'), as for Wells, is in the linguistic North, but East Anglia is not. The 'real' North, so to speak, is divided into the 'Lower North' (from the Humber–Ribble roughly to the Tees, but also including the north-west of England), i.e. Wells's 'middle north', and the 'North-east' (i.e. most of Northumberland and Durham): Wells's 'far north' (a label popularly given to Scotland, however).

What is most interesting about Trudgill's general North–South dividing line is that it almost certainly corresponds to the well-known southern limit of unsplit FOOT–STRUT as described in Chambers and Trudgill (1980), and Wells (1982). This has to be, along with the vowel in BATH, one of the most salient and most symbolic markers of Northern English pronunciation today, and both of which time and time again occur in popular discussions, conceptions and representations of Northern speech or speakers from 'oop North'. (Surprisingly, perhaps, the BATH vowel is not one of Trudgill's own diagnostic features.) In the history of Northern English they are relatively late developments, but are certainly significant in the period covered in this chapter for the delimitation of Northern English. The centring of the vowel in words like *butter* and *up*, and the lengthening of the vowel in words followed by *f, s*, and *th* as in *laugh, grass* and *bath* both seem to have become fashionable in London speech in the late eighteenth century, although Wells (1982, vol. 1) sees them as emerging in the mid- to late seventeenth century.[4] The FOOT–STRUT split at least was identified as an isogloss [SUM–SOOM] by the phonetician Alexander Ellis (1869–89). Remaining relatively stable for the past 100 years, nonetheless it only appears to have become a noteworthy social semiotic in the twentieth century, as with the short and long 'a' distinction, although comments are unfortunately sparse. This isogloss also has the Wash at one side, so to speak, but has its southern limit north of the other isogloss, gently sliding into the West Midlands with a dip round Greater Birmingham, and another near the Welsh border. Birmingham actually appears to be a kind of 'terminus' for both isoglosses in their historical spread northwards. In the late eighteenth century, as Wakelin (1972) convincingly argues, there would have been no big urban centres to the north likely to have been influenced by such fashionable pronunciations.

Over time then these vowels in particular have become the focus of condescension and derision on the one hand, and pride and solidarity on the other: depending, of course, on whether one is a Northerner or a Southerner.

For Southerners 'flat' vowels as in /grɑs/ are as metonymic as 'flat caps', and confirm the prevalent image of (all) Northerners as 'working class'. For Northerners, /grɑ:s/ would be talking 'posh' or 'la-di-da'. As Wells so aptly puts it:

> There are many educated Northerners who would not be caught dead doing something so vulgar as to pronounce STRUT words with [u] but who would feel it to be a denial of their identity as northerners to say BATH words with anything other than short [a].
>
> (1982: 354)

The short 'a' is presumably a particular 'hazard' because of its more limited distribution before fricatives, and in established lexical items at that. Even as late as the 1960s, if not later, 'elocution' lessons in Northern grammar schools aiming at the inculcation of Received Pronunciation (RP) and the eradication of a Northern accent concentrated on 'a' and 'u' in particular. Not surprisingly, to many educated Northerners, with the pull towards the metropolis/RP, these vowels have caused real existential conflict, a 'crossing-the-Rubicon' dilemma, in the fear of the betrayal of one's roots. So Alan Bennett, the Leeds-born playwright who went to Oxford in the 1950s, describes (1994) the 'fissure' between provincial and metropolitan, his two 'voices' of North and South; and describes how he

> tried to lose my Northern accent at one period, then reacquired it, and *now don't know where I am*, sometimes saying my 'a's' long, sometimes short, and 'u's' a continuing threat, words like 'butcher' and names like 'cutbush' always lying in ambush. Anyone who ventures *South of the Trent* is likely to contract an incurable disease of the vowels ...
>
> (1994: xiii) (my italics)

The poet Tony Harrison, also from a working-class Leeds background, vividly reveals his own sense of a cultural and linguistic divide in his poem *Them & [uz]*, which evokes memories of his school-days:

> We say [ʌs] not [uz], T.W!' That shut my trap.
> I doffed my flat 'a's (as in 'flat cap') ...
>
> (Harrison, 1987)

As the BATH and FOOT/STRUT isoglosses reveal, linguistic boundaries do not necessarily follow geographical boundaries such as rivers, as the previous discussion would suggest. Indeed, it is hard to see any such correlations, aside from the Birmingham-terminus hypothesis. The building of the M62 across the Pennines in the last quarter of the twentieth century may well in future have significant linguistic repercussions, although it generally follows the Humber–Mersey line. For the poet Simon Armitage

(1998), however, brought up in the south of Yorkshire, the M62 is already a salient 'frontier'. Roads and dialect divisions have in the past had some kind of association. King Alfred's own political north–south divide in AD 878, the Danelaw area, marked roughly by a line running diagonally from the Mersey to the Thames estuary, ran close to the Roman Watling Street. Because of the Danish settlements 'north' of this line (and with Norwegians in Cumberland), the North and the East Midlands gradually became linguistically distinct in terms of lexis, etc. from the West Midlands. Over 1000 years later, also running north-westwards from London is the M1. Since its opening, the phrase 'North of Watford Gap' has become popular – Watford Gap being a service station in Northamptonshire. It is possible, however, that many people who use this jocular expression do not actually know where it is; the currency of the phrase no doubt the result of its association, by a kind of 'folk etymology', with Watford in the similar expression. However, since Watford Gap is just south-east of greater Birmingham, and close too to Trudgill's Shropshire–Wash line and Wells's Severn–Wash line, as well as the Danelaw boundary, contemporary references may well be reflecting an interesting conjunction of lay and professional linguistic perceptions of a North–South divide.

'The far North': Scots and Northern English

From Roman times, the major route from London to Scotland in the 'far North' passed through York, Durham and Newcastle to Edinburgh, the route of much of the present-day A1 and the GNER railway. For many Northerners, Doncaster on the old A1 in south Yorkshire is the southern limit of the North; but for 'Geordies' the southern limit is Darlington on the Durham–Yorkshire border near the river Tees, if not actually Durham on the river Wear. For the Scots, however, the South begins at Newcastle on the river Tyne, if not actually at Berwick, on the river Tweed. Even today these sub-regions (and those in the North-West) mark significant dialects and accents within Northern English, despite the rather general labellings and delimitations of linguists such as Trudgill and Wells, and notwithstanding the urban varieties now superimposed (see pp. 61f.). As Beal details (1993: Ch. 6), for example, glottalling of the definite article as part of 'definite article reduction' is not found north of the Tees (and indeed is a typical Yorkshire stereotype), and nor, until quite recently, has been *h*-dropping, although this is now heard in Sunderland, on the Wear. In Teesdale streams are *becks*, in Northumberland and the border regions *burns*: *beck* reflecting Scandinavian influence, which Northumberland largely escaped, the Danes seeing the Tyne as their northernmost limit of settlement.

At the present-day, if the southern limit of Northern English seems flexible, its northern limit seems more assured, at least perceptually speaking, namely the political border between Scotland and England. Some linguists such as Crystal (1996a: 325, 328) and McArthur (1992: 893) would go so far as to say that this is a definite linguistic boundary, 'the most noticeable dialect distinction in modern British English', and the real 'North–South divide'. In the twenty-first century, therefore, especially with the recent restitution of the Scottish government, what was once part of a dialect of English is likely to have the status of a language like Gaelic. There is certainly an increasing tendency for English borderers to assimilate their speech to Northumbrian and Cumbrian English, and Scottish borderers theirs to Lowland Scots. [M] as in *which* and [x] as in /nixt/ 'night' have retreated over the border in the twentieth century. Yet given a time-span of nearly 1500 years in the history of Northern English, this political boundary has only relatively recently become a linguistic boundary. Northern English and Lowland Scots, known as *Inglis* in Scotland in the medieval period, retained close linguistic similarity well into the modern period, with Ellis (1869–89) assigning north Cumberland/Northumberland to Scotland linguistically; and even today their common origin is reflected in many phonological, lexical and grammatical features. For example, the auxiliaries *may* and *shall* are hardly ever used in Tyneside English, as in Scots, even in questions ('*Will* I put the kettle on?'); and *can/could* can be used as second modals, especially in negatives ('He *wouldn't could've* worked', i.e. 'be able to'). Other constructions in common include 'My hair *needs washed*'; and *for to* plus infinitives (see further Beal 1993: 193f.).

The strong and enduring literary tradition of ballad-making and recitation in the 'Border' regions from the Middle Ages well into the nineteenth century confirms this linguistic closeness. Words and spellings such as *mickle* 'much', *kirk* 'church', *baith* 'both', *sic* 'such', *twa* 'two', *wrang* 'wrong', *mair* 'more' reflect commonalities of pronunciation; participles in *-and* and forms such as *dinna* ('don't') reflect common morphology; others, such as *gang* 'walk', *bairn* 'child', *bonny* 'pretty', *ken* 'know', shared lexical items. In ballad diction, 'the North Country' could be either the North of England, or Scotland, although most usually the latter. Yet politically and ideologically, the ballads reveal conflict and antagonism, not solidarity, with their stories of cross-border feuds, raids and battles in wild terrain. Even in the eighteenth century, antagonism remains. In *Humphry Clinker* (1771) by the Scottish novelist Tobias Smollett, an epistolary tale of Matthew Bramble's pursuit of health cures round the spas of Britain, Bramble's nephew writes how 'from Doncaster northwards, all the windows of all the inns are scrawled with doggerel rhymes in abuse of the Scottish nation'.[5]

In one sense, the Union of Crowns (1603), and the Act of Union in 1700, should have strengthened the linguistic closeness between the border regions, yet, in actuality, it had the opposite effect in due course. Two 'standards' as models of language use developed: a Scottish standard based on the usage of the capital, Edinburgh, and the London standard. [See further Jones (1993) on eighteenth century developments.] This Scottish standard was aided by an inheritance of a strong literary standard, stretching from the so-called Scottish Chaucerian poets in the fifteenth century to Burns and Allan Ramsay in the eighteenth century. Indeed, the Cumberland ballad 'bard' Robert Anderson, a contemporary of Wordsworth, looked to this Scottish standard and Burns for much of his inspiration (see p. 57). Certainly, however, in the Early Modern period, as Blank (1996: 129) records, there were attempts made to 'anglicise' Scots, to bring it 'in line' with the language of London and the court (*Sudron*); James I/VI even going so far as to designate the border regions as the 'Middle Shires' (Blank 1996: 154). Moreover, during the eighteenth century, when the issue of 'standard English' became politically, pedagogically and culturally so crucial, as we shall see in the next section, educated Scottish people, like the Irish, were encouraged to abandon their 'barbarous' dialect, even by fellow Scots.

Attitudes to Northern English in the eighteenth century

Images of the ' barbarity' of Scots have recurred frequently over the centuries, as too of Northern English. Southern and metropolitan perceptions of the people(s) (uncivilised belligerent raiders, Gaelic-speaking or unintelligible tribes) and of the landscape (cold, mountainous, wild and relatively uninhabited) are inextricably associated with those of the dialect(s). John Ray (1670) records the proverb 'Cold weather and knaves come out of the north', also the home of the devil in folk-lore. Westmorland certainly scared Defoe (1724–26): 'the wildest, most barren, and frightful of any [region] I have passed over in England'. As well as its weather and landscape, the 'harshness' of Northern English itself has also been commented on. So as a model of pronunciation to avoid, Thomas Wilson in his *Arte of Rhetorique* (1553) describes how 'This man *barkes out* his English Northren-like, with "I say", and "thou lad"' (my italics). One of the best known comments comes from the Cornishman John of Trevisa (1380) in his translation of Higden's *Polychronicon* (1364) (itself based on William of Malmesbury's *De Gestis Pontificum Anglorum*, 1125) and repeated by Caxton 100 years later:

> All the language of the Northumbrians, and especially at York, is so sharp, slitting and frotting and unshaped, that we southern men can barely understand that language. I believe that is because they are near to strange men and aliens [i.e. the Scots] ... that speak strangely.

In Easther's preface to his *Glossary of the Dialect of Almondbury and Huddersfield* (1883) he states his belief that Yorkshiremen will never shake off the 'terrible roughness' of their speech; but he admires them for it.

One particular feature of Northumberland speech was singled out in the eighteenth century for its harshness, namely the so-called 'Northumbrian burr' or uvular 'r' [ʁ], this at a time when rhoticity was only gradually disappearing from London pronunciation. Its origins are a matter of dispute, local folklore attributing it to the imitation of Hotspur's speech impediment. (Shakespeare notes only his 'speaking thick' in *2 Henry IV*, Act 2, iii).[6] Daniel

Defoe (1724–26) appears to be one of the earliest commentators, calling it a 'shibboleth upon [the natives'] Tongues … [they] cannot deliver it without a hollow Jarring in the throat …'. Francis Grose in his *Provincial Glossary* (1787), in citing the proverb 'He has the Newcastle burr in his throat, adds that 'few if any of the natives of [Newcastle, Morpeth, 'and their environs'] are ever able to get rid of this peculiarity'. A popular song *On the Flight of the Young Crows from Newcastle Exchange* prophesies that 1783 will be a remarkable year, since

> The keelmen will stop cursing and drinking …
> Refining in language, improving in notes,
> Letter R will run smoother, and glib through their throats …
> Ralphs, Richardsons, Rogersons, uttered with ease …

A dialect poem *Canny Newcassell* in the same collection (Bell 1812) records how the lads of the city on their visit to London have 'wor [our] bur' made game of, in 'rum-gum-shus ['sharp'] chimes'. John Collier in his *Alphabet for Grown-up Grammarians* (1778) graphically describes it as a 'choaking guggle of a sound', in terms not unlike those found in the popular comic 'guides' to Geordie pronunciation from the late 1960s, e.g. Dobson (1969). By then fast approaching the status of a stereotype, to help characterise the Geordie working-class male, the Northumbrian burr is now mainly heard in the speech of older people in the rural areas of Northumberland.

The disparaging comments on the 'burr' in the eighteenth century clearly reflect an increasing sensitivity to matters of pronunciation, a sensitivity at the expense of 'provincial' speech. Since the mid-sixteenth century there had been moves towards a 'standard' in speech as well as writing, a standard based on the educated, polite and courtly members of London society, as the famous quotation from Puttenham (1589) cited on p. 47 above attests. With the acceleration of the pace in the eighteenth century, and a corresponding vogue for pronouncing dictionaries, this meant that the Northumbrian burr would become an obvious symbol or 'symptom' of rusticity and 'vulgarity', and provincial accents were generally seen as 'vicious' [James Buchanan's *Essay* (1764), cited Crowley 1991: 75f.]. There is plenty of well-documented evidence, in this period so crucial for linguistic ideologies which persist through the nineteenth century and into the late twentieth century, of a felt need and desire for a standardised writing and grammar based on London English (which was perceived as rational and logical), and this 'ideal' was propounded by schoolteachers even of Northern extraction (e.g. Fisher 1750), undoubtedly extra-sensitive to their sociolinguistic 'marginalisation'. Indeed, aside from London, Newcastle published more grammars during this century than anywhere else (Beal 1996: 364).

It is difficult to estimate the extent to which educated Northerners actually modified their accents: actors and preachers were more likely to do so, as today. John Walker (1791) strongly believed that even the best educated people in the provinces were 'sure to be strongly *tinctured* with the dialect of the county in which they live' (cited in Crowley 1991: 109) (my italics). Despite the growth of good Northern grammar schools in this period, wealthy *nouveau riche* businessmen and colliery owners certainly sent their sons south to acquire fashionable tastes and education, and this included ridding their language of Northernisms, and in particular the Tyneside rising intonation (Jewell 1994: 122f.; see also Mugglestone 1995: 424). Then as now a broad accent could hinder professional advancement.

The problem is, as historians of the language have recognised (see Barrell 1983; Crowley 1991), that no matter how earnest influential elocutionists and educationists such as Thomas Sheridan and Newcastle-born radical Thomas Spence were in advocating London English in the interests of supposed social equality and political unity, what this really meant was an increased awareness of social difference. To the provincial faults of illiteracy, vulgarity and even immorality could be added the Northern uncivilised harshness. It is not surprising, therefore, that by the nineteenth century and the rise of industrialisation 'working-class' connotations should supersede those of the peasant/labouring classes, and the political implications of the provincial–metropolitan divide become more significant. The class-tying of broad dialect becomes particularly associated with Northern English, with the rapid growth of Northern towns and cities, and has remained so until the present-day (see further p. 58f.).

'The real language of [Northerners]': the images of Romanticism

It has to be said, however, that not all attitudes to, or perceptions of, Northern English in the eighteenth century were entirely negative. As in the Renaissance, there were scholars, local historians and antiquaries who recognised the ancient history of dialects, and their 'purity'. Following John Ray's example (1674) with his *Collection of English Words* from the North, East and South of England, dictionary-makers such as Elisha Coles (1676) and later Nathaniel Bailey entered a not insignificant number of dialect words into their dictionaries, as well as 'general' North Country words. Bailey, for example, quite specifically identifies words from the six northern counties, e.g. *bumblekites* ('blackberries'), *thropple* ('throttle') and a *way bit* ('little piece') from Yorkshire (see further Axon 1883). Relying heavily on Ray was Francis Grose's *Provincial Glossary* (1787), intended to help people understand 'our ancient poets', but augmented by gleanings from his own travels and county histories, and including words from the West of England also. Words still heard in the North include *glum, hinny* ('honey'), *lugs* ('ears'); and the construction *I is* (in the North-East): also noted by Ray, e.g. *I's dazed* ('I'm very cold'). Even Defoe (1724–26) had to admit that the 'nations' of Northumberland 'value[d] themselves' upon the Northumbrian burr 'because, forsooth it shews the Antiquity of their Blood'. Samuel Johnson, in the *Grammar* attached to his *Dictionary* (1755, cited in Barrell 1986: 138), likewise acknowledging the 'harsh and rough' pronunciation of the northern counties, had to concede that their 'many words out of use ... are commonly of the genuine Teutonic race ... The northern speech is therefore not barbarous but obsolete'.

To a significant extent perceptions of the North and its language were changed during the eighteenth century by the vogue for travel by the fashionable middle classes, who saw, in Lucas's words (1990: 9), the landscape as a valuable 'regenerative alternative to the decadence of the society of the city'. Much of the topographical literature that was produced laid the foundations for the 'Gothic' and 'Romanticism'. The Lake District in particular was seen as a dramatic symbol of the sublime, with its natural untamed beauty that was at once awe-inspiring. Joseph Turner's paintings of crags and castles inspired by his own tour of the North in 1797 are paralleled in Mrs Radcliffe's prose *Description of the scenery of Skiddaw* (1794), and Elizabeth Smith's poem *Calm after a Hurricane at Patterdale* (d. 1803, reproduced in Bragg 1984). Thomas West, in his *Guide to the Lakes* (1779) notes how 'in parts so sequestered from the world, the vulgar language ... may be supposed to continue very little altered from what it has been for many ages'. Here was a language uncorrupted, the peasant in harmony with Nature.

In an Appendix to his *Guide*, West added 'Specimens of the Cumberland Dialect' from the poems of the 'ingenious and modest Relph; an author of some estimation in those parts [for his pastorals]'. Cumberland was renowned for its songs and ballads in the late eighteenth century, most of them composed to be sung to familiar airs in a broad dialect that approached a local literary 'standard' (but also influenced by the Scottish ballad tradition over the border). Robert Anderson from Carlisle, born in the same year as Wordsworth, was a popular poet in the region well into the nineteenth century. Calling himself the 'Cumberland Bard', the image he constructs of the people and his district is one of pride and friendliness, not barbarity or 'rudeness'. As the narrator says in *Canny Cumerlan'*, 'we help yen anudder; we welcome the stranger'. Local words and pronunciations abound in every verse: e.g. the distinctive 'intrusive *w*'-glide as in *fworgery, fwok* ('folk'), *cwoat* and *Borrowdale Jwohnny* (noted by Ellis 1869–89, part 3: 1309).

The title of the better known *Lyrical Ballads* by Wordsworth and Coleridge was clearly designed to evoke the popular genre of ballad-making that in the eighteenth century was also reaching the drawing-rooms of the middle classes in popular collections. Bishop Percy's *Reliques of Ancient English Poetry* (1765) has a preface in which he confesses he had wondered whether 'they could be deemed worthy of the attention of the public'; but Allan Ramsay's wonderfully titled *The Tea-table Miscellany* (1740) had reached its fifteenth edition by 1768, at least north of the border. (Percy's *Reliques* was reprinted many times during the nineteenth century, from London to Frankfurt.) Joseph Ritson's *Northern Garlands*, a collection of North-East poems first published between 1784 and

1802 in four volumes in Stockton-on-Tees, York, Newcastle and Durham, sold 500 copies in London in 1810.

However, in 'feed[ing] off the central fells and southern lakeland' in Bragg's terms (1984: ix), Wordsworth's and Coleridge's relations to the tradition of balladry, and to the Romantic ideology of the Northern peasant and his vernacular, are by no means straightforward. That Wordsworth certainly knew the poetry of Robert Anderson, for example, is attested by a letter to him dated Sept. 17th 1814 (see Hill 1984: 167–9). The very obvious fact that Wordsworth did *not* use the vernacular of the Lake District is generally glossed over by critics, on the grounds that he was however still avoiding the artificial 'poetic diction' of the mainstream literary tradition, and that he was following his own precepts of his *Preface(s)* and *Advertisement*. Here it is stated, for example, that the poems 'were written chiefly with a view to ascertain how far the language of conversation in the middle and lower classes of society is adapted to the purposes of poetic pleasure'. Moreover, the language of those who commune daily with Nature and with the 'best objects from which the best part of language is ordinarily derived' is 'more permanent' (Wordsworth 1800: *Preface* to 2nd edn). Smith (1984: 208) therefore argues that Wordsworth and Coleridge 'levelled' the dichotomy between 'primitive' and 'refined' language; and Adamson (1998: 598f.) argues that the traditional hegemony of the literary standard is broken, and that, 'naturalist' in their aims, they 'attempted to create the illusion that written language was in fact a transcript of oral language' by 'selecting features of conversational language'. However, Wordsworth's own careful 'selection of the real language of men' is uncomfortably like the Augustan editing of colloquialisms, regionalisms and other 'barbarisms', which Adamson herself refers to. It is hard to resist the view that this 'real language of men' was 'sanitised', purged of the living voice, for a sophisticated and larger-scale Establishment or metropolitan readership: in Wordsworth's own words, 'purified ... from what appears to be its real defects, from all lasting causes of distaste or disgust' (1800). Coleridge's paraphrase in chapter 17 of his *Biographia Literaria* (1817) echoes even more clearly the predominant ideology of the eighteenth century: 'purified from all provincialism and grossness'. Far from being radical, Coleridge himself proves to be reactionary: the 'rustic's language', so purified, will not differ 'from the language of any other man of common sense ... except as far as the notions ... are fewer and more indiscriminate'. He further makes analogies with the language of 'many classes of the brute creation' and of 'uncivilised tribes'. In sum, it is therefore hard to agree with Lucas (1990: 91f.) that Wordsworth had a 'desire to keep dialect alive'. And the time was yet to come for regionalisms to return to mainstream literature.

The Industrial Revolution: the growth of Northern urban dialects

It is generally argued that the growth of a 'standard' dialect tends to marginalise and 'erode' vernacular variation, just as literacy kills off oral traditions, and a 'standard' literary language marginalises dialect writing. However, even in the early twenty-first century a doomsday scenario of the 'death' of dialects has not yet arrived (see next section); and from the early nineteenth century onwards there is certainly plenty of evidence of a flourishing popular culture in oral and written Northern English that appealed to both working and middle classes alike and which remains to this day. The 'disproportionate improvement' (Jewell 1994: 143) in literacy levels in the North of England during the eighteenth century seems only to have intensified cultural production. Indeed, with the dramatic rise in urban populations in the North in the nineteenth century, most of them working class, came a corresponding increase in pamphlets, broadsides, 'almanacs' and other kinds of dialect writing rooted in oral traditions (Shorrocks 1996: 387; Dyson 1997). It is clearly no accident that the development of a working-class consciousness went hand in hand with the intensification of the regional, the locally patriotic, as manifested in the promotion of the vernacular, symbolic of the socially excluded and marginalised. Ballads and songs were not only collected but composed afresh in the local dialect and printed in local newspapers, or recited/sung in front parlours and performed in the theatres and later music-halls. So the *Lambton Worm*, still well known in the North-East, and based on a popular medieval legend, was a comic 'sham ballad' composed in 1860 (chorus: 'Whisht, lads, haad yer gobs/Ah'll tell yer all an aaful story ...'). Well known too on Tyneside were the songs of Ned Corvan (1830–65), George Ridley (1843–73) and of Joe Wilson (1841–75), who, like the other traditional song-writers and 'bards' from Cumberland and Lancashire, dealt with marital strife, rites and rituals and family life (e.g. *Geordy, Haud the Bairn*). Many of these popular ballads or songs have become present-day 'anthems', symbols of local pride, whether Ridley's *Blaydon Races* on Tyneside, or *Maggie May* in Liverpool (see also Beal 2000).

A long-standing popular genre was the 'dialogue', either in verse or prose, and associated with Northern English since the late seventeenth century. Skeat (1911) prints a broadside from York (1673) in rhyming couplets called *A Yorkshire Dialogue (between an Awd Wife, a Lass and a Butcher)*. Another *Yorkshire Dialogue* was written by George Meriton (York 1683). Such dialogues were usually lively rumbustious affairs, full of bickering and complaints between family members. Cawley (1959; see Meriton 1683) quite plausibly relates them to the fifteenth century Townley plays from the Wakefield area. They provide fascinating insights into the colloquial idioms and discourse markers of the kind that still mark localised ordinary conversation today. So the Lass's *wyah* and the Mother's *w-ya* look very much like the *Why-aye* or *Way-aye* of Geordie today, the variation in spelling even at the present time, of course, reflecting its primary occurrence in informal speech rather than writing, and hence non-standardised in spelling (see next section).

Like Meriton's, the earlier dialogue has an agricultural setting and reveals the hardships of the farming life: the ox fallen into the pig trough and broken his *cameril-hough* (hind-leg). Yet one also suspects, in Meriton's case, his own relish in the proverbs and expressive lexis. For example, the son bursts in to say: 'Fatther our Bull segg's pussom'd, hee's degbound' (i.e. our gelded bull is poisoned, he's swollen). ('*Wellaneerin, wellaneerin*' ['Alas, alas'] is the father's response.) And the daughter complains:

> Fatther I've gitten Cawd, I can scarce Tawk
> And my *Snutles* [nostrils] are seay fayer stopt, I can nut *snawke* [smell]
> Nor *snite* [blow] my Nose …[7]

In 1801 appeared *A Lonsdale Dialogue* by W. Seward, printed at Kirkby Lonsdale on the border of the West Riding of Yorkshire and Lancashire (reproduced in Skeat 1896). This is a homely prose dialogue between a couple engaged to be married:

> Malle: Naw, haw iz ta ta-nete?
> Harre: Gaily; haw's taw ta-nete?
> Malle: I kna-nat haw e iz. I sat up sa lang yesternete, at I can hardly hod my ene oppen …

Noteworthy features are: phonologically, the traditional Northern /i:/ for /ai/ as in 'to-night'; 'l'-vocalisation in *hod* for 'hold' (noted by John Ray in 1674); 'a' for 'o' as in *sa lang*; grammatically, 'I' plus 'is'; second person pronoun singular 'thou' forms for intimacy (*ta, taw*); and *at* for *that*, widespread in traditional northern dialects, but of disputed origin; and lexically, *gaily* for 'very well' (from Old French): cf. *gay/gey* in Cumbrian and Scottish English meaning 'very'. Read aloud, the dialect would sound quite familiar still in this part of Northern England, and the sentiments and colloquial vigour not out of place in the dialogue of the longest running television serial set in Manchester, *Coronation Street*:

> That's o at fellas thinks on, gittin a hauseful o'barns for t' wimen ta tack cear on.

Better known are the 'miscellaneous works' of 'Tim Bobbin' (alias John Collier of Urmston in Lancashire) (1775) containing two dialogues in broad dialect spelling (Tim Bobbin and his 'Buk'; 'Tummus and Meary') and his 'view of the Lancashire dialect'. This volume was popularly reprinted for the next century, not only in other cities in the North of England (Leeds, 1790; Salford, 1811; Rochdale, 1894) but also in London (1806, 1820). The dialogues were extensively annotated by Samuel Bamford, a radical poet and dialect writer, dubbed 'the Lancashire bard' (Hewitt and Poole 2000: 117), and the work was used as a source by Francis Grose (1787) in his *Provincial Glossary*. Noteworthy grammatical features include *hoost* ('she shall'); *If idd'n* ('if you would'); *Iftle* ('if thou wilt'); *I'r* ('I was'); and *te* ('thy', 'the', 'they'). In his 'Observations', however, 'Tim Bobbin' notes changes in his local dialect:

> But as Trade in a general way has now flourish'd for near a Century, the
> Inhabitants not only Travel, but encourage all Sorts of useful Learning;
> so that among Hills and Places formerly unfrequented by Strangers, the
> People begin within the few years of the Author's Observations to speak
> much better English. If it can properly be called so ...
>
> (Collier 1775: 10)

Bobbin's comments, and his own pseudonym, hint at a certain point of
fact, namely that in the eighteenth century there were many parts of the
North that had enjoyed increasing prosperity, especially in the manufacture
of cloth from wool and cotton, and a prosperity that was intensified with the
mechanisation of many of the processes. As Jewell (1994) records in more
detail, industrialisation generally came early to the North: a steam-engine
was in use in Northumberland in 1714, and the waterways and canals all over
the North were much exploited for trade. Sheffield was already famous for
its steel industry in the early eighteenth century, and the coal-mines of the
North-East were proverbial in the seventeenth century ('carrying coals to
Newcastle'). Until the mid-nineteenth century, Newcastle was the largest
industrial town in the country. As a result, much popular song and poetry
changed from pastoral and rural themes, and new 'sub-genres' developed
which reflected a more industrial and urban setting, just as new occupational
dialects developed alongside the traditional dialects of farming and fishing.

One such distinctive 'sub-genre' was what I shall term 'pitmen poems', in
want of a recognised label. Although there were poems in circulation in areas
such as the Forest of Dean, they are particularly associated with the Newcastle
area from the mid-eighteenth century to the end of the nineteenth century,
and the early ones collected in popular Newcastle-printed miscellanies such
as Ritson (1793f.) and Bell (1812). They are interesting linguistically not
only because of the broad dialect depicted in many of them, especially the
'dramatic monologues', but because of their use of coal-mining terms. These
terms would be in regular use well into the twentieth century, and can be
linked also with 'Pitmatic', the particular dialect of Durham miners south of
the Tyne, which survived until the decline of the coal-mining industry in the
1980s. From ballads such as *Weel May the Keel Row, The Collier's Rant, The Collier's
Pay Week, The Pitman's Revenge against Buonopart* and T. Wilson's *The Pitman's
Pay* (cited by the phonetician A. J. Ellis in 1890, who was clearly interested in
the speech of the 'pitmen') the miners emerge as a jolly-hearted set of
workmen, dutifully bringing home their wages at the end of the week, but
fond of drinking, dancing and fighting at the local *hoppings*. Terms specific to
the Northumberland–Durham coal industry include *keel* (flat-bottomed boat);
keel-bullies (men who carried coals to and from the ships); *tram* (coal-truck in
the mine); *hoggars* [kind of pump (word pre-dating *OED* of 1850s)]; *huddock*
(cabin of keel or coal-barge); *duddies* [work-clothes (still heard in the North-
East today)]; *motty* (metal tally on tub of coal); *marrows* ('mates' down the
pit), as in the first line of *The Collier's Rant* 'As me and my *marrow* was ganning
to wark'.[8]

Crowley (1989a: 156) estimates that between 1871 and 1901 the number of towns with populations of more than 50,000 doubled; it has to be stated also that most of these were north of Watford Gap. Since immigration for (working class) employment largely came from the (rural) hinterlands, and social networks were characteristically close, linguistically speaking the dialects of the Northern towns tended to remain conservative and locally distinctive. Even today, for example, sociolinguistic research into the accent patterns of Hull reveals that the pronunciation of the PRICE vowel as /aː/ before voiced consonants as in *bride, five* in working-class speech was reported in East Yorkshire 130 years ago (see further Kerswill and Williams 1999: 217; Williams and Kerswill 1999: 142f.). One significant exception was Liverpool, which, as a major port, was more cosmopolitan and had large-scale immigration from Irish workers in the nineteenth century. Its distinctive intonation today, and heavily aspirated 't's may in part be due to Irish influence. In the twentieth century, the dialect of the large conurbations has now tended to 'spread' out through the suburbs back to the hinterlands, as they have tended to become 'regional standards', or 'supra-local norms'. So middle-class Northerners today in the West Wirral may well look to Liverpool as a model for accent, rather than to the Cheshire of tradition on the one hand, and RP on the other (see further Newbrook 1999: 91f.)

In one sense, the loaded polarity we are used to of the 'North [negative]–South [positive] divide' should have been reversed in the nineteenth century as a result of industrialisation, since for the first time in history the North was more successful economically than the South, and there flourished a wealthy 'millocracy' (Crowley 1989a: 153; see further Jewell 1994: 112f.). The North's equivalent of the metropolis was Manchester: a 'cottonopolis' (Guest 1998: 88). But reports of the awful working and living conditions of the labourers, the dirt and pollution inevitably coloured popular/outsider perceptions, and so too the images of Northern cities as Dickensian 'Coketowns' full of chimneys and slag-heaps, an alien 'Other'. Despite the flourishing of dialect poetry (Hollingworth 1977 singles out Lancashire between 1856 and 1870), it was the novels of social realism and political intent that came to foreground Northern dialects in their dialogue against such industrial backgrounds and so provided insights into the relations between the vernacular and issues of power(-lessness) and class that are still relevant today.

What also crucially emerges, however, from the novels of Elizabeth Gaskell, for example, a key figure in this context, is the sense of dialect as a marker of (working class) solidarity, of an 'us' versus 'them' ideology, that also pervades the contemporary vernacular poetry and song and also the music-hall routines.[9] And perceptions of Northern 'harshness' and lack of sophistication in culture and language are overlaid in this period and beyond, for example in the gritty realist novels and films of the 1960s, with those of 'toughness' and 'resilience' in the face of hardships and unremitting toil. But this resilience is also strongly dependent on humour, friendliness and plain-speaking, which may account for the fact that contemporary research into attitudes to dialects reveal similar positive connotations for Northern varieties.[10] These are much exploited in advertising and tele-sales; and in Bourdieu's terms (1991), such 'markets' have begun to endow Northern dialects with cultural 'value' or 'capital'.

Conclusion: the future (study) of Northern English

Britain has essentially been an urbanised society for over 100 years; yet despite a steady increase in sociolinguistic studies in recent years, we still know relatively little about its urban dialects. A pioneer survey was that of the Tyneside Linguistic Survey first planned in the early1960s by Barbara Strang and her colleagues at the University of Newcastle, but no major publication has so far been produced. Granted that new urban varieties are still emerging, for example Sunderland and Middlesbrough, the fact remains that there are no significant studies of Manchester or Leeds, and certainly no studies of the language of the ethnic minorities that form such a large part of the population of cities such as Leeds, and particularly Bradford.

The tendency in dialectology at least, since its foundations in the late nineteenth century, has been to look in detail or extensively at rural dialects, in the context of repeated fears of their immanent disappearance in the face of the decline of an agricultural economy, the spread of standard English, improved communications, the development of BBC radio broadcasting and increased mobility, for example. Striking is the fact that the two major linguists in this endeavour were both Northerners, Joseph Wright and Harold Orton, who in addition to their major works (1898–1905 and in the 1960s respectively) both produced studies of their native village dialects [of Windhill in West Yorkshire (Wright 1892) and of Byers Green in County Durham (Orton 1933)]. Following the nice suggestion by Wells (1982: 351) we may ponder whether their interest was stimulated by the rich variety of Northern dialects around them.

Fears of extinction or disappearance, however, have also been expressed by sociolinguists even in relation to urban varieties. Occupational dialects of the Industrial Age are now themselves in danger of dying out: e.g. of the coal-mining, iron and steel and ship-building industries once dominant in the North. More generally, it has repeatedly been stated that the gravitation towards a prestigious 'standard', intensified by curriculum and educational policy since the late nineteenth century, has resulted in the stigmatisation of local forms of speech and the development of regionally 'modified standards', or what Trudgill and Chambers (1991: 2–3) term 'mainstream' dialects, urban middle-class varieties, modified towards standard English. It has also been stressed that there is the danger of more homogeneous varieties emerging, dialect 'levelling', as a result of the greater mobility and social mixing of populations in present-day towns.

All this is true, but for one thing dialect levelling is not new, and features are not necessarily modified in one direction. Historically, by a process of general regional diffusion, the -s ending of the third person singular present tense, a Northern feature, has come to be part of southern and standard English (see also pp. 45–6); currently, RP pronunciations such as /wɒn/ for /wʌn/ 'one' and /sɪtiːz/ for /sɪtɪz/ 'cities' and /ɑ/ for /ae/ show Northern influence. Moreover, away from the generalities of dialect levelling, the real linguistic picture is actually quite complex. In terms of the individual rather than the community, for example, older, working-class speakers tend to remain dialectally conservative. But dialect switching or 'bidialectalism' is also a common phenomenon – educated middle-class speakers switching into broader dialect at home or with friends. Swann (1996: 321f.) aptly calls this 'designer English', implying that even accommodation may be an artefact, accents and dialects more or less conscious constructs, important signals of identity and difference. In addition, the mechanics of dialect 'levelling' are not always straightforward. New pronunciations constantly emerge, for example, which appear to be neither a local nor a 'standard' feature, but a compromise perhaps. Historically, this may account for the general Northern /oː/ and /eː/ vowels arising amongst middle-class speakers resisting both the traditional /ʊə/ and /ɪə/ forms, but resisting too the 'posh' RP diphthongs /əʊ/ and /eɪ/ (see Orton 1933). Some emerging Northern vowels are difficult to account for: the front-rounded vowel /ø(ː)/ in Newcastle as in 'home' amongst young working-class and middle-class males is traditionally a feature of the North-East coast (see Rydland 1999), but it may be a 'hypercorrect' attempt at /əʊ/. And while sociolinguists plausibly suggest that 'Estuary English' rather than RP is now a model for the speech patterns of young people throughout the country (e.g. in relation to glottalling, and also TH-fronting as in 'fevver' for 'feather'), it is difficult to estimate whether these are permanent accent changes in say Liverpool, Hull and Middlesbrough, or merely a youth, street-wise fashion; or even indeed, revivals of a once quite localised feature.[11]

At the level of pronunciation it is clearly easier to argue for a resistance to standardisation, since historically this has not been an absolute requirement of the whole standardisation and codification process. However, as part of the ideology lying behind this (Milroy and Milroy 1985) there is a danger of assuming that even in grammar there is more uniformity or homogeneity than there actually is; and so assuming also that descriptions of the 'grammar of English' include regional grammars rather than just 'standard' English. One major drawback has obviously been the lack of attention paid to spoken grammar until relatively recently; but even in the huge corpus-based *Grammar* by Biber *et al.* (1999) it is stated that 'dialect differences are not as pervasive as we might imagine ... the core grammatical structures are relatively uniform across dialects' (Biber *et al.* 1999: 20–1); and the main 'vernacular' features are reduced to matters of morphology/morphophonemics (twenty of these), as distinct from syntactic (just two) (see Biber *et al.* 1999: 14.4.5.). Moreover, the emphasis is very much that such features are stigmatised, and lacking in prestige – hence marginalised. And the persistence in Biber *et al.* (1999) and other grammars of the generic synonym 'non-standard' for 'vernacular' does nothing to reduce their marginal status. While it can be convincingly argued that their corpus is unrepresentative, it is also interesting that grammatical variation is reduced to the level of the morphological, precisely the area concentrated upon in traditional dialect surveys such as Orton *et al.* in the 1960s. The fact remains that an extensive study of syntactic and pragmatic variation in regional varieties remains to be carried out (and see Milroy and Milroy 1993a: xiii).

Nonetheless, there is enough evidence from individual studies to reveal a rich picture of grammatical complexity in Northern varieties. Some traditional distinctions, for example *thou/thee* for intimate address, may well be declining in spread of usage across the region, although these forms are still to be heard in Sheffield today, for example. Other pronominal forms of address have emerged, e.g. *youse yees* (plural) in Liverpool and Newcastle (perhaps under Irish influence). Traditional to the North (and noted in Wright and the SED) but still a feature of Tyneside English (Beal 1993) is what Ihalainen (1994: 213f.) terms the 'northern subject rule', where the verb has -*s* ending in all persons, unless adjacent to a personal pronoun subject (so 'birds sing*s*'; 'they peel them and boil*s* them'). Perhaps surviving in rural areas is the five-term system of demonstratives noted by Wakelin (1972): *thir* 'these', *tho* 'those', *thon* 'that over there', *thon ones* 'those over there', *thonder* 'that yonder'. Alive and well in the Greater Bolton area (Shorrocks 1997) is a four-term system of affirmative and negative particles [*aye* (positive)–*yigh* (contradictory)–*now*–*nay* (contradictory)]. In Tyneside speech *div* and *divvent* are variants of 'do' in questions and negation (also here *dinna, dint*).

Many other features are clearly part of the expressive, emphatic and focusing resources of speech silenced in writing, such as discourse tags: 'I'm going out tonight, *me*' heard on Tyneside and in Yorkshire; 'You can't *but*' (as a warning or challenge) or 'I'll manage *but* [however]' on Teesside and Tyneside; 'she's canny *like* [so to speak]' in Middlesbrough; 'I will see you tomorrow *likely* [probably]' in rural Cumberland. 'He's gone for t' pick *HER* (stressed) up' in Bolton refers to the subject's wife, not mentioned in the co-text, but known in the context (G. Shorrocks, personal communication). Again, traditional dialectology in its concentration on phonetic, morphological and lexical information tended to ignore discourse features, even when recordings were made,[12] and ignored too the wide range of expressive exclamations which yet help to characterise a region as much as the accent. Interestingly, they are as characteristic of dialect stereotyping today in popular perceptions and the media, as particular phonemes are: e.g. *ee (by gum)* in Yorkshire; *by 'eck* in Manchester; *howay/hadaway* and *man* on Tyneside.[13]

Perhaps the most striking omission in contemporary dialectology and sociolinguistics is an extended study of intonation and related prosodies such as voice quality and tempo; again, noteworthy distinguishing markers of dialectal variation, and part of the popular perceptions of regional varieties in Britain. The Scouse velarisation, for example, is easily recognisable, and the rapid rate of delivery of Geordie leads to charges of incomprehensibility. The twentieth century saw marked advances in the recording of speech, but even Wells (1982) in his detailed study of accents has very little to say on intonation (similarly Wells 1984). Ellis (1869–89, vol. 5) at least noted the 'rising inflexion of the Newcastle pitmen', 'higher for questions than for simple affirmation' (and see also a brief comment by Watt and Milroy 1999: 31). It was dismissed as a 'most barbarous, monotonous and irritating twang' by J. B. Priestley (1934: 290). Cruttenden (1997) sees rising intonation as a general feature of 'urban Northern British' (which interestingly includes Birmingham!) but this hides the different pre-head patterns which distinguish Tyneside speech from that, say, of Liverpool (Farrar *et al.* 1999: 245f.).

In conclusion, it is probably true to say that there is more localised speech north of Watford Gap than south of it. Hence there is a plausible justification for Rawnsley's claim in his very first sentence (2000: 3) that 'the North of England evokes a greater sense of identity than any other region of the country'. In a period of growing political decentralisation (the establishment of a Scottish parliament has been followed by calls for a Yorkshire one), relations between regional identity (preferred and real) and dialect boundaries (actual and perceived) are likely to be even more significant. So long as Northerners want to be different from each other, or to show their allegiance to a particular social group, region or town, dialect differences will remain. Scouse or Geordie will simply redefine itself, or new isoglosses maintain a 'North–South' linguistic divide.

Notes

1 For a chapter on the cultural politics of Northern English in the Renaissance, see Blank (1996). This present survey forms part of an extended study of the cultural history of Northern English, in preparation. Thanks are due to Joan Beal, Helen Berry, David Fairer, Vic Gammon, Andrew Gibson, Lynette Hunter, Rowena Shuttleworth, Reiko Takeda, Clive Upton and John Widdowson.

2 Wright (1996: 272–3) sees this dialect boundary as marking the Northern limit of the great vowel shift. But it was only the back vowels that remained unaffected; for the front vowels the North appears to have had its own, earlier shift; see Wakelin (1972: 107–8) and Smith (1996: 99–101).

3 Wells (1984: 57) says /u:/ is 'no longer in urban Tyneside', but Watt and Milroy (1999: 29) find it in working-class male speech.

4 Northern 'u' was certainly noted as such by Walker in his *Pronouncing Dictionary* (1791). Mugglestone (1995) argues that long and short 'a' were both labelled as 'vulgar' and 'elegant' variously up to the mid-nineteenth century, and /a:/ is still a feature of southern speech generally, of all social classes.

5 Through the opinions of captain Lismahago the novel provides a defence of Scots in terms also used for Northern English (see pp. 55f.): 'true, genuine Old English', close to Chaucer and Spenser, free from the 'affectation and false refinement' of London English.

6 Heslop (1892: xxiv), who notes the Hotspur legend, doubts the burr is of 'Old Northumbrian' origin, but suggests a continental influence instead. Ellis (1890: 125) believes it of 'recent origin', of 'no dialectal value', but a 'defect of utterance'.

7 Also from Yorkshire is *The York Minster Screen* (1833), reprinted in Skeat (1896), which begins: [Mike Dobson:] 'Hollo, Bob Jackson, owr't the plague's thee boon' [where the plague's thee bound].

8 Noted by Orton (1933) in his native mining village of Byers Green, County Durham, and also the *Survey of English Dialects* (1962) for Northumberland. In Ray (1674) the word appears as a North Country word for one of a pair (of shoes or gloves). According to the *OED* its origin is unknown.

9 Both Melchers (1978: 113) and Easson (1985: 696) stress that the glosses Gaskell provided for her first novel *Mary Barton* (1848) not only helped her readers' potential ignorance but aimed to show the living continuity of the dialect with the past: John Barton and Job Legh speaking the 'true' English of Chaucer.

10 See Coupland (1988: 97), Mobärg (1989: 288f.) and L. Milroy (1999a: 189). However, Scouse is less favourably appreciated for such qualities than Yorkshire or Geordie, according to recent market research (see, for example, *Daily Telegraph* 1 January 1997) – a far cry from the 1960s when, with the Beatles and the 'Merseysound', Scouse acquired considerable cultural 'capital' in Bourdieu's terms (see p. 62). The Yorkshire image of friendliness and plain speaking was cultivated by the Labour Prime Minister Harold Wilson in the 1960s, turning his back on his earlier Oxbridge accent. The maintenance of an educated South Yorkshire accent by the former leader of the Conservatives William Hague is no doubt due to similar connotations.

   As far as I know, little research has been carried out on the relations between the positive connotations and general stereotypes of Northern dialects and their exploitation in working-class comedy acts on stage and later radio and television: this would include such names as Roy Castle (Huddersfield), Jimmy Clitheroe (Lancashire), Ken Dodd (Liverpool), Norman Evans (Manchester), George Formby (Manchester), Freddie Frinton (Grimsby), Jimmy James (Middlesbrough), Ken Platt (Lancashire), Sandy Powell (Rotherham) and Robb Wilton (Everton).

11 According to R. W. Bailey (1996: 78), Otto Jespersen when touring Britain in 1887 noted final glottal stops in Sheffield, Lincoln and Glasgow. Wakelin (1972: 98) notes TH-fronting in Leeds.

12 Orton (1933: 134) does at least comment on the characteristic North-East connective phenomenon still common today of final 't' shifting to /r/ before a word beginning with a vowel, e.g. *sirup* ('sit up'), *shurup* ('shut up') and *geraway man* ('get away, man', i.e. 'you don't say so') (see also Wells 1984: 56). And in an Appendix he transcribes some wonderful 'specimens' of conversations at the local football pitch. Another linking prosody noted as 'general Northern' for the late eighteenth century and early nineteenth century by Ihalainen (1994: 213) is the 'linking *v*' as in 'tiv another'. I have seen no references to its survival today, although I note its occurrence three times in a ballad called *Sedgefield Fair*, sung to Roy Palmer (1979) by a North Yorkshireman.

13 An item of national radio news that *ee!* had entered the revised *Concise Oxford English Dictionary* produced the headline in the *Daily Telegraph* 'Ba gum, there's an ee in t'Oxford Dictionary' (9 June 1999). J. B. Priestley (1934: 290) found 'objectionable' the constant 'Ay-ee, mon' or 'Ay-ee, yer b– – –' of the men's talk in Newcastle, and the never-ending 'hinnying' of the women.

4 The history of southern hemisphere Englishes

Elizabeth Gordon and Andrea Sudbury

Between 1800 and 1876 there was a great outward movement of peoples from the British Isles. The official number was more than 4 million (Simpson 1997: 7), but historians say that many more left whose departure was not recorded, with the true number perhaps being more than double that in the official statistics. This was part of a huge nineteenth century European diaspora involving around 50 million people (Belich 1996: 278). For most of these emigrants it was a one-way journey, and they never returned to the home of their birth.

One of the results of this great movement of peoples was that the English language was transported by the emigrants to countries in the southern hemisphere – Australia, South Africa and New Zealand. The Englishes spoken in these countries are much younger varieties than the older colonial varieties of English spoken in the West Indies, India and North America, and the beginning of the colonial period in Australia coincides almost exactly with the end of the colonial period in what were by then known as the United States of America.

The southern hemisphere destinations of Australia, South Africa and New Zealand were not 'empty' countries. The Europeans who travelled there, however, did so on the assumption that these new lands provided greater opportunities for success than they could achieve at home, and they gave little thought to the fact that these countries were already occupied and that European success would be achieved only by the dispossession of indigenous people.

The stories of those early settlers involve adaptation and survival in countries very different from the places they had left behind. They also involve the adaptation and development of their language. As we will show, the circumstances and conditions in Australia, New Zealand and South Africa were very different, and these differences are reflected in present-day Australian English (AusE), New Zealand English (NZE) and South African English (SAfE). At the same time the three varieties have remarkable similarities. Many a New Zealander travelling overseas will tell of being mistaken for an Australian, and occasionally for a South African. There are enough points in common in all three varieties for them to be described collectively as southern hemisphere Englishes.

Australian English

English in Australia

AusE is commonly defined as being homogenous, with no or very little regional variation. Whether this is the actual situation is perhaps questionable, since, on the whole, studies of AusE have focused on the variety spoken in New South Wales (NSW), the most populated state (Horvath 1985: 19). Certainly a number of recent studies suggest a more diverse situation, with the emergence of some regional variation (Bradley 1989, 1991; Oasa 1989). By contrast, social variation in AusE is well attested and has been represented in terms of a continuum ranging from Cultivated [most similar to Received Pronunciation (RP), least local], through General to Broad (furthest away from RP, most local) (Mitchell and Delbridge 1965; Lass 1987: 299).

Yet, for many groups of Australians the English they speak is influenced to a greater or lesser degree by their local community language, be it Greek, Italian or some other language. Traditionally it was assumed that the effect of community languages on the Australian-born children of non-English immigrants were minimal and such speakers spoke the same as children of English-speaking Australians (Blair 1989: 171). Research such as Horvath's (1985) study on the sociolects of Sydney has questioned this position. Aboriginal English is also distinctive from that spoken by the population of Anglo-European descent (Arthur 1996). Here, although we recognise that many varieties of AusE exist, both as second-language and first-language varieties amongst the multicultural ethnic groups in Australia, the sense in which we use AusE refers to 'the dialect spoken by (non-Aboriginal) native-born Australians ... [which] is the dominant form of English in Australia' (Blair 1989: 172).

Nineteenth century British settlement

English was brought to Australia at the end of the eighteenth century, with the arrival of the First Fleet to the shores of New South Wales in January 1788. Although 'rediscovered' by Captain Cook in 1770,[1] it was not until after the US War of Independence and transportation to North America ceased that Australia was considered as an alternative destination for convicted felons.

The First Fleet consisted of just over 1,000 people, 759 of whom were convicts, with four companies of Marines (Macintyre 1999: 31). Men outnumbered women by three to one. By the turn of the century there were some 5,000 British residents in NSW. Between 1793 and 1810 approximately 400 convicts per year were transported; this had increased to over 1,000 each year by 1815, and at its peak, between 1826 and 1835, over 5,000 convicts were transported annually (Inglis 1974: 8). By the time transportation stopped in 1852,[2] 160,000 convicts had been transported to Australia from Britain and Ireland. NSW and Van Diemen's Land (now Tasmania) were the main destinations for the convicts, though smaller penal colonies were established in other parts of the land.[3]

It is difficult to establish precise regional origins of the convicts. Although written sources record the place of trial for individual convicts, this is a poor guide to the place of origin for many of them, since other evidence suggests that at least one-third were tried outside their county of birth (Robson 1965: 20). Thus, although approximately one-third of all convicts were tried in Ireland, the actual number of Irish convicts is likely to be higher, with a substantial number of the London-, Lancashire- and Scottish-tried convicts actually being Irish-born (Robson 1965: 14, 20; Prentis 1983: 49). With this caveat in mind, Table 4.1 shows the most common counties where transported prisoners were tried.

The majority of the British convicts came from urban areas. Outside London these included manufacturing cities such as Birmingham and Manchester in the Midlands and North respectively (Inglis 1974: 8). For the most part they came from the lowest stratum of society and were predominantly unskilled and under 25 years old (Robson 1965: 14). As far as the convicts transported from Ireland were concerned, more came from rural areas, fewer had moved outside their counties of birth and there were more unskilled labourers amongst them than amongst their English counterparts (Robson 1965: 10).

Not all the white settlers to Australia in the early part of the nineteenth century were transported convicts. As well as the prison wardens sent out with the convict ships[5] and military personnel/officials, small numbers of free settlers chose to go to Australia. However, it was not until the 1820s that non-convict settlers came in any large proportions. Numbers increased from just 8,000 free settlers arriving in NSW in the 1820s, to 30,000 new arrivals in the 1830s and over 80,000 in the 1840s (Macintyre 1999: 75). The gold rushes of the 1850s, particularly in Victoria, saw the population of Australia increase dramatically: 'In one decade the populations of NSW, South Australia and Queensland doubled, whilst that of Victoria increased seven-fold' (Buxton,

Table 4.1 Percentage of convicts to Australia according to county of trial[4]

County	Percentage
London	17.9
Lancashire	7.0
Dublin	5.1
Yorkshire	3.7
Warwickshire	2.8
Cork	2.8
Surrey	2.7
Gloucestershire	2.6
Kent	2.2
Somerset	2.0

in Crowley 1974: 166). Numbers of 'new' Australians[6] increased from 430,000 in 1851 to 1,150,000 a decade later (Macintyre 1999: 87).

English-speaking settlers came from all over the United Kingdom and Ireland. Substantial groups came from the south of England. For example, between 1860 and 1892 approximately 18.5 per cent of settlers came from the south-west of England and 14.7 per cent from the south-east (Lucas 1987: 97).[7] Large numbers of Irish emigrants arrived, particularly after the Great Famine of 1846 (Roe, in Crowley 1974: 122). When the numbers of free and transported Irish immigrants are combined, it is estimated that by 1891 a quarter of the Australian population was ethnically Irish (Lucas 1987: 93). There were also significant numbers of Scottish immigrants. Although they predominantly came from Lanarkshire and the Lowlands (Lucas 1987: 97), there were sufficient Gaelic-speaking Scots to warrant some Presbyterian church services being conducted in Gaelic (Roe, in Crowley 1974: 122). One estimate for the proportion of Scottish immigrants to Australia between 1851 and 1900 is 14–16 per cent (Prentis 1983: 68).

The social origins of the free settlers was mixed, though very few came out from the highest social ranks (Inglis 1974: 19). Moneyed individuals were particularly encouraged to emigrate, but thanks to assisted passages many came out from the lower classes (Lucas 1987: 14). Amongst the middle-class settlers were high-ranking military and government officials, large landowners and 'mercantile capitalists' (Horvath 1985: 35). Included in the government-assisted migrants were many taken from the workhouses of urban Britain. One way of recruiting free settlers was a bounty system, such that agents were paid per migrant they sent to Australia. Workhouse residents were a prime source of people for the bounty hunters. Thus, as Macintyre observes, 'this process of "shovelling out" paupers produced an immigrant cohort that was hardly different in background and circumstances from the convicts' (Macintyre 1999: 77).

The origins of Australian English

Most accounts of the development of AusE seem to agree that a distinctive Australian accent developed very early, most likely amongst the first immigrant children born in Australia (Cochrane 1989: 178). In support of this is the absence of Irish and Scottish features in AusE.[8] Despite a sizeable number of settlers from these areas (see above), they may have arrived in Australia too late to have a significant influence on the developing dialect [in accordance with Mufwene's (1996) founder principle]. However, although there is some agreement as to *when* AusE emerged, there is less agreement concerning the *origins* of AusE. Several theories have been proposed – is it a transported English dialect, most likely Cockney, or is it a mixed dialect, and if so, where did the mixing occur?

AusE as transported Cockney

This hypothesis proposes that AusE is essentially late eighteenth-century London English which was transported to Australia by the early convicts and settlers as an already established dialect (Hammarström 1980; Cochrane 1989). Such a claim is based, in part, on the evidence that London provided the greatest numbers of immigrants in the early years of colonisation (Hammarström 1980: 53). However, as shown above, it is not necessarily the case that prisoners convicted in London came from London at all, thus it is unsafe to assume that all of the London-transported convicts spoke Cockney.[9] A further strand of Hammarström's argument is that, as London English would have been the prestige variety at the time of British settlement, it stands to reason that it would have been the model to aim for in the new society (Hammarström 1980: 53).

Linguistic evidence for the 'transported Cockney' position is based on comparisons between relatively modern Cockney and Australian pronunciations, particularly vowels.[10] Hammarström accounts for the differences between these dialects today as changes undergone in Cockney. He argues that AusE (and other transplanted varieties) are more conservative and thus will have changed less (Hammarström 1980: 42).

AusE as a mixed dialect

The alternative hypothesis is that AusE has its origins in dialect mixture and not in a transported English dialect. There are two aspects to the mixing pot theory:

1   AusE is a mixed variety consisting predominantly of south-eastern British English dialects which were mixed in Britain *before* transportation. Such mixing possibly took place in London (Turner 1972; Collins 1975).
2   AusE is a mixed variety with mainly south-eastern dialect features which were mixed *on* Australian soil (Bernard 1969; Blair 1975; Trudgill 1986). In fact, Bernard goes as far as to suggest that the same mixed variety developed in several different Australian settlements simultaneously (Bernard 1969: 66).

The dominance of London variants in the new Australian dialect is easily accommodated by these mixed dialect explanations – if the largest proportion of speakers came from the London and south-eastern region, it follows that the variants used by such speakers would have been more likely to be retained in the new dialect. This is made explicit by supporters of the mixing bowl theory (Blair 1975: 25).

South African English

English in South Africa

English is spoken as a home language by just 8.6 per cent of the South African population (about 3.46 million people).[11] Of those speakers, just over half are of European descent. Yet English enjoys a position in South African society far exceeding the number of native speakers. Roughly 45 per cent of the population spoke English (to some degree) in 1991.[12] English has enjoyed official status in South Africa since the early years of British settlement: it was made the sole official language of Cape Colony in 1822, a position shared with Dutch from 1910 (changed to Afrikaans in 1925). However, since 1994, after the first democratic elections in South Africa, English and Afrikaans have shared official language status with nine indigenous African languages (Gough 1995).

With such a multicultural society, it should come as no surprise that English in South Africa is not a homogenous variety. Five types of South African English have been identified, which may be crudely separated according to population groups (Branford 1996: 35). Within each type there is a continuum of varieties ranging from broad to close to standard British English.

What we refer to as *South African English* (SAfE) in this chapter is the variety spoken by the smallest of these groups, namely the English spoken as a first language by white South Africans. It is this native speaker variety which has been the focus of most studies of English in South Africa, and the main emphasis here is the history and development of this dialect.

The other types of South African Englishes are predominantly (with some exceptions) non-native varieties of English:

Afrikaans English is the variety spoken by South Africans of Dutch descent (including white and coloured people) who speak Afrikaans as a first language. English has been used by the Dutch settlers in South Africa for at least as long as English settlers have been there. Afrikaans English is distinguished by strong Dutch influence, particularly in its phonology, but also in its syntax (Branford 1996: 37–40; Watermeyer 1996: 99–124).

Coloured English is a particularly difficult variety to define, given the heterogeneity of the group of people usually described as coloured[13] (Branford 1996: 40). In fact, Malan notes that although the majority of people who speak such English are classified as coloured, other speakers, including some working-class whites, Indian- and Xhosa-descended people, also use this variety. For this reason, she prefers the term Cape Flats English (Malan 1996: 145). Of the 3.6 million people classified as coloured in the last census, the vast majority (82.1 per cent) stated their first language as Afrikaans. Thus, Coloured English is influenced by Afrikaans as well as Cape English (see Branford 1996; Malan 1996).

Black South African English is the term used to describe the English spoken by black South Africans, the majority of the population. Roughly 61 per cent of black South Africans claimed to have some knowledge of English in the

1993 RCM ('reaching critical mass') survey (Gough 1996: 53), with varying degrees of competence. However, less than 0.4 per cent of blacks reported that English was their first language in the 1996 census. As with the other non-native South African Englishes, Black South African English is influenced by the native African languages of its speakers, in both its phonology and syntax (Lanham 1996: xxii).

South African Indian English is spoken by those South Africans of Asian descent, predominantly the descendants of the indentured Indians brought to Natal from the 1860s (see p. 74). In recent years, English has rapidly been replacing Indian dialects as the first language of South African Indians, to the extent that in the 1996 census over 94 per cent reported that English was the language of the home (see Mesthrie 1996a and this volume).

Nineteenth century British settlement

English was first brought to South Africa towards the end of the eighteenth century when, in 1795, the British annexed the Cape, which had been in Dutch possession for 150 years.[14] Under the Treaty of Amiens, the British occupation was short lived, just 8 years, but the British returned in 1806 to reclaim the Cape (Thompson 1990: 52). At the time of the second British occupation there were already some 10,000 Europeans living at the Cape, predominantly Dutch, but also French Huguenots and Germans (Troup 1972: 47).

For the British, the value of the Cape was purely strategic and initially there were no plans to set up a settlement. Consequently, in the early decades of the nineteenth century only small numbers of British settlers, predominantly merchants, arrived at the Cape. In addition, there were administrative and military personnel, although it is likely that these inhabitants were transient (Lanham 1996: 20). Such British settlers became part of the upper stratum of Cape Town society and intermarriage with the Dutch elite was common. However, the British government became motivated to populate the Cape, partly as a cheap means of creating a civil defence force to secure the frontier between the colony and the indigenous Xhosa people. The government advertised for prospective settlers to farm the land, without revealing their planned 'defence' role (Lester 1998: 8). Over 80,000 people applied for the 4,000 or so passages. The first significant and organised groups of these settlers arrived in the Albany district of the eastern Cape in 1820. They subsequently became known as the 1820 settlers. These immigrants were selected from all areas of the British Isles and from all parts of society, excluding the aristocracy, and were almost a microcosm of nineteenth century Britain (Sparks 1990: 56). Many came from areas which were economically depressed in the aftermath of the European War. The greatest proportion of these came from the southern counties of England, with roughly 39 per cent coming from Middlesex alone. A further 11 per cent came from the other home counties. There were also significant groups from

Ireland (11 per cent) and Scotland (6 per cent) (Morse-Jones 1971: 5). However, the land was not good for agriculture and the situation was made worse by the fact that very few of the 1820 settlers had any agricultural knowledge since most came from urban areas (Keegan 1996: 63). Just 3 years later more than 60 per cent of these settlers had left their rural farms and moved to other parts of the country, particularly the urban centres such as Grahamstown, where they became artisans and merchants (Sparks 1990: 61).

New settlers continued to arrive in southern Africa in small numbers. However, the next major wave of British settlement came in the 1850s when large groups of settlers came to Natal, the Dutch settlement on the eastern seaboard, which had been annexed by the British in 1843. Between 1849 and 1852 some 5,000 immigrants had been brought out as agriculturists. A large proportion of these came from the Midlands, Yorkshire and Lancashire (Branford 1994: 434) and more of them came from the middle classes than did the Cape settlers (Thompson 1990: 97). As was the case with the earlier Cape settlers, those coming to Natal had little agricultural knowledge and within a few years most had moved from the land to the urban areas of Durban and Pietermaritzburg, where many became successful traders and artisans (Keegan 1996: 206). As well as new arrivals from Britain, many settlers came to Natal from the Cape Colony (Keegan 1996: 206). By 1870 there were 15,000 British settlers in Natal and just 3,000 Afrikaners (Thompson 1990: 97). In addition to the European settlers in Natal, a significant group of immigrants came from Asia. Ever since the British colonisation of Natal there had been a shortage of labourers in Natal and, since slavery had long been abolished, one solution to this was to bring out indentured labourers from the Indian subcontinent. Between 1860 and 1911 some 152,000 indentured Indians had been brought to Natal.

A third wave of white settlers was attracted to southern Africa in the 1870s and 1880s, when diamonds and then gold were discovered in the Transvaal and Witwatersrand regions respectively. For example, in Kimberley, the main diamond-mining centre, the population increased from 5,000 in 1870 to 50,000 by 1872. Forty per cent of the residents were European. The Witwatersrand experienced an equally sudden population boom. Johannesburg was transformed in just over a decade, from a tiny settlement when gold was discovered in 1886, to a major urban centre with over 75,000 white residents by 1899 (Thompson 1990: 120). Amongst this wave of immigrants were groups of miners from Cornwall, where the tin-mining industry was in decline (Thompson 1990: 118). As well as new settlers, many Cape Colonists and Natalians flocked to these areas.

Development of South African English

The two distinct waves of English settlement in South Africa resulted in the development of two quite separate varieties of nineteenth century South

African Englishes. The first was the English which developed in Cape Colony, the second was the variety of English which emerged in Natal.

Cape English was the first distinctive variety of SAfE to develop and has its origins in the first generation of African-born English speakers, namely the children of the 1820 settlers (Lanham 1995: xxi). Lack of attachment to and contact with Britain amongst this frontier society accelerated the formation of a local English (Lanham 1996: 20). Many of the Cape English features originated in south-eastern English dialects, particularly Cockney and lower middle/lower class speech (Lanham 1995: xxi). Dutch also had an influence on the developing dialect, both lexically and phonologically, as a result of the close association between the English and Dutch settlers on the Eastern Frontier (Lanham 1996: 21). The indigenous African languages, such as IsiXhosa, contributed a wealth of vocabulary items, particularly for native flora and fauna, to the developing variety (see p. 84).

One reason why a distinctive variety of English developed in Natal was because the demographics of the founding populations of the two British colonies were very different. In contrast to the Cape settlement, relatively few settlers went to Natal from the south of England. Instead, there was greater input from northern British dialect regions as noted above. There was also very little contact with Dutch speakers. In addition, the new British immigrants who came to Natal were more likely to come from the middle classes or higher. The population density in Natal was greater than that in the Cape and society was considerably more urban than the rural settlements of the Cape. Furthermore, unlike the Cape Colony, Natal was not a frontier society, making it easier for British social distinctions to be maintained (Lanham 1996: 21). This was facilitated by closer ties to Britain: 'The Natal settlers had a strong desire to remain English in every aspect of identity, social life, and behaviour' (Lanham 1995: xxi). As a consequence, although Natal English developed some local features, standard British English was perceived as the prestige model. Even at this stage, Cape English was denigrated as 'local' and carried low prestige (Lanham 1996: 21–2).

The discovery of gold and minerals in the last quarter of the nineteenth century led to increasing stratification of white South African society. Natalians fared better in the social ranking order than Cape colonials, finding it easier to mix within the highest status groups – they fitted in more with the new British immigrants, being considered 'more English' (Lanham 1982: 327); they also tended to be better educated and more skilled. The Cape settlers were more likely to be placed lower on the social hierarchy and were often associated with the Dutch (Lanham 1996: 23). RP was quickly established as the most prestigious accent in this increasingly hierarchical society. Since Natal English shared similarities with RP, it was recognised as not being significantly different from British English by other settlers (Cape Colonials, Afrikaners and other Europeans). For that reason it gained the status of an acceptable, local, informal standard (Lanham 1982: 328).

South African English today

The influence of RP in South Africa persisted until well past the Second World War and in certain spheres, such as the media, RP continued to be the target variety until relatively recently, as noted by a BBC correspondent in 1973:

> Listening to the radio is like switching on the BBC Home Service in the days before Suez ... the accents of the English services are impeccably upper middle-class. It's only when people are interviewed that you hear the authentic South African being spoken.
>
> (John Simpson, quoted by Lanham 1996: 24)

This RP model is essentially what Lanham originally identified as 'Conservative' in his tripartite classification of SAfE (Lanham 1978). However, for the majority of white English-speaking South Africans, access to authentic models of this prestige variety became increasingly more removed with time. This has resulted in more local variables (particularly from Natal English) becoming acceptable as standard norms (Lanham 1982: 331). In fact, 'Respectable' SAfE has become the accepted standard and has been described as 'probably the best reference accent for the country in general' (Lass 1987: 303). Many of the variables which characterise this variety have their origins in Natal variables.

The 'extreme' end of the SAfE continuum is the most 'local' – 'Extreme' SAfE carries low status and is stigmatised by much of the white English community (Lanham 1982: 331). Many of the features associated with 'extreme' SAfE are Cape variables or come from Afrikaans English.

New Zealand English

English in New Zealand

New Zealand is a remarkably monolingual country. Estimates based on the 1996 census suggest that 95 per cent of the population speak English and 85 per cent are monolingual English speakers (see Kuiper and Bell 2000: 13). Like Australia, there is little regional variation in New Zealand apart from the distinctively rhotic Southland variety of NZE in the southern part of the South Island (Bartlett 1992). Variation according to social class, however, is widely recognised, with sociolinguists adapting Mitchell and Delbridge's terms cultivated, general and broad for categories of NZE to represent social class variation (see, for example, Bayard 1995; Gordon and Deverson 1998). In more recent years an ethnically marked variety of NZE has been noted and is variously described as Maori accented English, Maori English or Maori Vernacular English (see King 1993; Bell 2000). In the past it has been generally accepted that the influence of the immigrant communities in New Zealand has been negligible. However, over the last decade there has been a considerable increase in the number of immigrants from Asian countries and, in Auckland especially, there is overwhelming evidence of migration from the Pacific Islands. While NZE has been the subject of a number of major research projects these have not considered the influence of present-day immigration.

Nineteenth century British settlement

The beginning of the main European settlement of New Zealand dates from 1840 when the treaty of Waitangi was signed between a number of Maori chiefs and representatives of the British government. For about half a century before this date New Zealand had been a rather lawless and ungoverned outpost of the Australian colony of New South Wales. By 1839 the total population of the country was about 2,000 people but, once Britain gained sovereignty over the whole country in 1840, the European population of New Zealand grew at a phenomenal rate. By 1858 Europeans outstripped the indigenous Maori people (56,000 Maori to 59,000 Europeans, Graham 1992: 52) and by 1881 they had reached half a million. The 1886 census showed that 52 per cent of the population was born in New Zealand (Graham 1996: 112).

Immigration to New Zealand occurred in three stages. The first period in the 1840s and 1850s was one of planned settlement, largely under the auspices of the New Zealand Company set up for purposes of land speculation under the direction of Edward Gibbon Wakefield. In the original Wakefield settlements (Wellington, Christchurch, Dunedin, Nelson, New Plymouth) attempts were made to control the social mix and nature of the colonists but this proved mainly ineffectual.

The second period of immigration came in the 1860s with the discovery of gold in Otago. Many miners came from the goldfields in Australia but others came from all over the world. The new immigrants also included large numbers of Irish Catholics, a group carefully excluded by the earlier planners (Akenson 1990: 24). In the North Island the period of the 1860s was one of conflict between Maori and Europeans (or *Pakeha* as they are known in New Zealand). Regiments of the British Army, which included soldiers from Britain, Australia and Ireland, came to fight in the New Zealand Wars and many remained after the wars had ended.

The last stage of immigration lasted between 1870 and 1885. This was a period when the government embarked on an ambitious programme of public works and development and actively recruited migrants from the British Isles. Over 100,000 immigrants (93 per cent from the UK) were brought to New Zealand in the 1870s. The majority of these came from the British Isles, and within Britain people from England made up the largest ethnic minority. The Welsh probably made up about 2 per cent and Scots made up 24 per cent of the total New Zealand population. The Irish who arrived somewhat later made up 19 per cent by 1881 (Belich 1996: 316-17).

The earliest settlers were regarded as the 'founding fathers and mothers' of European New Zealanders and achieved high social status in the new country simply because they were first to arrive. Their specific reasons for immigrating to such a distant country were various but all wanted to better themselves and provide better prospects for their children. At the same time they were certainly not abandoning their British roots. Their aim was to create a new Britain in the South Pacific in the context of British law, religion, education, social values and practices.

By the 1860s–70s there were more New Zealand-born than there were immigrants in the country. The New Zealand-born had only second-hand knowledge of Britain through the accounts of their parents and they did not have their parents' desire to make New Zealand a replica of Britain. While remaining loyal to Britain, the colony was developing its own character and the New Zealand-born considered themselves quite distinct from the immigrants who continued to arrive from Britain.

The British settlers who made their homes in New Zealand in the nineteenth century were mostly from the lower middle classes, or from labouring/agricultural backgrounds. Although there were attempts to encourage people who were rich and/or noble, these largely failed. Early New Zealand has been described as 'overwhelmingly a working settlers' society' (Graham 1996: 116). This does not mean that there were no social class distinctions, but rather that the distinctions were blurred. The first settlers were particularly concerned with survival and there are many graphic accounts of the hardships many endured (see Porter and Macdonald 1996). Those lower down the social scale were more likely to adapt their housing, dress, food and leisure activities to the colonial situation while those who were higher on the social scale were more likely to rely on British imports or follow British customs more closely in the new country.

The origins of New Zealand English

In the two or three decades from the first settlement in 1840 the foundations of New Zealand society were laid down. It is in this period that NZE was also established. Comments about vocabulary differences appeared very quickly. Samuel Butler, who later wrote the novel *Erewhon*, went to New Zealand as a young man in 1859. He wrote about the use of the term *flax bush* 'where we would have used *flax plant*'. He commented on farming terms such as 'mob' and 'outstation' adapted and imported from Australia where they had been used for the convict settlements (quoted in Turner 1966: 56, 145). Recent research has now demonstrated that the New Zealand accent also developed in those first three decades of settlement (Trudgill *et al.* 2000).

The first serious written account of New Zealand spoken English came from an amateur phonetician called Samuel McBurney in 1887. He was complimentary about the speech he heard in New Zealand and said that in the main it was better than heard in most districts at 'Home' – i.e. in England (Turner 1967; Gordon 1983). By the beginning of the twentieth century there were many written comments about New Zealand speech which were uniformly uncomplimentary, describing it as an ugly colonial twang just slightly better than the English spoken in Australia. School Inspectors wrote reports in which they complained that this new variety of English was the outcome of laziness and the evil influence of 'the home and the street'.

Until quite recently, written comments gave the only evidence available on early NZE. However, research into the spoken English of those first New Zealand-born *Pakeha* has now been made possible because of the discovery of an archive of recordings of about 300 elderly people collected in different parts of New Zealand in the 1940s. This is the basis of a major research project into the Origins and Evolution of New Zealand English (ONZE) at the University of Canterbury (Lewis 1996). It has demonstrated that some people born in the early 1870s had a recognisable New Zealand accent. The project has revealed a high degree of variability in the speech of the earliest speakers (born in the 1850s and 1860s) and, furthermore, has demonstrated that some people born in the early 1870s had a recognisable New Zealand accent (Trudgill *et al.* 1998).

The discovery of this archive of early spoken NZE has led to interesting speculation and theorising about the origins of the New Zealand accent and new dialect formation in general. It has caused the swift rejection of the theory promoted in New Zealand in the 1930s and 1940s (and similar to the explanation for AusE) that the accent was a version of London Cockney (Wall 1958).

Another single-origin theory which has been put forward more recently is that NZE was largely derived from AusE (Bauer 1994b; Gordon and Deverson 1998; Bayard 2000). Early commentators remarked on the similarity of the two varieties, and recordings of old New Zealand speakers in the ONZE project are often thought to be Australian. Because of the close connections between New Zealand and New South Wales before 1840 and then later at the time of the goldrushes, an Australian influence is to be expected. However, it is now considered that a single-origin theory whereby NZE came directly from Australia is too simple and does not account for areas in New Zealand where the New Zealand accent developed in spite of the fact that there was little or no Australian influence, nor does it account for the similarities not only between AusE and NZE but also between them and SAfE.

Southern hemisphere Englishes

Phonetics and phonology

At the phonological level AusE, and to a lesser degree NZE and SAfE, correspond more or less one-to-one with Standard Southern British English (Wells 1982: 595). The most distinctive aspects of the southern hemisphere Englishes are their phonetic characteristics. Here only the most distinctive southern hemisphere phonetic realisations are discussed.[15] Wells's (1982) lexical sets are used for points of reference for vowel realisations. A summary of the key features for all three varieties is given in Table 4.2.

Perhaps the most widely discussed southern hemisphere feature concerns the movement of the front short vowels in the lexical sets TRAP, DRESS and KIT.[16] For AusE, SAfE and NZE the TRAP vowel is realised in the area of cardinal 3 /ɛ/ and DRESS in the region of cardinal 2 /e/. However, it is the KIT vowel which distinguishes these southern hemisphere Englishes. In AusE KIT is most commonly realised as a high front vowel [i]. By contrast, in New Zealand the KIT vowel has centralised towards [ɨ] and for some speakers is even lowering towards schwa. This difference in the KIT phoneme has resulted in the stereotype that Australians eat [fiːʃ ən tʃiːps] whilst New Zealanders eat [fʌʃ ən tʃʌps] (Bell 1997). In South Africa both realisations occur and are loosely distributed allophonically, with certain environments (adjacent velar consonants, preceding /h/, word initially and preceding palato-alveolars) inhibiting centralisation (Taylor 1991).

The southern hemisphere English diphthongs serve to distinguish them from most northern hemisphere varieties as well as marking the different social varieties within the southern hemisphere. Two characteristics stand out: the first concerns the movement of the southern hemisphere diphthongs, commonly referred to as 'diphthong shift' (Wells 1982: 597).[17] In essence this describes a continuation of the great vowel shift with respect to the closing diphthongs, such that the onsets of the front diphthongs (FLEECE, FACE) are lowering and backing, whilst the back onsets (GOOSE, GOAT) are lowering and fronting (Wells 1982: 256). As far as the PRICE and MOUTH onsets are concerned, in AusE and NZE and for some South African speakers,[18] there is a crossover pattern such that the onsets are different for each vowel. PRICE has backed towards /a – ɒ/ and MOUTH has fronted towards /æ/. For some speakers these onsets are also closer, towards /ɔ/ and /ɛ/. The second characteristic feature of southern hemisphere diphthongs is glide weakening (Wells 1982: 614). In SAfE such weakening of the glide has led to monophthongisation, particularly for the MOUTH and PRICE diphthongs. Recent research suggests that glide weakening is on the increase in NZE (and AusE) (Trudgill *et al.* 2000).

The START and PALM lexical sets are realised with a long open front vowel [aː] in both AusE and NZE. This is also the case for the BATH set in New Zealand. In Australia, however, certain words in the BATH set, most commonly when the vowel is followed by a nasal, are realised with [æ], leading to a contrast between the vowels in *darts* [daːts] and *dance* [dæns] (see Wells 1982: 233). In the case of SAfE, the START/PALM/BATH vowels are one of the most distinctive features. Realisations are invariably backed, with Conservative and Respectable varieties favouring [ɑː]. Extreme SAfE has even backer realisations, in some cases with rounding [ɒː – ɔː] (see Branford 1994: 480).

All three varieties have lost the southern British English distinction between /ɪ/ and /ə/ in unstressed syllables. So, whereas *rabbit* is [rabɪt] in many

British varieties, AusE, NZE and SAfE favour [rabət]. This leads to a number of southern hemisphere homophones, such as *pack it* and *packet* [pækət] (Wells 1982: 602).

NZE is undergoing a further loss of vocalic contrast, namely a merger of the NEAR and SQUARE diphthongs.[19] For an increasing number of New Zealand speakers there is no distinction between pairs such as *here* and *hair* or *really* and *rarely*. Realisations come anywhere in the shared phonetic space of these diphthongs, with a tendency towards the closer onset vowel [ɪə] (Gordon and Maclagan 1990: 146).[20]

For the most part all varieties have similar consonantal realisations, although SAfE shows a certain amount of divergence from the Australian and New Zealand norms.

All three varieties are generally non-rhotic, with the exception of the Southland area of New Zealand (Bartlett 1992) and some extreme SAfE which may be influenced by Afrikaans (Lanham 1982: 338). AusE and NZE have both linking and intrusive /r/, unusually, however, this is absent in South African varieties. Furthermore, unlike the other southern hemisphere dialects, SAfE is marked by a lack of ING variation. /h/ dropping is relatively rare in all of these Englishes.

With respect to /l/, both AusE and NZE have a tendency towards dark /l/ in all environments. Recent research suggests that there is an increasing trend towards /l/ vocalisation in these varieties (Horvath and Horvath 1997, 1999). SAfE, on the other hand, tends more towards clear realisations.

/t/ is commonly voiced intervocalically in all southern hemisphere Englishes, though this is less widespread than in American varieties. /t/ glottalling seems to be spreading in New Zealand and Australia amongst younger speakers, particularly in word and syllable final positions (Bayard 1990; Holmes 1994, 1995a).

The southern hemisphere varieties have one characteristic prosodic feature, namely rising intonation at the end of statements. This intonation pattern, known as the High Rising Terminal (HRT), is particularly widespread in Australian and New Zealand Englishes.[21]

Lexicon

One very noticeable feature of these three southern hemisphere Englishes is the distinctive lexicons which have developed since colonisation.[22] Many words have entered these varieties to describe aspects of the new environments, particularly native flora and fauna, but also words to describe the practices and customs of the indigenous peoples. Some of these have subsequently spread into other varieties of English.

The English lexicons of Australia, South Africa and New Zealand have all been affected to some extent by the indigenous people in these countries. The situation in each country was different. The Australian continent was occupied by scattered groups of gatherer–hunters speaking over 200 distinct

Table 4.2 A comparison of key features of AusE, NZE and SAfE (from Sudbury 2000: 115)

Feature	Australian English	New Zealand English	South African English
KIT	[i]	[ɨ – ə]	Allophonic distribution [ɪ – i] / [ɨ – ə]
DRESS	[e] or closer	[e – ɪ] (sometimes diphthongised)	[e]
TRAP	[æ – ɛ]	[ɛ – ɛ̝]	[ɛ]
LOT/CLOTH	[ɒ – ɔ] some [ɔː]	[ɒ] some [ɔː]	[ɒ – ɔ]
STRUT	[ɐ] fronting	[ɐ] fronting	[ä – ɜ] central to back
FOOT	[ʊ]	[ʊ – ɤ]	[ʊ – u]
START/BATH/PALM	[æ – aː]	[aː]	[aː – ɒː]
NURSE	[ɜː – iː]	[œ̈ː – øː]	[œ̈ː – øː]
FLEECE	Tendency to diphthongise [ɪ̈i – əi]	Tendency to diphthongise [ei – ɨi]	[iː]
FACE	[ɛɪ – ʌɪ – ɑɪ]	[ʌɪ]	[ëi – əi – ʌe]
THOUGHT/FORCE/ NORTH	[ɔː]	[ɔː – oe] frequently diphthongised	[ɔː – oː]
GOAT	[ɐ̈ʊ – ʌʊ – ɒʊ]	[ä̈ʊ – ʌʊ – ɒʊ]	[əʊ – ʌʊ – ʌː]
GOOSE	[ʉː] tendency to diphthongise [ɵe – ɵ̈ʉ]	[ʉ] tendency to diphthongise [ɨʉ]	[u: – ʉː]
PRICE	[aɪ – ɒɪ – ɔː]	[aɪ – ɔː]	[ɒɪ – ɑː] [aɪ]
CHOICE	[ɔɪ – oɪ̞]	[oe – ɔɪ – ọ̈ɪ̞]	[ɔɪ – oe]
MOUTH	[au – æu – ɛu] some glide weakening	[æu – ɛu – æᵊ – ɛᵊ] some glide weakening	[æu] [ɑu] glide weakening

NEAR	[ɪə – ɪˠ – iː]	[ɪə – eə]	[ɪə – iː]
SQUARE	[ɛə – ɛˠ – ɛː]	[ɪə – eə]	[ɛə – ɛː – eː]
NEAR/SQUARE merger	✗	✓	✗
CURE	[ʊə – uːə – uː – ɔː]	[ʊə – uːə – uː – ɔː]	[ʊə]
HAPPY	[iː]	[iː]	[iː]
/ə/ in weak syllables	✓	✓	✓
/ɪ/ /ə/ merger	✗	✓	Allophones of the same phoneme
Vowel neutralisation before /l/	✓	✓	✓
H drop	✓ (variable)	✓ (variable)	✗
-ING	✓ (variable)	✓ (variable)	✗
/ʍ/ /w/	✗	✓ (retreating)	✗
Post-vocalic R	✗	✗ (except Southland)	✗
Linking/intrusive R	✓	✓	✗
T-glottaling	Not much	✓	✗
T-voicing	(lenition to [ɾ])	✓	✓
/l/ /ɫ/ allophony	Tendency to dark	Dark	Clear
/l/ vocalisation	✓ (some)	✓ (some)	✗
Disyllabic OWN	✓ (variable)	✓ (variable)	(Regionally variable)
WITH	[wɪð] (some [θ])	[wɪθ] (variable)	

languages and the dialects within them (Arthur 1996). In South Africa were the Khoikhoi (Hottentots), the Nguni group of languages, including Zulu, Pondo, Themba and Xhosa, and the Sotho-Tswana group, including Sotho, Venda and Lemba. In New Zealand, on the other hand, the indigenous people, the Maori, were largely an agricultural people speaking a single language (with dialectal variations), which meant that there was a single unified source of loan words from Maori into English. For the most part there are many loan words which are a familiar part of the lexicons in the individual countries, especially for flora, fauna and features of local topography, but few of these have moved into mainstream English. Exceptions are *kangaroo, budgerigar, koala, kookaburra, boomerang* (from Aboriginal languages into AusE); *kiwi, haka, moa* (from Maori into NZE); and *donga* (from Xhosa into SAfE). In the case of South Africa, contact with another colonial language, Dutch-Afrikaans, has also had a significant influence on the lexicon, with words such as *springbok, wildebeest, Boer, trek* and *apartheid* now used and understood world-wide.

Many lexical items from British English have acquired extended or new meanings in the southern hemisphere, while at the same time other British words have been discarded. Words referring to features of the landscape such as *brook, common, copse, field, green* (as in *village green*), *heath, meadow, moor, spinney, thicket* and *woods* are known only through English literature. In New Zealand the British English *field* is 'a paddock' and British *stream* is 'a creek'. The word *bush* (meaning a shrub in British English) is land covered with native rain forest in New Zealand, but in Australia it refers to the outback (Gordon and Deverson 1998: 63).

The colonists used existing words from British English for different species of flora and fauna in the new settlements. The New Zealand *beech trees* and *birch trees* are nothing like their British namesakes. The Australian *hawk* is a different bird from the English *hawk*, as are the New Zealand *robin, magpie, cuckoo* and *kingfisher*. In Australia words referring to the early convict settlements soon changed in meaning to become farming terms – *station* and *mob*, for example. The military term *muster* used for moving criminals transferred to the present meaning of mustering sheep and cattle.

Within the southern hemisphere Englishes a number of older dialectal words were also retained, which may have since been lost in their original dialects. For AusE and NZE such words are often the same or very similar (Bauer 1994b: 410). An example in both AusE and NZE is *skerrick*, as in 'not a skerrick' from Yorkshire dialect meaning 'nothing'. The Australian and New Zealand use of *spell* meaning 'a rest' is a British dialect term now obsolete in Britain, as is *larrikin* for a mischievous youth and *chook* for chicken.

In Australia the transportation era was a rich source of vocabulary, with much criminal slang being imported with the convicts. Although most of these criminal terms have since fallen out of usage, a few items still exist today, such as *swag* meaning knapsack (originally a thief's plunder or booty), *new chum*, a derogatory word for 'novice', and *old hand*, referring to someone with experience (see Orsman 1997).

In South Africa the political system of apartheid created many new meanings for existing English words as well as new coinings. Examples include words such as *Bantustans* or their official name *homelands* (areas reserved for occupation by black Africans with very limited self-government), *group area* (urban area for a specific ethnic group), *classification* (into racial groups) and *resettlement* (moving groups by force). Even words such as *coloured* have been politicised in SAfE (see Branford 1994).

Grammar

It is widely reported that there is little to distinguish the southern hemisphere varieties from other major world Englishes with respect to morpho-syntactic features: 'there are very few if any *major* grammatical features characterising Aus/NZE' (Lass 1987: 300, our italics). The exception here is perhaps SafE, which, at least in certain sociolects, has syntactic features which are the result of close contact with Afrikaans. For example the use of *busy* as a marker of progressive aspect in constructions such as *he was busy lying in bed* would appear to derive from the Afrikaans progressive aspect marker *besig om te* (Branford 1994: 490).

Of course, this is not to say that there is no syntactic variation in these varieties, but such features are not markedly different from features in other Englishes.[23] Thus, the following comments by Branford about SAfE may equally be applied to the other southern hemisphere Englishes:

> Colloquial varieties [of SAfE] have a number of apparently distinctive syntactic items and structures, but it is difficult in the case of many of these to determine whether they are in fact indigenous to SAfE, of English dialect origin, or merely characteristic of informal English generally.
>
> (Branford 1994: 488)

Notes

1 In fact, prior to Cook, much of the western coast of Australia had already been charted and named 'New Holland' by Dutch navigators in the mid-seventeenth century (Mcintyre 1999: 23).
2 This was 1868 in Western Australia.
3 The exception to this was South Australia, where no convicts made up the early white population.
4 Figures are based on Robson's sample of convicts transported to Australia (1965: 176–85).
5 As far as the regional and social backgrounds of the guards is concerned, it is likely that many of them had similar origins to the convicts themselves (Eagleson 1982: 420).
6 That is to say, excluding Aboriginal peoples.
7 Lucas bases these figures on Crowley (1951) and warns that they may possibly represent government assisted immigration, rather than the total immigration to Australia (Lucas 1987: 97).
8 However see Horvath (1985: 39); Trudgill (1986: 140) for possible Irish features.

9   A point clearly made by Bernard (1969: 64).

10 Hammarström, for example, bases his comparison on Sivertsen's (1960) study of Cockney English.

11 Figures given here are taken from the 1996 census web pages of Statistics South Africa.

12 This is an estimate based on the 1991 census (Schuring 1993, in Gough 1995).

13 'People considered to be of mixed racial ancestry' (Malan 1996: 125).

14 For English in South Africa prior to British colonisation, see Gough (1995).

15 For fuller phonetic descriptions of the southern hemisphere Englishes, see Bauer (1986), Branford (1994), Horvath (1985), Lass (1987), Trudgill and Hannah (1994) and Wells (1982).

16 For NZE, see Bauer (1979, 1992), Bell (1997), Trudgill *et al.* (1998) and Woods (1997) for hypotheses about the direction of this movement and discussion on whether it is conservative or innovative.

17 For a more contemporary perspective of this movement in terms of Labov's (1994) principles of vowel shifting, see Sudbury (2000: 103).

18 A number of South African speakers show the reverse pattern, where the onset of PRICE has fronted and MOUTH has backed (Wells 1982: 614, 621).

19 For example, see recent work by Bauer (1986, 1994b), Gordon and Maclagan (1990), Holmes *et al.* (1991), Holmes and Bell (1992) and Maclagan and Gordon (1996).

20 The conclusions of the Wellington Porirua Project, however, suggest that although /ɪ/ may have been the favoured onset in the early stages of the merger, /e/ seems to be increasingly favoured by some speakers (Holmes *et al.* 1991: 81).

21 For AusE, see Guy and Vonwiller (1984, 1989); for NZE, see Allan (1990), Britain (1992) and Warren and Britain (2000).

22 For more detailed descriptions of southern hemisphere English vocabulary, see Turner (1994), Ramson (1970, 1988) and Baker (1966) for AusE; Orsman (1997), Bauer (1994b) and Eagleson (1982) for NZE; Silva (1996) and Branford (1994) for SAfE.

23 For variation in AusE, for example, see Eisikovits (1981, 1987, 1989) for Sydney; Shnukal (1982) for Cessnock, NSW. In NZE, the Porirua Project (Holmes *et al.* 1991) considered non-standard syntactic features; also research by Sigley (1997), Hundt (1998), Britain (2000), Britain and Sudbury (in press), Quinn (2000).

5 'Deformed in the dialects'

An alternative history of non-standard English[1]

Shana Poplack, Gerard Van Herk
and Dawn Harvie

Introduction

Many salient non-standard features of contemporary English and its varieties
are widely held to be recent innovations, generated by rural, uneducated,
minority and other marginal speakers. This is particularly true of
morphological and syntactic features. *Ain't*, demonstrative *them* and a variety
of verbal inflections, among others, have become stereotypically associated,
and ultimately identified, with specific (non-standard) varieties. African
American Vernacular English (AAVE) is a prime example. Its distinctive
morphosyntax has spurred a massive long-term research effort to locate its
origins, typically, in the African mother tongues of the ancestors of current
speakers, and in attendant processes of creolisation and decreolisation.

Recent research (Poplack 2000a; Poplack and Tagliamonte 2001) has
proposed an alternative history for these forms, one that is firmly rooted in
the internal evolution of English vernaculars. We have argued that reliance
on the prescribed standard as a metric, coupled with inattention to the history
and evolution of spoken English, conspire to obscure the fact that many of
the non-standard features today associated with AAVE are not innovations,
but *retentions* of Early Modern English (and older) forms. Such retentions are
a by-product of the sociolinguistically peripheral status of the speech
communities in which they are used. This chapter describes the novel use of
existing resources that led us to these conclusions. The *Ottawa Grammar
Resource on Early Variability in English* (OGREVE) is a unique compilation of
reference grammars of the English language written between 1577 and 1898.
Though a number of other such bibliographies are available, most notably
Sundby *et al.* (1991), Görlach (1998) and Fries (1925), the OGREVE is unique
in its emphasis on linguistic variability of earlier times. The data of the
OGREVE, when properly exploited, enable us to: (1) infer the existence of
such variability, (2) trace the evolution of normative dictates associated with
key linguistic variables, and, perhaps most innovative, (3) discern hints of
linguistic 'conditioning' of variable usage from grammarians' injunctions.
Incorporation of these conditions as factors in the analysis of contemporary
variability enables us to test their current applicability and thereby ascertain
the history and provenance of the variable constraints operating on these

features. The OGREVE represents an important tool in ongoing investigations into the origins of key variables of Early African American English (Early AAE) (Van Herk 1999; Poplack and Tagliamonte 2001).

In ensuing sections we explain how early grammars and vernacular speech cross-validate each other as reliable sources of information on language variation and change. We first consider the relationship between the grammatical enterprise and language in use. We then describe the constitution of the OGREVE, and detail our methods for extracting clues to variability from even the most resolute advocates of the standard (e.g. Jonson 1640/1972). The next section describes the varieties of African American English whose analysis has been informed by the attestations of the OGREVE. We illustrate the utility of the materials by comparing the trajectory of two key variables throughout the grammatical tradition with their behaviour in Early AAE – the unmarked or variable past-tense forms of strong verbs, and -*s*-marking in the simple present tense. We show that not only the Early AAE variant forms, but, more important, the linguistic (and social) factors conditioning their occurrence are the legacy of centuries of variability in English. This bolsters our claims (e.g. Poplack and Sankoff 1987; Tagliamonte 1991; Poplack 2000a; Tottie and Harvie 2000; Van Herk 2000; Walker 2000; Poplack and Tagliamonte 2001) that many features of Early AAE that have been construed as alien compared with the modern-day standard in fact have their roots in the vernacular or regional English of earlier centuries.

'Ascertaining the English tongue'

The rising status of the English language through the Early Modern period led to calls for its codification, such as Jonathan Swift's *Proposal for Correcting, Improving, and Ascertaining the English Tongue* (1712), reproduced below:

> Persons, as are generally allowed to be best qualified for such a Work ... should assemble at some appointed Time and Place, and ... some Method should be thought on for *ascertaining* and *fixing* our Language forever, after such Alterations are made in it as shall be thought requisite.

Despite pleas like Swift's, English has never had an official regulatory body, such as those established for French or Italian. For some 300 years, however, the language has had its own *de facto* 'Academy'. Composed of the authors of grammar books, usage manuals, and style guides, this Academy has collectively contributed to the standardisation of the language (at least in its written form).

Grammarians and students of linguistic variation would seem to be uneasy bedfellows at best. The major focus of variation theory is on form–function asymmetry, especially where several forms compete to perform referentially identical functions. Grammars aim to furnish an ordered view of language, in which each form serves a single function and each function is represented by a single form. The normative enterprise, instantiated in grammars, dictionaries, usage manuals, or newspaper columns, carries the quest for form–function symmetry even further: not only is a particular form to be associated with a particular function, but competing forms are to be eradicated. A range of strategies, partially dependent on the prevalence of the forms involved, may be employed to achieve this goal. Variability may be ignored, degraded by associating one or more of the variants with boors, foreigners, or the illiterate, or explained away by imbuing variant forms with subtle semantic distinctions (Poplack 2000b). Paradoxically, however, systematic examination of the OGREVE reveals that grammatical injunctions of an earlier time may conceal the historical antecedents of many non-standard forms in the spoken language. This is invaluable information for students of dialect differentiation and linguistic variability.

Standardisation entails ironing out variability, usually by stigmatising as 'non-standard' the forms found in regional or working-class varieties. This is the point of departure for our analyses. Earlier generations of grammarians were willing (sometimes eager) to describe what they perceived as the linguistic chaos around them, if only to vilify it, as in Gill's (1619/1972: 121) observation (which provided the title for this paper): 'there is scarcely a verb which is not deformed in the dialects according to their hearer's vulgarity'. Our working hypothesis in analysing grammars of past centuries proceeds from the observation (elaborated on p. 95) that forms salient enough to have incited the opprobrium of grammarians were not only attested but probably widespread in contemporaneous spoken usage. Such attestations permit us to circumscribe the chronological extent of linguistic features, and thereby infer which ones are retentions and which are innovations.

Building the Ottawa Grammar Resource on Early Variability in English

In constituting the OGREVE, we took the designation *grammar* as a cover term not only for traditional prescriptive and descriptive grammars, but also for dialect grammars and usage manuals. This contrasts with more restrictive uses of the term in the study of the grammatical tradition (e.g. Sundby *et al.* 1991; Görlach 1998): 'a book intended for use in schools or for private reference which contains a description of the structure of a language at least on the levels of spelling/pronunciation and syntax' (Görlach 1998: 4). Our research agenda required that the stylistic coverage of the OGREVE extend to spoken, regional, and dialectal forms, which would not necessarily be fully covered in traditional grammars.

Annotated bibliography

Development of the OGREVE involved searching for potentially useful works through the establishment of broad initial criteria, followed by increasing restrictions on the materials. We first assembled an annotated bibliography of 641 early works on the English language or English linguistics, drawn from a range of sources. These included the Scolar Press English Linguistics 1500–1800 series, comprising a reprint of 365 titles, primarily of traditional grammars, as well as the Scholars' Facsimiles & Reprints series. We also consulted standard reference works on the evolution of the English grammatical tradition (e.g. Fries 1925; Alston 1965; Vorlat 1975; Sundby *et al.* 1991; Görlach 1998). Görlach (1998) provided us with many works not within the purview of Scolar Press, including Pegge (1803/1814), Jackson (1830), Smith (1855), Peacock (1863), Duncan (1870/1942), Brewer (1877), and Nesfield (1898); Sundby *et al.* (1991) gave us Harris (1752/1970) and Burn (1786/1805), and confirmed our selections of many works from Scolar Press.

Initial criteria for inclusion

Our goal of tracing variability throughout the English grammatical tradition dictated radically different criteria for inclusion from those of other compilations. Of the initial 641 works, 249 were retained based on their satisfaction of one or more of the criteria of accessibility, publication date, prestige, and possibility that variability would be mentioned. Accessibility was a practical concern. Many grammars were never reprinted, and the originals were too fragile to travel. Publication date between approximately 1550 and 1900 was partly determined by availability – sixteenth-century grammarians were more concerned with describing Latin and Greek than English – and partly by our research agenda, which focuses on the *evolution* of English variability. Our specific interest was in the language of emigrants to the New World, which may have provided a model for the first generations of African Americans. The criterion of influence on popular (educated) opinion required that we consider such well-known works as Jonson (1640/1972), Priestley (1761/1969), Lowth (1761/1967), and Murray (1795/1968). The fourth, most important, criterion was the mention of variability involving non-standard morphological and syntactic forms, insofar as this could be inferred from titles [e.g. *Common Blunders Made in Speaking and Writing, Corrected on the Authority of the Best Grammarians* (Smith 1855)] or descriptions ('somewhat of a ratbag' Görlach 1998: 256) in reference works.

Grammars excluded

Closer inspection of the 249 works retained at this stage revealed more than half to be unsuitable for our purposes, for a variety of reasons. Some works were not about grammar at all, including philosophical treatises on the nature of language or Utopian works aimed at creating new universal languages. An example is Francis Lodowyck's (1652/1968) *The Ground-Work of a New Perfect Language*. In many others, such as Burles (1652) or Farnaby (1641/1969), the subject matter (and, sometimes, the language in which they were written) was Latin or Greek. This is especially true of the period before 1750, when English was not yet considered worthy of serious study. Some works, especially post 1800, are simply too standard for our purposes, describing an increasingly codified English. Other works from the same period aimed at a lay audience furnish taxonomies of 'blunders', usually lexical or phonological. Rather than treat grammar as a system, they simply caution readers against shibboleths such as *ayn't*, *bran new* [sic], *leastwise*, *anyhow* (Smith 1855) or *scrunch*, *chaw*, *cuss*, *Vendsday*, *yeller* (Jackson 1830).

Grammars retained

Retained for the OGREVE were any and all grammars from which we were able to infer the existence of morphological or syntactic variability. These include works written in Latin, but about English, such as Cooper (1685), perhaps the first grammar to mention *ain't*, and Wallis (1653/1969). Usage manuals were also retained, if the 'blunders' in question involved grammatical features. This winnowing process left us with ninety-eight works relevant to variability in English, ranging from Henry Peacham's *The Garden of Eloquence* (1577/1971) to John Collinson Nesfield's *English Grammar, Past and Present* (1898). Figure 5.1 shows the distribution of the works constituting the OGREVE across time periods.

Although the distribution in Figure 5.1 results to some extent from accessibility, it is largely a reflection of the publishing history of grammars of English. Grammars published before the early 1700s are more likely to be concerned, directly or indirectly, with the structure of other languages, with English often used as a vehicle for teaching them. Increased efforts to standardise the language in the 1700s and early 1800s resulted in a surge of grammars in and about English. The rise in popularity of dialect works and usage manuals in the 1800s, especially later in the century, reflects the rise of scholarly interest in regional and working-class varieties (Crowley 1989a). The goal was to document regional and especially rural forms before they were levelled by modern technology such as the telegraph and steam engine. Urban working-class forms, on the other hand, were slated for eradication. Attestations of variability are most plentiful in these genres.

The ninety-eight grammars retained tend to fall into one of four categories. Highly *prescriptive* works, imposing norms of speech and writing, deal with variation in order to castigate it. Examples include Baker (1770), Cooper (1685), and, especially, usage manuals from the 1800s [e.g. George Duncan's *How to Talk Correctly* (c. 1870/1942)]. Jackson (1830: *passim*), for example, categorises a variety of non-standard features as 'low', 'very low', 'exceedingly low', 'vilely low', or 'low cockney', as well as 'ungentlemanly', 'filthy', 'ridiculous', 'disrespectful', 'blackguard-like', 'very flippant', or 'abominable'. Adams Sherman Hill admonishes that '[s]ome blunders in the use of verbs are, or should be, confined to the illiterate' (Hill 1893: 79). Other works (e.g. Miège 1688; Bayly 1772/1969) appear blandly *descriptive*, reporting the

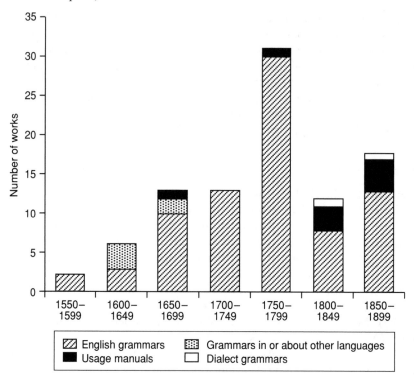

Figure 5.1 OGREVE grammars across time and genre

existence of forms that would mortify later writers, and sometimes even their own peers. Miège (1688: 110–111), for example, gives a list of common contractions that includes *int* and *ant*, forms of *ain't* that his contemporary Cooper (1685) qualifies as 'barbarous'. Juxtaposition of prescriptive and descriptive treatments is particularly valuable for our purposes, as it provides evidence that the non-standard uses were widespread enough to engender both censure (in the case of *ain't*, from Cooper) and placid acceptance (from Miège). Works retained largely for their influential nature, for example Lowth (1761/1967), make infrequent reference to non-standard forms, but are a good source of information on the type of variation salient to well-educated, highly standard speakers and writers (e.g. *got/gotten* variation in the participle). Still other works are veritable goldmines of social or regional non-standard forms. An excellent example is Joshua Pegge's *Anecdotes of the English Language: Dialect of London* (1803/1814). Pegge champions the existence of non-standard Cockney forms, such as *have took, com'd [<came], gone dead, ghostes, hisn, mought, aks [<ask]*, and *for to*, through reference to historical or logically analogous forms.[2] His detailed description of a non-standard variety was so far ahead of its time when it first appeared that some reviewers assumed it was a joke.

The OGREVE corpus is not intended as a representative sample of early grammars, nor even of all grammars mentioning variation of any kind. Rather, it is a distillation of the works we have found most relevant for the diachronic study of non-standard variation, the product of a research process that cuts across traditional conceptions of what constitutes a grammar. In fact, some of the most useful works for our purposes (e.g. Pegge 1803/1814) were deliberately excluded from other collections, or relegated to appendices. The diverse sources constituting the OGREVE represent diverse approaches to the codification of the English language. Although each provides a radically different view of linguistic variability over the duration, all are complementary ways of attesting to its existence.

Mining the OGREVE for variation

We examined the grammars retained for the OGREVE for mention of features associated with African American English. These included unmarked or verbal preterites, non-standard -s-marking in the present tense, and the periphrastic (*gonna*) future, among others. Relevant passages were photocopied and indexed to create a master reference of over 700 pages, which we used to inform analyses of contemporary variability. From this master reference, we constructed a computer database of all relevant quotations.

The goals, organisation and style of early grammars differ substantially from their modern counterparts, requiring us to develop methods to locate the relevant material. In this section we consider three issues that we addressed to maximise the usefulness of the OGREVE: (1) evaluation of the unequal treatment of forms in the grammars, (2) interpretation of evidence of the variability, and (3) tracing evidence of the conditioning of that variability.

Evaluating the grammatical treatment of forms

Simple frequency of mention in grammars does not necessarily indicate how widespread a particular form may have been in the speech community. Not every extant form, no matter how stigmatised by some, was equally salient to all contemporaneous grammarians.

A number of factors conspired in bringing a form to their attention. A relatively recent form will generally attract a great deal of attention, usually negative. Brainerd (1989) points out that grammarians grudgingly accepted preterite contraction (*loved*>*lov'd*), which was universal by the inception of the grammatical tradition, while negative contractions (especially *ain't*), which were both later and more sporadic, were vociferously opposed. Forms with analogues in classical languages rarely incurred much controversy. On the contrary, such forms were *usually* mentioned in connection with classical languages, e.g. early references to the English periphrastic futures (*going to* and *about to*) surface in descriptions of the Greek *paulopostfuturum* (Priestley

1761/1969). Presumably, this is partly a reflection of the pedagogy of classical studies of the time, and partly an attempt by early standardisers of English to link the language for status purposes to a supposed Greek origin. Likewise, grammars frequently mentioned the co-existence of a high-status innovation and an older variant with a long tradition in educated or formal use. Forms such as *thou*, third-person *-eth* or second-singular *-est,* and unstressed periphrastic *do* in the present and preterite, were all probably near-moribund in common usage for several centuries before grammars were willing to dispense with a reference to them, or to euthanise them as 'solemn' or 'ancient'. Preterite *gat* (<*got*) is another of the rare forms to proceed directly from uncritical acceptance to obsolescence.

The variability most appealing to early grammarians involved situations that lent themselves to the exercise of logic. Cases where one variant is argued to be 'better' (based on recourse to supposedly invariant classical or logical analogues) received ample, even disproportionate, attention. The most prominent discussions involve:

- maintenance of a distinction between preterite and participle forms in irregular verbs (e.g. *drank* vs. *drunk*) to ensure clarity;
- the use of *you was* in second-person singular contexts, where the incursion of the 'plural' *you* into the erstwhile context for *thou* is said to require the plural verb form;
- the *shall/will* distinction, a mainstay of nineteenth-century prescriptivism (*Will I?* is construed as illogical, as *will* indicates volition, which a speaker need not question of himself);
- negative concord, since 'two negatives make a positive';
- the subjunctive, whose conditioning was debated in early grammars and whose very existence required defence in later ones;
- split infinitives, impossible in Latin and therefore unsavoury in English; and
- present-tense concord with conjoined subjects, collective nouns, and existentials, where errors are ascribed to inattention to the plural nature of the subject of the sentence.

Factors such as recency and analogy with respected sources amplify the attention paid by grammarians to particular features, though some of them may not have been particularly frequent in informal speech. This mismatch is hardly surprising, given that the intended audience for these grammars, especially pre-1870,[3] rarely included the working classes, whose linguistic descendants supply the material for much contemporary sociolinguistic investigation. It was usually necessary, then, to go beyond grammarians' favoured preoccupations to seek evidence of the forms of interest to our research, as detailed in the remainder of this section.

Inferring the existence of variability from attestations in the OGREVE

The search for rare clues to the early use of variant forms in the OGREVE could not always rely on contemporary categorisations of linguistic structure. An eighteenth-century author who lists standard verb paradigms might only mention non-standard unmarked past forms under *vowel substitution* (e.g. Fisher 1750/1968); negation might be considered under *contraction* (e.g. Miège 1688). Zero relative clauses surface under *ellipsis*, historical present under *enallage*, and *ain't* under *blunders*. Tense distinctions may show up as *aorist* vs. *non-aorist*, verbal marking as *accidence*, and subjunctives as *conjunctives* or *optatives*. Optimum use of the materials required bridging the concerns and language of contemporary sociolinguistic enquiry with those of early grammatical classification.

The way a grammar describes a form, and the context in which it is mentioned, can help us infer how widespread it was at the time. Uncritical mentions in descriptive and prescriptive works are especially valuable to us, as they suggest that a particular form was sufficiently frequent and well entrenched to escape censure. Here we might include the extremely widespread levelling of preterite and participle paradigms until at least the 1800s, *come, run*, and other unmarked preterites in the 1600s, and the *going to* future, apparently throughout its history.

A mix of critical and uncritical mentions, as in the description of *ain't* in Cooper (1685) compared with that in Miège (1688), also suggests that a form was in widespread use, with attendant stigma perhaps of recent provenance or limited effect. Similarly, defence of a particular form through appeals to usage or 'habit' suggests that the form was both widespread and salient, but not sufficiently entrenched to ward off prescriptive censure. This category includes *you was* in Webster (1789/1967: 233–234) and *have went* in Pegge (1803/1814: 242).

Implicitly critical mentions, such as those associating a form with a particular region or class (thereby situating it outside the mainstream), often suggest that the form was not only widespread in the contexts in question, but probably salient enough to draw attention outside those contexts, especially if invoked often. This is the case with many of the examples mentioned in nineteenth-century dialect works, e.g. *mought* or variable *-s-* marking (e.g. Pegge 1803/1814; Peacock 1863).

Not all critical mentions of a non-standard form are admissible evidence of its status in the usage of the time. Some grammarians (notably Fogg 1792/1970) clearly use invented forms. These, however, are usually described as such, and occur almost entirely in tables of 'false grammar' meant as exercises for students/readers to correct. Even within such tables, some examples are drawn from (and credited to) well-known authors or prestigious newspapers, assuring us that the forms involved were widespread enough to have appeared in 'respectable' print. In other cases, authors take offence at uncommon forms, as with Smith's (1855: 5) injunctions against *you are mistaken* for *you mistake*. Thus, in the absence of clues to the contrary in the texts themselves, we do not assign undue weight to lone mentions. The strongest evidence for the early existence of a non-standard form resides in multiple attestations, both critical and non-critical. In general, if a form was frequently censured, or a standard form proposed in its place, we may infer that it was known, used and probably widespread.

Simple mention of a standard form (e.g. in tables of verb paradigms) does not imply the widespread use (or even the existence) of a corresponding non-standard form which the grammarian hopes to eradicate. Standard forms were often described simply to illustrate parts of speech or verb forms, or to educate foreigners. When, for example, Reed and Kellogg (1886: 239) give us paradigms like *run, ran, run ... see, saw, seen*, we learn nothing about the existence or frequency of non-standard preterite *run* or *seen*. On the other hand, when Smith (1855: 13) tells us that "*Says I*," should be "*Said I*," or "*I said*", we infer that preterite marking with the verb stem *say* was widespread enough to occasion comment. Likewise, Perley (1834: 76–79) suggests an English origin for such non-standard forms as *he was drownded in the river, it is hisn*, and *who done the work* simply by describing them as 'familiar'. He also illustrates the distance of these forms from standard(ising) English by referring to them as 'Vulgarisms ... familiar examples of bad English, particularly of false grammar ... It is hoped that the attention of instructors generally will be directed to this subject, so that their pupils shall talk, as well as write, good English' (Perley 1834: 76–77). The survival of many of these forms to the present day, and the tendency to see in them evidence of recent decay or incomplete acquisition, is clear evidence of the success of the prescriptivist enterprise in shaping language attitudes and beliefs. As we shall see in the section beginning on p. 101, its success in influencing language use has been far less resounding.

Table 5.1 graphically illustrates the widening gap between prescriptivism and praxis with regard to a locus of variability that has persisted over the centuries: variable or zero marking of past-reference verbs. Consider the treatment of a number of notoriously variable verbs (*run, ran, come, came*, etc.) in the fifty-six OGREVE works that mentioned them. Non-critical attestations of variability (represented as ○s) cluster in the earliest period, at the left side of the table. As the prescriptive enterprise intensifies, acceptance of variation decreases, as evidenced by fewer ○s. The reduction in the number of mentions in the middle of the table graphically illustrates how grammarians wrote formerly acceptable variation out of the story of standard English. As the standard becomes firmly entrenched (post 1800), we observe an increasing tendency to stigmatise the variable or non-standard forms as vulgar, provincial, or dialectal. The same variation, although presumably identical in use, has now been assigned a different place in the construction of standard English. Interestingly, these are the very variants that are seen by many today as incursions rather than retentions.

Table 5.1 The treatment of selected non-standard preterite forms in grammars represented in the OGREVE

	1577	1619	1640	1653	1654	1671	1674	1685	1688	1700	1711	1711	1723	1733	1735	1746	1750	1762	1765	1770	1771	1772	1784	1785	1785	1786	1788	1792	1793	1795	1797	1802	1803	1803	1810	1830	1834	1834	1846	1850	1851	1855	1863	1866	1870	1874	1877	1880	1886	1893	1898
eat		O	O	O		O			O	O	O	O	O	O		O	O	O	O							O					O	O	O	×				O	O		O	×	×	O	×	×		O		×	
run			O	O	O	O	O			O	O		O								×	O			×		×						×			×	×				O		×	×		×		O			
come(d)				O	O	O				O	O		O																				×										×								
say(s)	O																										O									×						×									
give								O	O																																										
done																																				×	×					×								×	
see(n,d)															O																					×	×	×					×	×							
have																																																			
go																																																			
be																																																			

Note
O, variable (non-standard form) not stigmatized; ×, variable (non-standard form) stigmatized.

Inferring the conditioning of variability from attestations in the OGREVE

Less frequent than simple attestations of a form's existence, but infinitely more useful for the purposes of variationist investigation, are references to the *conditioning* of a variable form – that is, statements in the grammars attributing the choice of a variant to particular linguistic or social factors. As the stated purpose of both descriptive and prescriptive grammars was to represent the way language was, or should be, spoken or written through the application of the scientific method (i.e. the discovery of immutable truths or inviolable laws), it is not surprising that few grammars were willing to go beyond the acknowledgement of non-standard variation in order to explain it. This makes the references we have found to the conditioning of variability particularly valuable, although the same caveats must apply to them as to attestations of the forms themselves.

Social conditioning

Early grammars were more likely to attribute variability to social than to linguistic factors, as this did not require the acceptance of inconsistencies within the language itself. Dialect grammars (e.g. Peacock 1863) attribute non-standard forms to the local dialect. Even in mainstream grammars, non-standard forms are sometimes associated with a particular region, often Scotland, Ireland, or the north of England. When they are further equated with the working classes (Beattie 1788/1968: 192–193), we may infer that they had spread into vernacular use in other areas. Non-standard forms are often directly linked to class rather than to region, as seen in associations with colloquial speech, lack of education and/or 'vulgar' usage (see Gill 1619/1972; Jackson 1830; Perley 1834; Hill 1893). Given the demographics of post-1600 British society and emigration, it is these non-standard forms that would have been most available for transmission to New World slave societies.

The frequency with which particular forms are qualified as 'Cockney' in the OGREVE requires elaboration. In general use, the term Cockney is associated with working-class Londoners. In grammars and usage manuals (e.g. Pegge 1803/1814), though, the term seems to be used with much broader reference. During the period covered by the OGREVE, standard English was becoming more closely associated with a specifically *London* elite: 'the conversation of the highest classes in London society is now looked upon as the standard of English pronunciation' (Graham 1869: 156) (cited in Crowley 1989a: 149). It follows that non-standard forms would also be defined in London terms,[4] 'the inhabitants of London have the disadvantage of being more disgraced by their peculiarities than any other people' (Gwynne 1855: 60). Most of the authors (and readers) of these early works were London-based. They had access to a term for non-elite speech and wielded it broadly. It seems likely that 'Cockney' in the OGREVE should be read as code for 'urban non-elite', without reference to a specific region. Sweet (1890: vi–vii) (cited in Crowley 1989a: 155) expresses clearly what the term was intended to convey and why: 'The Cockney dialect seems very ugly to an educated Englishman or woman because he – and still more she – lives in a perpetual terror of being taken for a Cockney.'

Linguistic conditioning

At the heart of the variationist enterprise is an attempt to divine the rules underlying the choice between two or more variants of a form, based on their conditioning. By 'conditioning' we mean the effect of certain linguistic contexts on variant choice. For example, auxiliary verbs in Early AAE questions (Van Herk 2000) are more likely to resist inversion to pre-subject position in negative or yes–no questions, as in (5.1) and (5.2) below, than in affirmative WH questions, as in (5.3). Thus linguistic environment conditions inversion.

(5.1)   He don't know the pastor?

$$(SE/003/965)^5$$

(5.2)   You have heard from him?

$$(SE/003/235)$$

(5.3)   What *do* you call them?

$$(ANSE/007/758)$$

Shared conditioning of variant choice across language varieties is far stronger support for a shared origin than is the simple sharing of variant forms, which may be generated by entirely different, underlying grammars (Bickerton 1975; Tagliamonte and Poplack 1993; Poplack and Tagliamonte 1996). Likewise, similar conditioning over time is the strongest possible evidence that a current form is the legacy of an earlier period. The most innovative aspect of our investigations into the OGREVE is this emphasis on tracing the conditioning of current variability.

One prime example relates to the ultimate stereotype of non-standard speech, the negator *ain't*. Research on *ain't* variability reveals that it surfaces almost entirely in present tense *be + not* and *have + not* contexts, in both British (Wright 1898–1905: III, 88; Cheshire 1982) and American dialects (Feagin 1979: 217; Christian *et al.* 1988: 169) as well as in Early AAE (Van Herk 1999; Howe and Walker 2000). In other words, *ain't* alternates with *has not* and *is not*, but not *was not*, *did not*, or *does not*. The OGREVE reveals that the identical conditioning was already in place over 300 years ago: Miège (1688: 110–111) gives *int* and *ant* as permissible contractions, but only for *isn't* and *hasn't*.

Another example of long-standing conditioning involves the use of *was* in contexts where present-day standard English would require *were*. Variationist research reveals that, among other contexts, second-person singular favours use of *was* in contemporary Scottish use, as well as in several varieties of Early AAE (Tagliamonte and Smith 2000). Thus speakers are more likely to say *you* [singular] *was* than either *they was* or *we was*. The OGREVE shows Noah Webster (1789/1967: 233–234) describing – and defending – just such a distinction:

> In books, *you* is commonly used with the plural of the verb *be, you were;* in conversation, it is generally followed by the singular, *you was.* Notwithstanding the criticisms of grammarians, the antiquity *and universality* [emphasis ours] of this practice must give it the sanction of propriety; for what but practice forms a language? This practice is not merely vulgar; it is general among men of erudition ... Whatever objections may be raised to this inflection, *it is the language of the English* [emphasis Webster's], and rules can hardly change a general practice of speaking; nor would there be any advantage in the change, if it could be effected.
>
> (Webster 1789/1967: 233–234)

Webster's restriction of non-standard *was* to second-person singular contexts is his sole concession to non-standard verb concord. It continues to apply in the Early AAE materials recorded some two centuries later (Tagliamonte and Smith 2000).

Given the gap between our concerns and those of early grammarians, it is remarkable that we are often able to find such clues to the presence and conditioning of non-standard features. It is the bridging of these seemingly polar opposites, the prescriptive tradition of past centuries and the variable data of sociolinguistically peripheral communities, that permits us to construct our alternative history of African American English.

African American English in the diaspora

The data on which the analyses of the next section are based come from varieties of English spoken in the African American diaspora. Prompted by conditions in the United States in the eighteenth and nineteenth centuries, thousands of African Americans dispersed to Canada, West Africa, the Caribbean and South America. Because the communities they established have remained isolated from the surrounding population as a result of geographic, linguistic, ethnic, social, educational, and religious differences, the linguistic structures used by the first settlers have survived into current generations. This provides a unique window onto an earlier stage of African American English, without which the various scenarios for the origins of contemporary AAVE cannot be fully assessed.

Our research programme investigates the speech of members of three such communities – one in the Samaná peninsula of the Dominican Republic

(Poplack and Sankoff 1987) and two in Nova Scotia (Poplack and Tagliamonte 1991) – first settled in the late eighteenth and early nineteenth centuries. The focus is on language *use*. Conclusions are based on systematic examination and empirical analyses of the language of 101 speakers of diaspora varieties of African American English, and thirty-five speakers of control varieties. The data analysed consist of hundreds of hours of high-quality recordings of informal conversations with community members, focusing on the elderly speakers most likely to preserve earlier linguistic features. The size and quality of the data set enable us to identify subtle conditioning factors whose direction of effect and statistical significance are revealed through analysis of thousands of tokens of each linguistic feature.[6]

A hallmark of this work is the cross-validation of linguistic findings across the diverse diaspora communities, further validated through comparison with the Ex-Slave Recordings – linguistic data collected in the 1930s and 1940s from African Americans born into slavery. This helps to rule out the possibility that features we take to be conservative are not the result of internal linguistic change, nor of post-settlement contact with surrounding communities. The sociolinguistically peripheral status of these communities, with respect both to each other and to mainstream developments, makes it likely that any linguistic features and conditioning they share descend from a common stock.

In fact, precise and subtle similarities surface with regularity in the three diaspora communities whose language we have studied, suggesting that their language can be taken as representative of an earlier stage of AAVE. Many of these Early AAE features have also been situated with respect to similar dialectal forms in Canada, Great Britain and the United States (as well as to superficially similar but structurally different forms in the creole varieties). The OGREVE has enabled us to trace, for the first time, the *developmental* aspect of these features, by establishing the trajectory of their linguistic antecedents through the English grammatical tradition. In the next section, we investigate the dialogue between the OGREVE and the Early AAE materials as they relate to two core features of the African American English tense/aspect system: the variable expression of past and present tense.

The results

Variation in past-tense marking

Variability between marked (5.4a) and bare (5.4b) past-tense verbs is a hallmark of AAVE.

    (5.4a)   A bunch of us *walked* up the stairs and *sat* down and Caroline *looked* up.

                                                  (ANSE/039/735)

(5.4b)   As they *return*, the doctor *went*. And when the doctor *went*, she *come* and she *work*, she *work*, she *work*.

(SE/002/1176)

Although bare forms were initially considered the result of phonologically motivated removal of the English past-tense marker {ed} in weak verbs such as *work* and *return* in (5.4b) (e.g. Labov *et al.* 1968; Fasold 1972), it was soon suggested (following Bickerton 1975) that the alternation between marked and stem forms conveyed different (creole) aspectual readings. Continuing attempts to address these suggestions (e.g. Winford 1992; Tagliamonte and Poplack 1993; Blake 1997; Patrick 1999) show that the unmarked past is typically construed as alien to the English grammar of past-tense marking, particularly when 'strong' verbs, such as *come* in (5.4b), are involved.

The data of the OGREVE are particularly relevant to the question of whether the alternation between bare and marked pasts signals specific aspectual and temporal distinctions, like those of creoles (Bickerton 1975; Winford 1992), or whether they are the product of simplification processes in weak verbs and inherent variability in strong verbs.

Inspection of attestations involving past-tense formation shows that alternation of preterite with present (usually zero) morphology has been attested in English since at least the sixteenth century. We first encounter the *enallage* of present for past in Peacham (1577/1971: no page numbers):

Enallage of tyme, when we put one time for another, thus. Terence. I come to the maydens, I aske who she is, they say, the sister of Chrisis, for, I came to the maydens, I asked who she was ...

Over a century later Miège (1688: 70) observed:

The Present Tense in particular is sometimes used for the Preter Imperfect. As, having met with him, he brings him to his House, and gives him very good Intertainment. There we say brings for brought, and gives for gave.

Enallage of Tense was also listed under Lowe's (1723–1738/1971: 7) *figures of syntax*: 'Then comes Alexander with all his forces' for 'Then came Alexander' (see also Collyer 1735/1968). Fisher (1750/1968: 125) described enallage of vowels ('sware, for swore; speak, for spoke') that resulted in present morphology on past reference verbs. Other grammarians seeking to explain the variation between zero and overt past inflection invoked the desire 'to give vividness and reality' (Bullions 1869: 39) to past events via the 'historical' present.

Most attempts to account for the variable expression of the English past tense in early grammars, however, invoke the verb-class membership of irregular verbs remaining from a vigorous Old English cohort of about 360

(Strang 1970: 147; Krygier 1994: 247). The number, membership, and very existence of such verb classes have been contested since at least the early seventeenth century, however. Some grammarians (e.g. Fenning 1771/1967: 65) simply provided long tables of verb conjugations, considering that more general rules for past-tense formation 'are so numerous and intricate, that they rather perplex the judgement than assist the memory of the learner'. Fenning's contemporaries Bayly (1772/1969) and Fogg (1792/1970: 144–146) arrived at twelve irregular verb-class distinctions, based on perceived correspondences between present, preterite and participle forms. Greenwood (1711/1968) described only two types of irregular verbs, while Gill (1619/ 1972) claimed that there should be three conjugations, as there were only three 'tenses' in English (present, preterite and perfect). Variability even within these classes is confirmed by Gill's (1619/1972: 121, emphasis added) comment on his 'third' conjugation: 'In this conjugation also belong almost all the common verbs of the second conjugation (not because of any peculiarity in our language, but because *common usage attempts anything*)'.

It is clear that, during much of the period covered by the OGREVE, expression of past time was so variable that even prescriptivists described it in detail. Table 5.1 traces some of these verb forms across fifty-six grammars over three centuries. The acceptance of currently non-standard variants illustrates grammarians' uncertainty over which verbs to assign to which classes. A mention of preterite *come* or *run*, for example, indicates a willingness to class them with verbs whose preterite form is the same as that of the participle (or the stem). The contemporary rigidity of prescribed verb-class membership, foreshadowed by the reduction in uncritical mentions of variation over time, is clearly a later development, one that conceals the variability of earlier English.

Our analyses of Early AAE past marking (Poplack and Tagliamonte 2001) tested the contribution of verb-class membership to the probability that a stem form would be selected in past-tense strong verbs. We divided 4130 strong verbs into the following classes: class I (stem = participle, e.g. *come/ came/come*), class II (preterite = participle, e.g. *meet/met/met*), and class III (stem ≠ preterite ≠ participle, e.g. *go/went/gone*),[7] after Christian *et al.* (1988). Initial results suggested that verb-class membership was, indeed, the primary determinant of stem form preterite marking. But closer inspection shows that the 'classes' are made up of disproportionate numbers of a few verbs, and that these in turn display idiosyncratic marking patterns.

Table 5.2 shows that 'verb class I' is made up largely of the verb *come*, which in most Early AAE varieties tends to surface in unmarked form. Preterite *come* is a stereotype of non-standard English dialects, attested in North America (Pedersen 1967; Feagin 1979), England (Tidholm 1979; Tagliamonte 1999), and elsewhere (Zettersten 1969; Ramisch 1989). It has figured prominently in the English grammatical tradition since 1577, as illustrated in Table 5.1. 'Verb class II' is also largely made up of a single verb, *say*, which in three of the four Early AAE varieties tends to surface in unmarked

Table 5.2   Distribution of stem forms of strong verbs according to lexical identity, verb-class membership and text frequency in four varieties of Early AAE

					ANSE			
	SE		*ESR*		*NPR*		*GYE*	
	%	N	%	N	%	N	%	N
Class I								
come/came/come	36	404	94	49	76	49	50	80
run/ran/run	38	8	100	8	67	6	78	9
become/became/become	100	8	–	–	100	1	–	–
Class II								
say/said/said	75	296	33	58	38	71	5	39
tell/told/told	18	192	0	25	14	22	–	–
send/sent/sent	34	77	0	7	–	–	–	–
make/made/made	3	70	11	9	0	11	28	18
bring/brought/brought	3	61	0	11	17	6	80	5
leave/left/left	8	59	0	7	–	–	50	10
build/built/built	17	47	–	0	0	1	–	–
buy/bought/bought	0	37	0	24	100	2	0	4
find/found/found	11	37	33	3	0	2	–	–
meet/met/met	3	31	–	0	–	–	–	–
teach/taught/taught	19	27	60	6	–	–	27	11
keep/kept/kept	8	26	0	5	100	2	–	–
think/thought/thought	9	11	17	6	0	10	0	8
hear/heard/heard	16	19	–	0	–	–	–	–
Class III								
go/went/gone	2	373	0	52	8	107	14	126
get/got/gotten	14	101	7	43	13	55	29	73
know/knew/known	9	98	19	16	50	16	39	56
give/gave/given	42	59	93	14	60	5	92	12
see/saw/seen	30	53	33	6	5	20	–	–
do/did/done	5	20	18	11	0	19	21	24
speak/spoke/spoken	10	20	–	0	–	–	–	–
break/broke/broken	0	21	25	4	–	–	–	–
Total	25	2488	30	537	23	535	27	574

Note
SE, Samaná; ESR, the Ex-Slave Recordings; NPR, North Preston; GYE, Guysborough enclave.
Reproduced from Poplack and Tagliamonte (2001).

form (Table 5.2). Like *come*, preterite *say* has a long history of use in English and English-derived varieties. *Say* figured (along with preterite *come*) in the enallage in Peacham (1577/1971: no page number): 'I come to the maydens, I aske who she is, they say, the sister of Chrisis.' *Say* also has a history of inflection with verbal *-s*, as in Samaná, invoking regional, uneducated, and/ or working-class speech throughout the English-speaking world.

The tendency for *come* and *say* to surface as stems is shared by *give* and *run*, in both Early AAE and the OGREVE (Tables 5.1 and 5.2). Other verbs, however, are almost always inflected (e.g. *went, have* and *be*). *Had* and *was* are so frequently marked, in both the OGREVE and in non-standard dialects, that they are typically excluded from quantitative analyses (Rickford 1986; Winford 1992; Tagliamonte and Poplack 1993; Blake 1997; Patrick 1999; Poplack and Tagliamonte 2001). So firmly entrenched are preterite *had, went*, and *was/were* that *no* unmarked, or present-tense variants, are attested for these verbs in the OGREVE (indicated by the shaded portion of Table 5.1). Lack of mention is not in itself evidence against the existence of past tense *have, go* and *is/are* – after all, some grammarians fail to mention non-standard forms. What is compelling, though, is the *relative* treatment of these verbs: *come, run, give* and *say* surface as stems; *had, was/were* and *went* do not. This profile parallels precisely the patterns for Early AAE summarised in Table 5.2.

The fact that some verbs occur largely in stem form, while others are nearly always inflected, argues that inflectional preferences are lexically based and not the result of more generally applicable grammatical tendencies, as would be expected of markers of tense and/or aspect. This bolsters our conclusion that both stem (and marked) forms of these verbs in Early AAE can be traced to an earlier stage of the English language.

The present tense

The near absence of present-tense -*s* on AAVE third-person singular verbs [as in *know* in (5.5a and b)] and its 'unpredictable' occurrence elsewhere [e.g. *treats* in (5.5b)] led early scholars (Labov *et al.* 1968; Fasold 1972) to conclude that this inflection was not part of the underlying grammar of AAVE.

(5.5a)   He *know* the first guy that *shoots* the deer and everything.

(ANSE/062/361)

(5.5b)   And they all treating me mighty nice, all the White folks that *know* me, they *treats* me nice.

(ESR/003/32–34)

As with variability in the expression of the past, researchers have long been at odds over how best to account for the function of verbal -*s* in AAVE. Explanations have included hypercorrect insertion (Labov *et al.* 1968; Fasold 1972), aspect marker (Jeremiah 1977; Pitts 1981; Brewer 1986) and narrative marker (Myhill and Harris 1986). The variable occurrence of verbal -*s* across grammatical persons and numbers is also well documented throughout the history of the English language. Alternation among inflections (including -*s*, -*þ* and zero) of the simple present-tense paradigm has been attested since the Old English period (Jespersen 1909/1949; Holmqvist 1922; Brunner 1963; Curme 1977; Wakelin 1977). Competing variants have traditionally been associated with distinct regions and social classes: Northern British dialects were the driving force. Verbal -*s* originated in the spoken language, and apparently remained a marker of popular, colloquial, or dialectal speech until at least the early seventeenth century (Jespersen 1909/1949; Holmqvist 1922; Strang 1970; Barber 1976; Curme 1977; Nevalainen and Raumolin-Brunberg 1996b).

Precursors of this variability, and suggestions of the factors that may have constrained it, are also amply evident in the OGREVE. Lack of concord across the present-tense paradigm is attested from the earliest grammars, despite disagreement over which persons take -*s*. Hume (1617: 27–32) (who occasionally uses non-concord -*s* in his own prose) favours second- and third-person singular:

> The second person is of him that is spoaken to; as, *thou wrytes*. The third person is of him that is spoaken of; as, *Peter wrytes* (1617: 27) ... *I wryte, thou writes, he wrytes* (1617: 30) ... *I have bene, thou hes bene, he hes bene* (1617: 32)

Mason (1633: 44) describes a regularised plural paradigm: '*we be ... ye are or be ... they be,*' (1633: 58), as does Aickin (1693: 13): '*we was, ye was, they was*'. The highly prescriptive Cooper (1685: 139) suggests the singular form everywhere but in second person singular: '*I was, thou wast, he was, we was, ye was, they was*'. Well over a century later, Beattie (1788/1968: 192–193) remarked on the (still) opaque nature of the standard agreement rule, reproduced below:

> Custom has made this third person plural necessary, by determining, that the verb shall agree in number with its nominative. But if custom had determined otherwise, we might have done without it ... if custom had not subjoined a plural verb to a plural nominative, or to two or more singular nominatives, there would have been no fault in the syntax.
> (Beattie 1788/1968: 192–193)

Most grammarians ascribe the variability to confusion over the number of the noun phrase, and thus the appropriate inflection for the verb. Particular offenders included existentials, conjoined subjects and, especially, collective nouns such as *multitude* or *parliament*. Virtually all the post-1750 grammars consulted in the construction of the OGREVE (including those not retained) discuss these features, often with the same invented examples, in the same order, with the same section numbering. The analyses reported in Poplack and Tagliamonte (2001) reveal that these distinctions, despite their salience to grammarians, do not begin to account for the extent of variability in Early AAE. But a less-well-documented constraint that has recently begun to figure prominently in discussions of verbal -*s* plays an important role. This is what has come to be known (after Ihalainen 1994: 221; Klemola 1996: 49, 179–180) as the *Northern Subject Rule*.

Murray (1873: 211) formulates the rule as follows: 'When the subject is a noun, adjective, interrogative or relative pronoun, or when the verb and subject are separated by a clause, the verb takes the termination -*s* in all persons', illustrating with the thirteenth- and fourteenth-century Scots and Northumbrian data in (5.6) and (5.7).

(5.6)   The burds *cums* an' *paecks* them but They *cum* an' *teake* them.

(5.7)   Fuok at *cums* unbudden, *syts* unsaer'd.
          'Folk that comes unbidden, sits unserved.'

The early associations of non-concord -*s* with the north and the working classes effectively guaranteed its marginal status in older grammars, since early grammarians, especially prescriptivists, concerned themselves largely with the middle-class language of the metropole. We can, however, trace explicit reference to the Northern Subject Rule at least as far back as Beattie (1788/ 1968: 192–193), who invokes not only the variability (*coffer-lids* that *close* vs. *two lamps … lies*), but also its social and geographic provenance:

> in old [i.e. Early Modern] English, a verb singular sometimes follows a plural nominative; as in the following couplet from Shakespeare's Venus and Adonis, She lifts the *coffer-lids* that *close* his eyes, Where lo, *two lamps* burnt out in darkness *lies*. The same idiom prevails in the Scotch acts of parliament, in the vernacular writings of Scotch men prior to the last century, *and in the vulgar dialect of North Britain to this day: and, even in England, the common people frequently speak in this manner*, without being misunderstood.
> (Beattie 1788/1968: 192–193, emphasis added)

Note that although Beattie links the form to the north, including Scotland, he also describes its use among the 'common people' of the rest of England. The Northern Subject Rule may well have been used across a wider range of classes in the north than elsewhere, but by the end of the eighteenth century it was clearly no longer restricted to that region, at least among the lower social strata.

The fact that the Northern Subject Rule involves a combination of type of subject [noun phrase (NP) vs. pronoun] and adjacency (proximity of the NP to the verb) makes this condition on variability particularly amenable to empirical test. Table 5.3, adapted from Table 7.6 in Poplack and Tagliamonte (2001), demonstrates that these effects remain operative in Early AAE, as well as in many other -*s*-preserving dialects.

Table 5.3 depicts a variable rule analysis of the contribution of the terms of the Northern Subject Rule to the probability that -*s* will be selected in approximately 1188 third-person plural contexts admitting the simple present tense. In each one, adjacent pronouns (5.8), were distinguished from non-adjacent pronominal and noun-phrase subjects (5.9).

(5.8)   He *live* with mama thirty, thirty-two years …

(ESR/013/339)

(5.9a)   The inside box with the coffin what *sits* down in the grave.

(ANSE/015/904)

(5.9b)   Every time somebody I know *die*, that's when I get the urge.

(ANSE/053/1252–3)

The well-documented propensity for -*s* to appear on verbs whose subjects are non-adjacent, and to be avoided when the subject is an adjacent personal pronoun (5.8), is apparent in the conditioning of variable -*s* usage in most Early AAE varieties. This is particularly true of the third-person plural contexts displayed in Table 5.3, which dialectologists cite as most relevant (Wakelin 1977; Ihalainen 1994; Schendl 1994). The identical constraint hierarchy shared by three out of four Early AAE varieties and its parallels to the conditioning of -*s* variability described in the OGREVE confirm that the effect of subject type and adjacency in Early AAE present-tense marking is a legacy of English. These findings suggest that verbal -*s* must already have been inherent in the language of British colonists which constituted the target for first generations of African Americans in the United States. That language was transmitted, along with the constraints conditioning its inherent variability, to ancestors of the Early AAE speakers.

Summary

In this chapter, we have detailed the construction of the OGREVE, a corpus

Table 5.3   Four independent variable rule analyses of the contribution of factors selected as significant to the presence of verbal -*s* in *third-person plural* in four varieties of Early AAE

					ANSE					
	SE			ESR		NPR			GYE	
Corrected mean	0.260			0.064		0.114			0.068	
Total *N*	699			72		173			244	
Northern subject rule	*Prob*	%	N	*Prob* %	N	*Prob* %	N	*Prob* %	N
Non-adjacent pronoun or NP	0.59	37	151	0.70 17	24	0.41 12	57	0.78 20	80
Adjacent pronoun	0.47	25	512	0.39 4	46	0.56 16	97	0.35 4	160

Note
SE, Samaná; ESR, the Ex-Slave Recordings; NPR, North Preston; GYE, Guysborough enclave; NP, noun phrase. Adapted from Poplack and Tagliamonte (2001).

of nearly 100 grammars of the English language published since 1577. Its purpose is to discern the existence and conditioning of prior variability from works whose professed aim was to eradicate it. By tracking attestations of variation in multiple works from differently constituted genres (mainstream and dialect; descriptive and prescriptive), we situate forms within the trajectory of the development of English. Despite the apparent gulf between a research agenda emphasising analysis of linguistic variability, and the concerns of these early grammars, which promote invariance, we have succeeded in exploiting the unacknowledged dialogue between prescription and praxis.

Linguistically principled investigation of the OGREVE, informed by systematic analysis of linguistic variability, has enabled us to propose an alternative history for African American English, a thoroughly studied yet still misunderstood non-standard variety of English. We traced Early AAE patterns of linguistic variability through the OGREVE, discovering, operationalising and empirically testing diachronic clues to their conditioning. The results of this exercise revealed numerous and non-trivial similarities between Early AAE and the English historical record. This in turn suggests that many aspects of Early AAE described as innovation, incomplete acquisition or contact-induced change are in fact retentions of once robust features since eradicated from the accepted standard.

The OGREVE is very much a work in progress. As our research programme continues to develop, new sources will be added, new data will be drawn from those already consulted, and new studies will be informed by the insights gained from work to date. The development of resources such as the OGREVE requires a substantial commitment of time, energy and intellectual curiosity. We hope to have shown how analysis of the resulting materials, by revealing the variability inherent in earlier English, can enrich the study of any language variety derived from it.

Notes

1 Construction of the OGREVE was generously supported by the Social Sciences and Humanities Research Council of Canada (SSHRCC) in the form of research grants to Shana Poplack. Dick Watts and Jürg Schwyter first brought the Scolar Press Collection to our attention, and participants in LIN 7942: *Language variation & linguistic ideology* unearthed a number of other important sources. Staff at the Inter-Library Loans Department of the University of Ottawa and the supplying libraries kindly acceded to most of our requests for references. Their contribution to this project is gratefully acknowledged.

2 All these features are widespread in African American English, white North American dialects and Caribbean creoles.

3 Universal mandatory education in Great Britain began in 1870, thus increasing the exposure of dialect users to the standard, and presumably vice versa (Crowley 1989a).

4 Note that there is a similar tendency to refer to a current non-standard variety, despite its wide geographical reach, as 'Estuary' English.

5 Codes in parentheses identify: (1) the corpus: Samaná English (SE), Ex-Slave

Recordings (ESR), African Nova Scotian English (ANSE); (2) the speaker; and (3) the location of the utterance in the recording, transcript, or data file.

6 For detailed analyses of these materials, we refer the reader to Poplack (2000a), Poplack and Tagliamonte (2001).

7 An invariant class IV (*hit/hit/hit*) was by definition excluded from the variable analysis.

6 Building a new English dialect

South African Indian English and the history of Englishes[1]

Rajend Mesthrie

Introduction

The imperial and colonial predispositions of the British in the modern period set off linguistic processes which made the mostly linear history of English up to that point rather more complex and challenging for the historian. The growth of English is certainly tied to the rise of the United Kingdom as a major shipping and capitalist power from the eighteenth century on. That English has always co-existed with other languages is often downplayed in traditional accounts; in the history of global language English this oversight takes on particular significance. Whilst some handbooks now tack on descriptions of extra-territorial varieties in Canada, the USA, Australia and South Africa, the history of English has gone beyond the linguistic practices of the descendants of Anglo-Saxons in colonial environments. The colonised, dispossessed and economically dominated have their histories of English too. The sailor, merchant, soldier, slave driver and/or missionary were initially responsible for the introduction of English abroad: later, teachers as we know them came to be involved. Sometimes the teachers were soldiers, as two brief examples from British rule in Africa show. Caleb Shivachi (1999) cites the role of the Kings' African Rifles in disseminating a knowledge of English in east Africa in the early twentieth century. In nineteenth century Natal (South Africa) in an early attempt to provide education to Indians on some sugar estates, discharged soldiers from the Indian army were recruited, since they had acquired some knowledge of an Indian language. This project was soon abandoned for, as the Superintendent's report of 1880 wryly put it, 'their conduct was not such as to command the respect of those among whom their work lay' (Brain 1983: 205). The first generation of missionaries who followed upon the early traders and slave drivers were in quite a few territories either L2 (second language) speakers from Holland, Germany and France, with a varied competence in English ranging from the minimal to the competent (Mesthrie 1996b, 1998), or broad dialect speakers (Moorhouse 1973; Mesthrie 1992a: 21). Input from standard southern British English and/or Received Pronunciation (RP) was in the first generation of missionary contact in Africa very rare.

Conditions of learning in the earliest period were thus hardly optimal. The initial imposition of English may seem an exaggeration in view of the desirability of the product today. Yet in territory after territory, from Wales to the Cape, India to Sri Lanka, a common practice in introducing English in schools was to silence the local languages. Whilst one may have some sympathy for an overworked teacher (of whatever background) trying to introduce an unknown language to unenthusiastic locals, the methods in territory after territory often smacked of raw power. Not only were local languages banned from classrooms, but children caught using them, even in playgrounds, were severely punished (for examples see Romaine 1989: 217–218; Phillipson 1992; Crystal 1997; Mesthrie 1999).

The adoption of English in the long run mirrored the advantages and weaknesses of colonisation. English brought Western education and access to some of the cultural and scientific elements of the West. In countries such as India and South Africa it enabled developing local leaderships to communicate with each other beyond the confines of traditional ties to region, and linguistic and ethnic group and ultimately led to new ideas of nationhood. The darker side of the spread was the devaluation of local languages and the destruction of local cultures. It has for some time become problematic to talk of *the* English language. Sociologically speaking it might make better sense to think in terms of an 'English language family'. This cover term spans a number of varieties with very different histories, functions and structural characteristics. Estimates of the size of this family range from 1.2 to 1.5 billion – this being Crystal's (1997: 61) 'middle of the road estimate' of the number of people with a 'reasonable competence'. The number of native speakers within this group is in the region of 337 million – i.e. one-quarter to one-fifth of the total (Crystal 1997: 60). English is most used today in interactions between non-native speaker and non-native speaker, rather than in any other possible combination. The English language family may be said to comprise the following members:

1   Colonial standards in the UK, the USA, Australia, New Zealand, Canada and South Africa, the territories having a large settlement of 'traditional' English speakers.
2   Regional dialects, involving identifiable subvarieties within the above territories, e.g. the broad division between north and south linguistically in England.
3   Social dialects, which involve particular varieties characteristic of social groups within a territory, e.g. Cockney within London, Appalachian English in the USA.
4   Pidgin Englishes, which are relatively simplified varieties arising from contact between groups of people not sharing a common language: e.g. pidgin English in the Cameroons and Nigeria. However, pidgins may expand and take on a greater range of functions within a society, as in the case of Papua New Guinea.

5   Creole Englishes, which typically arise from a rather special situation in which a pidgin started to be used as a first language and underwent considerable expansion in the process, e.g. Creole English in Jamaica.

6   ESL (English as a second language): these are forms which have arisen in countries where English was introduced in the colonial era in face-to-face communication or in the education system in a country in which there is, or had once been, a sizeable number of speakers of English. In ESL countries such as Kenya, Sri Lanka and Nigeria English plays a key role internally in education, government and administration.

7   EFL (English as a foreign language): this refers to English as used in countries in which the influence of English has been external, rather than via a large body of 'settlers'. For such countries English plays a role mainly for international rather than intra-national communication (Japan, China and Germany). Whereas ESL countries produce literature in English, EFL countries do not. The real distinction between ESL and EFL countries is that the former play cricket, the latter do not.[2]

8   Immigrant Englishes: in the context of migration to an English-dominant country, second-language varieties of English might retain their distinctiveness or merge with the English of the majority depending on the social conditions. Thus whilst English in Mexico is of the EFL variety, Chicano English of Mexican immigrants shows greater affinity with general US English, though it is still a distinctive variety.

9   Language-shift Englishes: these are varieties that arise when English replaces the erstwhile primary language of a community. Frequently the linguistic properties of ESL become stabilised; so that even though English is an L1 (first language) for many groups of native American Indians, the Irish in Ireland and Indian South Africans, the new first language retains a distinctiveness and sense of continuity with the ancestral languages and cultures.

As with all taxonomies for human behaviour this scheme for types of English conceals a great deal of flexibility: Loreto Todd's caution not to expect sharp edges and watertight compartments in language seems apt. Population demographics and ensuing political struggles can lead to shifts in linguistic balance: as with the complex and ongoing historical relation between Spanish and English in California. An ESL variety may start to become a language-shift English, as is currently happening in Singapore. A further disaffection with the above classification is that it treats English in, say, present-day Norway and China as of the same type: these are EFLs. Yet the rise of the European Community has surely made English in Europe something between ESL and EFL. We might note that Holland has started to play cricket competitively too!

The central position in the field of 'World Englishes' (or 'New Englishes') is that these are not necessarily incomplete systems, dependent upon – and falling short of – the norms of native British or US English.[3] As spoken by the most fluent and educated speakers a New English such as that of Sri Lanka or South Africa has a linguistically and socially valid identity. Such varieties have become the *de facto* targets of acquisition: a child acquiring spoken English in Singapore acquires Singaporean English, not British English. Since an important function of ESL is to communicate with people from the same country, external native speaker norms are not entirely relevant. Interactional sociolinguistics, the branch that has gained the most ground in the last two decades, stresses that communication of a message is only part of the function of any act of speech. At the very same time speech is used to maintain relationships, to signify or defuse power and to communicate aspects of one's social identity: who we are, where we come from, where we hope to be going, and what relations we hope to establish with the people we happen to be speaking to. Such questions usually carry local not global answers. For these purposes sounding like a native speaker from the metropolis is seldom appropriate, unless one wants to distance oneself from one's utterance.[4] Sounding like a colonist or representative of the ex-colonial order might be feasible if one wishes to strategically withdraw from unreasonable requests being made by a fellow ESL speaker, or from the obligations imposed by common bonds like ethnicity, or if one needs to don the mantle of authority.

The second principle of New Englishes research – related to the first – is that these varieties must of necessity fit into the linguistic ecology of their region. There is frequently an interplay between the New English and these local languages via code switching. The linguistic ecology demands such blending. Research in east Africa by Carol Myers-Scotton (1993) has shown how sophisticated the process actually is, how delicate the resulting change of function of the speech act can be, and how the consequent balance between speaker's and listener's rights and obligations can be changed or maintained.

This chapter offers an overview of a clear-cut case of a language-shift English, which because of political circumstances (state-enforced segregation) stabilised as an L1 while interaction with native speakers was limited. Rigid segregation led to a fossilisation of South African Indian English (SAIE) at the stage that L2 was turning into L1. As a result SAIE offers the historian and linguist a unique chance of studying the linguistics of language shift.

South African Indian English: historical background

SAIE is today spoken by about a million people. Its origins ultimately lie with the abolition of slavery in the British empire in the 1830s, which created a labour vacuum that the colonial authorities filled by importing Asian labourers. The chief source of this cheap labour was India, resulting in large Indian communities in Mauritius, the Caribbean, Fiji and South Africa. Whilst there were no slaves to be freed in South Africa, the reluctance of the indigenous Zulu menfolk to work as agricultural labourers led to the import of 152,184 Indians from various parts of India (present-day provinces of Bihar, Uttar Pradesh, Andhra Pradesh and Tamil Nadu) between 1860 and 1911.

These were speakers of a range of north Indian languages, which coalesced into a South African form of Bhojpuri (simply called 'Hindi' in South Africa), as well as of Dravidian languages of south India, chiefly Tamil and Telugu.[5] Muslims spoke one of the above varieties and/or a form of Urdu. A non-labouring class of traders settled in South Africa, becoming part of the Indian community: these were mainly speakers of Gujarati and Konkani. The dynamics of demography and prestige of these languages and their speakers was such that no one language predominated or had sufficiently greater prestige than the others to count as a lingua franca. (This was unlike the island of Fiji, where the demographics dictated that Fiji Hindi emerged as the lingua franca of the Indian community.) With the growth of Western-oriented education and job opportunities, English (which was not initially known amongst the majority of immigrants) became an important second language for some speakers within a generation. (Other lingua francas included Fanakalo – a pidgin form of Zulu – and to a lesser extent Bhojpuri and Tamil.) Males were quicker in acquiring English via outside employment and because of the reluctance of parents in the early phases to send their daughters to school. Bughwan (1970: 503), the first researcher on SAIE, believed that English was transmitted to Indians by native speakers of the language – British missionaries, British teachers and English-speaking sugar-estate owners. This is a rather optimistic view of the social conditions that prevailed in the colony. We can instead posit four main possible sources of input to the learner:

1   schooling, with teachers being native speakers of English;
2   schooling, with teachers being non-native speakers of English;
3   contact with native speakers of English in Natal;
4   contact with non-native speakers of English (chiefly Indians).

Written records suggest that all four sources were significant in shaping SAIE. As far as education in the nineteenth century was concerned, it would appear that the number of non-native English-speaking teachers was at least as great as that of mother-tongue English teachers. This includes the missionaries, many of whom were of continental European origin (see further Mesthrie 1992a: 19–22).

For the first 90 years or so English was a second language, known only to some members of the Indian community. The 1936 census records suggest that 40 per cent of Indians knew English. Of this 40 per cent more males were learning English than females (roughly 7:3); more urban than rural speakers were learning it (roughly 3:1); and more were learning English at school than at home (roughly 17:1). Even prior to the apartheid era Indians went to schools at which they were in the majority, and their teachers were largely (but not solely) Indian. The National Party, which came into power in 1948, sought to make Indians one of the four recognised 'race' groups of the country and began enforcing rigid segregation in the 1950s. This had consequences for the 'crystallisation' of an Indian dialect of English.

By the late 1950s when, despite apartheid, educational conditions actually improved, English began to be introduced in the home and neighbourhood by children. In some homes a rapid inversion of roles took place. Whereas the first- and second-born child might have arrived at school with no knowledge of English, their subsequent influence in the home was in some instances so significant as to cause the last or second-last child in large families to arrive at school with English as dominant language. In the 1960s and 1970s English became the first language of a majority of Indian schoolchildren. A process of shift is under way, with the Indian languages surviving with some difficulty. This process can be thought of as gradual or rapid, depending on one's defining criteria. As 1960 was exactly 100 years since the first immigrations, the process might seem a gradual one; but as 1960 was also less than 50 years since the last shipload, the shift is perhaps not all that gradual.

In some homes parents (especially rural mothers) learnt English from the youngest children, rather than vice versa. This process, which I call a 'closed cycle of reinforcement' in language shift, continues today, though it is now manifest in the interactions between grandparents (especially grandmothers) and grandchildren. That is, those grandparents with little or no schooling who spoke an Indian language to their children a generation ago are now forced to learn English in order to be intelligible to monolingual grandchildren. (In some homes grandchildren are lucky enough to receive input from grandparents in an ancestral language, but this is increasingly rare.) The closed cycle of reinforcement is remarkable for its potential two-way influence: the grandparent learns from, and with, the grandchild, and in turn reinforces the grandchild's child-language. As one of my interviewees discussing his wife's knowledge of English put it, 'Now with her purposes too, her grandchildren all growing y'see, now she must communicate with them in the language they understand [English]. So she goes along with that language. *They teach the grandparents how to speak the language*' (emphasis mine).

SAIE and other Englishes

The kind of English that stabilised was, as I have already indicated, a very special one, given that the policy of apartheid (1948–1991) kept Indian children away from first-language speakers of English descent, in hospitals, homes, neighbourhoods, public facilities, schools and even universities. The result is that, whilst being quite South African in some respects (aspects of lexis and phonology), it is a recognisably different variety of South African English. This difference is not always evident to the wider society, since SAIE speakers adopt more careful and formal styles in public interaction. In this regard language-shift Englishes differ from L2s, since they develop style and register flexibility to cover the domains formerly reserved for the ancestral language(s). SAIE is also similar to the English of India (in aspects of pronunciation, lexis and syntax) but in many ways significantly different. Similarities are the result of several factors: shared mother-tongues; input from a very small percentage of indentured workers (of Christian background) and traders from India; and from the early English teachers specially brought from India. There are four salient items related to education that SAIE shares with Indian English, which are probably a reflection of the influence of these early teachers: *tuition(s)* 'extra lessons outside school that one pays for'; *further studies* 'higher education'; *alphabets* 'the alphabet, letters of the alphabet'; *by-heart* 'to learn off by heart' (e.g. *Don't by-heart your work*; *He by-hearted his work*).

The main difference between SAIE and Indian English is that the former is not a predominantly 'educated' or 'elite' variety. In contrast to Indian English, which has been characterised as 'bookish', 'Latinate' and imbued with a 'moralistic' tone (Kachru 1983: 39), SAIE is hyper-colloquial, sometimes in situations demanding a measure of formalese. Although SAIE has many overlaps with Indian English, some of its features are not quite as prominent as in the latter. In particular, retroflexion of consonants such as [t] and [d] is not the salient characteristic that it is in Indian English, and appears to be receding in SAIE. Likewise, the strong aspiration and murmur associated with consonant articulation in Indian English is receding in SAIE. This probably reflects the greater influence of South Indian languages, in which these features play only a minor role, on SAIE than on general Indian English. One salient feature that SAIE still shares with Indian English (IE) is the use of a syllable-timed rhythm rather than stress-timing, especially in colloquial styles.

SAIE shares similarities with L2 varieties of English throughout the world, in some of its characteristic simplification and regularities. This includes the use of grammatical elements that are, from the viewpoint of the L2 learner, more salient than their standard English equivalents. For example, instead of the perfective construction in *I've eaten*, SAIE speakers at their most casual say *I finish eat*. (Compare this with Singapore English use of perfective *already* – Williams 1987.) Another example is the (salient) form *never* for the standard perfective negative *haven't*: thus in informal SAIE *You never see him?* is the equivalent of standard *Haven't you seen him?* Similarities with other New Englishes extend to the use of an invariant tag, *isn't*, in negative questions. Thus *He came there, isn't?* is equivalent to standard English *He came there, didn't he?* (The actual form of the negative tag varies in New Englishes – e.g. *no, isn't it, is it*, etc. SAIE *isn't* is clearly a clipping of IE *isn't it*.) But, once again, there are differences between SAIE and other New Englishes.

One of the most significant is that it is now a first language for a majority of its speakers; another is that it did not originate mainly in educational contexts.

Vocabulary and culture

At its most formal, SAIE lexis differs only slightly from general South African English; at its least formal, it is exceedingly different. The differences found in informal speech are catalogued in my *Lexicon of South African Indian English* (Mesthrie 1992b), a work comprising about 1400 items characteristic of this dialect. Entries describe specific lexical items from a variety of sources, points of grammatical usage (e.g. *y'all* as plural second-person pronoun), specific pronunciation traits (e.g. *bagit* for 'bucket' among many older speakers), adolescent slang and proverbs (e.g. *to want mutton curry and rice everyday*, which means 'to expect a good time/the best always'). The majority of lexical items are drawn from Indian languages in the sphere of kinship, religion and culinary practices. Interestingly, some of these still vary from home to home, depending on the ancestral language. A good example is the word for 'spicy food', for which the adjective *hot* is ambiguous. Speakers wishing to describe spicy food, rather than food that is hot in terms of the temperature, use one of the following, depending on the ancestral language: *karo* (Tamil); *karum* (Telugu); *thikku* (Gujarati); *thitta* (Hindi/Bhojpuri); *thikka* (Urdu). (The last term is now known in several English-speaking territories thanks to the culinary item *chicken thikka*, probably first introduced from India and Pakistan into British English.) Since these terms are used in primarily domestic settings, they are not widely known. In public discourse a term like *pungent*, *chilli-hot* or just *hot* may be used. *Pungent* is interesting for the (Bakhtinian) way that cultural and other tussles turn up in language. Its disparaging overtones are not known to SAIE speakers, who must have taken this term from colonial Natal English speakers. The latter are known to have been in the habit of making unflattering remarks about the smell of curry in Indian homes. Three areas of vocabulary are listed below: the lexis of love (which has a Victorian flavour about it, hinting at a time when love was not spoken about directly), some salient semantic shifts and common lexis now known to all SAIE speakers, drawn from a variety of Indian languages.

The lexis of love:

future (n.): 'husband or wife-to-be';
interested in: 'in love with';
get in touch: 'have a romantic involvement';
proposed: 'affianced, engaged';
disappointed: 'jilted in love';
spoilt: 'carrying a child out of wedlock';
marry out: 'to marry outside one's traditional subethnic group'.

Some semantic shifts in SAIE:

lazy: 'unintelligent' (in addition to usual standard meanings);
interfere: 'to molest';
hint: 'to speak ill of' (not necessarily obliquely);

independent: 'stand-offish, haughty';
raw: 'uncouth, vulgar';
healthy: 'fat, overweight' (not a conscious euphemism);
goodwill: 'compulsory payment to landlord to secure accommodation'.

Lexis drawn from Indian languages:

isel: 'a winged termite, flying ant' (Tamil, Telugu);
dhania: 'coriander' (Bhojpuri, Gujarati, Urdu);
bhajia: 'spicy fried snack' (Bhojpuri, Urdu);
nikah: 'Islamic wedding ceremony' (Urdu);
thanni: (a popular card game) (Tamil);
jhanda: 'flag hoisted by some Hindus after prayers' (Bhojpuri).

Such vocabulary retention represents a complex case of substratum influence from several languages once characteristic of different members of the speech community.

The sociolinguistic continuum in SAIE

SAIE today is far from homogeneous: it is a continuum of varying styles and strategies. A sociolinguistic description of SAIE can be best effected by dividing this continuum at three salient points, resulting in sublects which I call the basilect, mesolect and acrolect. These terms are well known in creole studies where basilect denotes the 'deep' creole furthest removed from the colonial language; acrolect, the creole variety closest to the colonial language; and mesolect, the broad range of varieties between these two extremes. Importing terms from creolistics is, I believe, not controversial, since creolisation is a special case (under extreme social conditions) of the process described in this chapter: the acquisition of a second language as a first language, under conditions of minimal contact with target-language speakers.

As far as SAIE is concerned the basilect follows a largely nativised norm, influenced as much by substrate phenomena and (possibly universal) strategies of L2 communication as by the norms of colonial Natal English. The basilect is today typically used by older speakers with little education, who acquired English as a second language. However, it is spoken with all the fluency of an L1. The acrolect follows fairly closely upon the norms of colonial Natal English, except for its phonetics and two or three syntactic constructions (described later). The mesolect(s) mediate between these two extremes by a host of interesting syntactic strategies (also discussed later). In second-language acquisition terms the lects are essentially interlanguage varieties stabilised (or fossilised) at various points of an interlanguage continuum. Moreover (and this is what makes SAIE a particularly interesting variety), these lects have been pressed into service as first languages – see Mesthrie (1992a: 32–33) for the reasons thereof.

A brief exemplification of speech typical of each lect follows:

Basilect

Question: How often (do) you go to Durban?
Response: Where we go! Hardly we go, visit Durban too. Sometime 'olidays, my 'usband take his brother's house, an' his sistern-law there, an' all of his connection. My connection, all staying Merebank. Sometime holidays we go, but this year 'oliday we had, y'know, like we had some problem an' all, like we want to go visit, I don' like to stay that two–three weeks an' all – they living 'ard life like us too, they earn little bit money too. We must think too, we just can't go sit down, y'know, like brother or sister, anybody can be, like Durban-side they must pay water, this-thing rate, lights, that-all they must pay ... [55-year-old, rural, female, working class].

(Loose standard English equivalent: We don't go. We hardly ever go to visit people in Durban. Sometimes during holidays my husband takes us to his brother's and sister-in-law's house or to other relatives. My relatives live in Merebank. We sometimes go on holidays, but this year we had some problems; even if we want to visit, we have to consider that to stay for two or three weeks is an imposition, since they live a hard life, with a little money only. We must be considerate; we can't just pitch up and remain there for long. Even if it's our own brother or sister, or anyone close we have to realise that in Durban people have to pay for services like lights, water, etc.)

Mesolect

Question: Tell me about the time you had a heart attack.
Response: ... I went an' bought one soda water. So I had a soda water in the cafe, I took my coat out, took my jersey an' all out, I chucked it on the table. I sat, sat, sat – I said no', I felt I must reach home. I didn't trust anybody to drive that van because it was lent to me from somebody else. So somehow or other I managed, I jumped into the van, an' I drove the van an' came, I just came an' parked here an' lied down. My son was here, this second, third fellow of mine. Phoned by Dr T. G. Singh, while I'm lying on the bed, I donno what happened, the wife gave me little bit of sugar-water. I just drank that sugar-water, and, eh, just when I finished the sugar-water I became normal ... [60-year-old, urban, male, working class].

Acrolect *(regarding nursing–patient relationships in a small town)*

> Well, you see because it's a small town, and everybody knows me, then automatically they become more demanding, because – eh – they feel, well, everybody knows me and – just go to Mary and we'll ask her; doesn't matter if she's on holiday or it's a Sunday, or – y'know – something like that. And now I find that I'm not only doing the medical part of it and trying to work; they come to me when they're getting married, to design their dress; or their children are having parties. Y'know I've become part of everybody's family, which is nice in a way [30-year-old, female, urban, middle class].

In addition to the three main lects, another turned up in my fieldwork conducted in the late 1980s, which I labelled pre-basilectal. It involves a small number of (second or third generation) speakers whose command of English is makeshift, and who have difficulties in expressing themselves in English, even about domestic topics. Pre-basilectal speech is difficult to follow, even for one who understands all the nuances of the basilect. In Mesthrie (1990) I discuss the similarities and possible links between the pre-basilect and Butler English, a rudimentary pidgin of South India. This is the earliest interlanguage form discernible within SAIE and forms an important foil for the proper understanding of the more focused and stable basilect.

A recent development in post-apartheid society is the rise of a small group of young people who have attended, or currently attend, private schools in which the norms of prestige varieties of (White) South African English prevail. Depending on the age of such 'dialect immersion', and the nature of their social networks and especially peer groups, many of these can be described as post-acrolectal speakers. They use an essentially non-SAIE system, but may belong to the SAIE speech community, albeit tenuously. For example, in a discussion with me one young woman in her twenties expressed a consciousness of moving in two social worlds in a way that was not possible a generation ago. She believes herself to be bidialectal, speaking SAIE in her residential neighbourhood and general South African English with her former school and university friends of whatever ethnic background. Announcers on Radio Lotus, a station aimed at an Indian listenership, are usually acrolectal (with strong concessions to general 'announcer-speak'). On the other hand, Indians trying to break into national radio and television use a conspicuously post-acrolectal variety.

Putting the main lects in boldface, the SAIE continuum may be presented as follows:

pre-basilect – **basilect** – **mesolect** – **acrolect** – post-acrolect

The ratio of speakers of these lects in my fieldwork was respectively 1:4:12:3:0.[6] My classification of speakers is based on their overall linguistic performance in the informal interview situation. One further feature of post-apartheid policy might affect this: for the first time in about 80 years it is possible for Indians to enter the country legally. This could enable a slight reinforcement not only from Indian languages, but from Indian English too.

If we were to characterise SAIE as one focused system (and this is probably not feasible), that system would be closer to the mesolect than the basilect. The mesolect carries less stigma than either the basilect or the acrolect. That is, in informal situations an SAIE speaker has to strike a balance between not sounding too basilectal (with its undertones of lack of sophistication, being rural, aged, etc.) or too acrolectal (which could be interpreted as 'putting on airs', being cold, distant, etc.). A similar pattern has been observed for creolophone societies. Washabaugh (1977: 334) describes three 'pressures' that adult speakers in a post-creole continuum are caught up in: (1) a pressure to avoid basilect forms; (2) pressure to acquire the acrolect; and (3) pressure to use a casual style in informal situations.

These pressures have far-reaching consequences in the syntactic behaviour of SAIE speakers. The few glimpses of pressure (3) that were revealed on tape were illuminating, however. One acrolectal speaker, after being drawn into the interviewer's confidence, and wishing to be friendlier than she had sounded up to that point, asked two questions: *'Religion – you got that, eh – Catholic?'* and *'It must be a really bad experience?'* The personal tone accompanying these remarks was suggestive of a desire to be friendly and helpful, and was enhanced by the use of syntactic properties that are atypical of the acrolect: topicalisation, absence of *have* before *got* in the first question and non-inversion of auxiliary and subject in the second. Conversely, a mesolectal speaker not wanting to sound overdeferential, uneducated and easy-going (and powerless) might well increase the use of 'formal' constructions such as *do*-support, auxiliary inversion, perfective *have*, etc. (with possible hypercorrections).

Another speaker (a college lecturer), whose interview style can best be described as upper-mesolectal to acrolectal showed similar patterns of style shifting in a generally relaxed interview. In the middle of the session she turned to her husband, who had just returned from shopping, and asked *'You bought cheese, Farouk?'* Once again, an intimate style required a switch away from the acrolect constructions (*do*-support, in this instance). The reply of the husband, a high-school English teacher, was even more revealing. Not realising that the tape was running he said, in an ultra-casual style, *'No, but lot butter I bought'*. This single utterance contains a number of basilectal features that he himself might harangue against in the classroom: a pre-dilection for topicalisation; *lot* for 'a lot of' (or 'much' in classroom English); and a basilectal pronunciation, [nɔː] for acrolectal *no* (= [noʊ]. Such back-sliding has been noted for other New Englishes – see Ho and Platt (1993) for Singapore.

Another argument for not considering the SAIE system to comprise a bipolar 'dialect plus standard' mechanism comes from a study of the acrolectal end of the continuum. The acrolect is not the same as standard English or the (White) South African English variety used in Natal. In terms of both accent and syntax there are subtle boundaries which few speakers traverse. Only a few speakers are genuinely bidialectal in SAIE and South African English. These tend to be young professionals employed in prestigious commercial houses – where they come into contact with South African English employers and clients – a few radio and television announcers and the new generation of private school goers. Those who carry the South African English dialect home run the risk of being gently ridiculed ('Your mummy's using her Standard Bank accent') and, in my observation, switch to the mesolect in intimate styles.

The acrolect

What are the syntactic features that the acrolect shares with the basilect and mesolect and that mark off the acrolect from general South African English?

1   *y'all* as plural pronoun form. This form, which is below the level of social consciousness for most SAIE speakers, occurs in informal letters (where it is usually spelt *you'll*) and formal speeches. It has a genitive form *y'all's*.

2   Copula attraction to *wh-* in indirect questions, which results in sentences such as those in examples 6.1 and 6.2:

   (6.1)   Do you know what's/what is roti?[7]

   (6.2)   I don't know when's/when is the plane going to land.

   In sharp contrast is the (standard) South African English equivalent with the copula occurring after the subject noun phrase (NP) of the embedded clause. The equivalent of example 1 above would have stress on sentence-final is: '*Do you know what roti is?*'

3   The use of *of* in partitive genitive constructions beyond standard English contexts:

   (6.3)   The trouble with him is he's got too much of money.

Linguistic processes typical of the basilect

In comparison with the early interlanguage forms characteristic of the pre-basilect, the basilect displays a much more focused and developed structure.

This can be characterised in terms of two broad processes: (1) expansion of inner form and (2) complexification of outer form.[8]

Expansion of inner form

This refers to the development of 'core' structures that enable the basilect to function as a full linguistic system. In comparison to the pre-basilect, the basilect has structures such as relative clauses, a stable system of prepositions and topic–comment principles. From a sociolinguistic point of view what makes the basilect remarkable is that such grammatical machinery has been developed by using its own resources, rather than by recourse to structures from standard English or other dialects and offshoots of British English. I will exemplify this claim by examining complementation and co-ordination in the basilect.

Complementation

Among the more striking differences between basilectal SAIE and standard English complementation are the following:

1   Sentence-external placement of modal-like modifiers.

   (6.4)   **Lucky,** they never come (= 'We were lucky that they didn't come').

   (6.5)   **Must be,** they coming now (= It must be that they're coming now/they must be on their way').

2   This pattern is extended to constructions that would require raising and the use of infinitives in standard English:

   (6.6)   They told I must come an' stay that side (= 'They asked me to come and live there').

   (6.7)   I like children must learn our mother tongue (= 'I'd like our children to learn our mother tongue').

   (6.8)   Then Ram told Devi's mother must tell I must come (= 'Then Ram asked Devi's mother to ask me to come').

   Like examples 6.4 and 6.5 these show the pattern 'modal-like element + *s*', with the structure of '*s*' unchanged. Although the usual English pattern with *to* infinitives and raising does occur in the basilect, they are not as frequent as patterns exhibited in sentences such as 6.6–6.8.

3   The use of clause-final *too* as a hypothetical marker in conditional clauses.

> (6.9)   It can be a terrible house **too**, you have to stay in a terrible house (= 'Even if it's a terrible house, you have to live in it').

> (6.10)   Very sick an' all **too**, they take them to R. K. Khan's (= 'If they're very sick, they are taken to R. K. Khan Hospital').

Co-ordination

Both the basilect and pre-basilect often favour the paratactic stringing of clauses instead of overt co-ordination markers:

> (6.11)   She was calling, she was telling ... (= 'She called and said ...').

> (6.12)   Born over there, I'm brought up over there (= 'I was born and brought up over there').

When co-ordination is marked, a variety of strategies arise. The ones that are 'created' rather than 'inherited' (from Natal English) are exemplified below.

1   Use of *too* clause-finally: there were a few instances of these in the corpus.

> (6.13)   I made rice **too**, I made roti **too** (= 'I made both rice and roti').

> (6.14)   You walk into town **too** its difficult, you wanna do shopping **too**, its difficult (= 'If you want to walk in town and do your shopping, it's difficult').

> (There are parallels in such clause final marking in Indic and Dravidian languages – and rigid verb-final languages generally.)

2   Use of salient phrase-final quantifiers:

> (6.15)   I speak English, Tamil, **both** (= 'both X and Y ...').

> (6.16)   ... rose-water, vicks, coconut oil, **nothing** (= 'neither X nor Y nor Z ...').

> (6.17)   We had to take out our shirt, tie, vest, **everything** (= 'all of X, Y, Z ...').

> (6.18)   They must have one cup porridge, water, **anything** (= 'one of X, Y ...').

Complexification of outer form

Whereas the previous examples focused on the development of essential core structures ('inner form') in the basilect, in this section I will exemplify the fleshing out of syntax by psycholinguistic processes which do not always derive from the English input. Such 'fleshing out' may lead to an increase in redundancy, making an interlanguage more like a native language.

Double marking of clause relations

In shifting from parataxis to a less paratactic state the same conjunction may be repeated before each clause.

> (6.19)   **But** it'll come, **but** too late (= 'It'll come but too late').

> (6.20)   **So** when I was a baby, **so** my father-an'-them shifted here to Sezela (= 'When I was a baby my father's family moved here to Sezela').

Occasionally, the repeated conjunction occurs in the clause-final position:

> (6.21)   We go Howick **now**, we feel different **now** (= 'When/if we go to Howick today we feel that it has changed').

> (6.22)   But if I tell somebody **now**, they'll say he's bluffing **now** (= 'If I were to tell someone this today, they'd say I was lying').

More usually, different conjunctions occur in each clause:

> (6.23)   **Though** I visit very often to Durban, **but** I don't like it.

> (6.24)   **But** sincing the weather wasn't promising too, **then** we decided to come today (= 'Since the weather was also not very good, we decided to come today').

Sentences 6.23 and 6.24 show that an initial conjunction may co-occur with a final one within the same clause. Double marking of clause relations is a common feature of New Englishes (see Williams 1987), including South African Black English.

Use of target language forms with non-target meaning, function and distribution

This is an often-remarked upon characteristic of creole expansion that would appear to have some relevance in second-language acquisition (Andersen 1983: 31–32). It is a pervasive feature of basilectal syntax and morphology; though for reasons of space only two areas will be covered: (1) aspect and (2) changes in parts of speech.

1   Aspect marking: the verbs *stay* and *leave* are used in non-target language ways to convey aspectual distinctions. *An' stay* after a verb signals a habitual sense; *an' leave him/her/it* is a completive marker.

    (6.25)   We'll fright an' stay (= 'We used to be afraid [for a long while]').

    (6.26)   When mother-all here, we'll talk mother, and laugh an' stay (= 'When my mother and others were alive we used to talk merrily [at length]').

    (6.27)   She filled the bottle an' left it (= 'She filled the bottle completely').

    (6.28)   We whacked him an' left him (= 'We beat him up thoroughly').

    This construction, which is not a very common one, might be part of a larger tendency to replace adverbs by verbs in sentences denoting habitual action:

    (6.29)   He'll run an' come (= 'He'll come running').

    (6.30)   They only laugh and talk (= 'They always speak happily/in a laughing manner').

    Sentences 6.25 and 6.26 show another aspectual difference from standard English: the use of the reduced form of *will* to denote past habitual action (equivalent to standard English *would*). The most striking innovation in aspect marking in SAIE is, however, *should* for standard English 'used to', probably based on an original confusion between the fast speech forms of *used to* and *should* ([stu] and [səd] respectively – see Mesthrie 1992a: 130–133).

2   Change of part of speech: an interesting change is shown by the use of *here* as a sentence-final exclamatory tag, as in examples 6.31 and 6.32:

    (6.31)   I don't like it, **here**!

    (6.32)   He's troubling me, **here**!

    There are two plausible etymologies for the tag. The first involves a change of part of speech of the phrase *do you hear/you hear?*, which must have been reduced to *hear* and reinterpreted as *here*. Native-speaker intuitions – including my own – suggest a current identification with *here* rather than *hear*. The two forms are also phonetically distinct: *here* = [hjæ]; *hear* = [hje]. Furthermore, the syntactic contexts in which the form may occur has been extended to include declaratives (indicating disapproval, a complaint or anger) instead of the predominantly imperatives of the target language. A second possibility is that the form *here* comes from colloquial English dialect sentences such as *Here, you wouldn't be pulling my leg, would you?*, where it acts as a focus marker: i.e. an attention-getter, with a vague sense of misapprehension or a warning. If this is the case, then it would count as an archaism, since the form is not common in general South African English. Nor has the construction been reported for any other New English. I have, however, encountered an example in a recent Indian film (*Kuch Kuch Hota Hai*), in which an Anglo-Indian character, called 'Colonel', says in English *Daadi gone mad here* (= Granny has gone mad; *here* = [+ EXASPERATION]). This raises the possibility of the survival or change of part of speech passing from British dialects to South Indian English to SAIE (where South Indians are in a slight majority).

We have already seen the adverb *too* in a variety of functions. Two of these functions have been described already: as a clause-final hypothetical marker, and as an occasional marker of co-ordination. Yet another function is as focus marker:

(6.33)   This weather **too**, it's terrible (no other terrible thing mentioned).

Whereas the focus falls on the NP in sentence 6.33, it is on the main clause in 6.34:

(6.34)   We were very small when they died **too** (no other dead – or small – persons mentioned).

In the basilect (and to a lesser extent, the pre-basilect) some words have changed (or extended) their word-class affiliation, without a significant change in semantics:

(6.35)   We from born we staying here (*born* n.).

(6.36)   We very unity people this side (*unity* adj.).

(6.37)   From small he's like that (*small* n.).

(6.38)   Very sin to see that thing (*sin* adj.).

(6.39)   He offed it! (= 'He put it off') (*off* v.).

(6.40)   Who's look-aftering the baby? (*look-after* v.).

Instances of adjective/noun overlap are probably traceable to Dravidian influence (see Mesthrie 1992a: 208).

Characteristic processes in the mesolect

While basilectal syntax consistently shows the creation of core grammatical machinery, the mesolect is characterised by processes of restructuring of such basilectal forms in the direction of the acrolect. Three processes will be illustrated:

Replacement of form, without change of meaning

One characteristic of decreolisation that has some relevance to change in SAIE is the manner in which restructuring takes place. Bickerton (1975) suggests that when new forms in the mesolect are acquired from the acrolect, they at first retain the 'old' meaning, function and distribution of the forms they are replacing. Slobin (1973: 184) suggests that this is in fact a general principle of L1 acquisition – 'a far reaching principle [for L1 acquisition] which could be phrased as follows: *new forms first express old functions, and new functions are first expressed by old forms*' (emphasis in original). The process is noticeable in mesolectal SAIE.

A few mesolectal speakers expressed emphatic co-ordination on the lines of (example 6.41):

    (6.41)   My dad was a soccerite **as well**, he was a musician **as well**. (= 'My dad was both a soccerite and a musician')

This appears to be based on the basilectal pattern of OV-ordination with *too* occurring at the end of each clause – see sentence 6.13. Speakers who produce sentences such as 6.41 conceive of *too* as non-standard (or, at least inappropriate in certain styles) and replace it with the standard English form *as well*. The resulting pattern illustrates the retention of the basilectal pattern, despite seeming more acrolectal to the speakers.

A similar phenomenon occurs with certain lexical items and idioms. The basilectal phrase for a bin, *dirty box*, is stigmatised in the classroom, and in an effort to sound less basilectal some speakers use the phrase *dirt-box*. Likewise, the basilectal phrase *to make dirty* (= 'to litter') is realigned as *to make dirt*, which is syntactically standardish without being a standard English idiom.

Addition of features

A related modification of basilectal features in SAIE involves addition rather than replacement. The result is, once again, less basilectal but not more standard, though it might feel so to mesolectal speakers.

Sentences 6.42 and 6.43 illustrate two patterns in the basilect involving absence of the copula (the basilect generally favours a zero copula after *that*). Whereas 6.42 shows simple absence of the reduced form *'s* after *where*, 6.43 shows an attempt at compensating for copula absence by use of the deictic *that* at the end of the clause.

(6.42)   Where that place – Chatsworth? (= 'Where's that place, Chatsworth?').

(6.43)   Paan that (= 'That's paan/it's paan'; *paan* = 'betel leaf').[9]

In attempting to avoid this basilectal pattern some speakers (usually mesolectal) produce intermediary sentences which incorporate both basilectal and acrolectal forms:

(6.44)   Where's the place is, Chatsworth?

(6.45)   It's paan that (compare 6.43).

We have seen that one of the features of SAIE that occurs in all lects is the attraction of the copula to *wh*-forms in indirect questions (for example, even acrolectal speakers say: *Do you know when's the plane going to land?*). Acrolectal speakers may use the standard equivalent without attraction in slightly formal styles. Interestingly, a few times in the corpus (only) mesolectal speakers produced the copula in both 'attracted' position as well as in its original trace position:

(6.46)   You see where's the bridge is?

For different reasons, no basilectal or acrolectal speaker would produce such a hypercorrection. (Acrolectal speakers have the standard construction; basilectal speakers do not wish to sound acrolectal.)

Near misses

A third process, suggestive of an intermediary stage between the basilect and acrolect in SAIE, involves what I call 'near misses'. Speakers use forms that are close to the standard, but differ in minor details: a divergent use of a preposition from the acrolect, an overgeneralised environment for a rule, a re-subcategorisation of a verb, a novel form of an old idiom, etc. These are typically mesolectal since they involve neither the creation of a form (as one often finds in the basilect) nor its exact 'inheritance' from standard English (as one finds in the acrolect). Speakers have learned a form, but not completely. In situations involving monitored speech they are easily able to produce a standard form, but in spontaneous discourse, under either very relaxed or very tense situations, display several 'near misses'. By contrast, forms typical of the basilect often involve not-so-near misses. The first of our two sets of illustrations concerns items that are recognisably part of the dialect (chiefly the mesolect).

1a Prepositions:

> (6.47)   He's got no worries of anyone ('about').
>
> (6.48)   I'm not fluent with Afrikaans ('in').
>
> (6.49)   I was good in arithmetic ('at').

1b Adverbials, adjectives and quantifiers: *for really* 'really, truly', *farest* 'furthest', *worst* 'worse' (in addition to its usual meaning), *more worse* 'worse'

1c Lexis and idioms: *sincing* 'since (because)', *catch up* 'catch on', *can't stick the heat* 'can't stand the heat', *play fools* 'play the fool', *long-cut* 'long route, long way', *to run a mock* 'to run amok, to revel',[10] *to pick somebody out* 'to pick on someone (verbally)'

> Some of the 'near misses' involve a conflation of two target-language items, or the influence of one over another. Thus *sincing* seems to be based on both *since* and *seeing*; *long-cut* is formed by analogy with *short-cut*, etc. Such neologisms, overgeneralisations and recategorisations are very common in the New Englishes generally. Sey's grammar (1973) of Ghanaian English and Nihalani *et al.*'s (1978) lexicon of Indian English give examples which suggest that these processes occur to a much greater extent than in SAIE. Indeed, these are the most salient feature of those varieties of English. In SAIE they are one of a widely varying set of processes, and not the most divergent of these from standard English.

2   Another interesting set involves items that are 'one-off' errors, used by mesolectal speakers in the interviews. Although the individual items exemplified in 6.50–6.52 are not characteristic of the dialect, the process is widespread enough in the mesolect to warrant attention.

> (6.50)   I accompany all the vegetables with spices (= 'I mix the vegetables with spices').
>
> (6.51)   I overlooked it (= 'I neglected to do it').
>
> (6.52)   You'll find one person is linked relatively to a number of people (= 'related to a number of people').

This class of near misses is psychologically interesting, since the speakers would have little difficulty in using the correct forms in most situations. Yet there seems to be an asymmetry between the passive command of English and the productions of mesolectal speakers in semi-formal speech.

The gap between the basilect and acrolect is a wide one in SAIE, and the mesolect mediates via a series of strategies. In connection with second-language data, the point to be made is that the analyst should be sensitive to the characteristic processes found in different (frozen) interlanguage stages.

Conclusion

In this chapter I have concentrated on the building of a new dialect of English in the process of language shift. I have shown that this involves (1) the creation of new structures via psychological processes common in second-language acquisition, (2) the retention of some features from the substrate languages, chiefly Bhojpuri-Hindi and Tamil and of some features of the English of India, (3) the inheritance of many superstrate structures from standard English, via the classroom and colonial Natal English. Other influences arising from language contact can also be discerned, such as the indirect influence of Zulu (often via Fanakalo pidgin) and Afrikaans (often via South African English). A close study of syntactic etymology in the dialect is a rewarding occupation for the historian of language that I have not pursued here, except in asides, mainly for lack of space.

It is true that, as language shift progresses, English education increases within the community and desegregation applies, more and more speakers will command the upper mesolect and acrolect. This will not lead to the immediate disappearance of the basilect, however. For one thing the basilect does have some covert prestige, and is seen by some parents and grandparents of the working class as a natural medium for conversation with young children. A great deal of backsliding in casual style amongst SAIE speakers also leads to the continued use of some basilectal constructions. Male teenage slang seems to draw on non-English sources for its vocabulary, but on the basilect for its syntax. A good history of English in its colonial and post-colonial incarnations will have to pay attention to a symphony of lects within any New English.

Notes

1 This chapter is a revised and updated account that draws upon Mesthrie (1995 and 1999) in parts.
2 Except for Malaysia, which ought to play the game, but doesn't.
3 The term 'World Englishes', as used in the literature and – especially – the journal of that name, denotes all members of the English language family as I have characterised it, except the first three.
4 Here I adapt the old distinction between metropolis and colony. The term 'metropolitan' English is thus a useful term for native British and US English (insofar as these exert considerable influence in one way or another on all other Englishes).
5 I sometimes use the hyphenated form 'Bhojpuri–Hindi' to link these two varieties – the former, a vernacular; the latter, its heteronymous literary and cultural standard.

6 The zero should not be interpreted literally; it signifies that no post-acrolectal speakers turned up in the interviews. The actual proportion is close to zero.
7 Roti is flat, round, unleavened bread.
8 I owe this classification to Valdman (1977: 155), who discusses these processes in relation to creolisation.
9 This construction might appear to resemble elliptical expressions (with copula deletion and rightward movement of the demonstrative) in informal English, e.g. *Good pass, that* (in football commentary) or *Nice bread, this* (casual or intimate style). The SAIE construction does not have an adjective, nor the semantics of approval or disapproval, that such sentences typically express.
10 This is not just a phonetic innovation. Some speakers use phrases such as *He was running a big mock over there*. *Mock* seems to mean 'revelry, doing things without the consent or approval of elders, taking advantage of a situation, taking advantage of the opposite sex'.

7 The story of good and bad English in the United States

Dennis R. Preston

Nonstandard US English (NUSE) has a threefold identity. First, there are linguistic forms which never or rarely occur in the speech or writing of educated, middle- to upper-status speakers.[1] Such forms are traditionally the ones regarded as nonstandard by linguists. This, however, suggests a class- or status-based etiology for Standard US English (SUSE), a characterization which the democratic–populist ideology of the country would seem to deny.

Second, certain linguistic features which occur in the speech of the best-educated, highest-status speakers from some regions or from some ethnic groups are regarded by the general public as nonstandard, although nonlinguists prefer such terms as *substandard* or simply 'bad English' or 'sloppy speech'. This second category derives from the stereotype of such groups as being made up primarily of poorly educated and lower-status persons, which suggests that nonstandardness on the basis of status is recognized in practice if not in ideology, as mentioned for the first category. For example, 'sick *at* my stomach' is used by southerners of all educational levels, but, since it is 'southern', it may be perceived as nonstandard by nonsoutherners, who get 'sick *to* their stomachs' and probably see everything southern as 'substandard'.

At the same time, however, some features which may be used in a very limited regional area go unnoticed, by hearers from outside the region as well as the local speakers themselves, so long as the speakers do not belong to one of those groups about which negative stereotypes are held. For example, users of 'need + past participle' (e.g. 'my clothes need washed') occupy a relatively narrow band through the Midwest (though the form is perhaps somewhat more widely distributed than previously thought, as suggested in Frazer *et al.* 1996: 263). Since these Midwesterners are not prejudiced against linguistically (or in other ways) by themselves or others, the users of this form are seldom mocked for it and are, in fact, surprised to find that it is not universally distributed.

Since the object of this survey will be folk or public notions of nonstandardness, rather than only those recognized by linguists, I will include comment about both sorts, but I will try to point out which is which, although it is not always possible to do so absolutely. In some cases it may be possible to find items which are straightforwardly nonstandard in one region but standard in another, and in such cases the perceived nonstandardness would not derive from negative stereotypes. Visitors to Michigan, for example, are often amazed at the degree to which preterit-participial levelling has advanced among educated speakers (e.g. *grow/grew/grew*; *go/went/went*).

The third type of NUSE consists of the casual or informal features of language use. Even though they are used by the best-educated and highest-status speakers and among groups about whom no negative stereotypes are held, they are considered by many nonlinguists to be nonstandard. The very best-educated speakers say 'gonna' in rapid, casual speech, for example, but many such speakers are unaware of their own usage. This type may also include items which could more properly be called *slang*, *jargon*, and *obscenity*, to name perhaps only the most obvious classes. For example, the slang vocabularies (or even some typical speech habits) of younger speakers, even the best-educated and highest-status ones, are regarded as nonstandard.

NUSE, therefore, appears to refer to (1) lower-status usage, (2) usage among prejudiced-against groups, regardless of status, although uniform low status is often mistakenly attributed to such groups, and (3) rapid, colloquial, slangy, and obscene use. For linguists, of course, only type (1) is considered nonstandard, although there may be some hedging on type 3.[2]

How have linguists and nonlinguists come to believe such radically different things about NUSE (and SUSE)? After all, linguists and nonlinguists have long been in agreement about language which is 'bad' because it obfuscates, is halting, is repetitive, is over- (or under-)qualified, or lacks coherence. Linguists, however, may say that even language which exhibits such apparently deplorable characteristics might be 'good' – i.e. effective – if that was the impression the speaker/writer meant to convey, but, even in such cases, one could argue that what is at stake is simply the appropriate or effective choice of 'bad language'. In West African Wolof culture, for example, Irvine (1975) has shown that upper-status speakers are supposed to appear linguistically reserved, even inarticulate.

Before we can even approach the question of how such divergent views of standardness in US English arose historically, we shall have to tackle the problem of Ungarinyin. Rumsey (1992) contrasts 'Western languages' with Ungarinyin (an aboriginal language in north-western Australia), noting, for example, that English uses both direct and indirect reported speech (e.g. *She said, 'I'm going to Menaggio'* versus *She said she was going to Menaggio*) but that in Ungarinyin there is no such thing as indirect reported speech. Rumsey concludes that a Western ideology of language – that language and its use are not one and the same – is not viable for speakers of Ungarinyin. Westerners, he contends, believe that language has an out-of-context existence which is somehow separate from use. For speakers of Ungarinyin, language structure and use are inseparable; language itself does not really exist except in use.

I do not know about other 'Western languages', but, for US English, Rumsey could not have said it better. For speakers of that variety, language appears to exist not only free of context but also free of cognitive and social reality. In short, it is other-worldly.

Consider the following linguistically mysterious conversation:[3]

> D: Oftentimes a gift is something like you you go to a Tupperware party and they're going to give you a gift, it's - I think it's more: impersonal, - than a present.
>
>   [
> H: Uh huh.
>
>   [
> G: No, there's no difference.
>
>   [
> D: No? There's real- yeah there's really no difference.
>
>   [
> G: There is no difference.
> D: That's true. Maybe the way we use it is though.
> U: Maybe we could look it up and see what 'gift' means.
>
>   [
> D: I mean technically there's no difference.
> ((They then look up *gift* and *present* in the dictionary.))

(Niedzielski and Preston 1999: 313)

H (a non-native speaker of English) has asked D and G (young adult native speakers of US English) about the difference in meaning between 'gift' and 'present'. D begins, perhaps like any serious lexicographer, by investigating contrasting situations to uncover any subtle nuances of meaning. He is reminded by his partner, however, that that is not the right path, and he hastens to agree that there is 'really no difference'. He goes on, however, to add the amazing (for linguists at any rate) comment that there may be a difference – but only in 'the way we use it'.

Rumsey, therefore, has it right but does not go far enough. These speakers of US English not only see a difference between 'use' and 'language' but obviously assign a priority (whether 'really' or 'technically') to 'language'. Figure 7.1 shows what I believe to be the ordinary speaker of US English's theory of language. The flow (as the arrow on the right shows) is down from 'the language' into the performances of those who use 'good language'. (Ignore for the moment the other possibilities.)

I believe this 'flow', however, is not from a socially (or even historically) determined repository of language norms. 'The language' is a Platonic ideal, one whose existence is not due to a process which has determined its shape from prior or recent performances of 'good speakers' or even from honoured texts or language experts. These latter, like the perspicacious philosopher, may see rather more clearly what only dances flickeringly on the cave wall for the rest of us and then record its essence in such places as 'The dictionary'.

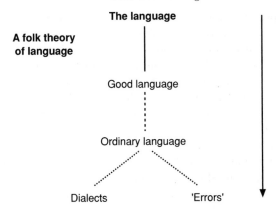

Figure 7.1 The typical US nonlinguist's theory of language[4]

This folk theory of language does not derive from D's comments on 'gift' and 'present' alone but from the investigation of a great deal of 'folk linguistic' material (e.g. Niedzielski and Preston 1999). I believe this theory will make plausible a very large number of beliefs held by nonlinguists about the nature of English – beliefs which have been derived from respondent comments and experimental tasks which touch not only on such 'essential' linguistic features as synonymy (as in the 'gift' – 'present' discussion) but also on language structure, acquisition, education, social stratification, and many other areas.

We can begin with some simple proof on the basis of the US proverbialism – 'Ain't ain't a word'. Although there may be a little nervous selfconsciousness in this, it is a perfect illustration of the ideology outlined above. Everyone knows there is a word 'ain't' and that it has widespread use, but that is not enough to redeem it for 'language' status. Use, in short, will not qualify linguistic items for existence in 'the language'. And, if an item is not in 'the language', then it cannot surface in 'good language', the only completely enfranchised use.

But what of the 'nervous selfconsciousness' of this little proverbialism? Speakers of US English are not all 'fancy-pants'; in fact, they have a democratic horror of snobbishness, and it would be unusual if this populist strain of national character were not built into language. It surfaces, as Figure 7.1 shows, as 'ordinary language', the variety many fall back on for everyday use, acknowledging, however, its (minimal) waywardness. Some time ago Wolfram and Fasold pointed to this strange dichotomy between US regard for 'the language' (and its realization in 'good language') and the norms of everyday use.

> Standard American English, in the *informal* [emphasis in the original] sense, or in the informal standard form of any language, must be distinguished not only from substandard forms but also from superstandard forms. There is general agreement about what forms of a language are preferred above others within a language community, even

when the preferred forms are not used. It is typical for people to be slightly schizophrenic about their use of language. They acknowledge that some aspects of their use of language are not 'correct': they can tell you what the 'correct' form is, but they never actually adopt it. At an emotional level, these admittedly correct forms are rejected by some speakers because they are *too* [emphasis in the original] correct. These speakers do not adopt such forms and at unguarded moments will even make negative value judgments about speakers who use them, not because these forms are 'bad English' or because the speakers who use them are considered uneducated, but because the forms are 'too snooty' and the speakers 'too high-falutin'. Of course, the same speakers may smugly reject other vocabulary, grammatical constructions, and pronunciations as 'poor English' and tend to consider people who use them as uneducated or stupid. Both the superstandard and substandard forms can be considered 'nonstandard' (although elsewhere we reserve this term for what we are now calling 'substandard'); that is, they are not the standards by which the speaker actually regulates his [sic] speech – they are not effective standards. Everything in between substandard and super-standard represents the effective informal standard to which the individual's speech actually conforms.

(Wolfram and Fasold 1974: 19)

Conversations with nonlinguists confirm that there is perhaps more overt awareness of this dichotomy than Wolfram and Fasold (1974) might have imagined.

G: You go to school, and you learn what's called
proper English. (.hhh) And this is your written ((G uses an
aspirated 't' in 'written' here; it is not his normal usage)) English.
And it's also what's considered proper. But once you take that=
                                                  [
H: Uh huh.
                                                  [
?:   ((whispering))
G: =back home, everybody's home is a little different. And from the
culture of economics. What you: how you were raised and all that,
(.hhh) y- you may speak different-ly that what- actually wa[s]
given to you. (.hhh) You have like we have normally in English you
have to match up the appropriate verb with the appropriate tense.
Uh there are certain verbs that when we use a helping verb or
'have', 'has', or 'had', (.hhh) we use a special verb, for example.=
                                       [
H: Uh huh.

G: =(.hhh) When you get back HOME, uh some don't use the=
                                    [
H: Uh huh.
G: =corre- some do NOT use the correct verb, with it. But when
they're speaking they do not think anything about it. (.hhh) If they
would go back into the classroom now, and they were to take that
same test, (.hhh) they would have to use the correct verb. But
when they go home and SPEAK, they will not use that verb.
Because to do so, somebody'll look at you and say 'Oh you're=
[[
H: Uh huh.   Uh huh
G: =trying to be uppity, huh.' 'You're trying to be smart, huh.'=
                        [
H: Uh huh(h).
G: =In other words trying to look down on your- on uh on your el-=
[
H: Oh what I-, what I mean i-
G: =elders. Trying look down (.hhh) trying to say that I'm better th-
than uh than you are.
                            (Niedzielski and Preston 1999: 149–150)

Speakers of US English do not want to seem 'uppity', but, as G notes, they
are aware that their casual, spoken usage is 'incorrect'. On the other hand, it
is possible for linguistic complications to mislead even those who overtly claim
to be users of this more casual standard. S, for example, appears to be an
'anti-whomer', but he apparently fails to note the strong attraction for 'whom'
directly after a preposition even in his own speech.

X: 'Who do you speak with' or 'Whom,
with whom do you speak'.
S: 'With whom do you speak' is correct.
X: How about 'Who do you speak with'?
S: It's not correct, but it's familiar. - It's used.
                                [
X: What do you mean by 'familiar'.
S: It's something that Americans say every day. It's something that
we say so much, that we're used to saying, we don't think about it.
When someone's on the phone, they hang up the phone and you
say 'Who were you speaking with.' It's just something we
understand - automatically. That's all. He means to ask me is this?
So I say I was speaking with this person.
                            [
X: So when do you speak 'whom,' do
you speak with 'whom'. What kind of situation do you speak in=

140   *Dennis R. Preston*

```
                              [
   S:                  Because (  )-
   X:   =this way.
   S:   Ah. Ah hah. For me, - I never use it.
   X:   Oh, I see. - Why.
                  [   ]
   S:              Because-
   S:   Because I'm never in a sit- - situations where I'm dealing with -
        anyone with whom I need to be that polite.
   X:   So that's a very polite way.
                     [
   S:                Very. (#10)
```
                         (Niedzielski and Preston 1999: 162–163)

Wolfram and Fasold are surely right when they note that the 'effective norm' of speech is developed in contrast to the standard, but it is also clear that the drive for 'ordinariness' may even cause speakers to make claims about usage which are overstatements about their casual use as well.[5] The 'ordinary language' of Figure 7.1 is, therefore, a first step away from the essential nature of the language itself, but it is not a completely unattractive one.

In spite of this linguistic populism, speakers of US English are quite ready to identify speakers whose language is not simply 'ordinary' or 'casual' but downright 'bad'. Speakers from south-eastern Michigan, for example, an area of high linguistic security, when asked to characterize 'correct' and 'incorrect' English in the USA on a purely geographical basis, responded as in Figure 7.2.

Michigan (and only Michigan) scores in the 8.00 range, a testimony doubtless to its security, and areas nearby also fare well in Michiganders' estimation. The South, however, is obviously some sort of linguistic sink-hole, and New York City and nearby New Jersey are also places where Michiganders do not believe good English is to be found. A means-scores trip from Michigan to Alabama takes us from the heady 8.00 of Michigan, through a two-digit drop in Indiana (6.00), on to a middling 5.00 for Kentucky, a crummy 4.00 for Tennessee, and a bottom-of-the-barrel 3.00 for Alabama. It is not necessary to recount here the well-known popular culture perception of all things Southern (and its historical background) which help feed this linguistic prejudice. It is quite obviously the case that, in spite of professional linguistic belief to the contrary, some speakers of US English believe that standardness is a regional as well as social factor. One conversation with Michigan respondents will confirm much of what is shown in Figure 7.2.

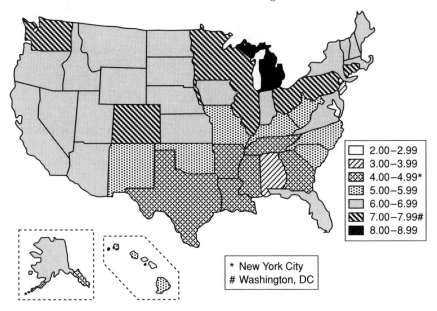

Figure 7.2 'Correctness' of regional English from the point of view of south-eastern
Michigan respondents (1 = least correct; 10 = most correct) (Preston 1996:
312)

H: But which city you think is the - standard English for, I mean,
from-
    [
D: From from well - we think, yeah, we think the Midwest.
     [
S: (   )
                  [
G: Detroit. ((laughs))
H: Midwest?
    [
S: The Midwest no, cause dad Cal- I I've been to California=
                          [
D: (   )
                              [
G: California-
S: =a lot more than you, California talks the same way as here.
There's no accent. I can't tell the difference.
       [
D: Right - that's true I can't either when I'm in California.
                                   [
S: So like
the the Western - the North, North and the South would=

```
              [                        ]
D:                They talk a little slower though.
S:   =would basically be the two accents, with little tiny dialects here
and there.
G:   That's true.=
S:   =Like the New Yorkers ((laughs)).
```

```
H:   Oh you know what, I've always thought Northern part English is
standard. So, that's wrong right?
G:   I think so Northern English.
             [
D:        (                 ) - Yeah I think so, I think that's correct.
                                      [
S:                                     Yeah North- Northern English
(        )
        [
H:   Northern part English is c- is standard English (            )?
                                                    [
D:                                                   Yeah, yeah.
                                                    [
G:                                                   That's right=
                                                    [
S:                                                   Yeah=
G:   =- what you hear around here.
S:   -=standard.
                         [
D:                        Because that's what you hear on the
TV - like newscasters. If you listen to the - the naˈional=
[
H:   ((laughs))
D:   =newscast of the national news - on Channel 7 som- they=
                                 [
G:                                Uh huh
D:   =sound they sound like we: do, they they sound sort of (   )=
                                                         [
H:                                                        (  )
D:   =Mid- Midwestern, like we do.
```
(Niedzielski and Preston 1999: 97–98)

Although Michiganders may deviate from the 'good language' of Figure 7.1
(in their populist zeal) they fall from grace only as far as 'ordinary language',
but their rankings of other regions for linguistic 'correctness' and such
conversations as the one just cited show that speech from other regions (the
'dialects' of Figure 7.1) deviates even further from 'the language'. Such speech
is simply on a par with 'errors', and the folk theory suggested in Figure 7.1
enfranchises such evaluations.

When speakers of US English are forced to reveal their specific categorizations of questionable items, these forces can again be observed. The following sentence was one of several submitted to university students in south-eastern Michigan for evaluation (Al-Banyan and Preston 1998):

The award was given to Bill and I.

This sentence fails to use *me*, although the first person pronoun is the (conjoined) object of the preposition *to*. The use of nominatives in conjoined constructions has a long history (e.g. Shakespeare's 'All debts are cleared between you and I'), but many speakers who have been corrected for using objective forms where nominatives should occur (e.g. 'Me and Bill went to the store') have overgeneralized (or 'hypercorrected') and used the nominative everywhere in such conjoined constructions.

The respondents who were given this sentence, however, were asked to rank it on a much more sensitive scale than one which would have them recognize it as simply 'good' or 'bad'. They were given the following five options:

1   Circle an **a** if you would never use this sentence (called 'Never' in the following analysis).
2   Circle a **b** if you would use this sentence only with close friends and/or family (called 'Informal' in the following analysis).
3   Circle a **c** if you would use this sentence in general conversation, in classes, in stores, and with people you don't know well (called 'General' in the following analysis).
4   Circle a **d** if you would use this sentence only in writing or in very formal speech situations, like a job interview or a lecture (called 'Formal' in the following analysis).
5   Circle an **e** if you would use this sentence in all situations (called 'All' in the following analysis).

In terms of the concepts introduced in Figure 7.1, option **a** should identify 'real' nonstandards (i.e. 'dialects' or 'errors'), **d** and perhaps **e** 'good language', and **c** and perhaps **b** 'ordinary language'.

The respondents were also asked to provide data of their own with the following instruction:

After you rate this sentence, use the space where it says 'What you would use' for your second response:

•   If you gave the sentence an **a**, write the sentence you would use most frequently in all situations.
•   If you gave the sentence a **b** or a **c**, write the sentence you would use in writing or in very formal speech situations.

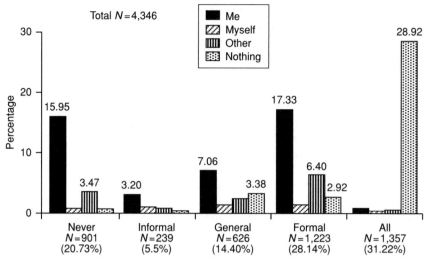

Figure 7.3 Responses to 'The award was given to Bill and I' (Al-Banyan and Preston 1998: 34)

- If you gave the sentence a **d**, write the sentence you would use in less formal situations.
- If you gave the sentence an **e**, write in nothing at all.

The 'expected corrections' coded for this sentence were **me**, **myself**, **other**, and **nothing**. Figure 7.3 shows the results for this task. Here it appears to be very likely that hypercorrection (i.e. avoiding the 'Bill and me' of nominatives even in a position directly after a preposition) has even more fully established itself among university-age respondents in the USA than one might have suspected. Thirty-one per cent find this sentence acceptable for 'All' situations and 28 per cent prefer it for 'formal' use; that is, more than half believe it is 'good language'. The prescriptively preferred 'me' is given by 17 per cent for formal and 16 per cent for those who say they would never use 'I'. They are clearly far back in second place to those who must be in the vanguard of this emerging standard.

Of course, this reveals that use – and not the Platonic ideal which I contend rests at the bottom of US English folk linguistic belief – is what eventually provides the language with its standards, but I believe it even more subtly shows the power of a belief in an 'exterior standard', one which the respondents to this sentence believe they are adhering to even in the face of its 'unnaturalness'.

The real proof, however, for the folk theory elaborated in Figure 7.1 lies, I believe, in the regard many speakers of US English have for speakers of nonstandard varieties. Here is what a Michigan respondent believes about African-American English (AAE):

M: Yeah, ah see that - that's what upsets me. You can see a really - an educated Black person, I mean I- you know I don't care what color a person is. It doesn't matter to me. - And you can underSTAND them and you can TALK to them and - Look at on the news, all the news broadcasters and everything. They're not talking ((lowered pitch)) 'Hey man, ((imitating African-American speech)) hybyayhubyhuby.' You can't understand what they're saying. And - I just don't think there's any excuse for it. It's laziness and probably - maybe it is you know, because they are low class and they don't know how to bring themselves up or they just don't want to.

(Niedzielski and Preston 1999: 131)

M is 'upset' by AAE, and this fact might take this discussion in two directions, both worth pursuing. The first, essentially nonlinguistic, suggests that many in the USA are affronted by distinctiveness or difference. They are affronted since they believe that those who are different (and who make any claim that that difference has led to prejudices against them) have simply not taken advantage of the opportunities they have had presented to them, presumably 'advantages' which would have made them 'non-different'. I believe we must understand this sociopolitical interpretation before we go on, but, for my purposes here, it is also clear that a theory of language must rest behind such political ideology and that theory must make it convincing that nonstandard speakers have 'simply' not taken advantage of the opportunity to 'bring themselves up'.

M first suggests that acquisition of standard behaviour is not impossible since 'educated' African-Americans, for example those on news broadcasts, have obviously acquired intelligible varieties. But critics of M might suggest that those African-Americans were especially privileged and that many others have not had the opportunity to acquire the variety she admires.

M would not be sympathetic to this, I believe, since she finds that there is 'no excuse for it' and that it is just 'laziness'. For a moment she seems to soften her criticism with a sort of social construction of the situation; African-Americans may not speak 'properly' because they are 'low-class' and 'don't know how to bring themselves up', but, at the end, she returns to a position which puts the blame fully on them – 'they just don't want to'.

For this criticism to obtain in its strongest form, speakers of nonstandard varieties must have access to the variety M expects of them, and her assertion that they 'just don't want to' or her reference to their 'laziness' must indicate a sort of recalcitrance, for, if the task amounted to a complex one, M might be tempted to be more sympathetic. As we shall see in further folk commentary, that is not the case, for learning 'good' (or at least 'ordinary') 'language' is not only just *easy* – knowledge of it is *already present*. Consider the following remarks from a European-American school teacher from south-eastern Michigan (who works in a largely African-American school):

146   *Dennis R. Preston*

G: And so somebody got it in their head that what was actually
SPOken should be the correct English. (.hhh) And then through the
idea of saying well it's racist not to teach it and started pushing it,
(.hhh) they tried to push that as an (deliberately) actual correct way
to speak. ((pause)) And thank God for most of us it died. It didn't
work.

Because it IS improper to say. The=
                                   [
H: Yes.
G: =children themselves – all of us at time may say the improper
endings. We may say it. (.hhh) But we recognize it is somebody
says to us 'Is it correct,' you say 'No,' you know, 'This is the
correct way (to) speak.' (.hhh) But- to sit and TEACH it incorrectly I
don't think is right. Cause you DO say 'I have gone,' You do not
say 'I have went.'

(Niedzielski and Preston 1999: 233–234)

There is a great deal that might be gleaned from the first part of this
conversation, for G is obviously responding to various attempts (and perhaps
even in-service programs which he has experienced) to make teachers aware
of the structural and social properties of what would have been known then
as 'Black English' (i.e. AAVE, AAE or, most recently, 'ebonics'). It is clear
from his comments, however, that he too, like the general public, has
misunderstood the educational effort of that time as one which intended
schools to 'teach' Black English.

The more important part of this conversation for the concerns raised here,
however, is the latter. G appears to believe that children (intuitively?) know
what is correct. It is what you 'DO say'. Somehow, at least for D, but I suspect
for many, the 'knowledge' of 'good language' is easily accessible. That children
would be speakers of the variety of their speech communities and have
difficulty recognizing, not to mention producing, alternative forms seems
not to be a viable interpretation.

Even members of the AAE community appear to hold to the belief that
very young AAE speakers know and are capable of using 'better' language:

J: And I used to teach Black children. And I had a difficult time
understanding what they were saying. And I found out later though
that they were - it was intentional, because they could speak - like
we speak. And they wer- because: I - was having difficulty with this
o(h)ne little bo(h)(h)y. He was twe(h)lve. (.hhh) And - I - was
supposed to test him, for uh reading problems. And I couldn't=
                                                              [
H: Uh huh.
J: =understand what he was saying. And so I called uh the=

```
                                    [
H:                                  Oh:?
J:    =teacher next to me was Black. (       ) next to me. (.hhh) So I=
                                    [
H:                                  Uh huh.
J:    =did go over and get her, and I asked if she would help me.
      (.hhh) And she came in and she- - just- said to him, she said 'You
      straighten up and talk - the right way. She's trying to help you.'
      ((laughs))
             [
H:       So uh you mean uh - he shou- can: - I mean, he know=
               [
J:             (       ) understood what he mean( ).
H:    =how to -
J:    talk correctly
           [
H:         talk to correctly. But he won't.
                     [
J:                   Well, she said he did, but he wouldn't.
```
                          (Niedzielski and Preston 1999: 131–132)

J goes further than G in believing that African-American children have not
only knowledge of 'good language' but also the capacity to use it. In fact, only
their recalcitrance causes them to speak in an 'unintelligible' way. Since J's
experience was confirmed by an African-American teacher, one can imagine
that her suspicions were deeply confirmed.

The repercussion of such belief (undoubtedly related to the similarly
common folk misunderstanding that regional varieties are diminishing in
the USA as a result of radio, TV, educational opportunity and the like) is that
in educational environments in the USA, children are punished (in some
form or another) for speaking the language they brought to school with them,
but, except in a very few instances, *no careful and systematic plan for instructing
NUSE-speaking children in an alternative variety is in place in the United States.*

Why should there be? The people who do not speak at least 'ordinary
language' are simply those who have failed to put out the minimum effort
required to have 'accessed' that variety. Perhaps more importantly, at least
from a 'moral' perspective, the people who do not choose to pay sufficient
attention to 'the language' to guide their behaviour are those who lead
unregulated lives. Anyone who has taught Linguistics 101 will attest to the
fact that one of the most difficult concepts to convey to neophytes is that all
languages and language varieties are regulated. 'The language' has rules
which are fully instantiated in 'good language'; 'ordinary language' chooses
to ignore a select few of these, although one might suspect that those ignored
at this level are regarded by many speakers as 'unimportant' ones, perhaps
even ones only the picky really care about, as suggested in the characterization
of the 'superstandard' cited from Wolfram and Fasold above. The levels below

that (which I have called 'dialects' and 'errors' in Figure 7.1) are simply without rules. For M, therefore, and I believe many others, language is like a great deal of other behaviours. Those who fail to follow its easily acquired rules are those who live irresponsible lives.

M and others will not have to seek far in current US ideology outside language to find grounds for their linguistic folk beliefs. US right-wing politicians, pundits, and thinkers all believe that individual responsibility, regardless of upbringing, opportunity, or denial of opportunity, need only be exercised to achieve the sort of life they imagine every US citizen wants. I have taken the liberty of substituting a linguistic concept (in square brackets) for an economic one in the following characterization of that conservative belief, but I believe it does no great disservice to the original.

> As used by the right, character has meant primarily a set of virtues associated with personal responsibility – self-control, duty, deferred gratification. Conservatives blame [bad language] on bad character (the poor lack self-control, discipline, and the will to sacrifice) rather than on social and economic conditions … . The failure to find, keep, and advance in ['good language'] is seen as an individual and moral – not a social – failing.
>
> (Bertram and Sharpe 2000: 44)

By placing language itself outside both social environments and cognitive embedding, folk linguists in the USA are able to posit an easily accessed exterior standard, one which good people will access with little effort and place themselves where they belong – in the mainstream of US society.[6]

Since this book is historical, however, we must go on to ask the relevant question: how did the folk linguistic theory which supports this attitude to SUSE and NUSE arise? In the earliest days of the Republic, Noah Webster stepped forward as the champion of things linguistically US. As a rural schoolmaster shortly after the Revolutionary War,

> He found himself teaching an ancient text, Thomas Dilworth's *New Guide to the English Tongue* (1740), which for its inadequate pedagogy was offensive to a Yale-trained teacher and which by lauding kings, queens, and parliaments was offensive to any man who hated the British kings, their taxes, their women, and their works. He decided to write a great *Grammatical Institute* which would purify the American language and promote American patriotism.
>
> (Laird 1970: 264–265)

More importantly,

> He was as much patriot as pedagogue. … [T]hough Webster came back with the militia from Saratoga, 'in a sense he never took off his uniform.

He continued to fight the British all his life' (Evans 1962: 11). He believed
in the new American nation; believed that its government, its home life,
its religion, its language, and its government were right before God ... .
(Laird 1970: 277)

At this early period in the development of attitudes towards language
correctness in the USA, it is easy to see threads of populism (things said by
'good Americans' as opposed to 'evil Britons') entwined with an appeal to
universals or factors outside social reality.

There may have been, therefore, a 'romantic' attempt to establish an
'American language' (e.g. Drake 1977: 14–15), one perhaps more oriented to
usage in the new country, but, although that effort may survive in the populist
selection of 'ordinary language', it gave way to a new prescriptivism. Although
that prescriptivism may have had some intellectual background in the mid-
nineteenth century (Drake 1977: 17–30), it found new ideological bases in
the twentieth.

That ideology is, put simply, an extension of the belief that things American
are correct; therefore, the ideals (including the language) which lie behind
them are reified in the Platonic way I have described here. This nearly
religious fervour found perhaps no greater expression in the popular press
than when the now infamous Webster's *Third New International Dictionary* was
published in 1961. That debate is well documented (e.g. in Sledd and Ebbitt
1962), but the ideological framework of the debate is extremely well
exemplified in both the professional identity of the author (the Right
Reverend Richard S. Emrich, the Episcopal Bishop of Michigan) and the
expressed detail of the following:

If a sentry forsakes his post and places an army in danger, the penalty is
severe. If a guardian ceases to guard and neglects his duty to children,
there are few who would not condemn. If a great dictionary forsakes its
post as the guardian of our language, how can one avoid disappointment?
... [T]he editor has failed to see that one cannot in this life avoid taking
sides: one cannot be neutral. In the contest between good language and
poor language, the new dictionary has cheapened the language. What
led the editors to abandon standards and judgments? If men assume the
responsibility of publishing a dictionary (a trust from Noah Webster), do
we not expect guidance, though imperfect, in good English? Because
language changes and new words are added, does it follow that standards
do not exist? Cannot a language, like everything else, be weakened and
corrupted? ... Dean Inge of St. Paul's, London, was known as the 'gloomy
dean' because he had no optimistic illusions about the modern world. He
did not believe that what was new was necessarily good. He was one of
the first to attack bolshevism at a deep level. He said that traditions,
disciplines, and standards were necessary in politics, but that the
bolsheviks were foisting on the world the naïve belief that a bright future

could be built by firing squads, mass trials, propaganda, etc. (Castro). Old disciplines and standards may be dismissed. 'Nonsense!' said the 'gloomy Dean'.

The bolshevik spirit, he said, is to be found everywhere, not just in Russia. Wherever our standards are discarded in family life, the care of the soul, art, literature, or education, there is the bolshevik spirit. Wherever men believe that what is, is right; wherever they discard discipline for an easy shortcut, there is bolshevism. It is a spirit that corrupts everything it touches. ... [W]ith all of its virtues and prodigious labor and excellence of printing the greatest of all American dictionaries has been corrupted at center. The greatest language on earth has lost a guardian.

(Emrich 1962)

Somehow in American public life, the correlation between Americanism and godliness (and the 'evil' atheism of such states as the former USSR) has allowed the creation of the sorts of ideals expressed in the Platonic theory of language one finds at nearly every social level and in every speech community in the United States. (And this review almost explicitly notes the Platonic existence of the ultimate correct form of the language by noting that even the well-intentioned dictionary-maker can give advice which is still 'imperfect'.)

Perhaps this ideology has its roots in the diversity of the United States and the early developed fear and distrust of things 'foreign'. As the 'English only' movement of today continues to reveal, people of the United States have long been wary of the 'loss of English' and, hence, the 'heritage' and 'cultural values' which have been inextricably associated with the tongue. In their introductory essay in *Language in the USA*, Ferguson and Brice Heath (1981) document impassioned pleas to avoid the loss of English by eighteenth, nineteenth and twentieth century pundits, almost at decadal intervals.

This ideology, whatever its exact historical basis, has permitted the development of the folk theory of language which reigns today. It is one quite obviously diametrically opposed to that of professional linguists and may even contribute to the folk trivialization of linguistics in United States' popular and even academic venues. Certainly the field has had little or no impact on legislation, education, and other important areas in which scientific considerations of language ought to hold sway. For the time being, then, the history of nonstandard English in the United States is a reflection of the unfortunately xenophobic character (in the domestic as well as external sense) of many of its residents. The populist urges which keep many speakers short of 'good language' are nevertheless overwhelmed by their continued faith in a cognitively external variety which determines what the perceived to be 'rule-free' nonstandards are, and, worse for the body politic, who the inattentive and recalcitrant speakers are who fail to at least sip from the fountain of 'the language' or 'English' undefiled.

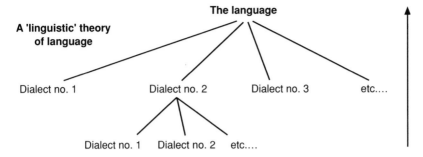

Figure 7.4 A linguist's theory of language

Notes

1 The determination of SUSE on the basis of the social identity of a group of speakers (determined by some factor other than the language they spoke) was perhaps not effectively realized until C. C. Fries' 1940 *American English Grammar*.

2 The 'appropriateness' distinction between cultural levels and functional varieties (Kenyon 1948) suggested that the two concepts should not be confused [i.e. a 'standard speaker' (cultural level) would have a continuum of usage which ranged from the formal to the casual (functional variety)]. Later sociolinguistic studies, however, would show that such levels and varieties are related in a systematic way; as Labov (1972: 240) put it, it would not be easy '... to distinguish a casual salesman from a careful pipefitter'. In an even stronger statement of this interrelationship, Bell (1984) notes that stylistic variation [i.e. Kenyon's (1948) 'functional varieties'] derives from a speech community's status varieties [i.e. Kenyon's (1948) 'cultural levels'] as speakers adjust their performances in various environments according to what Bell calls 'audience design', itself a notion related to 'accommodation'.

  As some others have pointed out, however (e.g. Fairclough 1992), accommodation to the 'standard' (obviously a part of any doctrine of 'appropriateness')springs from class enforcement as well as sensitivity to social surroundings and may, therefore, lead to a general criticism of at least some accommodation as a power-based speech strategy.

3 The transcription system used here is generally that of Gail Jefferson (as outlined, for example, in Schenkein 1978).

4 A linguist's theory of language, on the other hand, locates language as a cognitive reality for each individual speaker and then catalogues the social by-products of the similarities (and dissimilarities) among those grammars. Figure 7.4 shows such a theory.

5 Trudgill (1972) has made this interpretation famous with the label 'under-reporters', a condition he finds more often among men, who seem to need to lay claim to more nonstandard usage than they actually use; in his interpretation, this allows closer association with 'covert prestige' (i.e. the prestige which stems from non-sanctioned sources) and its obvious 'macho' value.

6 This article does not address the question of how US English folk belief arose. Milroy and Milroy (1999) believe this ideology grew out of the multilingualism of earlier US history and is a by-product of the 'levelling' or 'melting-pot' attitude which large numbers of culturally and linguistically different people met in the late nineteenth and early twentieth centuries.

  Those who seek a more thorough historical treatment should seek out two books which provide detailed treatment of the changing attitudes towards standards and usage in the history of the US: Drake (1977) and Finegan (1980).

Part II

The history of communicative and pragmatic aspects of English

In the second part of the book we turn our attention to pragmatic, sociopragmatic, sociolinguistic and discourse-oriented approaches to the historical study of English. We are, of course, aware that the contributions in Part II barely scratch the surface of the enormous amount of work which still needs to be done in this area, work which might offer numerous other stories to tell. We trust that the reader can at least catch a glimpse of the kind of research being carried out on exploring the historical dimensions of language use, although it is our opinion that much more of this kind of work should be undertaken.

Much has either been written directly about the ideology of the standard language (Milroy and Milroy 1999; Milroy, J. 1999, 2000) or has been inspired by the work of the Milroys as well as by work by Crowley (1989a,b) and Leith (1983), e.g. Watts (1999a,b, 2000), Fitzmaurice (2000), Mugglestone (1995), Bex (1999), Davis (1999). No one has yet explicitly linked the ideology of the standard to the ideological discourse of politeness in the eighteenth century. In Chapter 8 Watts suggests strongly that the ideology of the standard language is part and parcel of an ideology of politeness and that there is an uncanny similarity between John Honey's notion of 'educatedness' at the end of the twentieth century and that of politeness. His contribution is thus a retelling of the story of the standard which links eighteenth century ideas about the value of 'standard English' to certain late twentieth century ideas.

Sharon Millar's chapter also takes as its starting point the eighteenth century. Her ideas about the importance of oral eloquence during that century and well into the nineteenth make it plain that the ideology of the standard, or, as Watts puts it, the ideology of politeness, extends to the spoken language towards the end of the eighteenth century and has had an enormous effect on perceptions of the standard language, or 'correct English', right up to the present day. The 'story' that Millar tells is one of social elitism and exclusion and fits very neatly into the ideological paradigm that was first set up by the Milroys.

Chapter 10 by Terttu Nevalainen deals with the status of oral English in centuries during which a faithful representation of speech was not possible and, more importantly, with the status of women's writing in the period from the fifteenth to the eighteenth centuries. She asks whether gender differences in the use of English are noticeable in the writing of women during this period, thus challenging male-dominated assumptions (e.g. by Wyld and others) that the influence of women on the history of English was negligible. The chapter turns out to be an important new telling of the relationship between women's language and the development of alternative styles of English. An added problem posed by Nevalainen's contribution is how we can extrapolate away from written texts to gain some idea of how speakers of English may have used the language in forms of oral interaction. The problem is not solved here, but, then, on the other hand, it is hardly likely ever to be solved. This, however, should not stop us from using written sources in an attempt to reconstruct forms of oral interaction.

Andreas Jucker's chapter (Chapter 12) goes in the same direction, although it does not focus on women's language. Jucker deals with the development of discourse markers through the history of English, i.e. his focus is on the spoken language. Until recently no one has thought it necessary to investigate the processes of pragmaticalisation in the same way and with the same intensity as grammaticalisation has been studied. That it is indeed an important area of research is evidenced by the role such metapragmatic elements play in the oral production of any language. If this aspect of language structure is neglected, we might develop histories of written forms of English and entirely ignore what went on in ordinary everyday social interaction between speakers of varieties of English in earlier periods of time. A focus on discourse markers and the important process of pragmaticalisation is thus a new approach and promises to provide a corrective to such erroneous views of the connection between written and oral language.

8   From polite language to educated language

The re-emergence of an ideology

Richard Watts

The obsession with politeness

Eighteenth century British society, or at least the middle and upper sections of it, was obsessed by the idea of politeness. There were references in countless publications to 'polite behaviour', 'polite language', 'polite education', 'polite literature', even to 'polite philosophy'. The historian Paul Langford, in a book with the intriguing title *A Polite and Commercial People: England 1727–1783*, says of politeness that it was in a sense 'a logical consequence of commerce' (Langford 1989: 4). In theory, politeness was a question of morals, but this didn't always correspond to its practical significance in acquiring 'material acquisitions and urbane manners' (ibid.: 5). What it conveyed to those who were seeking to acquire it were the trappings of 'upper-class gentility, enlightenment, and sociability' (ibid.: 4). Contemporary commentators on eighteenth century society were 'as much intrigued by the impact of affluence on manners, as by its material consequences. In a word, they charted the progress of politeness' (ibid.: 71).

In this chapter I want to discuss the social, and ultimately political, implications of the ideology of politeness on the development of Standard English in the eighteenth century, and then to focus on a rather odd re-emergence of that ideology under the guise of the term 'education' in the writings of John Honey in the late 1980s and 1990s (Honey 1988, 1989, 1997). I shall argue that the acquisition and use of Standard English appeared to guarantee social climbers in the eighteenth century access to the world of politeness, the result being that 'polite language' came to mean 'standard language'. Today, however, the acquisition and use of Standard English English[1] is misused at least in certain powerful circles in Britain, as a guarantor of access to the world of education. In both cases, the world of politeness and the world of education are presumed to provide access to the corridors of political and cultural power, although this is rarely, if ever, stated explicitly.

What I want to offer, therefore, is the rough outline of a history of the link between Standard English and hegemonic social and political institutions. I shall argue that this link is still on today's political agenda in Britain even though, like a chameleon, it has changed colour in the meantime. I shall start by exploring attitudes towards language, language users and politeness in the first 80 years of the eighteenth century by quoting from a variety of writers on language and philosophy. Towards the end of the chapter I shall draw parallels between the links made between politeness and language in the eighteenth century and those made between education and language now.

In the spirit of this book I wish to challenge the accepted wisdom of histories of 'the English language' – meaning, of course, histories of Standard English[2] – constructed by the academic establishment. Histories of English tend conveniently to gloss over the cynicism of a belief in 'the legitimate language', a belief which has systematically and consistently devalued other varieties of English and constantly added greater value to Standard English. In doing so, I am treading a path which others have beaten before me, notably Milroy and Milroy (1999), Smith (1984), Mugglestone (1995), Jim Milroy (1999, 2000), Leith (1983), Bauer (1994a), even though, apart from McIntosh (1998) and Klein (1986, 1994, 1995), commentators have been strangely silent about the existence of an 'ideology of politeness'. I shall start in the second half of the eighteenth century with Samuel Johnson.

The language of 'affectation'

In 1777 Samuel Johnson was asked to write biographical prefaces for a collection entitled *The English Poets*, which was compiled by a group of London booksellers. One of those prefaces in particular aroused a storm of protest amongst the friends of the dead poet Thomas Gray, who had died in 1771. It is generally thought that their protests were aimed at the way in which Johnson criticised Gray's poetry rather than his treatment of the details of the poet's life. Yet Johnson does not hesitate to quote Mason, Gray's biographer, with respect to Gray's 'affectation in delicacy, or rather effeminacy'. And he doesn't have any scruples about telling the reader how Gray was pestered by students at Peterhouse College, Cambridge, where he lived, and forced by the indifference of the college governors to move to Pembroke Hall. The portrait of the poet delineated by Johnson in the first part of his 'Life of Gray' is by no means positive, and it prepares the way for an attack on the poet's literary abilities in the second half.

Johnson's comments on Gray's 'Ode on Spring' set the tone for the rest of his critical appraisal of Gray as a poet:

> His Ode on Spring has something poetical, both in the language and in the thought; but the language is too luxuriant, and the thoughts have nothing new.
>
> (Johnson, in Bredvold *et al.* 1935: 561)

From this point on Johnson proceeds to dismantle Gray's poetry. Referring to 'The Progress of Poetry' he makes the following comment:

Gray seems in his rapture to confound the images of 'spreading sound' and 'running water'. A 'stream of music' may be allowed; but where does 'music', however 'smooth and strong', after having visited the 'verdant vales', 'roll down the steep main', so as that 'rocks and nodding groves rebellow to the roar'? If this be said of music, it is nonsense; if it be said of water, it is nothing to the purpose.

(Johnson, in Bredvold *et al.* 1935: 562)

His concluding comment on 'The Bard' reads as follows:

These odes are marked by glittering accumulations of ungraceful ornaments; they strike, rather than please; the images are magnified by affectation; the language is laboured into harshness.

(Johnson, in Bredvold *et al.* 1935: 564)

By the time Johnson wrote the prefaces to *The English Poets* he had already become an established authority on the English language, a reputation justly acquired through the publication of his dictionary. Apparently, this authority allowed him to make judgments on the language of the poets whose work was represented in the collection. He says that Gray's language is 'too luxuriant'; he criticises Gray's use of metaphor in 'The Progress of Poetry'; and says of 'The Bard' that 'the language is laboured into harshness'. But he does not consider it necessary to define what he means by the term 'luxuriant', nor to explain why it is that the metaphorical comparison of music with the water in a mountain stream is 'nonsense'. Nor does he indicate what he understands by his own sentence 'the language is laboured into harshness'.

Now, as a writer of poetry himself, we must assume that Johnson the critic could have explained his own critical terminology – although he obviously considers it superfluous to do so. The reader either accepts Johnson's criticism or, in challenging it, reveals a lack of affiliation to authority in judging linguistic standards.

Johnson was by no means the only 'expert' on language in the second half of the eighteenth century to place himself above the writers of literature by passing critical judgments on their creative linguistic ability or even the grammatical accuracy of their writings. But we must allow Johnson the writer to pass judgment on his peers. In the case of grammar writers, however, the freedom to pass critical judgment on writers of literature appears strange in the modern world. For example, in his 1761 grammar Robert Lowth castigates a whole range of authors, even the editors of the authorised version of the Bible, for mistakes. He goes so far as to suggest that contemporary editions of certain works should be prepared in which those 'mistakes' are eradicated.

In his 'Preface' Lowth justifies the writing of his grammar in the following words:

A Grammatical Study of our own Language makes no part of the ordinary method of instruction which we pass thro' in our childhood; and it is very seldom that we apply ourselves to it afterward. And yet the want of it will not be effectually supplied by any other advantages whatsoever. *Much practice in the polite world*, and a general acquaintance with the best authors, are good helps, but alone will hardly be sufficient: we have writers, who have enjoyed these advantages in their full extent, and yet cannot be recommended as models of an accurate style.

(1761: vii, italics mine)

The reader is advised to get as much 'practice in the polite world' as s/he can, but is warned that the best authors will 'hardly be sufficient', since many of them 'cannot be recommended as models of accurate style'. An example of his critical stance towards established authors can be seen on page 43 of the grammar where, in discussing *less* and *worse*, Lowth aligns himself with Johnson and takes Addison and Dryden as models of what *not* to do:

'*Lesser*, says Mr. Johnson, is a barbarous corruption of *Less*, formed by the vulgar from a habit of terminating comparisons in *er*.' 'Attend to what a *lesser* Muse indites.' Addis. *Worser* sounds much more barbarous, only because it has not been so frequently used:
'A dreadul quiet felt, and *worser* far
Than arms, a sullen interval of war.' Dryden.

(Lowth 1761: 43)

Of course we could argue that there is a significant difference between Johnson and Lowth. The former focused his attention on 'errors' of style whereas the latter was hunting down 'errors' of grammar. Nevertheless, the number of cases in which those with the 'authority' to judge in matters of language in the second half of the eighteenth century had no qualms about doing so leads us to the conclusion that matters of correctness, propriety, aestheticism and moral delicacy were uppermost in the minds of intellectuals concerned with language at that time. They set the tone for social climbers wishing to acquire those attributes of polite society that were enshrined within forms of language. In addition, literary critical discourse, the public discourse of essay writing and the discourse of grammar writers, dictionary compilers, elocutionists, etc. are important aspects of a larger ideological discourse which Milroy and Milroy (1999) refer to as 'the ideology of standardisation'.

But there is another reason for me quoting precisely those passages from Lowth. He assumes that the reader of his grammar will not have had any instruction in English grammar at school, but aspires to acquire 'a liberal education'. This is put very explicitly on pages viii–ix of the preface:

[A knowledge of English grammar] is with reason expected of every person of a liberal education, and much more is it indispensably required of every one who undertakes to inform or entertain the public, that he should be able to express himself with *propriety* and accuracy. It will evidently appear from these Notes, that our best Authors for want of some rudiments of this kind have sometimes fallen into mistakes, and been guilty of palpable errors in point of Grammar.

(Lowth 1761: viii–ix, italics mine)

Lowth's grammar thus takes on the function of a self-help for social climbers, for those who wish to 'inform or entertain the public'. They are admonished to gain some 'practice in the polite world' and to aim for 'propriety' as well as accuracy, otherwise they will reveal themselves as members of 'the vulgar' in their 'barbarous' use of language. At the very beginning of his preface Lowth tells his potential readers that '[t]he English Language hath been much cultivated during the last two hundred years. It hath been considerably polished and refined ...' (1761: i). The tell-tale word here is 'polished', which is a variant of 'polite' (from the Latin past participle *politus* meaning 'polished'), and the implication is that those who have had a liberal education and are members of the 'polite world' have carried out the polishing. The social aspirations of the emergent middle classes in eighteenth century British society were intimately linked to membership in polite society. This is neatly summed up by Langford (1989: 63):

> Nothing unified the middling orders so much as their passion for aping the manners and morals of the gentry more strictly defined, as soon as they possessed the material means to do so. This was a revolution by conjunction rather than confrontation, but it was a revolution none the less, transforming the pattern of social relations, and subtly reshaping the role of that governing class which was the object of imitation. The aspirants sought incorporation in the class above them, not collaboration with those below them.

Similar quotations can be drawn from almost all the grammars, books on elocution, style and self-help manuals throughout the eighteenth century to those we have taken from Lowth and Johnson. Before commenting briefly on a selection of quotations from various authors, I shall return to Johnson's comments on Gray's poetry. Johnson accuses Gray of producing 'images ... magnified by affectation' and of using language which is 'laboured into harshness'. Part of what I call the 'ideology of politeness' sets up 'affectation' as the opposite of 'politeness' (see Watts 1999a). If we can interpret Johnson as accusing Gray of using the language of affectation, is he then implying that Gray was not a member of polite society, i.e. that he was a middle-class social climber? If so, the discourse is less the discourse of eighteenth century literary criticism than that of social affiliation and social discrimination.

Politeness and language in the eighteenth century

Daniel Defoe

On the eve of the eighteenth century, in 1698, Daniel Defoe published *An Essay on Projects*. One of the projects with which Defoe was concerned was the establishment of an English language academy akin to the Académie Française.[3] The patron of such an academy was to be King William III, and its function would be to promote the refinement of the English language such that 'the true glory of our English style would appear, and among all the learned part of the world be esteemed, as it really is, the noblest and most comprehensive of all the vulgar languages in the world'. The work of the society would be

> to encourage *polite* learning, to *polish* and *refine* the English tongue, and advance the so much neglected faculty of correct language, to establish purity and *propriety* of style, and to purge it from all those innovations in speech ... which some dogmatic writers have the confidence to foster upon their native language ...
>
> (Defoe, in Bredvold *et al.* 1935: 3, italics mine)

Defoe wishes to exclude from his putative society clergymen, physicians and lawyers – all those who had received their education at Oxford or Cambridge. Instead, he would have it 'wholly composed of gentlemen', twelve of whom should be elected from the nobility, twelve from the gentry and twelve on the basis of 'mere merit'. His aim in suggesting that an academy of the English language should be de-institutionalised away from the universities and streamlined to fit the needs of polite, genteel society is 'to banish pride and pedantry, and silence the impudence and impertinence of young authors, whose ambition it is to be known'.

Defoe's project represents one of the first suggestions for the creation of a model of 'the English language' which has as its aim the advancement of polite learning, i.e. the propagation of the customs and behaviours of a distinct, socially privileged section of English society. In addition, the link with the 'polite' levels of social structure is meant to 'polish and refine' the English language and to provide a yardstick by means of which a standard of correctness can be established and a 'purity and propriety of style' can be maintained.

However, we should be under no illusions as to what Defoe was aiming at here. Those who were meant to set the standards of language correctness and propriety of style should be members of genteel, polite, or 'polished', society, i.e. the socially privileged, the educated, but not professional classes, those with wealth and power enough not to have to fend for a living; in a word, socially privileged amateurs.

Anthony Ashley Cooper, the 3rd Earl of Shaftesbury

What was 'polite learning' for Defoe, or 'polite society' for Lowth? How did writers in the eighteenth century understand the concept of politeness? What were its connotations? Clearly, it did not mean what we understand by the term today. The modern, twentieth century understanding of politeness is that it consists of mutually shared forms of consideration for others. Being polite means that the speaker has access to sets of strategies for constructing, regulating and reproducing forms of cooperative social interaction. Generally, it involves maintaining the participants' positive faces during ongoing socio-communicative verbal interaction.

Certainly, some of these features of the notion of politeness are also shared with the eighteenth century conceptualisation of the term. But the differences are more striking. Carey McIntosh (1998: 160) suggests that '[politeness] measured in part the distance a person or community had come from savagery'. So while consideration for others was still at the centre of the concept of politeness, there was also a desire not to shock others but to please and gratify them. This could often be achieved by simulating interest in others and by creating, very often deliberately setting out to create, a favourable impression on them.

The architect of an ideology of politeness during the first decade of the eighteenth century was without doubt Anthony Ashley Cooper, the 3rd Earl of Shaftesbury. For the earlier part of the century Lawrence Klein (1986, 1994, 1995) has illustrated the importance of the concept of politeness for public life in both Britain and France. He has shown how Shaftesbury's philosophy, which was to exert such an influence on the development of later writing in the century, was based on his conception of politeness. He also describes in detail the emergence of a philosophy of politeness in Shaftesbury's works which we may refer to as 'the gentrification of politeness'. In 1711 Shaftesbury published a selection of his works under the title of *Characteristicks of Men, Manners, Opinions, Times: An Inquiry Concerning Virtue or Merit*. In *Characteristicks* Shaftesbury sets out a programmatic manifesto of 'polite philosophy'. He forges a political discourse that legitimates the Whig regime of the 1690s and, in doing so, legitimates the language of that discourse, i.e. Standard English. 'Polite philosophy' created a system of beliefs and values, i.e. an ideology, which served as a discursive model for the social class of the gentry and later for the emergent middle classes in the eighteenth century.

Shaftesbury characterises the kind of society he envisages as polite as follows:

> Our joint endeavour, therefore, must appear this; to show 'that nothing which is found charming or delightful in the polite world, nothing which is adopted as pleasure or entertainment, of whatever kind, can any way be accounted for, supported, or established, without the pre-establishment or supposition of a certain taste.'
>
> (Shaftesbury, in Bredvold *et al.* 1935: 267)

The essential condition for what is 'charming and delightful in the polite world' is good taste. But what did Shaftesbury mean by the terms 'polite' and 'good taste'? After all, if you need good taste to achieve politeness, how do you achieve good taste? The implied answer in the following quotation from Shaftesbury is that it is inborn, it is an attribute of the true gentleman:

> Whoever has any impression of what we call gentility or politeness is already so acquainted with the decorum and grace of things that he will readily confess a pleasure and enjoyment in the very survey and contemplation of this kind. Now if in the way of polite pleasure the study and love of beauty be essential, the study and love of symmetry and order, on which beauty depends, must also be essential in the same respect.
>
> (Shaftesbury, in Bredvold *et al.* 1935: 273)

So the eighteenth century ideology of politeness was composed of the following values: decorum, grace, beauty, symmetry and order. These values were transformed into the social symbols for membership in the class of the gentry that the upwardly mobile emergent middle classes eagerly sought to attain. In a word, they became features of the legitimate language, 'standard English'.

Joseph Addison and Richard Steele

These social symbols were nowhere more clearly expressed than in the two periodicals *The Tatler* and *The Spectator*, the former initiated by Steele and the latter by Addison. *The Tatler* and *The Spectator* exerted an enormous influence over writers in the eighteenth century, although they appeared during a relatively short time-span between 1710 and 1712, with another eighty editions of *The Spectator* appearing in 1714. The terms 'polite' and 'politeness' themselves appear relatively infrequently in both periodicals, but their significance lies in the fact that Addison and Steele were concerned to 'popularise' the ideology of politeness by raising issues that touched upon the social symbols listed above in as many numbers as possible. They were also concerned to make the periodicals available to as wide a reading public as possible.

The character of Mr Spectator provides a filter through which various forms of social behaviour representing those values are presented, commented on and evaluated in what amounts to an effort to 'construct' a polite social order. Their purpose was not to question the social order itself nor to put it to the test in any way, but to create a common feeling for it. In a very real sense, they might therefore be called the 'propagandists' of the ideology of politeness.

The measure of success that the 'propaganda' of *The Spectator* achieved in constructing a model of 'polite language' was considerable, as Susan Fitzmaurice points out (2000: 201):

The combination of authority and expertise results in the citation of *The Spectator* as representative of the best in English prose and thus as a candidate for the model *par excellence* of polite language of the period. By the second half of the century, quotations from the periodical, with Addison invariably identified as the source of the quotation, come to be the staple fare offered by grammars characterising polite language. This kind of citation presents the linguistic aspect of good manners and behaviour. The grammarians cite and change *The Spectator*'s language to demonstrate how elegant language might be improved by grammatical correctness.

Evidence of the interest shown in the writing of grammars that try to offer some form of access to polite language by the editors of *The Tatler* and *The Spectator*, i.e. Addison and Steele, can be found in *A Grammar of the English Tongue* by Charles Gildon and John Brightland, which was published in 1711. The 'narrative' persona in *The Tatler* is the fictional Isaac Bickerstaff. This same Isaac Bickerstaff (alias Richard Steele) mysteriously appears as the 'Censor' in the frontispiece of the grammar. Bickerstaff gives an 'approbation' of the grammar and enjoins the general public to buy and read it since '[t]he *Text* will improve the most Ignorant, and the *Notes* will imploy the most Learned'. A notice of Gildon and Brightland's grammar is given in Nr. 234 of *The Tatler*.

Jonathan Swift

It is certainly the case, then, that *The Tatler*'s and *The Spectator*'s, particularly Addison's, influence on the construction of an ideology of politeness, or rather of an ideology of 'polite language', was immense. We have already seen how Lowth lashes out in his footnotes at Addison, Pope, Dryden, Swift and even Milton. As early as 1724 Hugh Jones also lists these authors (apart from Milton) as being those whom the reader of his grammar should consult as models of polite language. But there is a certain uneasiness about Swift and Pope being lumped together with Addison. Fitzmaurice (2000: 200) suggests that 'Swift's *Examiner* found little in [*The Spectator*] to attract his ire'. That might very well be the case but it does not change the fact that Swift's political leanings were Tory rather than Whig and that *The Examiner* was a competitor of *The Spectator*. She also suggests that Swift and Addison were members of a social network that included Congreve, Steele, Pope, Halifax, Wortley and Lady Mary Wortley Montagu. This, too, is undoubtedly true, but she admits to the weakness of the links between Swift and Pope and the others in the network. I shall therefore look at Swift's references to polite language in his *Proposal for Correcting, Improving, and Ascertaining the English Tongue* in a little more detail in this section.

Milroy and Milroy (1999) consider Swift's pamphlet to be the beginning of what they call the 'complaint tradition', in which those who set themselves up as authorities on the correct forms and uses of 'standard English' complain about declining standards, deterioration in the language, the moral degradation of imperfect users of the language, etc. To the extent that the argument of the entire text hinges around Swift's perception of the language as being 'extremely imperfect',[4] they are, superficially, correct. But there are a number of points which seem to have escaped the notice of commentators.

To begin with, Swift's *Examiner* was a rival Tory periodical to Addison's *Tatler* and Steele's *Spectator*. For this reason, we might expect Swift not to concur in his judgment concerning polite language and the ways to achieve it. Second, Swift also published a satirical pamphlet on *Polite Conversation*, which in modern editions of Swift's work often appears in the same volume as his *Proposal*. Third, when he begins his 'letter' to the Earl of Oxford by suggesting that consultation with 'some very judicious Persons' has persuaded him that 'nothing would be of greater Use towards the Improvement of Knowledge and Politeness, than some effectual Method for *Correcting*, *Enlarging*, and *Ascertaining* our Language', the contemporary reader might find it difficult to take him completely seriously. After all, he omits 'judiciously' to say who those 'very judicious Persons' were. Were they perhaps Addison and Steele? Fourth, given the connotations of social climbing associated with politeness and polite language and given his Tory leanings, is it not a little ironic when he accuses the Court of being the 'worst School in England' for standards of correctness and propriety in speech and that 'our young Nobility' should learn correct English so that 'they may set out into the World with some Foundation of Literature, in order to qualify them for Patterns of Politeness'? Fifth, if this really were a letter addressed to the Earl of Oxford, why should it be printed, as a pamphlet, 'for BENJ. TOOKE, at the *Middle-Temple-Gate, Fleetstreet*. 1712'. Sixth – although this might be splitting interpretive hairs – why is the letter given the date 'Feb. 22, 1711–12? Was it 'sent' in 1711 or 1712? Or was it sent at all?

There are several more questions concerning Swift's text that could be asked here. My major point is that no one, to my knowledge, has really challenged the assumption that Swift meant the letter to be taken seriously. Nor has anyone deconstructed the text with a view to interpreting it as an ironic commentary on 'the Pretenders to polish and refine [the language]'. Precisely because it is a text by Swift, this would seem to be the most obvious thing to do. At all events, the jury is still out on this question.[5]

Hugh Jones

Hugh Jones's *An Accidence to the English Tongue* is reputed to be the first grammar written in the American colonies, although it was printed in London, where Jones had returned by 1724. Strangely enough, Jones himself does not call *An Accidence to the English Tongue* a 'grammar', although he obviously has a didactic purpose in mind when he lists the potential users ('BOYS and MEN, as have never learnt *Latin* perfectly, and for the Benefit of the FEMALE SEX: Also for the *Welch, Scotch, Irish,* and *Foreigners*'). He describes it as 'A *Grammatical* ESSAY upon our LANGUAGE, Considering the true Manner of *Reading, Writing,* and *Talking* proper *English*'. The borderline between a prescriptive grammar and an instruction manual on how to behave verbally in polite society all but disappears here. This is reflected by the structure of the book, in which forty-one of the sixty-nine pages comprise four 'parts', containing the 'grammar'. The remaining 'part' spans the final twenty-eight pages and deals with 'Of English Discourse, or Speech', 'Of Composition', 'Of Rhetorick', 'Of English Verse', 'Of Delivery' and 'Of Disputation, and Conference' (this last section on its own spanning almost twelve pages). If we ask ourselves who has 'the true Manner of *Reading, Writing,* and *Talking* proper *English*', the answer, in Jones's terms, is simple: 'BOYS and MEN, as have learnt *Latin* perfectly'. Put differently, Jones's model of perfection in the use of the English language is composed of those *male* members of society who have had, in Lowth's terms, a 'liberal' education, i.e. the gentry and the aristocracy.

As one would expect, the twenty-one pages devoted to 'the true Manner of *Reading, Writing,* and *Talking* proper *English*', and in particular the final twelve pages, have numerous references to politeness, learning and good manners, e.g.

> Our Language affords us *Choice* of *Words,* and *Variety* of *Expression*; in which we should *imitate the Learned* and *Polite,* the *Correct* and *Pure* ...
>
> (Jones 1724: 62, italics in the original)

> *Reading* promotes *profitable* and *pleasant Learning* and *Knowledge*: a *fine Hand* is beautify'd with *good Composure*; and an *elegant Composition* is compleated by *handsome Delivery*. So that *good Manners, correct Writing, proper English* and a *smooth Tongue,* are requisite *Qualifications,* sufficient to render a Person (of but tolerable good Endowments) completely *accomplished* for *Conversation.*
>
> (Jones 1724: 64–65)

> *Practice* is highly instrumental in *advancing* Persons to any *Degree* of *Perfection* in our *Language*; Great *Improvement* being made by *learned Conversation,* and *ingenious* and *polite Correspondence* ...
>
> (Jones 1724: 65–66)

Those who should be imitated – the gentry – are not only polite; they are also 'learned'. The promotion of learning and knowledge is through '*good Manners, correct Writing, proper English* and a *smooth Tongue*'. The aim set out by Jones is to 'advance persons to a degree of perfection in English', and this can be achieved by '*learned Conversation,* and *ingenious* and *polite Correspondence*'. The link between John Honey's definition of 'standard English' as the language of the 'educated' and those writing within the ideology of politeness in the eighteenth century emerges particularly strongly from Jones's *Accidence.*

Thomas Sheridan

As the eighteenth century progressed, a new focus for Standard English began to emerge: the correct pronunciation and oral production of English. One of the major figures associated with elocution in the second half of the century was Thomas Sheridan, who published a pronouncing dictionary in 1780. In 1762, however, he had already published the texts of a course of public lectures delivered on the subject of elocution, together with three other related texts: 'Two Dissertations on Language', 'The Heads of a Plan for the Improvement of Elocution' and 'A Dissertation on the Causes of the Difficulties, Which occur, in learning the English Tongue'.

The lectures were a huge success, drawing large audiences at which Sheridan collected subscriptions for the publication of the text.[6] At the beginning of *A Course of Lectures on Elocution* (1762) a list of subscribers is provided which numbers well over 200 names, only a tiny fraction of which give evidence that members of the aristocracy bought the book. The overwhelming majority of subscribers, as far as one can tell by title and profession, appear to have come from the rising middle classes, or what Langford calls 'the middling orders' with their 'passion for aping the manners and morals of the gentry more strictly defined'.

As with Hugh Jones, the model set up by Sheridan is that of 'polite society'. In Lecture II he refers to the two pronunciations current in London, one in the city 'called the cockney' and the other 'at the court-end' called 'the polite pronunciation' (Sheridan 1762: 30). The problem for Sheridan's audience is that 'court pronunciation is nowhere methodically taught, and can be acquired only by conversing with people in polite life'. How he imagined that his enthusiastic audiences could gain access to 'conversing with people in polite life' is not stated anywhere in his text. He even follows this point by stating that 'court pronunciation' is 'a sort of proof that a person has kept good company, and on that account is sought after by all, who wish to be considered as fashionable people, or members of the beau monde'. So we are left with the uncomfortable feeling that Sheridan does not consider his audiences capable of reaching these heights in any case.

At a later point in Lecture II he maintains that:

> ... all who have an opportunity of being informed of that pronunciation, most used by men of education at court, will have the best authority on their side; as that is indeed the only standard we can refer to, in critical cases, as well as others.
>
> (Sheridan 1762: 36)

The standard which Sheridan is taking is 'men of education at court'. Those in polite society are taken as the authority on 'standard English' pronunciation. Notice here how Sheridan, like Jones, creates an explicit link between 'politeness', 'learning' and 'standard English'.

To dispel any doubts concerning this link, consider the following argument used in 'The Heads of a Plan for the Improvement of Elocution' to justify authoritative statements about 'correct' language usage:

> All *barbarous* nations agree in not *studying* or cultivating their languages, and this is one of the characteristical marks of barbarism. All *civilized* countries agree in studying and cultivating their languages, and this is amongst the first proofs given of their politeness.
>
> (Sheridan 1762: 217, italics mine)

A binary opposition is set up between 'barbarous nations' and 'civilized nations', the hallmark of the latter being that the language of those nations is studied ('learning') and cultivated ('standardised'). Learning and standardisation are then classified as the hallmarks of politeness.

The number of cases in which the two notions of 'politeness' and 'learning' are intimately connected with 'standard English' could be multiplied almost indefinitely in the eighteenth century. Sometimes the standard is set in accordance with the language of the gentry, sometimes with the language used at court. We frequently find references to the social symbols of politeness, decorum, grace, beauty, symmetry and order, as these were articulated by Shaftesbury and made popular by *The Tatler* and *The Spectator*, and their representation in 'standard English'. The binary opposition often made between 'barbarism' and 'civilization' also occurs frequently and is particularly popular as an argument to justify 'polite language' as 'standard language' towards the end of the century.

The ideology of politeness in eighteenth century Britain created a social revolution. For the members of the middle classes, who were rapidly becoming more affluent, more mobile and more self-confident, being 'incorporated' into polite society was the goal of their social aspirations. Collaboration with those less affluent and less fortunate than themselves was never their goal. It is hardly surprising that they sought access to the prestigious ideological discourse of politeness, nor that they saw language, the acquisition of 'standard English', as an explicit means to gain that access. But it is also hardly surprising that those in control of that discourse, paying lip-service to the aspirations of the middle classes, presented it as an attainable goal whilst at the same time doing everything they could to thwart those ambitions. By shifting ground in the specification of how Standard or 'polite' English was to be understood, assimilation to the standard language remained always just out of reach of the middle classes (see Crowley 1989b; Mugglestone 1995; Bex 1999). So an alternative way of understanding the Milroys' ideology of standardisation would be to see it as forming a major part of the ideology of politeness in the eighteenth century. The legitimate language, 'standard English', was an indispensable attribute of anyone belonging to, or aspiring to belong to, 'polite society'.

But what happened to the close connection between 'standard English' and polite society when the concept of politeness shifted ground towards the end of the nineteenth century to refer to social behaviour displaying mutually shared forms of consideration for others regardless of the social class from which the interactants come? References to polite language continued to appear throughout the nineteenth century, and a link was frequently made between the social elite, Standard English and concepts such as 'a liberal education' and 'learning'. There are even sporadic references to polite language in the early part of the twentieth century, but by and large it is the term 'education' which conveniently takes over from politeness in the twentieth century to characterise the elitist nature of the legitimate language – Standard English.

In the efforts of the Conservative Party governments of the 1980s and early 1990s to reintroduce the teaching of grammar and 'standard pronunciation' into the National Curriculum for English the term 'education' appears to have emerged in place of the eighteenth century concept of politeness. Outside the media the strongest apologist for the link between education and Standard English is John Honey, and I shall finish off this alternative look at the development of 'standard English' by discussing the re-emergence of the ideology of politeness in the guise of the ideology of education in the final section of this chapter.

A wolf in sheep's clothing: from politeness to education

Understanding the historical origins of the ideology of standardisation as the mainstay of the ideology of politeness may help us to gain an alternative perspective on the heated debate over 'standard English', of what it is or what it should be, of its status and its perceived 'market' value with respect to other varieties of English, of its genesis, etc. Honey (1997: 3) maintains that '[s]tandard English is now a battlefield', Honey himself having been in the fray for most of the time during which the battle has been waged. The metaphor is not inappropriate, since we could argue with some justification that the ideology of standardisation, in Britain at least, has always been one of repression, of potential and often real violence, and of political power.

Enough has been said about Honey's controversial book to make any further lengthy comment on my part superfluous,[7] but it might be helpful to suggest that, in broad terms, it forms part of a heated and rather 'British-centric' dispute over the status of 'standard English' and the ways in which it is taught. The dispute has been carried out between, on the one hand, the political establishment, certain powerful sections of the media, certain members of the teaching profession and those of the writing profession and, on the other, the education establishment (school boards, examination bodies, academic departments of education in the universities, etc.) and linguists, applied linguists and sociolinguists inside and outside the universities.

The basis of Honey's argument is the lack of formal 'grammar' teaching in English and his placement of blame for this situation on the shoulders of linguists and sociolinguists who have supported the notion of linguistic equality, 'the notion that all languages, and all dialects of any language, are equally good' (Honey 1997: 5), is summed up in the following excerpt:

> It is perfectly true that a higher social position is often, though by no means always, available to users of standard English, but, independently of that, a whole range of benefits may accrue to those who can handle standard English – access to a vast literature, the ability to handle complex technology, the ability to exploit the resources of an educational system – which are not automatically of relevance to the user's social status. The defining quality symbolised by the use of standard English is not social rank as such, but instead of *educatedness* ...
>
> (Honey 1997: 131)

What Honey does not point out is that acquiring this mystical and elusive quality of educatedness, which he continually highlights as the goal of teaching 'standard English', i.e. the acquisition of 'the real rules which operate among the educated' (Honey 1997: 179), is propagated as the way to gain access to 'social rank'. On the contrary, he alleges that 'prominent British academic linguists have worked to deny or reduce access to this especially valuable variety for British children' (1997: 192), and he constantly expresses his belief in the superior qualities of 'standard English' as against other varieties, in both structural and functional terms.

The ominous solution that Honey almost imperceptibly slips into his argument is that 'a form of authority' should be set up to watch over Standard English. Honey is careful not to call it an 'academy', but that is clearly what he understands it to be:

> So what the English language needs is a form of authority that can easily be appealed to for guidance as to the uses which are acceptable compared with those which are not – an authority based not on an individual's irrational likes and dislikes but on the concensus of educated opinion.
>
> (Honey 1997: 163)

The solution is ominous because it was precisely this sort of demand which was voiced by Defoe in 1698 'to encourage polite learning'. The discourse and the basis on which it was originally constructed have been reproduced and reconstructed institutionally from then till the present day. Although it has taken on many different shapes and found many different modes of expression, it remains what it always was: elitist, essentially backward-looking, powerful and latently violent. Perhaps it is the realisation that the discourse is still with us that is so depressing about the current dispute over Standard English.

Let us have a brief critical look at points in Honey's book in which 'standard English' is explicitly connected with 'education' and 'educatedness'. His first move is to declare that Standard English is the language of the educated and to maintain that *Language is Power* (Honey 1997) is written in Standard English, which is a way of avoiding the necessity to define his terms. On pp. 33 and 35 he equates 'educatedness' with 'literacy', suggesting that, by being educated, one is in the 'mainstream of society'. But he implies that Standard English is an expression of the principal values of the 'mainstream', and that by not speaking Standard English it may not be possible to reach the mainstream:

> ... standard forms are the expression of a complex of values associated with being in the mainstream of society, and with educatedness, which in its turn is associated with literacy.
>
> (ibid.: 33)

> ... standard English is perceived by all – and resisted by some – as the language of literacy and of educatedness.
>
> (ibid.: 35)

As the book progresses, Honey moves into a position in which 'standard English' is an avowedly value-laden term which 'is the badge of literacy and education' (ibid.: 114).

But how does Honey understand 'education'? On p. 39 he begins to make his position clear:

> ... there is a long-standing and now overwhelming association, right across British society, between the use of the grammar, vocabulary and idioms of standard English, and the concept of 'educatedness'.

The statement is entirely unsubstantiated by any evidence at all, but it is interesting to note how Honey smuggles 'grammar, vocabulary and idioms' into his notion of 'educatedness'. In point of fact, 'education' is never explicitly defined throughout the whole book, although there are plenty of indications as to how the reader is intended to understand it.

Whatever type of 'educatedness' Honey associates with a command of Standard English, it leads to respect for the educated even from 'those who do not themselves possess it'. The implication is that those of higher social status are 'educated'. The 'real rules' of 'standard English' 'operate among the educated' and are insufficiently well known by those who pass judgment on it, by which Honey means linguists, sociolinguists and educationalists in academic institutions (ibid.: 179).

Honey finally gives the reader some insight into his category of 'educated people' by referring to an article published by him in *English Today*:

> But in October 1995 I published in the journal *English Today* evidence drawn from more than fifteen years of recording examples of educated people who use the supposedly 'incorrect' forms – 'to my wife and I',

'between you and I', 'for we British', etc. My fifty examples came *from prominent literary figures*, from *university professors* (including *well-known professors of English*), *distinguished Oxbridge theologians* ('for we who are in chapel today'), *politicians* (including several party leaders, and three education ministers) like Paddy Ashdown, Lord (David) Owen, George Walden ('the likes of you and I'), Sir Rhodes Boyson, Paul Channon and Mrs Thatcher ...

(ibid.: 161, italics mine)

Honey's scale of values with respect to 'the educated' include politicians, none of whom is from the Labour Party, well-known literary figures and university professors including professors of English, presumably at Oxbridge as are his 'theologians'. The class of the 'educated' for Honey is in no way identical to the gentry or the aristocracy as was the case in the eighteenth century, but it still contains a fairly liberal sprinkling of those who wield power in late twentieth century Britain.

The shift to a connection between 'standard English' and 'educatedness' is therefore nothing less than a wolf in sheep's clothing, the wolf being what was referred to in the eighteenth century as 'polite society'. 'Standard English' remains linked to notions of social climbing, prestige, elitism and exclusivity. It is presented as a means of bettering oneself socially. But there is one major difference between the connection between the ideology of standardisation and the ideology of politeness in the eighteenth century and that between the ideology of standardisation and the ideology of education at the end of the twentieth. The discursive practices of the eighteenth century ideology of standardisation were largely successful in constructing what came to be seen as 'standard English' precisely because that ideology was part of a wider ideology of politeness.

In the second half of the twentieth century the ideological discourse of education as John Honey and others see it is out of step with the course taken by the public education system in England and Wales, even given the National Curriculum imposed by the Conservative Party government of the 1980s and early 1990s. No one argues against the significance of 'standard English' in that system, just as long as it is seen to be a highly codified and statusful dialect which is not bound by a unique phonological system and which has the flexibility of being used in a range of oral as well as written registers (see Trudgill 1999).

If Honey's ideology of education is interpretable as a re-emergence of the ideology of politeness, it no longer includes an ideology of standardisation such as existed in the eighteenth century. The discourse shaping that ideology has been overshadowed by other forms of discourse about language that are related in other, more complicated ways with public education in Britain. At this point, a word of caution should be voiced. To judge by the reactions of the press, the government and certain self-appointed guardians of 'standard English' in the late 1980s the ideology of standardisation is not dead yet, and to understand why that is so, we need to trace its progress as a part of the ideology of politeness from the beginning of the eighteenth century. An alternative approach to the development of Standard English which undertakes to do this throws an interesting new light on the current rearguard battle over its present-day status.

Notes

1 I have used the term 'Standard English English' as does Trudgill (this volume) to indicate its status as a dialect of English restricted to England (rather than to other parts of the British Isles). Most of the time, however, I shall simply refer to Standard English, which I will capitalise to indicate that the nomenclature is used to refer to a variety of English.

2 See the comments made in the short introductory chapter with respect to the equation 'history of English = history of Standard English' and J. Milroy (this volume).

3 Hence Defoe's suggestion predates Swift's *Proposal for Correcting, Improving, and Ascertaining the English Tongue* (1712), in which a similar proposal is made, by 14 years.

4 Swift maintains, for instance, that '[the language's] daily Improvements are by no Means in Proportion to its daily Corruptions; that the Pretenders to polish and refine it, have chiefly multiplied Abuses and Absurdities; and, that in many Instances, it offends against every Part of Grammar.'

5 If it were to return a verdict of 'satire', it would not greatly weaken Milroy and Milroy's argument, but it would reconstitute Swift's letter as a text attacking politeness and polite language.

6 The connection that Langford makes between commerce and politeness is underscored in the case of Sheridan by the fact that they were also a huge success financially. It is also possible to argue that Sheridan was deliberately, and one might also say cynically, using the aspirations of middle-class audiences to climb the social ladder by acquiring a Standard English pronunciation and mode of oral delivery.

7 See the epilogue by Crowley to Bex and Watts (1999).

9 Eloquence and elegance

Ideals of communicative competence in spoken English

Sharon Millar

Where grammar ends, eloquence begins.

(George Campbell)

The theme of this chapter is the development of ideals in relation to verbal expression in spoken English. The perspective taken is that of three of the spoken 'arts': oratory, conversation and reading aloud. These skills had considerable cultural and social significance, but they have not been given a great deal of attention in histories of the English language. In part this is the result of the traditional emphasis on the written channel, meaning that general ideals applicable to speech as well as writing, such as eloquence, tend to be narrowed down to written varieties, such as literary prose (see for example Leith and Graddol 1996). Even in histories of pronunciation, the spoken arts do not make much of an appearance since these are generally concerned with phonological descriptions or the standardisation of accent, where emphasis is usually placed on sociolinguistically significant, allophonic realisations (see for example Mugglestone 1995; MacMahon 1998).

The limited mention of spoken skills is not, I believe, due to their inherent lack of interest for histories of the language. It is more a question of focus. So, for instance, Baron (2000) mentions oratory and reading aloud since her concern is with the evolution of written English and its relation to the spoken medium. Some historians, such as Burke (1993), Cmiel (1990) and Jamieson (1988), have taken an interest in matters of communicative competence, specifically conversation and public speaking, in the belief, not held by all historians, that language is a significant element of social and cultural history. I would argue that a focus on the spoken arts can contribute to a cultural history of the English language in a number of ways. Firstly, since oratory and conversation dealt with communication, they give us an insight into contemporary ideals of public discourse and how these evolved. These ideals touched many aspects of linguistic structure as they essentially dealt with style, both linguistic and cultural. Secondly, as dimensions of legitimised communicative competence, forming part of what Bourdieu (1991) terms 'cultural capital', i.e. skills valued by the powerful and influential in society, the spoken arts were affected by and contributed to standardisation processes, a relationship which merits some investigation. Finally, given the proficiency dimension of the spoken arts (how to become a good orator, reader, etc.), we are given insights into the contemporary understanding of language teaching and learning.

More specifically, this chapter will examine one of the overarching ideals of the spoken arts, namely eloquence, in terms of both its functions and forms. Its relationship with correctness and standardisation will also be explored. To put it another way, I am taking a rhetorical perspective on aspects of the history of English given that the tradition of classical rhetoric influenced notions of public discourse from the Renaissance through to the nineteenth century. The time-frame of the chapter is primarily the eighteenth and nineteenth centuries, although forays into earlier periods will be made to illustrate continuity in thinking. Both Britain and the USA (referred to here as 'America') will be considered.

I begin, however, with some remarks on data. Given that this chapter deals with precepts and beliefs about language, historical sources such as conduct, elocution and public speaking manuals can be usefully appealed to. Such manuals give us an idea of the writers' (meta)linguistic and sociolinguistic awareness, although they tell us little about actual use. An obvious difficulty for the historical study of spoken competence is data on usage. Reliance on printed representations of the spoken word is a necessity but, although informative, has its dangers. Take, for example, the farewell speech made by Abraham Lincoln in his hometown of Springfield in 1861. The version given in Fehrenbacher (1964: 149), which is taken from a contemporary newspaper, the *Illinois State Journal*, begins as follows:

> Friends, No one who has never been placed in a like position, can understand my feelings at this hour, nor the oppressive sadness I feel at this parting. For more than a quarter of a century I have lived among you, and during all that time I have received nothing but kindness at your hands. Here I have lived from my youth until now I am an old man
> ... .

The same 'speech' in the *Penguin Book of Historical Speeches* (MacArthur 1995: 363) is noticeably different:

> No one, not in my situation, can appreciate my feeling of sadness at this parting. To this place, and the kindness of these people, I owe everything. Here I have lived a quarter of a century, and have passed from a young to an old man ... .

This version is purportedly that which was partly written out by Lincoln and partly dictated by him afterwards (Basler 1969). Clearly, the historian of language risks drawing different conclusions depending on which 'speech' happens to be selected as data. What is interesting is that both versions are presented as authentic spoken language, i.e. as what Lincoln actually said. This same trend is apparent in the reporting of other types of oral culture, such as oral narrative. For instance, the narrative of John Slover is claimed to be 'from his mouth as he related it' in 1782. Yet, in the extract below, it is difficult to gauge how much was subjected to the editorial process and how much was genuine oral narrative.

> Death by burning, which appeared to be now my fate, I had resolved to sustain with patience. The divine grace of God had made it less alarming to me, for on my way this day I had been greatly exercised in regard to my latter end.
>
> (*Narratives of a Late Expedition Against the Indians* 1783: 21)

Despite their problematic nature, these printed representations of 'speech' are sociolinguistically significant in that they would have cultivated the perception of the spoken language as being not that different from the written in terms of discourse organisation, e.g. coherence and choice of words and sentence constructions. Indeed, as we shall see, the practice of the spoken arts encouraged the notion that speech was spoken writing: the means by which the visual was made audible.

Oratory, conversation and reading aloud as public discourse

Before focusing on the concept of eloquence, I will give a brief overview of the significance of the spoken arts in the public domain of the eighteenth and nineteenth centuries.

Oratory

The public nature of the spoken arts is perhaps most apparent in relation to oratory. This was, after all, public speaking for a civic purpose. It was traditionally linked with three main areas: government and politics, law and the Church, and their associated occupations. Popular oratory or speaking, that is public address not necessarily tied up with state institutions, only became widespread in the eighteenth century with the creation of a public sphere. This new space became populated with political clubs, reading societies, special interest associations and coffee houses, all types of voluntary organization which 'opened the public sphere to expressions of public opinion' (Becker 1994: 5). The emergence of public opinion in the eighteenth century was significant for oratory as it generated interest in oratorical performance and rhetorical skills. In England, for example, increased public attention was directed towards parliamentary debates so that by the 1770s 'MPs, once prized as "knowing Parliament men", were now public orators' (Langford

1989: 706). Their audience was not the handful of parliamentary colleagues actually present in the House of Commons, but the literate public, whose curiosity about names and issues was fanned by the ever-expanding press, which reported, often illegally, on parliamentary proceedings. Newspapers helped create an audience by proxy at a time when mass political oratory was rare, at least in eighteenth-century England, although realisations about the significance of the 'mob' were increasing (Rudé 1964). Mass audiences, however, did have access to a different type of oratory: evangelical preaching, such as that of John Wesley. In America, too, the public ear and eye were turned towards oratory: interest in certain court cases, for example, was so great that trials had to be held in large auditoriums and proceedings began to be published (Bohman 1943).

The expansion of the public sphere continued in the nineteenth century with the development of more and more literary clubs, debating societies and, in America, the lyceum movement. The lyceums organised the public lecture on a commercial basis, thus succeeding in establishing lecturing as a profitable career (Aly and Tanquary 1943; Scott 1980) and raising the profile of oratory. Lyceum lectures enjoyed enormous, if temporary, popularity among all classes of Americans, who were eager to acquire knowledge: 'going to lectures … is the next most important duty to going to church' commented an English observer (Davidsen 1974: 359). The expansion of the public sphere, which encouraged participation in public speaking, not just as speaker, but also as listener, brought with it moral implications. As potential markets for spoken skills opened up, the study of rhetoric was redefined from the more exclusive art of oratory alone to the general art of communication (Cmiel 1990; Johnson 1993). The opportunity to be eloquent was now available to the literate populace generally and availability brought obligation in its wake. Hence, Bell (1887: 1) could argue that ability in public speaking was the 'professional duty of the clergyman and advocate' and the 'social duty of the private citizen'.

Conversation

The term conversation originally referred to general dealings with others – social intercourse – and could also mean the company or society one kept; the narrower definition of interaction or talk alone developed during the nineteenth century. The blossoming of conversation as an art with distinct cultural value took place in the eighteenth century and related to fundamental social changes well under way in Britain and other parts of Europe. Social distinctions traditionally based on birth and land, such as 'gentleman' and 'lady', were being redefined as wealth and property began to be acquired by the non-gentry and lost by the gentry as a result of urbanisation, universal acceptance of primogeniture, growth in trade, availability of land once held by the Crown or the Church, and opportunities presented by colonial policies. In consequence, behavioural definitions of social categories took on paramount importance. Sir Richard Steele (1709: 2189–90) believed an essential aspect of gentlemanliness to be the ability to converse: the gentleman was a 'man of conversation', blessed with good judgement, whose conversation is

> a continual feast, at which he helps some, and is helped by others, in such a manner that the equality of society is perfectly kept up.

The key word here is 'equality'. Eighteenth-century notions of 'taste' and 'politeness' were in theory egalitarian: 'independent of class, birth and rank: good taste would produce "good society"'(Becker 1994: 73). This ideal equality could be acted out in the new public space of the coffee house and the assembly rooms. Here people could meet and 'converse', i.e. express ideas, discuss music, the arts, literature and language, and in so doing create and define a polite and refined public. It was within this consensual framework of politeness that conversational ideals, such as eloquence, would be established for the gentry and aspirants to gentility. So conversation had a dual function: that of cultural consolidation and cultural differentiation. The equilibrium upset by social mobility had to be regained through defining the new social elites in terms of some shared criteria, while simultaneously accentuating the differences between these groups and others. As Borsay (1989: 284) emphasises, it was vital that 'the newly established frontiers should be doubly fortified. An expanding and competitive elite was only tolerable if accompanied by more intensive segregation within society in general'.

The situation in eighteenth-century America was different from that in England, but here too there were concerns about traditional categories in flux. Post-revolutionary America disliked the hierarchical values of the old world, but the social levelling that ensued was a source of distress for the educated elites. Old notions of the educated gentleman versus the un-educated, common man were maintained, but came under considerable pressure in the nineteenth century when it was assumed that everyone could be a gentleman or lady. However, more genteel notions of the lady and gentleman still existed and were appealed to in many an American elocution manual. Vandenhoff (1845), for example, talks of 'elegant and accomplished ladies' (Vandenhoff 1845: Preface) and 'the educated gentleman' as opposed to the 'vulgar and unpolished man' (Vandenhoff 1845: 16).

Reading aloud

As a public activity, reading aloud overlapped with particularly religious oratory. Complaints about the lack of eloquence in eighteenth-century Britain, for instance, often referred to the inability of the clergy to read aloud (Shortland 1987). Steele (1711: 78) notes in relation to reading the Common Prayer that

> It is indeed wonderful, that the frequent Exercise of it should not make the Performers of that Duty more expert in it. This Inability, as I conceive, proceeds from the little Care that is taken of their Reading, while Boys and at School, where when they are got into Latin, they are look'd upon as above English, the Reading of which is wholly neglected, or at least read to very little purpose ...

Part of the problem in relation to spoken English abilities, specifically oratory and reading aloud, was that English at this time was not a recognised scholarly subject, except in the dissenting academies. The eighteenth-century debate in Britain about poor spoken language skills had, thus, a subtext promoting the educational status of English in relation to the classical languages. In contrast, in America, quite a number of academies based on an English rather than a Latin curriculum were already flourishing by the end of the eighteenth century (French 1964).

However, reading aloud in English came to be seen as more than just a professional skill; it was also an accomplishment and an indicator of status within polite society. American elocutionist Ebenezer Porter (1827: 13–14) believed that 'No one is qualified to hold a respectable rank in a well-bred society, who is unable to read in an interesting manner, the works of others'. The exclusiveness implied by this comment is obvious. At a time when literacy was far from universal, cultural capital was located not just in the ability to read, but to read aloud, and well.

Methodologically, reading aloud was linked to conversation in that the preferred manner of reading was that which most resembled 'natural' conversation. One should read as one speaks. The distinction between reading and conversation and their relationship to each other was often muddied, however. For John Walker (1781: 29) reading was 'artificial speaking', that is:

> Reading ... is to speaking what a copy is to an original picture: both of them have beautiful nature for their object; and as a taste for beautiful nature can scarcely be better acquired than by a view of the most elegant copies of it, speaking, it is presumed, cannot be more successfully taught, than by referring us to such rules, as instruct us in the art of reading.

So (good) speaking or conversation was the norm for reading, but the former was acquired by studying the latter. Logical or not, this premise has been a cornerstone of elocutionary method for over two centuries.

Although practised in the public domain, the skills of oratory, conversation and reading aloud blurred the dichotomy of public vs. private. Conversation, for example, could be private interaction taking place in the public eye and in public hearing. Reading aloud could be done to an audience in the privacy of one's home. Indeed, reading aloud to family and friends was a popular form of home entertainment for the genteel, especially in the Victorian era. In America, the 'parlor book', an anthology of literary pieces, was produced for precisely this purpose (see Rickert 1978). From a linguistic perspective, the public and private were, theoretically, to be collapsed. One was supposed to speak in public as one did in private: good linguistic habits were to be cultivated and practised in the private sphere and then transferred to the public. Hugh Blair, one of the most influential eighteenth-century British rhetoricians, argued for this sequential ordering as follows:

> If one has naturally any gross defects in his voice or gestures, he begins at the wrong end, if he attempts at reforming them only when he is to speak in public. He should begin with rectifying them in his private manner of speaking; and then carry to the public the right habit he has formed. For when a speaker is engaged in a public discourse, he should not be then employing his attention about his manner, or thinking of his tones and his gestures. If he be so employed, study and affectation will appear.
>
> (taken from *On Public Speaking* 1904: 171)

That there was to be no separate style for private and public domains was more than just a question of method. It reflected the neoclassical perception of moral character, which was holistic in nature. Man was an indivisible whole, not a context-dependent persona with a multiplicity of identities (see Cmiel 1990).

Eloquence

Eloquence was the ideal of classical rhetoric and one which was transferred to the Western European context as a matter of course during the Renaissance. It is a concept which has inspired learned treatises, such as Hume's *Of Eloquence* from 1742, and appeared in the titles of many an elocution or public speaking manual, e.g. *On Public Speaking. What eloquence is and how to acquire it* (1904). It is also a concept which has provoked harsh criticism over the centuries. Nowadays, although not the evaluative notion it once was, it still makes the occasional appearance. For instance on the back cover of Casperson (1999), praise from a reviewer reads as 'Wow! This book is all you need to be elegant and eloquent in business today'.

Defining eloquence is a difficult enterprise because of its diverse and changing nature: eloquence did not mean the same thing to all people throughout history or even within a given period. Linguists have tended to view eloquence as a property of language; Joseph (1987: 104) sees eloquence as the goal of elaboration, 'one of the most significant processes constituting standardization'. This view is perfectly legitimate, but is only one side of the coin. Eloquence was primarily a property or ability of speakers (and writers) and from that perspective 'implied far more than the ability to handle words deftly; it invoked larger concerns about audience, personality, and social order' (Cmiel 1990: 24). In this sense, eloquence was not about elaboration, but manipulation, involving control of others, the self and, as I will argue later, language.

In order to disentangle some of the many strands that make up eloquence, I will approach the concept in terms of its functions and then consider a few of its linguistic manifestations.

Functions of eloquence

These can be broadly characterised as a means of persuasion and/or a means of linguistic display. In addition, eloquence had an important symbolic function, relating to general behaviour and moral character.

Persuasion

This function of eloquence was primarily associated with oratory and, later, public speaking. Since eloquence as persuasion dealt with audience management, its instrumental benefits in terms of influence, fame and fortune had long been stressed. In the eighteenth century, eloquence as persuasion was to be cultivated as a practical skill, vital to certain occupations and indeed the health of democratic government. Hume (1825: 92–3) considered the sorry state of oratorical eloquence in England surprising, given the nature of English government:

> Of all the polite and learned nations, England alone possesses a popular government, or admits into the legislature such numerous assemblies as can be supposed to lie under the dominion of eloquence. But what has England to boast of this in particular?

His contemporary, Lord Chesterfield, felt that an improvement in oratorical skills was necessary to defend the constitution. The Americans similarly equated oratorical eloquence with liberal forms of government; for John Adams 'eloquence is cultivated with more care in republics than in other governments' (Cmiel 1990: 40). In addition to links with free speech, persuasive eloquence was coupled with humanistic values. 'To guide men toward virtue and worthwhile goals' (Gray 1963: 498) epitomised the spirit of Renaissance eloquence, and this altruistic spirit, if in a weaker version, endured into the nineteenth century. For instance, Lord Brougham, rector of Glasgow University in the 1820s, saw oratory as the means

> to diffuse useful information ... to further intellectual refinement ... to hasten the coming of the bright day when the dawn of general knowledge shall chase away the lazy, lingering mists, even from the base of the great social pyramid.
>
> (*Great Orators, Statesmen and Divines* 1881: 142)

What should be remembered, however, is that eloquence as a persuasive ability, be it in the pursuit of democracy, civic altruism or professional advancement, lay primarily in the domain of professionals and, thus, male elites. The public platform was not readily open to women, even of elite status, and those who dared to be public speakers met with considerable hostility (see Jamieson 1988). Females were taught rhetorical skills (see Lunsford 1995), but such teaching was undertaken in a different manner than that used for males and intended for very different purposes. *The Little Female Orators* (1770) gives an account of 'evening entertainments at a boarding school for young ladies four miles from London'. Every Saturday night, a pupil was to address the others on 'some moral and entertaining subject'. These included books they had read, the use of the fan and the importance of dress. Each talk was followed by observations by the governess, who generally discussed the suitability of the topic chosen and its moral implications. In Troy Female Seminary in America, elocution was a required course, the textbook being Hugh Blair's 'Lectures on Rhetoric'. The girls composed their own speeches and the best were read out, not by the authors, but by the teacher or a classmate. If a classmate was chosen, she was not to raise her eyes from the paper and the voice was to be kept low. In contrast, boys were trained extensively in declamation and self-presentation (O'Connor 1954: 29). Similarly in Oberlin College, the first college in America to open its doors to women, female students were not allowed to debate in the rhetoric class nor to read the commencement address at graduation. Only in 1874 did the college permit women to 'engage in the same Rhetorical Exercises as the gentlemen' (Conway 1995: 206).

Display

Eloquence as display refers to the sophistic trend in rhetoric to focus on manner rather than matter, shifting the emphasis away from communication between speaker and audience to self-expression. In so doing, it did not dispose of eloquence as persuasion, just relocated it. Functioning as a stylistic ideal, eloquence could still persuade, but it could also be applied to a wider range of linguistic activity, e.g. written, especially literary, composition, conversation and reading aloud. Renaissance writers equated eloquence with wisdom and decorum, the notion of what was fitting. In terms of language, decorum was 'the adjustment of separable objects to each other: the speaker fits his words to his subject, his audience, his occasion, his purpose' (Waswo 1987: 194). In other words, decorum focused on language style, that canon of rhetoric which was the most influential at the time, given the activities of the figurists and the views of the Ramists, who defined rhetoric exclusively in terms of style and delivery (manner), regarding content and argumentation (matter) as issues of logic. Waswo (ibid: 196) argues that this separation of matter from manner encouraged a behavioural understanding of decorum, hence eloquence, since the demand 'for an apparent semantic integrity which, because it is not conceivable as such in rhetorical terms, becomes a demand for moral integrity, for behavior that is appropriate and "fitting", whether political, personal, or social'.

The Renaissance understanding of eloquence is apparent in the eighteenth century, particularly when related to written genres. Cleric and rhetorician George Campbell saw eloquence as the matching of form to function (see Kennedy 1980) while the elocutionist Thomas Sheridan equated eloquence with elocution, thus highlighting delivery and spoken language, be this oratory, conversation or reading aloud. For Sheridan, elocution and eloquence were 'the graceful management of the voice, the countenance, and gesture in speaking' (Sheridan 1762: 19). Mohrmann (1983: 65) advocates that elocution was a 'natural development of Renaissance thought' since the notion of decorum included concerns about delivery. Sheridan's use of the adjective 'graceful' can, thus, be interpreted through Renaissance eyes to mean 'decorous'.

Symbolism

The symbolic nature of eloquence is testified by the behavioural aspects of decorum mentioned above, but the symbolism of eloquence has existed from classical times; the belief then was that an eloquent speaker was inherently a good man. During the Renaissance and beyond, the idea was given a slightly different slant in that the cultivation of eloquence was seen as simultaneously cultivating the ideal type: the virtuous, decent, learned, graceful gentleman, whose behaviour followed scrupulously the dictates of decorum. Eloquence implied self-control and so was a hallmark of social elegance, given that bodily and emotional self-discipline were perceived as part of being 'civilized' (Burke 1993; Elias 1994). In the eighteenth century, the symbolic role of eloquence gelled seamlessly with another significant cultural ethos – that of politeness (Klein 1989).

As a symbol, eloquence helped assert and confirm changing social identities. In the eighteenth century, the social category which was particularly affected by change was that of the 'middle station', to use Daniel Defoe's term; this was the social space occupied by all non-gentry and all non-manual labour. Those people in its upper echelons, the above middling people such as merchants, the professions and bankers, and their wives, represented the new category of gentleman and lady and they were anxious to assert this through elegant and refined behaviour. It was they who co-opted much of the literature on conduct and it was their interest that led to more 'bourgeois' values being propagated in the conduct books of the day. They even began to produce such literature themselves (see Carré 1994). In America, the symbolic function of eloquence was similarly propagated through conduct literature, most of which was borrowed from England. Hence old-world notions of linguistic refinement were imported to the new world. These fluctuated in popularity throughout the nineteenth century. Patriotic feelings fed the production of practical etiquette books written by and for Americans and expounding American values. In contrast, upsets to the social equilibrium, caused by the acquisition of vast wealth across the social spectrum in the aftermath of the Civil War, encouraged interest in old-world linguistic refinement, both as a marker of genteel taste among the nouveau riche and as a marker of polite superiority among those with a distaste for these new 'vulgar' rich (Cmiel 1990). Eventually, notions of gentility were ousted by the ever-increasing concern with financial success, a trend apparent in the self-help literature of the early twentieth century, and one which continues today. The beginning and end of the twentieth century saw the art of conversation defined in exclusively functionalist terms as a means to manage interpersonal relations for the purpose of self-advancement in business (see Lasch 1978).

Forms of eloquence

The forms of eloquence have provoked disagreement throughout history. The conflict usually referred to in the history of English is that between the over-elaborate and ornate written style of some Elizabethans and the plain, unadorned style demanded by more Puritanical elements. In this debate, eloquence was often seen as synonymous with ornate choice of words and use of rhetorical figures. However, the conflict about the forms of eloquence can also be seen in terms of defining formality levels, and by extension models of refinement, for spoken public discourse (see Cmiel 1990). It is this perspective I adopt here.

Style, formality and politeness

Waswo (1987: 193) notes in relation to Renaissance eloquence that 'the equation of good utterance and good matter is therefore a standard of judgement for highly formal usage'. Despite the down-grading of matter in the equation, this link with formality was still the case in the eighteenth and nineteenth centuries. Manuals of conduct, elocution and public speaking advocated very formal linguistic styles in relation to refined, decorous, polite behaviour. As an illustration, I will consider prescribed pragmatic strategies and proscribed phonetic processes of reduction.

Pragmatic concerns were central to eloquent conversation; decorum demanded 'fitting' behaviour and what was 'fitting' was defined by notions of refinement and politeness. This requirement was particularly acute when dealing with superiors or the more sensitive speech acts, such as accusing, apologising, condoling. Of particular importance was 'phraseology', where indirectness was the prescribed norm. The conduct books generally recommended elegant circuitry. For instance, Adam Petrie (1720) advised readers to jot down all 'elegant and ornate' sentences that might come their way and provided some examples that would be useful when talking (or writing) to a superior: 'you was pleased to put your self to the trouble to tell me so' or 'may I presume to desire the favour of your doing so and so' (taken from McIntosh 1986: 86). Expressing disagreement with a conversational partner was seen as requiring utmost tact and, in the light of the advice given, considerable verbiage. *How to Shine in Society* (1867: 20) informs readers that

> when you are compelled to dissent from anything that has been said, state first how far you agree with the speaker, and how happy you are to accord with him so far, then how unwilling you are to differ with him.

Expressing condolences similarly demanded verbosity. According to the *Young Man's Own Book* (1838: 232), saying 'I am sorry for your loss' is 'civil', but 'vulgar'. A better alternative, given that 'phraseology' distinguished 'a man of fashion', was:

> I hope, sir, you will do me the justice to be persuaded, that I am not insensible to your unhappiness, that I take part in your distress, and shall ever be affected when you are so.

The need to be discreet and aware of the needs of one's conversational partner was constantly emphasised. 'Never ask a question', advised *Etiquette for Gentlemen* (1841: 54), as the obligation to reply might cause awkwardness. So, replace 'How is your brother today?' with 'I hope your brother is quite well'. Interestingly, this same 'brother' example is to be found in Mrs Duffey's American etiquette book (1877), reminding us that conventionalised notions of politeness in one culture may well have been borrowed from another. Worth noting in this respect was the influence of French perceptions of 'politesse' on English ideals (Burke 1993).

Some evidence that these prescriptions reflected norms of usage can be gleaned from contemporary satirical comment. Jonathan Swift in his *Polite Conversation* from 1738 parodies excesses of elegance and their codification in conduct books by providing his readers with a collection of polite expressions, which sum up 'the whole Genius, Humour, Politeness, and Eloquence of England' (Swift 1963: 23) and which

> will easily incorporate with all Subjects of genteel and fashionable Life. Those which are proper for Morning Tea, will be equally useful at the same Entertainment in the Afternoon, even in the same Company, only by shifting the several Questions, Answers, and Replies, into different Hands; and, such as are adapted to Meals, will indifferently serve for Dinners, or Suppers, only distinguishing between Day-light and Candle-Light. By this Method, no diligent Person of a tolerable Memory, can ever be at a Loss.

> (Swift 1963: 38)

Steele too railed against conversation 'nowadays so swell'd with Vanity and Compliment and so surfeited ... of Expressions of Kindness and Respect' (Burke 1993: 112).

Turning to phonetic concerns, these focused on the traditional norm of distinctness. Key aspects of a lack of distinctness were omitting and changing 'letters', seen generally as 'faults' or 'defects' of pronunciation or enunciation. The very use of the word 'letters' is testament to the now-acknowledged fact that literacy (print awareness) has effects on certain types of phonological awareness (see Goswami and Bryant 1990). Atwell (1868: 13), for example, considers omission (*an'* for *and*) and substitution (*git* for *get*) as major 'errors in articulation'. For Holme (1898: 11), omitting final consonants in words and syllables was a fault both 'grievous' and 'fatal'. Hartley (1870: 35) warned his readers not to change 'the sound of *a* in such words as *than, that, was*, etc. into an indistinct sound of *u*; the *e* into *u*, in such words as *wicked, moment*, etc.' Russell (1851) and Gladstone (1893) expressed similar concerns, adding coalescence (e.g. /dʒ/ in *educate, would you*) and syllabic consonants to the list. What bothered elocutionists were the connected speech processes so characteristic of rapid, spontaneous speech.

The value of phonetic distinctness was explained variably in terms of function, aesthetics and politeness or refinement. Functional reasons related to 'the understanding', i.e. intelligibility, a factor which was emphasised greatly in the context of public speaking. When Thomas Sheridan (1762: 40) expressed his bafflement at the lack of interest in teaching people how to speak their own language, he homed in on the intelligibility dimension:

> it is a disgrace to a gentleman, to be guilty of false spelling, either by omitting, changing, or adding letters contrary to custom; and yet it shall be no disgrace to omit letters, or even syllables in speaking, and to huddle his words together, as to render them utterly unintelligible. Yet surely, exactness in the latter, is a point of much more importance ... the words of one who speaks in public ... may be ... addresseed to many hundred hearers; who must lose the benefit or purposed end of the discourse, in proportion as it is indistinctly pronounced.

However, for Sheridan (1762: 44) indistinctness also offended the conventions of politeness since it demanded 'a more than ordinary attention, which is always painful to the hearer'. So lack of clarity meant lack of consideration for one's listeners and, as such, rendered the speaker 'impolite'. American elocutionist Vandenhoff (1845: 16) expressed his concerns in terms of lack of 'polish', i.e. refinement: 'Pronunciation distinguishes the educated gentleman from the vulgar and unpolished man' and was to be based on 'the custom of the polite and elegant part of the world'. Note, in this case, pronunciation meant articulation and accentuation (not social or regional accent).

From a theoretical perspective, the norm of politeness advanced in conduct manuals and assumed in elocution manuals was generally that of negative politeness, which is associated with restraint and distance (Brown and Levinson 1987). It is also clear that notions of politeness were tied up with distinct notions of style: negative politeness involved pragmatic indirectness and phonetic explicitness. This relationship between the formality of style and politeness has been noted before. Wheeler (1994), for example, argues that negative politeness equates with formal style, which is characterised by avoidance of contraction, ellipsis, reduction of vowels and omission of consonants. Positive politeness, which satisfies our needs to be appreciated and is associated with solidarity, is thought to equate with informal contexts and styles (see Holmes 1995b). These equations, however, are best seen as tendencies. For instance, the act of condolence involves in many ways positive politeness, but can be phrased in highly formal language. Note the example of condolence above where the flowery verbosity is expressing solidarity.

Of course, stylistic correlates of any behaviour or context are not predetermined, but are the consequence of social and cultural change. Similarly, specific features are not inherently formal or informal, but derive this from macro- and micro-context. The styles considered suitable for the public domain have always been a source of disagreements. Conversation in eighteenth-century England oscillated between the ceremony of hierarchy and the directness of equality within polite circles. Public discourse in nineteenth-century America witnessed a struggle between old-world ideas of refinement and a new populism, which saw politeness as rapport rather than distance (Cmiel 1990). The result of the tension was not an informal style, but a stylistic hybrid, which mixed the refined with the vulgar, the formal with the informal. Evidence for this can be gleaned from the practice of, and reception to, certain public speakers. For example, when reviewing the oratorical style of Wendell Phillips, the *Andover Review* noted

> With an indifference to the foppery of culture he would put to frequent use the colloquialisms 'well', 'can't', 'wasn't', 'don't', 'won't', 'wouldn't', 'shouldn't', but from his refined lips they seemed almost to gain authority and propriety.

(Yeager 1943: 359)

It appears that contracted verbal forms in public discourse were gaining acceptability, even 'propriety' if uttered by the right sort of person. Arguably, they were on their way to losing all connotations of 'colloquial', a damning prescriptive category at the time, to become less stylistically marked, both in terms of (in)formality and politeness, in the public domain.

Eloquence, correctness and standardisation

Since classical times, eloquence has been linked to correctness. 'Virtues' of style and delivery included purity and clarity, both of which related to grammatical and phonetic correctness. Padley (1985) observes, regarding grammar writing in Europe generally, that inculcation of correct usage was a hallmark of rhetorically oriented grammars in the Renaissance. Classical notions of correctness were applied to English by those rhetorical handbooks which dealt with vices and faults of style. Puttenham (1589), for example, listed barbarism – bad spelling and mispronunciation, such as foreigners saying *dousand* for *thousand*; solecisms – misuse of grammatical rules; and 'rusticitie'. Classical thinking was used as not only a blueprint for the grammatical classification of English, but for some evaluative and prescriptive concepts as well.

The question is to what extent eloquence (as a speaker characteristic) and matters relating to public spoken discourse fed into contemporary ideas of standardisation, bearing in mind that correctness notions in language, and the prescriptive behaviour that accompanies them, are independent of the standard language concept (see Millar 1998). We might expect some interaction between eloquence and standardisation since both dealt with formal usage.

Evidence that rhetorical concerns nurtured the discourse of standardisation in England can be seen in the types of argument given for the establishment of a language academy for English by, for example, Thomas Sprat and Jonathan Swift. One major argument revolved around the need to protect style, especially written style, from the excesses of the elites. For Sprat the academy was to be 'a fixt and Imperial Court of Eloquence according to whose Censure all Books or Authors should either stand or fall' (Sprat 1667, taken from Waswo 1987: 200). Unlike Sprat, Swift's concerns were not solely related to the written language, as is testified by his *Polite Conversation* in which linguistic affectation is approached from the broad perspective of ethics and manners (Berger 1994). Interestingly, features frequently condemned by the pro-academy lobby, be it monosyllables, especially in past tense forms (*drown'd*, *drudg'd*), or 'unusual Coupling of Syllables and Sentences' (Defoe 1697, taken from Knowles 1997: 114) illustrate a long-established rhetorical concern: phonoaesthetics and the oratorical qualities of written composition.

Questions of an academy aside, eloquence, or the lack of it, was a prime motivating force behind the production of one of the major pronouncing dictionaries of the eighteenth century, that of Thomas Sheridan (1780). Thomas Sheridan's key interests were the 'revival of the art of speaking' and the reform of education, through which English was to be given precedence over the Classics and the spoken word precedence over the written (see Benzie 1972; Shortland 1987). To do this, English had to be made eloquent through codification in order to be a suitable vehicle for oratory; and oratorical skills were necessary to regenerate society and make England great. As Sichel (1909: 240–1) put it 'he would mend mankind by rhetoric'. In other words, Sheridan's concerns about refining English cannot be divorced from his obsession with spoken language skills. Other elocutionists, such as James Burgh (1781: 4), did not accept that English was inherently unsuited to oratory, but did consider the lack of interest in oratory and the English language as a source of national indignity:

> it is greatly to our shame that while we do so little for the improvement of our language, and of our manner of speaking it in public, the French should take so much pains in both these respects, though their language is very much inferior to ours, both as to emphasis and copiousness.

For elocutionists, the need to 'stabilise' English had a utilitarian imperative, with a nationalist dimension.

Not surprisingly, elocution manuals contained social and regional prescriptions, which fed into the growing standard language concept. These focused on segmental and, on occasion, non-segmental features of accent. As the former are well documented in histories of the language, at least in Britain, I will focus on the latter. Concerns here centred on provincialism, that arch-enemy of standardisation, being non-metropolitan, non-urbane and non-national. The crux of the provincial suprasegmental problem was intonation or 'inflections'. The standard typically appealed to with regard to inflections was John Walker's system from 1781. Its geographical basis, London, was recognised and accepted, although the system itself was criticised. Hartley (1870: 9) advised his readers:

> Walker's system is nothing more or less than an analysis of the manner in which the best speakers who are free from provincial accent, modulate their voices ... Understand and feel what you speak or read, and if you are free from provincial accent, you will inflect correctly.

Later in the same work, when talking about raising the voice to be heard, he stated 'if the object is attained by using the rising inflection, the delivery is incorrect and Scottish' (Hartley 1870: 31).

Knowles (1883: xxxi–xxxii) took exception to Walker's claim that the inflections related to meaning, but, like Hartley, did not question the overall geographical model:

> we beg leave to correct the erroneous position, that the inflections are essential to the sense. They are no such thing ... and for this palpable reason – the English, Scotch and Irish use them differently, and yet not the smallest ambiguity follows with regard to the communication, or the production of thought. ... The system is ... an analysis ... of the manner in which the best speakers in London modulate the voice, and as such, is highly important – assisting us to get rid of one source of that peculiarity which constitutes provincial speech – a misapplication of the inflections.

The importance of suprasegmental features to the concept of standard is difficult to estimate. Intonation certainly played a role, but what about pitch, rate, loudness and voice quality? These have always been vital to the perception of elegant, polite speech and norms relating to them have long been prescribed in the conduct literature. Such cultural norms, however, are generally not seen as part of the standard language concept; we tend not to talk of a standard 'voice'. Yet in reality we know relatively little about people's attitudes to suprasegmental features; neither do we know what happens suprasegmentally when people standardise their accents.

Perhaps the main contribution of eloquence to standardisation processes was that it defined formal uses of the language and, in so doing, helped define standard uses of the language. The link between formality and the standard language was of paramount importance in the eighteenth century. Johnson (1752: 395) tells his readers that

> I have laboured to refine our language to grammatical purity, and to clear it from colloquial barbarisms, licentious idioms, and irregular combinations. Something, perhaps, I have added to the elegance of its construction and something to the harmony of its cadence.

Those constructing the standard language did so within notions of a 'propriety' of style. Informality did not go unrecognised, but tended to be referred to in ambivalent if not negative terms. Sundby *et al.* (1991: 46), in their study of eighteenth-century prescriptive grammars, list under 'colloquial' labels, such as 'common style, discourse, conversation, speech', 'familiar', 'popular style', 'careless', 'impetuous' and 'slovenly'. Associations of carelessness and lack of forethought did not rest easy with notions of correctness, precision, purity and elegance – all qualities of the perceived standard. Modern-day sociolinguistic statements regarding the informal styles of the standard language and the 'logical independence of dialect, accent, register and style' (Andersson and Trudgill 1990: 172) would not have made a great deal of sense at this time. Incorporating informality into the construct that was the standard language was a development, and one which is still ongoing. Take, for example, the use of slang, which, in British English, is variably perceived as either non-standard or standard usage by non-linguists and linguists alike. For instance, Crystal (1992: 335) defines slang as 'informal, nonstandard vocabulary' while Andersson and Trudgill (1990) view slang as merely informal usage. Similarly, Andersson and Trudgill (ibid.: 178) classify narrative 'this' (e.g. *I was in the garden and this bird flew by*) as a device of informal style, considering it unsuitable for more formal types of writing, but 'highly recommended ... in informal contexts'. In contrast, Hudson and Holmes (1995) classify the same feature as non-standard in spoken English and suggest that it has no equivalent in standard English.

Conclusion

In taking a rhetorical perspective to the history of English, this chapter has highlighted the interplay between cultural and language style in the context of specific types of speech event. The concept of eloquence encapsulated both behavioural and linguistic ideals for the literate, polite speaker communicating with the literate, polite listener. As such, it touched on all aspects of linguistic structure and was a much broader concept than that of the standard language. Arguably, language standardisation has been given too much emphasis in the history of English. Of equal importance were linguistic styles, those 'cultural practices that are encouraged, perpetuated, challenged, and discarded through time' (Cmiel 1990: 16).

10 Women's writings as evidence for linguistic continuity and change in Early Modern English

Terttu Nevalainen

Honored Deare Brother,

You are, I see, resolved, I must never answer you in your owne language, tis pride enouf to understand itt; and equall comfort to find my stamering understood so well by you.

(CEEC, Tixall: 25; Winifred Thimelby to Herbert Aston, 1660s)

LOVELESS: Will you then make no difference, *Amanda*, between the Language of our Sex and yours? There is a Modesty restrains your Tongues, which makes you speak by halves when you commend; but roving Flattery gives a loose to ours, which makes us still speak double what we think:

(Vanbrugh 1697: 25)

Introduction

The section heading 'The history of non-formal styles and registers in English' raises a number of questions to do with the reconstruction of the spoken language of the past. As audio recordings only go back a century or so, historical linguists' data sources are necessarily limited to written materials. With no direct access to even interviewed speech, let alone to the vernacular,[1] there are obvious problems in using written data sources to access the less formal end of the stylistic continuum at any given time. And the further back in time we go, the narrower the range necessarily becomes.

The history of the English language is therefore largely based on formal and/or literary texts. Until recently, most of these texts were produced by men, which makes the history of English to a great extent a male domain. There are only a few notable exceptions such as Henry Cecil Wyld's *A History of Modern Colloquial English* (3rd edn, 1936). Wyld basically assumed that people wrote as they spoke – except in the case of spelling. Spelling was standardised quite early and no longer reflected the actual pronunciation of English in Tudor and Stuart times. Looking for materials that could reveal the writer's pronunciation, Wyld has this to say about the sources best suited for studying the spoken word of the sixteenth century:

> If the language of books is less individual than that of private letters, it is because in writing a serious literary work, destined for the public, the author was less unrestrained and followed the conventional spelling of the day – rather an elastic one at the best, or the worst – more rigidly than in familiar correspondence.
>
> (Wyld 1936: 113)

Apart from a range of published works written by men, Wyld makes frequent use of personal correspondence produced by men and women alike. It was important for him to get as close as possible to the spoken idiom because his aim was to trace the ancestry of 'Received Standard English' and answer the question 'How soon did men begin to feel that such and such forms were "right" in the spoken language, and that others should be avoided?' (Wyld 1936: 5). He gets closest to spoken forms in personal letters written by women:

> The letters of women, as we saw in the fifteenth century, and shall see again in the seventeenth and eighteenth centuries, are far less carefully spelt as a rule than those of men, and tell us more concerning their actual mode of speech.
>
> (Wyld 1936: 113)

Tudor and Stuart women's letters proved a real goldmine of information for Wyld's investigation because women did not have the same access to formal education as men in those days. Even within the upper ranks, girls were commonly taught reading skills but often no more than elementary skills in writing (see, for example, Cressy 1980: 142–174).

But over and beyond bad spelling, Wyld was not really interested in male and female differences in language use. By contrast, they are of considerable interest to historical sociolinguists today. I will discuss gender variation in domains of language structure and use other than phonology. The focus of this chapter will be on two areas where gender differentiation has often been attested in modern English speech communities: (a) discourse styles and (b) language change. They will be introduced in more detail in the third section (pp. 195–197). My historical material comes from the Early Modern English period, conventionally delimited to the two centuries from 1500 to 1700. Some references will also be made to fifteenth-century English. The Early Modern English period is the earliest from which women's writings have survived in sufficient quantities for this kind of empirical research.

My research question in the empirical part of the chapter is whether there is really need for language histories to pay systematic attention to the ways women and men used English in the past. Can we, first of all, reconstruct similarities and differences in male and female usages in a reliable way? And, secondly, if we can, are they linguistically interesting enough to be included in *general* histories of the language, not just in *alternative* ones? I shall begin by briefly presenting some of the data sources available for historical studies of women's language in the next section, including the *Corpus of Early English Correspondence* (CEEC; *c.* 1410–1682), used in the empirical studies to be discussed in the fourth section (p. 197).

As in most linguistic studies, the comparisons between male and female usages will be made on the basis of the writer's sex, but no biological or determinist interpretation of the findings is implied. The term *gender* will therefore be used to indicate that social factors such as power differences and social roles are likely to provide the more immediate explanations for the ways in which the two sexes used language in the past.

Textual resources

The reasons for the shortage of data of all kinds from earlier periods are well known, and shared by all historians. As Clark and Souden (1988: 18) put it: 'In a less than ideal world the historian has to take pot luck in terms of documentary evidence'. So much of the original evidence has simply disappeared in the course of time. On the other hand, whatever was produced in earlier times was often restricted to certain social groups and professions that required full literacy skills, both reading and writing. Because they were more abundant to begin with, these writings have also had a better chance of surviving. They typically consist of legal, political and religious documents and utilitarian writings of different kinds.

Published writings

As formal education was for a long time a male prerogative, women's writings are generally much rarer than men's. This imbalance in quantity is also reflected in the data collections used by language historians to be discussed below. It is telling that less than 2 per cent of the texts that were published in England in the early modern period were written by women. Figure 10.1 presents the relative frequency of women's writings in the estimated total published material in the seventeenth century by half decade (based on Bell and Crawford 1985: 266). Although the number of women's publications more than doubled in the latter half of the century, the total of all editions of women's writings does not exceed 900 for the whole of the century.[2]

Private writings

The situation looks a little brighter at least in terms of continuity when we move on to non-published writings. The first personal letters written by women go back to the turn of the fifteenth century. Among the very earliest are the letters by Elizabeth Despenser, Lady Zouche, written in 1402 and 1403. But only a handful of the fifteenth-century women's letters that have survived were in fact written by the women themselves (O'Mara 1996). Amanuenses were employed by the Paston women, for instance. But 200 years

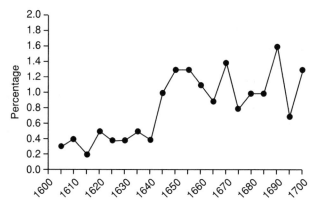

Figure 10.1   Relative frequency of women's writings in the estimated total number of publications in the seventeenth century (after Bell and Crawford 1985: 266)

later, in the seventeenth century, we can readily assume that all gentlewomen knew how to write, and did write their own letters (Heal and Holmes 1994: 252–254). A number of letters written by women of the middle ranks have also been preserved from the sixteenth century onwards.

The other genres that provide early material written by women are diaries and occasional memoranda. It is, however, a sign of the low overall rate of literacy of the female population that no examples have survived of female diaries below the level of the middle ranks from the Stuart period or earlier (Mendelson 1985: 183).

The Corpus of Early English Correspondence

Despite the fact that female letters and diaries have been preserved from the Early Modern English period, they may not necessarily be accessible to the historical sociolinguist. The reason is that a number of them have not been made publicly available in an edited form. And many of those that have been edited have had their spelling modernised by the editor.

The electronic resource used in the studies to be discussed in the fourth section (p. 197) is the *Corpus of Early English Correspondence* (CEEC). Its 1998 version was compiled by the Sociolinguistics and Language History team at the University of Helsinki between 1993 and 1998.[3] It covers the period from the early fifteenth century to 1682, and consists of about 6,000 personal letters in original spelling written by 777 people in all. The average proportion of women's letters is 20 per cent of the total. The vast majority of the women represented in the corpus come from the gentry and the nobility. Our access to gender differences below the gentry is largely restricted to the professional and merchant ranks in the sixteenth and seventeenth centuries. The role of gender in the propagation of linguistic changes can therefore rarely be systematically tested among the middle and lower ranks.

What can be done is, however, most valuable. The correspondence corpus allows us to test hypotheses of gender advantage in language changes that supralocalised, and eventually diffused throughout the country among the higher ranks in the early modern period. As will be shown in more detail in the next section, the changes that are promoted by women in modern speech communities are typically supralocal ones. The corpus also enables us to explore register variation by observing the relative distance between the letter writers and their addressees. It ranges from various relations within the nuclear family to friends and more distant recipients (Nevalainen and Raumolin-Brunberg 1996a; Nurmi 1999; Palander-Collin 1999).

Sociolinguistic 'universals' of language and gender

Language and gender research has generated a great deal of controversy over the last 30 years.[4] But there are also areas of research that tend to produce consistently similar results across speech communities and under different communicative conditions. Two of them will be discussed here, although I would hesitate to call them 'gender universals', at least not in any panchronic sense (which presumably was not the idea of the original researchers either). They are differences observed between women's and men's discourse styles (see below) and their roles in language change (see p. 196).

Discourse style

Previous research shows that men and women can diverge linguistically in ways that basically amount to different discourse styles. Janet Holmes (1998) formulates a list of six potential sociolinguistic universals, which relate to different aspects of communication: function, solidarity, power and status. Her list of generalisations is given below, beginning with the least contentious one, different patterns of language use. Some scientists would even argue that these developmental differences have a biological basis (Chambers 1995: 102–145) – in which case they could be assumed to be truly universal.

1   Women and men develop different patterns of language use (Holmes 1998: 462).
2   Women tend to focus on the affective functions of an interaction more often than men do (ibid.: 463).
3   Women tend to use linguistic devices that stress solidarity more often than men do (ibid.: 468).
4   Women tend to interact in ways which will maintain and increase solidarity, while (especially in formal contexts) men tend to interact in ways which will maintain and increase their power and status (ibid.: 472).
5   Women use more standard forms than men from the same social group in the same social context (ibid.: 473).

6   Women are stylistically more flexible than men (ibid.: 475).

The second tendency is a functional one, and contrasts interpersonal (= affective) and informational (= referential) meanings. In Western speech communities women are more oriented to affective meanings when they are talking to others, while men tend more to referential meanings. The third tendency suggests that women are more positively polite than men and use more discourse devices that take the interlocutor's positive face wants into account (see further Brown and Levinson 1987). The fourth one is closely related to the third and implies a contrast between solidarity and power. In formal, status-enhancing situations it can be measured in terms of global discourse features such as interruptions and amount of talk.

Tendencies 5 and 6 refer to power and social status. Women are found to use more standard-language forms and standard pronunciation than men from the same social group. This may be interpreted in terms of women wanting to appear more statusful than men. But, as Holmes (1998: 474) points out, the interpretation would contradict the fourth tendency. She therefore interprets it in the light of her sixth tendency, women's greater stylistic flexibility: women's ability to adapt to the appropriate style of speech for social dialect interviews. All researchers would not agree with this interpretation, but would view the 'Sex/Prestige pattern' as one of the most robust sociolinguistic universals in its own right (Hudson 1996: 195).

Language change

Another set of generalisations that can be tested with historical data is the role of gender differences in language change. It is a common finding in modern sociolinguistics that women rather than men are in the vanguard of linguistic change. William Labov (1990: 213–215) has formulated two basic principles to describe the roles women and men tend to assume in language change. The first one relates gender to prestige and the diffusion of linguistic changes, and the second to linguistic innovations.

1   In change from above, women favour the incoming prestige form more than men.
2   In change from below, women are most often the innovators.

The two principles do not preclude changes in which men are in advance of women, but these constitute a small minority. Principle 1 is the better documented of the two. It relates to the diffusion of language changes, and suggests that women adopt prestige innovations more readily than men. Principle 1 is especially noticeable in the lower middle class, but it is also observed in societies that are not overtly stratified.

Principle 2 is concerned with the actuation of linguistic changes. While the actual innovators of individual changes cannot usually be located, the principle argues that it is nevertheless possible to approach the issue. The changes from below the level of social awareness it refers to are often traced to upper working-class women, especially in sound changes.

There is also considerable agreement in recent research suggesting that the kind of language change that is particularly associated with women is *supralocalisation*, i.e. the spread of a linguistic feature from its region of origin to the neighbouring areas. Today supralocal processes are typically recorded in phonology. Milroy and Milroy (1993b), Docherty *et al.* (1997) and L. Milroy (1999b) come to the conclusion that strictly localised linguistic forms tend to be preferred by males, whereas the high-frequency variants used by females typically gain a supralocal status. Janet Holmes's studies of New Zealand English support this. Holmes (1997: 131), too, subscribes to the view that the success of innovations, both prestige and vernacular, crucially depends on their being adopted and endorsed by women.

Women's language and linguistic change

Coupled with the general observation of women being readier to adopt linguistic innovation than men, supralocal developments clearly emerge as processes worth testing in the context of Early Modern English as well. Since at that stage the English language did not have one prestige variety that could be called the Standard, least of all in phonology, it makes little sense to approach any potential gender differences in terms of a standard norm. But supralocal processes did exist and can be documented for this stage of the language, too. Many of the grammatical features that were to be codified as part of Standard English in the eighteenth century were simply supralocal features, both prestige and vernacular, from earlier centuries.

Returning to Holmes's interpretation of the 'Sex/Prestige' pattern (see p. 196), it is not too difficult to imagine the leading role of women in supralocal processes as a natural consequence of their greater linguistic flexibility and stylistic adaptability. But before we can postulate a hypothesis like this for Early Modern English, we shall have to demonstrate that there *were* systematic stylistic differences between the two sexes at the time.

Markers of involvement and discourse styles

The issue of male and female discourse styles was addressed by Minna Palander-Collin (1999) using the *Early English Correspondence Corpus* as her data. The analyses that she carried out can be related to the second and third 'gender universals' proposed by Holmes (1998), i.e. that women tend to focus on the affective functions of an interaction more often than men do, and that women tend to use linguistic devices that stress solidarity more often than men (see p. 195).

A number of markers of personal involvement were studied by Palander-Collin in seventeenth-century male and female correspondence, including first- and second-person pronouns (i.e. 'ego' and 'other' involvement), modal auxiliaries expressing possibility and first-person evidential, 'private' verbs (e.g. *assume, believe, doubt, find, guess, suppose* and *think*). For this part of her study she used a socially and temporally matched set of eight men and six women, most of them members of the upper gentry.

Second-person pronouns, markers of addressee orientation, can serve to illustrate the similarities and differences between male and female styles. Passages equally rich in second-person pronouns can easily be found in male and female data, as illustrated below by examples 10.1 and 10.2. The first extract comes from a letter written in 1627 by Lady Brilliana Harley to her husband Sir Robert Harley. The second extract is from Sir Thomas Wentworth's letter to one of his closest personal friends, Christopher Wandesford, dating from 1624. All second-person pronoun instances are shown in bold in the extracts.

(10.1)   … but this day has bine very dry and warme, and so I hope it was with **you**; and to-morowe I hope **you** will be well at **your** journis end, wheare I wisch my self to bide **you** wellcome home. **You** see howe my thoughts goo with **you**: and as **you** haue many of mine, so let me haue some of **yours**. Beleeue me, *I thinke* I neuer miste **you** more then nowe I doo, or ells I haue forgoot what is past. I thanke God, Ned and Robin are well; and Ned askes every day wheare **you** are, and he says **you** will come to-morowe. My father is well, but goos not abrode, becaus of his fiseke. I haue sent **you** vp a litell hamper, in which is the box with the ryteings and boouckes **you** bide me send vp, with the other things, sowed up in a clothe, in the botome of the hamper. I haue sent **you** a partriche pye, which has the two pea chikeins in it, and a litell runlet of meathe, that which I toold **you** I made for my father. *I thinke* within this muthe, it will be very good drinke. I sende it vp nowe becaus *I thinke* carage when it is ready to drincke dous it hurt; thearefore, and please **you** to let it rest and then taste it; if it be good, I pray **you** let my father haue it, because he spake to me for such meathe. I will nowe bide **you** god night, for it is past a leauen a cloke.

(CEEC, Harley: 3; Brilliana Harley 1627)

(10.2)   … **Yow** maie aduise herein with Sir Henry Fane, who is acquainted with the busines, and (if I bee not farr wide) will giue **yow** all the helpe and furtherance hee can; but bee close, for this is I tel **yow** *El mio secreto*. Here **yow** haue a little sprinklinge of Italian, but as for Latine not a word, since it seemes **your** store in that language is all spent and know except **yow** afford mee some in **your** letter, **yow** gett none in myne, reservinge it for more sublimated spiritts then moue in **your** heauy fatt carcaise; yet beginne assoone as **yow** dare, I will a warrant **yow** haue as hott as **yow** bringe and soe **yow** shall find itt ... I haue allmost finished my this yeare's building, which dun, I shall then apply my selfe with such sages as **your** selfe to build upp the polliticall walles and repaire the ruinous breaches of the comon wealthes and I trow shew **yow** too that deseruedly I hold my selfe a maisterpeece in architecture and turne 2 or 300 of **yow** to scoole againe, like a companie of poore fellowes as **yow** are. Am I not now as good as my word? and haue I not enlarged my penne ouer this side too and draw out my lynes as lastingly as a silke worme? Beleeue it, *I thinke* few men could haue made so much of so little and so fare **yow** well, **your** euer most assured freind and affecconate kinsman, Th. Wentworth.

(CEEC, Wentworth: 214–215; Thomas Wentworth 1624)

But individual examples do not necessarily tell the whole story. A more reliable result can be obtained by calculating the overall frequencies of a given feature over a large body of data and normalising them to a fixed amount of data, say 10,000 words. Palander-Collin (1999: 242) shows that Brilliana Harley in fact uses the most second-person pronouns among her six female writers (513 in 10,000 words), while Thomas Wentworth is one of the two men to employ it more than 350 times per 10,000 words – 375, to be precise. On average, women use 368 second-person forms per 10,000 words, but men only 293.

Second-person pronouns turn out to be indicative of the use of the other markers of personal involvement as well: although individual variation is in evidence, women also score systematically higher overall frequencies than men in the use of first-person pronouns (690 vs. 556 times per 10,000 words), possibility modals (95 vs. 84 per 10,000 words), and private verbs in the first person (57 vs. 39 per 10,000 words) (Palander-Collin 1999: 247).[5]

Palander-Collin also tested some of these findings against a larger body of male and female correspondents by analysing the single most frequent 'private' verb, the epistemic expression I THINK, with data from 136 men (551,800 words) and seventy-seven women (240,200 words). The chief aim of this analysis was to find out whether the relationship between the writer and the recipient of the letter was responsible for the observed differences in style. Although the correspondence in the CEEC is personal, written by one individual to another, the distance between the correspondents varies. Four major categories of recipient can be distinguished in the CEEC data: (1) nuclear family members (i.e. parents, children and spouses), (2) other family members, (3) close friends and (4) other, more distant recipients. The overall results for the period 1600–1681 are shown in Table 10.1.

The results are consistent: women use I THINK systematically more than men. The male range – with friends receiving the highest frequency – is in fact very narrow, while considerably more variation can be found in women's letters, with the highest frequencies in the nuclear family. If we break down

Table 10.1 The gender distribution of I THINK (per 10,000 words) in four seventeenth-century registers (after Palander-Collin 1999: 240)

Addressees/writers	Family, nuclear	Family, other	Friends	Others
Men	9.4	9.7	10.2	8.9
Women	22.3	17.1	14.2	19.4

the nuclear family data from the eight male and six female informants discussed above, the male average of I THINK in letters written to spouses is higher (13.5 per 10,000 words) than in letters either to parents (7.6 per 10,000 words) or children (7.3 per 10,000 words). The rank order remains the same in women's data but the frequencies are much higher: letters to spouses receive the highest frequency (27.1 per 10,000 words), those to parents come second (22.7 per 10,000 words) and letters to children third (16.2 per 10,000 words) (Palander-Collin 1999: 243).

There are three instances of I THINK in Brilliana Harley's letter extract in 10.1 (italicised in the text). Of the three, the first one is most likely to have been employed in the 'find' sense to express the writer's opinion, as is the sole instance of I THINK in the last sentence of Thomas Wentworth's letter extract in 10.2. Both are preceded by a conventional appeal to the listener, *believe me/it*. The third instance of I THINK in Harley (*I sende it vp nowe becaus I thinke carage when it is ready to drincke dous it hurt*) may have been employed to convey the writer's belief rather than her opinion. An in-depth study of possible semantic differences between female and male uses of these and other private verbs could throw more light on Holmes's sixth universal of women's stylistic sensitiveness. But the mere fact that these involvement features are used much more liberally by women than by men in comparable circumstances does speak in favour of systematic stylistic differences in earlier English, too. More studies, both qualitative and quantitative, will of course be needed to support the case but these first findings are encouraging.

Supralocal processes of language change

This section tests the hypothesis of women being the leaders in linguistic change by systematically comparing female and male data on ongoing changes during the Early Modern English period. All the changes to be examined are processes of supralocalisation. They are, moreover, features that were to be codified as part of Standard English in the eighteenth century. It is often the case that standardisation was superimposed on features which had gained a supralocal status well before the era of normative grammar. The data to be discussed in this section clearly support the hypothesis of women being the leaders in grammatical changes. But they also indicate that there were domains of language use, and consequently of language change, that lay outside the leading influence of women.

The role played by gender was tested by analysing a number of processes of linguistic change in the sixteenth and seventeenth centuries in quantitative terms (for details, see Nevalainen and Raumolin-Brunberg forthcoming). Ten of them will be discussed here. They can be characterised grammatically in different ways. Most of them involve morpheme replacement in that a form originally used in a given regional or social dialect is generalised in the literate social ranks throughout the country. The majority of these forms originated in the south. But there are notable exceptions such as the third-person singular present indicative suffix -*s*, a form of northern origin that replaced the southern -TH in the sixteenth and seventeenth centuries (see example 10.3, below). Similarly, the replacement of the possessive determiners MINE and THINE by the short forms MY and THY first began in the north (see example 10.4). Sometimes a widely used form associated with the City of London came to be abandoned in favour of a form propagated by higher social circles. This is what appears to have happened with the complex relative pronoun THE WHICH, which was replaced by the simple form WHICH (example 10.5). The following illustrations, from both women and men, present recessive forms in (a) and incoming forms in (b); this pattern will also be followed in the rest of the examples. John and Sabine Johnson in 10.4 and 10.5 were husband and wife and came from the ranks of well-to-do merchants.[6]

(10.3a) This **hath** changed my resolucon, for I intend now to staie here a fortnight longer ...
(CEEC, Wentworth: 215; Thomas Wentworth 1624)

(10.3b) I haue sent you a partriche pye, which **has** the two pea chikeins in it ...
(CEEC, Harley: 3; Brilliana Harley 1627)

(10.4a) At my departing from Callais, amongest other thinges that I desired you to take pains in **myne** absens from thens ...
(CEEC, Johnson: 582; John Johnson 1546)

(10.4b) The couart shal be cepte here on Fryday next. **My** ounckell Bryand and Mr. Douse wel be here at yet;
(CEEC, Johnson: 623; Sabine Johnson 1546)

(10.5a) Your letter by Mr. Brudenell I have receyved, for **the which** I thancke you.
(CEEC, Johnson: 266; Sabine Johnson 1545)

(10.5b) Victor hath gotten a byll of him **which** is signed by hys aunt, Joes Diricken's wyfe, ...
(CEEC, Johnson: 323, John Johnson 1545)

Some morpheme replacements resulted in more transparent or analytical forms. One of them is the spread of ITS, the innovative possessive form of the neuter personal pronoun, combining IT with the possessive -S. It was introduced at the end of the sixteenth century to compete with the historical neuter possessive HIS and its paraphrases THEREOF and OF IT (see example 10.6). Another process that increased analyticity in the English pronoun system was the replacement of relative adverbs in WH- by phrases consisting of a preposition and a WH-pronoun (e.g. *whereof* vs. *of which*; see example 10.7).[7]

(10.6a) ... the newes of your Lordship's good helth espetially understanding by Mr Greene that **the** state **therof** hath these hollydaies bene somthing ill desposed and uncertaine.
(CEEC, Wentworth: 38; Thomas Wentworth 1623)

(10.6b) Geometry had **its** beginning first in our knowledge since the flood from Aegypt, and there's good reason for it.
(CEEC, Conway: 38; Anne Conway 1651)

(10.7a) I shall ryght hertely desier you that we maye mete as we have done, trusting that these holydaies ye wil be hier, **wherof** bothe my wyf and I wold be glad.
(CEEC, Johnson: 231; John Johnson 1545)

(10.7b) I perceve that you arrived in savety at Callais, and that the plage is well seased, the Lord be prased, **of the which** I am glad to here;
(CEEC, Johnson: 289; Sabine Johnson 1545)

When a grammatical morpheme acquires a new function, the process may be seen not only as its functional expansion but also as a case of restructuring the system it is a member of. In our data these cases include the spread of the object pronoun YOU into the subject function and the disappearance of the historical subject form YE in the sixteenth century (see example 10.8). Another kind of generalisation took place when multiple negation disappeared between the fifteenth and eighteenth centuries: negative concord with negative indefinites (NOT plus NO/NEVER, etc.) was replaced by a system with a single negator followed by non-assertive indefinites (NOT plus ANY/EVER, etc. example 10.9). This process extended the use of these forms from other non-assertive contexts such as comparative and conditional clauses (IF ... ANY, EVER, etc.) to overtly negative ones.[8]

(10.8a) ... glad of Ratchelle's amendement. I praie you comme not moche at her yourself, leest **ye** get the dysease yourself.
(CEEC, Johnson: 395; John Johnson 1545)

(10.8b) Mr. Douse is nowe at London for the same mater: if **you** spake with hym, **you** shall knowe all.

                      (CEEC, Johnson: 245; Sabine Johnson 1545)

(10.9a) Har answar was that she wold **not** set har myend to **no** man tell she was delyvered and choirched ...

                      (CEEC, Johnson: 396; Sabine Johnson 1545)

(10.9b) ... for in good faithe I promes youe I had **no** joye of **annything**.

                      (CEEC, Johnson: 1250; John Johnson 1551)

Some of the changes directly affected clause and phrase structures. The demise of multiple negation was followed by another syntactic change, the rise of inverted word-order after clause-initial negative conjunctions and adverbs (NOR, NEITHER, NEVER) in Early Modern English (see example 10.10). Phrase structures were affected when the OF-phrase object of the gerund began to be replaced by a direct noun-phrase object (example 10.11). This process steadily increased the verbal characteristics of the gerund phrase from the sixteenth century onwards. Finally, ONE began to appear after adjectives used as nouns in Late Middle English. This use of ONE as a prop-word to mark the head of a noun phrase gained momentum and was generalised in the early modern period (example 10.12).[9]

(10.10a) Your gold that you sent me by Ambrose is not yett exchaunged, **nor I can** gett but xlvj *s st.* for an once therof ...

                      (CEEC, Johnson: 121; Otwell Johnson 1544)

(10.10b) I perceyve youre opinion of owre monneyes, which dissentyth not partely from others I have herd of beffore; **neither dyd I** suppose anny better sequele of it.

                      (CEEC, Johnson: 1476; Anthony Cave 1551)

(10.11a) ... bicause that she hathe bene with me a longe time, and manye years, and hathe taken great labor, and paine **in brinkinge of me up** in lerninge and honestie ...

                      (CEEC, Royal I: 154; Elizabeth I 1548)

(10.11b) I assure you, you ar wel worthy of suche traitors, that, whan you knewe them, and had them, you betraied your owne seurty **in fauoring ther liues**.

                      (CEEC, Royal I: 58; Elizabeth I 1590)

(10.12) I with all your lytell **ons** be in helthe, the Lord be prasid ...

                      (CEEC, Johnson: 668; Sabine Johnson 1546)

The illustrations in examples 10.10 and 10.11 do not focus on gender variation as such but rather on two facts shared by all these processes of change. First, both recessive and innovative forms could be used by women and men alike. So in example 10.10, two male contemporaries, the wool merchants Otwell Johnson and Anthony Cave, use both inverted and direct word order after clause-initial negative elements. The change is under way, and at this point it is the direct word-order (10.10a) that is generally the more frequent of the two. The second point to be made is that one and the same person could well use both recessive and innovative forms. The illustrations in example 10.11 contain two gerunds by Queen Elizabeth I: 10.11a shows the recessive object form with *of*, and 10.11b the incoming one without it. The instance in example 10.11a was penned by Princess Elizabeth in her teens, but since the construction was receding very slowly it frequently occurs in her later correspondence, too. In fact the older structure still prevails in the language today. The same is true of ONE shown in example 10.12. Although the use of the prop-word continues to expand in the Late Modern English period, we still have noun phrases such as *the rich* and *the poor* without a prop-word head.

Turning now to the evidence provided by the CEEC on these ten changes, a clear pattern emerges: of the ten processes, seven are led by women and three by men. They are specified in Table 10.2.

There is no single linguistic pattern associated with the changes promoted by either gender, but both morpheme replacements and innovative forms and processes are involved. The chronology of the processes varies, too. Some, such as the spread of YOU in the subject function, were completed in the sixteenth century, many in the seventeenth, while a few, such as the object of the gerund, had not run their course even by the end of the millennium.

What they all appear to have in common is that their gender alignment is not altered as the process advances in the early modern period: a change continues to reflect the same gender difference until it nears completion.

Table 10.2 Gender advantage in ten Early Modern English processes of change (based on Nevalainen and Raumolin-Brunberg forthcoming)

Gender advantage/process of change	Female	Male
1 Spread of -s	+	−
2 Spread of MY/THY	+	−
3 Rise of YOU	+	−
4 Spread of prop ONE	+	−
5 Rise of ITS	+	−
6 Rise of direct object of gerund	+	−
7 Loss of relative adverbs	+	−
8 Spread of WHICH	−	+
9 Loss of multiple negation	−	+
10 Rise of negative inversion	−	+

Note
+, led; −, not led.

Usually the difference appears in our data when a change has passed its incipient stage and can be labelled, following Labov (1994), as young and vigorous. The incoming feature is then used more than 20 per cent of the time.

The women in the CEEC need not, however, be the innovators of the changes that they are shown to lead. In many cases this is not very likely. These literate women mostly come from the gentry, but there is evidence to suggest that many of the linguistic changes originated from the middle or lower ranks. But it is significant that these upper-ranking women were an innovative force in their own social ranks and systematically adopted the forms and structures in question earlier than their male social peers.

This is true with the exception of the three changes at the foot of Table 10.2, which were promoted by male writers: the generalisation of the simple relative pronoun WHICH; the replacement of multiple negation by single negation followed by non-assertive indefinites; and the introduction of (subject–auxiliary/verb) inversion after clause-initial negative adverbs and conjunctions. In the last case our material is not very plentiful, but male advantage is clearly attested when the change is progressing from the young and vigorous stage to mid-range.

There are more data on WHICH and the disappearance of multiple negation. Both can be associated more or less directly with literate and educated usage. Single negation with non-assertive forms is particularly promoted by educated and professional men such as the administrators at the Royal Court. It was also the male Court circles that favoured the use of WHICH instead of THE WHICH. As the change reached mid-range in the latter half of the fifteenth century, the incoming form could receive institutional support from the printing press, which had been established in Westminster. What the changes promoted by male writers had in common at the time is that they were closely associated with circles whose linguistic practices were only indirectly accessible to women. A recent study (Rissanen 2000: 125) indicates that the use of non-assertive forms with negatives, for instance, was a feature of the legal language as early as the latter half of the fifteenth century.

Discussion

As pointed out in the introduction, past histories of English have rarely taken an interest in women's writings. When texts produced by women are considered at all, it is typically to make use of their spelling variation in order to learn more about the pronunciation of the English language, specifically of the precursor of the standard, as in Wyld (1936). In the previous section, the view was challenged that linguistic differences between male and female writers were necessarily *only* a matter of education or, in the case of women, the lack of it. To argue the point, I turned to personal letters that have come down to us from the early modern period, and examined stylistic variation and grammatical changes in progress in the light of the findings reported in Palander-Collin (1999) and Nevalainen and Raumolin-Brunberg (forthcoming).

Systematic gender variation could indeed be found in the way a number of linguistic devices were used to mark personal involvement. Men and women displayed precisely the kind of differences that have been found by modern researchers: as far as the affective (interpersonal) functions of interaction were concerned, female and male patterns showed consistent quantitative differences. The patterns consisted of involvement markers such as first- and second-person pronouns, modals and private verbs. The findings persisted when a closer analysis of four addressee categories was carried out with the epistemic expression I THINK. Besides showing lower frequencies in all the addressee categories, male writers displayed a much narrower range of variation than female writers.

Consistent gender differences could similarly be detected in processes of language change. Women were systematically ahead of men in most of the processes examined. For a number of reasons these differences cannot be interpreted purely in stylistic terms – men being closer to the standard that was taking shape, for instance, as Wyld found with spelling. The case was, in fact, precisely the opposite: the 'non-standard' features promoted by women later found their way into Standard English. Unlike in spelling, high-ranking men, too, adopted these incoming forms, albeit at a slower rate than women. The generalisation of these syntactic and morphological features cannot therefore be readily understood in terms of the modern 'Sex/Prestige' interpretation.

Written registers normally differ from spoken, but there are also some that closely approximate colloquial speech both today and in the past. As shown by Biber (e.g. 1995: 280–300), this list is headed by drama and personal letters. Although we have a case for arguing that early modern men typically used a less interactive register in their correspondence than women, it is unthinkable that their basic syntax and morphology were consistently less colloquial than women's. We should also bear in mind that, just like today, not all linguistic changes were conscious in earlier English either, but most of them spread naturally from below the level of social awareness. An example of such a change is the subject form YOU. The merchant Otwell Johnson regularly used the form in his letters to his sister-in-law Sabine Johnson, and Sabine similarly favoured YOU in her letters to both Otwell and John Johnson, her husband. But John, Otwell's brother and fellow merchant, hardly used the incoming form at all in his numerous letters to either of them (see examples 10.8a, 10.8b and 10.10a above).

While spelling is something that has to be taught in all ages, vernacular changes take place outside the classroom (besides, in Tudor and Stuart classrooms, boys did not learn English but Latin). Both ideologically and institutionally it would therefore be misleading to draw a direct parallel between modern notions of Standard English and the situation in early modern England. In this era before explicit codification and prescription, closer analogies can perhaps be found in supralocal usages, and notions such as Alexander Gill's (1619) *communis dialectus*, 'General Dialect', which he contrasts with other regional and social dialects. As we have seen, both regional and social differences can also be reconstructed using the correspondence corpus. A case in point is the spread of the northern third-person singular -*s*, which was slower in reaching East Anglia than the capital region. Women were also found in the vanguard of the change in East Anglia (Nevalainen *et al.* 2000).

Historical gender differences in language use may therefore perhaps be understood in the more fundamental sense of *difference* argued for by many modern sociolinguists: women are not just reflecting the general usages of their time, they are creating them (for modern parallels, see for example Milroy and Milroy 1993b: 65; Holmes 1997: 135). But, as our data have also shown, not all supralocal usages were spread by women in early modern England. The features promoted by men, such as the disappearance of multiple negation, were connected with professional or educated usage. They were favoured by the institutionally educated section of the male population in their private correspondence as well.

A satisfactory sociohistorical account of gender would need to compare male and female patterns of mobility and social networks, range of social roles, privileges and obligations. This would clearly go beyond the limits of this chapter. Let me therefore conclude by focusing on an issue that has already been touched upon and relates to all the others: education. It was used above to explain the male advantage in changes that were associated with professional language use. But education may have had an effect on the use of the vernacular, too. It is worth quoting a contemporary early modern view by citing the anonymous author (probably Mary Astell or Judith Drake) of *An Essay in the Defence of the Female Sex* (1696: 57–58):

> For Girles after they can Read and Write … are furnish'd among other toys with Books, such as *Romances, Novels, Plays* and *Poems*; which … give'em very early a considerable Command both of Words and Sense; which are further improv'd by their making and receiving Visits with their Mothers, which gives them betimes the opportunity of imitating, conversing with, and knowing the manner and address of elder Persons. These I take to be the true Reasons why a Girl of Fifteen is reckon'd as ripe as a Boy One and Twenty and not any natural forwardness of Maturity as some People would have it. These advantages the Education of Boys deprives them of, who drudge away the Vigour of their Memories at Words, useless ever after to most of them, and at Seventeen or Eighteen are to begin their Alphabet of Sense, and are but where the Girles were at Nine or Ten.

The author refers to popular views on maturational differences between boys and girls (*natural forwardness of Maturity*) but emphasises the role of linguistic contacts, upper-rank girls being early on exposed to a wider range of linguistic variation than boys. This, combined with the stylistic flexibility attributed to women – one of the potential universals proposed by Holmes (1998) – may be partly responsible for women's sensitivity to usages outside their local spheres.[10]

Conclusion

Systematic empirical studies based on personal correspondence indicate that male–female differences can be observed in Early Modern English. Moreover, they lend support to the kinds of gender difference seen today in patterns of language use and in processes of linguistic change. In the latter, it was women who were found to promote most of the supralocal processes discussed in this chapter.

Linguistic gender differences in earlier periods of the English language definitely merit the interest of language historians. The extent to which this history can be reconstructed is an empirical matter. Despite obvious material limitations, only the tip of the iceberg has been studied so far. Historical sociolinguistics and pragmatics will be instrumental in providing new perspectives for more balanced – and exciting – histories of the English language in the future.

Notes

1 Sociolinguists typically use the term 'vernacular' to refer to language used by speakers when they are not being observed by the linguist: 'the language used by ordinary people in their everyday affairs' (Labov 1972: 61–62, 69) and 'the style in which the minimum of attention is given to the monitoring of speech' (Labov 1972: 208). For further discussion, see for example Milroy (1992: 66–67).
2 Seventeenth-century women's published texts fall into such categories as religion (prophecy, prayers, Quaker literature), literature (songs, plays, poems, fiction), translations, political writings (pamphlets, educational writings, group petitions, philosophy), advice (practical advice of various kinds, mother's advice), lives (autobiographies, personal justifications, confessions), advertisements and various formal documents (Crawford 1985: 268–274). The Brown University Women Writers Project aims to make accessible an electronic database of women's writing in English from 1330 to 1830. Their online database was published in 1999 and covers a period from 1400 to 1850. For more information, see http://wwp.stg.brown.edu/project/.
3 This 1998 version of the CEEC was compiled by the Sociolinguistics and Language History team at the Department of English, University of Helsinki: Jukka Keränen, Minna Nevala, Arja Nurmi, Minna Palander-Collin, Helena Raumolin-Brunberg and Terttu Nevalainen. The copyright of the corpus and its published sampler version CEECS, available on the second ICAME CD-ROM, is the property of the project team.
4 See, for example, the collections of articles in Coates (1998) and Bergvall *et al.* (1996), especially the review article on prestige speech forms by James (1996). Labov (2001) also deals extensively with the matter.
5 It is interesting to compare these figures with those obtained from written dialogues of different types. Culpeper and Kytö (2000: 184–185) analysed four

types of dialogue from the period 1600–1720, and got the following average frequencies, here normalised to 10,000 words:

	Witness depositions	Trial proceedings	Prose fiction	Drama (comedy)
First-person pronoun	105.5	578.9	371.8	643.8
Second-person pronoun	62.9	297.3	210.8	443.0

With the exception of second-person pronouns in comedies, the women studied by Palander-Collin exhibit higher frequencies of both first- and second-person pronouns than the four speech-based genres, whereas the male usage approximates that of trial proceedings. Private verbs were also counted by Culpeper and Kytö, but their figures, based on sixty-eight verbs (and all persons), are not directly comparable with those analysed here, which were based on thirty-two items used in the first person (Palander-Collin 1999: 246).

6 There is a vast literature on the history of the third-person forms. For some recent corpus-based contributions, see Kytö (1993) and Nevalainen *et al.* (2000). On the possessive determiners in Middle English, see Mustanoja (1960: 157), and on WHICH/THE WHICH, Raumolin-Brunberg (2000).

7 On the history of ITS, see Nevalainen and Raumolin-Brunberg (1994), and analytic and synthetic tendencies in English, e.g. Danchev (1992).

8 For discussions of YE and YOU, see also Lutz (1998) and Nevalainen (2000), and on the disappearance of multiple negation Nevalainen (1998) and Iyeiri (1999).

9 Inversion after initial negatives is discussed by Nevalainen (1997) and Bækken (1998: 267–281), the English gerund by Fanego (1996) and the history of prop-word ONE by Rissanen (1997).

10 For contemporary early modern attitudes and commentary on gender, see Gowing (1996), Mendelson and Crawford (1998), Foyster (1999) and Okulska (1999).

11 Discourse markers in Early Modern English

Andreas H. Jucker

Introduction[1]

The following extract is taken from Shakespeare's *The Merry Wives of Windsor* (MWW):

> (11.1) *Evans*:   But that is not the question: the question is concerning your marriage.
>
> *Shallow*: Ay, there's the point, sir.
>
> *Evans*:   *Marry*, is it; the very point of it – to Mistress Anne Page.
>
> *Slender*: *Why*, if it be so, I will marry her upon any reasonable demands.
>
> (MWW I.i.220–226)[2]

Words such as *marry* and *why* at the beginning of the third and fourth utterance, in the way they are used here, are discourse markers. It is difficult to say what exactly they mean, and it is difficult to translate them into other languages. They are part of the interaction between the two speakers. In some sense they convey the speaker's attitude towards what is going on at the moment. *Marry* is a mild oath; it emphasises the utterance in which it occurs. And *why* conveys the speaker's surprise at the previous utterance.

There is extensive research literature on discourse markers in Present Day English, but so far only a few studies have been devoted to their historical development. This has several reasons. Such elements are typical of the spoken rather than the written language. As such they are less likely to occur in historical data. Moreover, research into the history of English has tended to focus on pronunciation, the structure of words and the structure of sentences, but not on the communicative aspects of the language and on the interaction between speakers of the language.

However, many discourse markers are regularly attested in several types of historical data. In the Early Modern English period, they are particularly common in plays, fiction and trial records. These genres have in common that they represent spoken language in a written form. Plays consist entirely or almost entirely of dialogues to be spoken by actors. In fiction, authors often include accounts of conversations between the characters of the narrative. And trial records give a more or less faithful account of the spoken interaction in the courtroom.

It is debatable how closely fictional dialogues in plays and fiction resemble the real spoken language of the time, but they contain many features that are absent from other types of language and that are similar to features that in Modern English are part of spoken language. The same features also occur in the transcriptions of court records, which purport to be accounts of actual spoken language. In these cases, too, we cannot be sure how accurate the rendering of potential discourse features is, because we have insufficient knowledge of how much the court clerks edited the words they wrote down. It is reasonable to assume that some utterances were transcribed very carefully, for instance if the words of a libel case had to be reported. In other cases some features, such as hesitations or repetitions, will have been edited out as irrelevant performance errors.

However, these limitations of the historical data should not be seen as serious impediments, because the concept of 'spoken language' as a coherent and homogeneous entity is in any case unrealistic or rather counterfactual. Spoken language occurs in many different contexts and in many different discourse types, and even for Modern English, where the data situation is much better than for older stages of the language, any description has to take into account the internal variation between different types of discourse. The descriptions of individual discourse markers that are offered here should therefore not be seen as imperfect statements about the 'real' spoken language in earlier centuries. They are attempts to describe how playwrights and authors of fiction chose to represent dialogues, and how court clerks transcribed the spoken reality of court proceedings.

Discourse markers: definition and delimitation

There is very little agreement among scholars working on discourse markers as to which elements should be included and which elements belong to some other category. I will adopt a prototype approach with a list of features that are typical for discourse markers. Prototypical discourse markers will exhibit most or all of these features; less prototypical markers will have fewer features or exhibit them to a limited extent only. The following list of features is based on Brinton (1996: 33–35) and Jucker and Ziv (1998: 3). It distinguishes between defining criteria on the level of phonology, syntax and semantics, and descriptive features on the functional and stylistic level.

I shall start with the phonological level, for which we lack direct evidence in historical data. Discourse markers are generally short and often phonologically reduced. The discourse marker *you know*, for instance, is often pronounced with a reduced first syllable, which in the written form is sometimes represented as *y'know*. In Early Modern English *I pray you* is variously abbreviated to *pray you* or just *pray*, and *in faith* is abbreviated to *faith*. Discourse markers often form a separate tone group, and many of them are marginal forms and hence difficult to categorise in terms of traditional word classes. In historical data this criterion is more difficult to apply since there is no way of checking the actual pronunciation beyond the orthographic representation, which may or may not reflect the phonological reduction.

The next set of features concerns the syntactic level. Discourse markers tend to occur at the beginning of sentences, and they are generally not part of the syntactic structure, or they are only loosely attached to it. The omission of a discourse marker does not render a sentence ungrammatical, or – in other words – discourse markers are generally optional. In example 11.2, *you know* is fully integrated into the syntax of B's utterance. *You* is the subject and *know* the verb, which takes the direct object *two languages*. If the two words were left out, the sentence would be incomplete and probably not understandable. In this case, *you know* is not a discourse marker. In A's utterance, on the other hand, *you know* could be dropped without affecting the understandability or the basic truth of the sentence. Here, *you know* is a discourse marker that collocates with the discourse marker *like*.

> (11.2)   B: So *you know* two languages, English and ... Spanish?
>   A: Well, I know Spanish, but I don't consider myself *like*
>   *you know*, fluent or anything
>
> (12A1i)

In historical data, this criterion is again often more difficult to apply than in modern data. There are numerous cases in which it is difficult to decide whether a particular element is part of the grammatical structure or not. Punctuation is an unreliable guide in such cases because it was generally added by later editors (Blake 1996: 124). Extract 11.3 gives an exchange between Rivers and Lady Gray in *The Third Part of King Henry the Sixth* (3H6):

> (11.3)   Riu.   Madam, what makes you in this sodain change?
>   Gray.   *Why* Brother Riuers, are you yet to learne
>   What late misfortune is befalne King Edward?
>   Riu.   *What* losse of some pitcht battell gainst Warwicke?
>
> (3H6, IV.v.1-4)

The spelling given in 11.3 is taken from the Folio version of 1623. Lady Gray's utterance starts with the discourse marker *why*. It collocates with the vocative *Brother Riuers*, to whom Lady Gray addresses a yes/no question. She wants to know whether Rivers already knows of the King's misfortune or not. In the Oxford compact edition *why* is followed by a comma, which suggests that the vocative, *Brother Rivers*, is bracketed off so that Lady Gray asks for the reason why Rivers is yet to learn about King Edward's misfortunes.

The quarto version of this play, moreover, has a comma after the initial *what* in Rivers's second utterance. The comma suggests that *what* is a discourse marker standing outside the syntactic structure of the question. The lack of a comma, on the other hand, suggests that it is part of the question (see Blake 1996: 124).

Perhaps the most important feature for discourse marker status can be found on the semantic level. Discourse markers tend to have little or no semantic content or propositional meaning, which means that a true sentence is true, and a false sentence is false, whether or not it contains a discourse marker. The prototypical discourse marker *well* satisfies this criterion, while the more marginal discourse markers *y'know* and *like* have some residue of semantic meaning.

In addition to the above features on the levels of phonology, syntax and semantics, discourse markers tend to share features on the functional and stylistic level. They are generally multifunctional, that is to say they operate on several linguistic levels simultaneously. The discourse marker *well*, for instance, often functions both on the textual and on the interpersonal level. Discourse markers are more typical for oral rather than written discourse, and they are generally associated with informality. They tend to be very frequent in spoken discourse, and speakers are often unaware of how frequently they use them.

Distribution of discourse markers in Early Modern English

The distribution of discourse markers in the Early Modern English text samples in the Helsinki Corpus (see Chapter 10) is – not surprisingly – very uneven. In fact, there are only three genres in which discourse markers occur with any noticeable frequency at all: in the genres plays, fiction and trial records. In the plays they have an average frequency of 9.2 discourse markers per 1,000 words. The corresponding values for fiction and trials are 4.0 and 1.5 respectively.

All the other genres in the Helsinki Corpus have very few discourse markers or none at all. In the genres biographies, handbooks, autobiographies, sermons, translations of Boethius and private letters they average between 0.5 and 0.7 tokens per 1,000 words. In educational texts, the Old Testament, diaries and travelogues they average approximately 0.1 tokens. And in histories, legal texts, the New Testament, official letters and scientific writings no discourse markers are attested at all. This breakdown indicates that the frequency of discourse markers is a direct correlate of the amount of (representations of) spoken language that is likely to occur in any particular genre. But it must be stressed that this is not the only influencing factor. Trial records and plays both consist almost entirely of representations of spoken language, while in fiction the spoken language is interspersed in non-dialogic prose, but nevertheless fiction has a much higher incidence of discourse markers than trial records.

The distribution across time also varies. The Helsinki Corpus distinguishes between three Early Modern English periods of 70 years each: From 1500 to 1570, from 1570 to 1640 and from 1640 to 1710. There is a considerable and mostly consistent increase in the frequency of discourse markers throughout the three subperiods. The trial records show an increase from 0.6 in the first subperiod to 0.9 in the second and to 3.1 in the final subperiod. The respective figures for fiction are 1.5, 3.7 and 6.7. The most impressive increase, however, is attested in the plays. Here there is an increase from 4.1 in the first subperiod to 11.7 in the second with a very slight decrease to 11.0 in the final subperiod. All the other genres taken together remain on a very low level throughout the three subperiods. They average between 0.2 and 0.3 in all three subperiods (see Figure 11.1).

Figure 11.1 gives the aggregate values for five discourse markers across the three genres plays, fiction and trial records in the three Early Modern English subperiods of the Helsinki Corpus. Four of the five discourse markers show an increase in frequency from a low level to a much higher level. The increase is particularly pronounced for the markers *O/oh* and *pray/prithee*. It is least pronounced in the case of *well*, but even here there is a steady increase. In the case of *marry*, on the other hand, there is a steady decrease in the frequency. However, the aggregate values hide the considerable differences that exist between the three different genres. The relevant values for the three individual genres are shown in Figures 11.2–11.4.

The patterns for the plays and for fiction are fairly similar. They both show very pronounced increases for *O/oh*, but the increase for *pray/prithee* is more marked in the plays than in fiction. The values for *well* are higher in

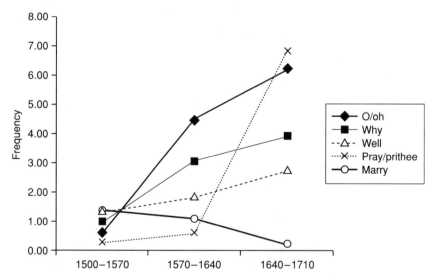

Figure 11.1 Frequency of five Early Modern English discourse markers (number of tokens per 1,000 words) in the genres plays, fiction and trial records in the Helsinki Corpus

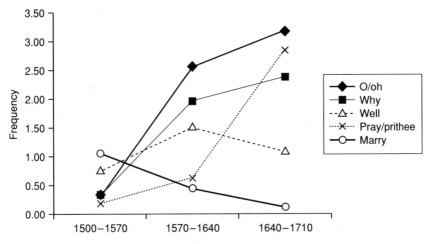

Figure 11.2 Frequency of five Early Modern English discourse markers (number of tokens per 1,000 words) in the play samples of the Helsinki Corpus

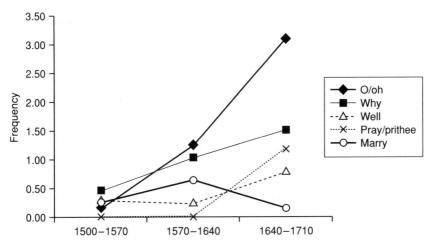

Figure 11.3 Frequency of five Early Modern English discourse markers (number of tokens per 1,000 words) in the fiction samples of the Helsinki Corpus

the plays than in fiction, but the development in both cases is not consistent. The values for *marry* start out at a higher level in the plays. In fiction they show an initial increase from the first to the second period, but in both genres they end up with equally low values in the third period. The trial records are noticeably different. All markers have relatively low frequencies except for *pray/prithee*, which shows a very high level in the third period. *O/oh* has a moderate peak in the second period, and *well* has a peak in the third.

It appears that the distribution of discourse markers is highly genre specific. The sample analyses on pp. 217–229 will show that the reason for this seems

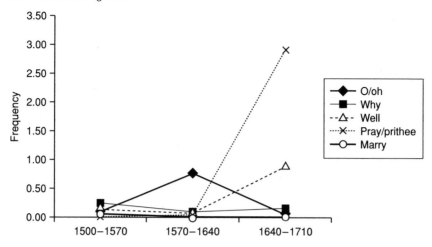

Figure 11.4 Frequency of five Early Modern English discourse markers (number of tokens per 1,000 words) in the trial record samples of the Helsinki Corpus

to be the preference of individual markers to occur in specific speech acts. *Pray* and *prithee*, for instance, occur almost exclusively in questions and requests, both of which are pervasive in trial records.

Pragmaticalisation and subjectification

The previous section has shown that individual discourse markers may become more popular and increase their frequency, or they may gradually become less popular and eventually fall out of use. In addition discourse markers may change their functions in the course of time. This poses the interesting question of whether all discourse markers undergo the same kind of development or whether every single marker develops in an entirely new and unpredictable way.

In fact, it seems that several discourse markers derive from lexical material with propositional meaning. Thompson and Mulac (1991) and Aijmer (1997) describe the development of the matrix clause *I think (that)* to the discourse marker *I think*. Thompson and Mulac (1991) call this a process of grammaticalisation in which a main clause construction becomes lexicalised as an epistemic adverb. Aijmer (1997), however, argues that the term grammaticalisation should be reserved for cases such as *(be) going to*, in which a lexicalised structure develops into a grammatical marker of futurity. In the case of *I think*, on the other hand, a lexicalised structure is recruited to serve a pragmatic function that involves the speaker's attitude towards the hearer. For this process Aijmer uses the term 'pragmaticalisation'. An element undergoing such a process loses its semantic or truth-conditional meaning (semantic bleaching) and at the same time increases its potential for conversational implicatures and its attitudinal meaning (pragmatic strengthening).

Traugott (1989, 1995) has proposed the notion of 'subjectification' as a pragmatic motivation for processes of grammaticalisation and pragmaticalisation. It entails multidimensional processes involving correlated diachronic continua. She argues that meaning changes tend to be unidirectional, which she defines as:

> the tendency to recruit lexical (propositional) material for purposes of creating text and indicating attitudes in discourse situations; in other words, the tendency for 'meanings to become increasingly based in the speaker's subjective belief state/attitude toward the proposition'.
>
> (Traugott 1995: 47)

Discourse markers have their individual histories, and at any given time some discourse markers serve more textual functions and others serve more interpersonal functions. And for every individual marker different functions may co-exist at certain periods and may even co-occur in the same text. Below I will try to place five different discourse markers that were prevalent in the Early Modern English period both on a cline of pragmaticalisation and on a cline of subjectification.

Illustrative analyses

O, oh: exclamation and information management

O – together with its spelling variant *oh* – is the most frequent discourse marker in the data samples of the Helsinki Corpus in the Early Modern English period. It is the most frequent discourse marker both in the genres plays and fiction in this period. In the genre trials, on the other hand, it ranks only third. According to the *Oxford English Dictionary* (OED), it goes back to Early Middle English but did not exist in Old English. It occurs in front of a noun or name in the vocative or independently expressing a variety of emotions, such as appeal, entreaty, surprise, pain, lament and so on.

(11.4) 2 Prom.:   What time of the year is 't, sister?
       C. Wench.:   *O*, sweet gentlemen,
       I am a poor servant, let me go.
       1 Prom.:   You shall, wench,
       But this must stay with us.
       C. Wench.:   *O*, you undo me, sir!
       'Tis for a wealthy gentlewoman that takes physic, sir;
       The doctor does allow my mistress mutton.
       O, as you tender the dear life of a gentlewoman!
       I'll bring my master to you; he shall show you
       A true authority from the higher powers,
       And I'll run every foot.
       (*Chaste Maid in Cheapside* II.ii.133–141)

In this extract two informers (called promoters) stop a country wench because she appears to be carrying meat with her, which is illegal during the time of the Lent prohibition. The second promoter asks her for the time of the year. She realises the real purpose of the question and implores them to let her go. In her first utterance, she addresses them with the vocative *O, sweet gentlemen*. The first promoter allows her to leave but indicates that she must relinquish her meat. In her second utterance, she uses *O* twice in her desperate appeal to the two promoters to let her keep the meat.

Taavitsainen (1995: 453–458) notes that in Early Modern English in addition to its occurrence with vocatives and exclamatory sentences *O* is often used in mild swearing or at the beginning of a negative remark or a violent protestation. She provides the following examples (Taavitsainen 1995: 455):[3]

(11.5)   What a Herod of Jewry is this? *O* wicked, wicked world! One that is well-nigh worn to pieces with age to show himself a young gallant!

(MWW II.i.20–22)

(11.6)   Yell.:   [*To Touchwood Junior*] What is 't you lack?
Touch.Jun.:   [*Aside to Moll*] *O*, nothing now; all that I wish is present; –

(*Chaste Maid in Cheapside* I.i.167–168)

(11.7)   Lady.:   Thou liest, brevity!
Sir Ol.:   *O*, horrible! Dar'st thou call me 'brevity'?
Dar'st thou be so short with me?

(*Chaste Maid in Cheapside* II.i.147–148)

If these analyses are compared with accounts of *oh* in Present Day English, a change of focus can be observed from the exclamatory function to a function as a marker of information management.

According to Schiffrin (1987), for instance, *oh* is a marker of information management. It typically occurs in repair sequences or as an information receipt.

It marks shifts in speaker orientation (objective and subjective) to information which occur as speakers and hearers manage the flow of information produced and received during discourse. Orientation shifts affect the overall information state of a conversation: the distribution of knowledge about entities, events, and situations. Although *oh* is a marker of cognitive tasks, its use may have pragmatic effects in interaction.

(Schiffrin 1987: 100–101)

Extract 11.8 gives a relevant example.

(11.8) Freda: Sometimes he got a notice for staying out past curfew.
Recently. In August, that was.
Val: *Oh* curfew? What's curfew?
Freda: A certain time that children have to be in.
Val: *Oh* your children. *Oh* I see. *Oh* it's personal. *Oh* I-... I
thought there might be police or something.

(Schiffrin 1987: 81)

Val precedes both her request for clarification (her first utterance in this
extract) and her acknowledgement of the clarification (her second utterance)
by *oh*.

Jucker and Smith (1998: 180–82) following Heritage (1984) also analyse
oh as a marker of a change of state of information. Heritage (1984: 336)
maintains that *oh* is basically a response cry and backward looking. For the
same reason, Jucker and Smith classify it as a reception marker. *Oh* occurs in
response to new information or in repair sequences (Heritage 1984; Schiffrin
1987).

Heritage (1984: 336) observes that *oh* is particularly prevalent in question–
answer sequences, but that it does not occur in non-conversational or quasi-
conversational question–answer sequences, such as medical consultations,
news interviews or courtroom examinations. This conforms to the small
number of instances in trial records in the Early Modern English data.

It appears from the examples given above that *oh* had a more exclamatory
function in Early Modern English and that it has a more text-structuring
function indicating the process of information management in Present Day
English. To this extent, the Early Modern English *oh* is an interjection rather
than a discourse marker, while Present Day English *oh* is a proper discourse
marker. It had already reached the end of the subjectification cline in Early
Modern English, and it was already fully pragmaticalised.

Why: surprise and protest

The discourse marker *why* can occur both as a preface to a question or as a
preface to a statement. It indicates that the speaker cannot understand what
has just gone before. According to the speaker the previous utterance does
not seem to make sense. In the words of the OED: 'As an expression of surprise
(sometimes only momentary or slight; sometimes involving protest), either
in reply to a remark or question, or on perceiving something unexpected'.
The OED lists examples from the early sixteenth century to the end of the
nineteenth century.

Culpeper and Kytö (1999) analyse *why* as a hedge, not as a discourse marker,
but this categorisation overlaps largely with my understanding of a discourse
marker. They argue that in trial proceedings *why* often occurs at points of
acrimony. It signals a break-down in the question–answer sequence. Judges

use it to express disbelief in a witness's evidence, and the witnesses use it to present an answer as if it were a self-evident truth. Or it occurs when the speaker indicates surprise at his/her interlocutor's lack of understanding. It seems to say 'don't you understand?'; 'don't you see?'; or 'isn't this obvious?'

When *why* prefaces a question, it indicates some kind of perplexity on behalf of the speaker.

(11.9)   Touch. Jun.:   Brother, I have sought you strangely.
        Touch. Sen.:   *Why*, what's the business?
                              (*Chaste Maid in Cheapside* II.i.124–125)

When the discourse marker *why* prefaces a statement, it indicates a certain amount of incredulity that the following point needs uttering at all. To the speaker what is to follow seems self-evident and without need of explanation. It 'introduces a statement which appears to draw the logical conclusion from what has gone before'; it has the sense of "'Well, that's settled, we're in agreement'" (Blake 1996: 128).

(11.10) Maid: There's a gentleman,
                  I haply have his name too, that has got
                  Nine children by one water that he useth:
                  It never misses; they come so fast upon him,
                  He was fain to give it over.
        Lady: His name, sweet Jug?
        Maid: One Master Touchwood, a fine gentleman,
                  But run behindhand much with getting children.
        Sir Ol.:   Is't possible?
        Maid.   *Why*, Sir, he'll undertake,
                  Using that water, within fifteen year,
                  For all your wealth, to make you a poor man,
                     You shall so swarm with children.
                          (*Chaste Maid in Cheapside* II.i.173–183)

In this example a maid tells Sir Oliver Kix and his wife of a man who purports to have a solution to their unfulfilled wish for a child, but both of them seem to be incredulous and rather slow in joining in the maid's enthusiasm. In her third utterance the maid has to make her claims more explicit. The introductory *why* expresses her exasperation at their apparent lack of understanding.

(11.11) 2 Prom.:   I am so angry, I'll watch no more today.
        1 Prom.:   Faith, nor I neither.
        2 Prom.:   *Why* then, I'll make a motion.
        1 Prom.:   Well, what is't?
                       (*Chaste Maid in Cheapside* II.ii.170–172)

The two promoters, who make a living of catching people who break the Lent prohibition, have been tricked by a country wench. She abandoned her basket with what the promoters believed was a sheep's head but turns out to be a baby. The promoters are now obliged to adopt the baby and provide for her. At this point they decide to give up catching prohibition breakers for the day.

(11.12) but as I am your Maid, I am not bound to you, and therefore I take the greater priviledge, but if you'd Marry me, I know # what I know. *Tom. Why*, what do you know Joan? suppose I should Marry thee: *Ione*. Indeed Sir, I'de be the lovingest Wife that ever was made of flesh and blood, I'le be so kind. *Tom*. How kind wouldst thou be? *Ione*. Ah master, so kind as my mistris us'd to be to you, # if not kinder, you may remember Sir that in her days I us'e to lye in the Truckle bed; O then master. *Tom. Why* what then Jone. *Ione*. Oh dear master, ask me no more questions,

(*Penny Merriments*)

In extract 11.12 Tom's servant, Joan, insinuates in various ways that he would be much better off if he were to marry her and have her as a wife rather than as a servant. Tom gets increasingly impatient at the opaque allusions and keeps asking her to be more explicit. Two of these questions are accordingly prefaced by the discourse marker *why*.

The discourse marker *why* has become rare in Present Day British English. In a random sample of the *British National Corpus* only five out of 1,000 occurrences of *why* turned out to be discourse markers. In Present Day American English it still seems to be common. As a discourse marker, *why* functions mainly on the interpersonal level. It is fully pragmaticalised and subjectified because it expresses the speaker's emotions and attitudes towards the utterances of his or her interlocutor. In Early Modern English and in Present Day American English it co-existed and co-exists with *why* in its propositional function. It is interesting to note that in Present Day British English the pragmatic function has receded almost entirely, while the propositional function is still an integral part of the language.

Well: frame and face-threat mitigator

A precursor of the discourse marker *well* is already attested in Old English, where it occurs in the form *wella*. As such it is used as an attention signal that can be paraphrased as 'listen to what I have to tell you'. It always occurs in contexts that are related to the spoken language, for instance in fictional writing at the beginning of a speech or at the beginning of a conclusion after an exposition (see Jucker 1997: 96–97). In this use it is similar to Old English *hwæt*, which is often used at the beginning of a poem or at the beginning of speech (see Brinton 1996). Both *hwæt* and *wella* in its function as an attention signal did not survive beyond the Old English period.

In Middle English, *well* made a new start. Here it is only found in one structural pattern. It always introduces direct reported speech as in the following examples.

> (11.13)   This Cook, that was ful pale and no thyng reed,
>   Seyde to oure Hoost, 'So God my soule blesse,
>   As ther is falle on me swich hevynesse,
>   Noot I nat why, that me were levere slepe
>   Than the beste galon wyn in Chepe.'
>   '*Wel*,' quod the Maunciple, 'if it may doon ese
>   To thee, sire Cook, and to no wight displese, ...
>
>   [*The Manciple's Prologue* (MancPro) IX 20-29]

> (11.14)   I woll have nothynge upon me but my shyrte and my swerde in
>   my honde, and yf thou can sie me, quyte be thou for ever.' 'Nay,
>   sir, that woll I never.' '*Well*,' seyde sir Launcelot, 'take this lady
>   and the hede, ...
>
>   (*Morte Darthur*)

In these examples as in all other Middle English examples, *well* functions as a text-structuring element. It collocates with reporting clauses containing either the verb 'say' or 'quethe' in the form *sayd*, *seyde* or *quoth*, and it can always be paraphrased as 'if this is so'. The speaker acknowledges the previous utterance by his interlocutor and draws an appropriate conclusion. This usage does not seem to be a direct continuation of the Old English *wella*. It is more likely that the Middle English discourse marker *well* derives directly from the adverb *well* meaning 'in a way appropriate to the facts or circumstance; fittingly, properly' (OED2, well adv. sense 5; see Jucker 1997: 99). Thus the Middle English data show the first stages of the pragmaticalisation process.

In Early Modern English the functions of *well* diversify. All the examples in the Helsinki Corpus from texts before Shakespeare still follow the Middle English pattern, but in Shakespeare's plays *well* is used both with a textual function, marking a topic boundary, and with an interpersonal function, marking a potentially face-threatening situation. The following passage in Shakespeare's *Merry Wives of Windsor* is particularly rich in occurrences of *well*:

> (11.15)   Quick.:   ... Have not your worship a wart above your eye?
>   Fent.:   Yes, marry, have I, what of that?
>   Quick.:   *Well*, thereby hangs a tale. Good faith, it is such
>   another Nan; but (I detest) an honest maid as ever
>   broke bread. We had an hour's talk of that wart. I
>   shall never laugh but in that maid's company! But,
>   indeed, she is given too much to allicholy and musing;
>   but for you – *well* – go to.

Fent.   *Well*; I shall see her to-day. Hold, there's money for
         thee. Let me have thy voice in my behalf. If thou seest
         her before me, commend me.

Quick.   Will I? I' faith, that we will; and I will tell your worship
         more of the wart the next time we have confidence,
         and of other wooers.

Fent.   *Well*, farewell. I am in great haste now.

                                        (MWW I.iv.146–161)

These instances have both a text-structuring and an interpersonal function.
They can no longer be paraphrased in a consistent fashion. Mistress Quickly
starts her second utterance of this extract with *well* in response to a question
that she does not want to answer. Towards the end of the same utterance, she
switches gear and gives Fenton a piece of advice. He responds by suggesting
that he does not really need the advice. He already expects to meet Anne
Page later the same day. In Fenton's last utterance in this extract, he wants
to finish the conversation.

Extract 11.16 is taken from the records of the Trial of Lady Alice Lisle.
The Lord Chief Justice allows Alice Lisle to produce a defence witness.

(11.16)   *L. C. J.*:   Look you, Mrs. *Lisle*, that will signify little; but if you
                        have any Witnesses, call them, we will hear what they
                        say: Who is that Man you speak of?

          Lisle: *George Creed* his Name is; there he is.

          L. C. J.:   *Well*, what do you know?

          Creed: I heard *Nelthorp* say, that my Lady *Lisle* did not know
                        of his coming, nor did not know his Name; nor had
                        he ever told his name, till he named himself to Col.
                        Penruddock when he was taken.

          L. C. J.:   *Well*, this is nothing; she is not indicted for harbouring
                        Nelthorp, but *Hicks*.

                                        (Alice Lisle)

The Lord Chief Justice prefaces his question to the defence witness, George
Creed, with *well*. As a text-structuring device it marks the beginning of a
new interaction, even if it turns out to be a very brief one. His response to
Creed's statement is again prefaced by *well*, which in this instance indicates
his dissatisfaction with what Creed had to say. It does not – according to him
– relate to the charges brought against Alice Lisle.

Fuami (1997) has analysed the use of the discourse marker *well* in
Shakespeare's *The Merry Wives of Windsor*. He notes that the Quarto and the
Folio editions of this play differ considerably in the way in which *well* is used.
The much longer Folio text has considerably fewer occurrences of *well*. Fuami
suggests that the earlier Quarto text uses more colloquial language because
it was a version of the play that was used for less sophisticated audiences. In

this sense, *well* can be considered to be a style marker indicative of colloquial or less formal style.

In Present Day English four basic functions can be distinguished. *Well* can be used as a frame marker, a face-threat mitigator, a qualifier and a pause filler. As a frame marker it indicates the beginning of a new topic. As a face-threat mitigator it indicates some problems on the interpersonal level. The face of the speaker or the hearer is threatened. In this function it prefaces disagreements, rejections of offers or refusals of a request. As a qualifier, it indicates a problem on the content level, in particular when an answer is not optimally coherent with the preceding question. The speaker may not have the necessary information or she may wish to challenge a presupposition of the question. As a pause filler, finally, *well* is used to bridge interactional silence.

If we ignore Old English *wella*, which does not seem directly related to the later development of the discourse marker *well*, the oldest function is the one as a frame, which goes back to Middle English. In Early Modern English it adopted the additional function of a face-threat mitigator. In the pragmaticalisation process it adopted additional and more interpersonal functions, that is to say it also underwent subjectification. The remaining two functions developed later (see Jucker 1997). However, it must be noted that this development of *well* could also be the result of the availability of relevant sources. *Well* may have been used as pause filler, for instance, for a very long time, but only in contexts in which it was unlikely to be recorded in written texts.

Pray, prithee: polite requests

The discourse markers *pray* and *prithee* are short forms of *I pray you* and *I pray thee*. In Early Modern English these and similar forms (*pray you, I pray, I prithee*) were used in questions and requests to add deference. They render an utterance more polite and less imposing. The verb 'to pray' also regularly occurs in its religious use of making a devout and humble supplication to God or some other deity. Busse (2000) investigates these forms in Shakespeare's plays. He notes that the most frequent form is *I pray you*, which occurs 233 times in the whole corpus (excluding plays of dubious authorship). The other forms, *pray you, pray (other), pray, I pray thee, I pray, pray ye, we pray you, I pray them, I prithee* and *prithee* are less frequent. The forms *pray* and *prithee* are attested seventy-one and ninety-two times, respectively, in the same corpus. However, in my own counts I have only included abbreviated and pragmaticalised forms *pray* and *prithee* but not the full forms with both subject and object.

Kryk-Kastovsky (1998: 48) reports that *pray* and *prithee* are the most frequent pragmatic particles, as she calls them, in her data of two extracts from trial transcripts, i.e. the Trial of Titus Oates and the Trial of Lady Alice Lisle. In the former she counted twenty-six instances of *pray* and only one of *prithee*, while in the latter transcript she found twelve instances of *prithee* and only one of *pray*. Kryk-Kastovsky also points out that it is only the interrogator who uses *pray* and *prithee*. This is not surprising since the defendants and the witnesses are not in a position to ask questions, and therefore there is no need for them to use these discourse markers. *Prithee* is fairly rare throughout the Early Modern English text samples of the Helsinki Corpus. It occurs in only six out of eighty-one text files; it is restricted to four genres. In addition to trial records it is attested in fiction, plays and private letters. Moreover, it occurs only in the third subperiod of Early Modern English (1640–1710). In other genres neither *pray* nor *prithee* are particularly frequent discourse markers. They seem to be particularly suited to the formality of the court-room situation and to the inquisitive speech acts that are used by the interrogators.

It would seem plausible that *prithee* is a less deferential version of *I pray you*, since it incorporates the familiar address form *thou*. However, Brown and Gilman (1989), who analyse politeness formulae in four of Shakespeare's tragedies (*Hamlet, King Lear, Macbeth* and *Othello*), conclude that *prithee* functions as an in-group identity marker and, therefore, has to be classified as a positive politeness strategy. *Pray you*, in contrast, is a deference marker. Busse (2000) modifies their results and argues that the dichotomy is not clear-cut. There is a considerable amount of overlap between the two categories. He also finds that *prithee* collocates not only with *thou*, as is to be expected, but also regularly with *you*. He concludes that 'the first component was phonemically reduced, and *-thee* lost its morpheme status and became part of a monomorphemic word' (Busse 2000: 216).

The following are relevant examples.

(11.17) *L. C. J.:*   *Pray*, when he came to Town again, where did he lodge?

                                                                   (Titus Oates)

(11.18) *Mr. At. Gen.:* *Pray* swear Mrs. *Duddle*, and Mrs. *Quino*.

                                                                   (Titus Oates)

(11.19) *Mr. Sol. Gen.:* *Pray* will your Lordship give my Lord and the Jury an account, when Mr. *Ireland* came to your House, an how far he travelled with you afterwards?

                                                                   (Titus Oates)

(11.20) *L. C. J.:*   What say'st thou? *Prithee* tell us what the Discourse was?

                                                                   (Alice Lisle)

(11.21) *L. C. J.:*   *Prithee*, I do not ask thee what thou did'st not, but what thou did'st?

                                                                   (Alice Lisle)

(11.22) *L. C. J.*:   *Prithee*, let me ask thee one Question, and answer
                            me it fairly; Did'st not thou hear *Nelthorp*'s Name
                            named in the Room?

                                                                    (Alice Lisle)

(11.23) *L. C. J.*:   *Prithee* be ingenuous, and let's have the Truth on't?

                                                                    (Alice Lisle)

These examples are all taken from trial records. Examples 11.17–11.19 are
taken from the Trial of Titus Oates and examples 11.20–11.23 are from the
Trial of Lady Alice Lisle. It can be noted that all instances are utterances by
the interrogators. In the trial of Titus Oates, the interrogators strongly prefer
the marker *pray*, while in the Trial of Lady Alice Lisle the Lord Chief Justice
prefers *prithee*. All utterances in these extracts are either requests or questions.
In example 11.18 the Attorney General gives the instruction for two witnesses
to be sworn in. Otherwise all examples are questions, which can also be seen
as requests, i.e. requests for information. The utterances are followed by a
question mark irrespective of their syntactic form.

The following examples are taken from genres other than trial records.
Examples 11.24 and 11.25 are taken from fiction and 11.26 and 11.27 are
taken from plays.

(11.24) I say Jone I could find in my heart to make thee Mistriss of my
         household, and Lady of my family, all which you know Ione is
         honour in abundance, but first I say you must subscribe and
         consent to my divers causes and considerations. *Ione. Pray* master,
         what be those causes & considerations, # I'le do any thing rather
         then lose my longing.

                                                              (*Penny Merriments*)

(11.25) I will Sir upon this condition, that you will grant # me two things
         that I shall ask you. *Tom*. Ay, ay, Joan, any thing I say, any thing,
         prithee # speak quickly, for I begin to be in haste now.

                                                              (*Penny Merriments*)

(11.26) Yell.:   Of what weight, sir?
         Touch. Jun.: Of some half ounce; stand fair and comely
                       with the spark of a diamond, sir; 'twere pity
                       To lose the least grace.
         Yell.:   *Pray*, let's see it.
                                         [*Takes stone from Touchwood Junior.*]
                       Indeed, sir, 'tis a pure one.
                                         (*Chaste Maid in Cheapside* I.i.170–174)

(11.27) Touch. Sen.:   I have no dwelling;

I brake up house but this morning. *Pray thee*, pity me;
I am a goodfellow, faith, have been too kind
To people of your gender; ...
(*Chaste Maid in Cheapside* II.i.90–93)

This discourse marker is no longer used in Present Day English. It is a case of pragmaticalisation from *I pray you* to *pray* and from *pray thee* to *prithee*. In the full form the phrase still has propositional meaning. In its abbreviated form, the meaning is primarily pragmatic. In Early Modern English both the full form and the pragmaticalised form coexist. In this case, therefore, the fully lexical structure with propositional meaning (*I pray you/thee*) co-occurs with its derived forms as discourse markers (*pray* and *prithee*) that have undergone a partial pragmaticalisation and subjectification process.

Kryk-Kastovsky (1998) speculates about the reasons for the disappearance of *pray* and *prithee*. She suggests that *pray* was ousted by the French *please* because *please* in contrast to *pray* was devoid of religious connotations and was, therefore, more appropriate for an increasingly secularised public life. Busse (2000), on the other hand, suggests that in colloquial speech a shift in indirect requests can be observed. While in Early Modern English the emphasis was on the expression of the speaker's sincerity (*I pray you*), it turned to the expression of doubt whether the addressee is willing to perform the act (*please*) (Busse 2000: 233).

Marry: obvious answers

In the Early Modern English text samples of the Helsinki Corpus, the discourse marker *marry* is almost entirely restricted to the genres plays and fiction, and even in these genres it is not particularly frequent. It has a history as a religious invocation and is thus the result of a pragmaticalisation process. It is first attested in the second half of the fourteenth century, and – according to the OED ('marry') – goes back to 'the name of the Virgin Mary used as an oath or an ejaculatory invocation'. The OED entry goes on to suggest that in the sixteenth century *marry* had become a mere interjection and was no longer perceived as a religious invocation. Fischer (1998: 36) hypothesises that there is a general tendency for religious oaths to develop into pragmatically weaker assertions or interjections and to lose their religious association in the process. He uses the OED on CD-ROM as a database and searches all the quotations, not just the entry for 'marry', for occurrences of this discourse marker. The first examples occur – according to the periodisation of the Helsinki Corpus – in the third Middle English subperiod (1350–1420). There is a steady increase up to a peak in the second Early Modern English subperiod (1570–1640). Afterwards the occurrences decline rapidly. Fischer notes that the OED's bias towards literary language may underrepresent the actual occurrences in more speech-based genres. Additionally it should be mentioned that the peak in the second Early Modern English period may be exaggerated.

This period includes the Shakespeare quotations and has a much higher number of illustrative quotations than earlier or later periods. Fischer's figures are not normalised to take account of the different amounts of data for each of his subperiods. In any case, the discourse marker was archaic or obsolete by the nineteenth century.

Fischer (1998: 44) postulates the following functions for the discourse marker *marry*:

> As a discourse marker *marry* performs a series of well-defined functions. It may initiate an utterance, but is found most often at the beginning of a second turn, indicating that this turn is the second part of an adjacency pair. As such it may be an answer to a question, or a (sometimes emotionally coloured) reaction to a statement. *Marry* generally signals some emotional involvement (sometimes quite weak, sometimes strong), which is hard to pinpoint, however.

He goes on to note that there do not seem to be any significant changes in the functions of *marry* over time.

The following are relevant examples:

(11.28) Chat: Nay, how prouest thou that I did the deade.
         D. Rat: To plainly, *by S. Mary*. This profe I trow may serue, though I no word spoke. *Showing his broken head.*
         Chat: Bicause thy head is broken, was it I that it broke? I saw thee Rat I tel thee, not once within this fortnight,
         D. Rat: No *mary*, thou sawest me not, for why thou hadst no light, But I felt thee for al the darke, beshrew thy smothe cheekes, And thou groped me, this wil declare, any day this six weekes. *Showing his heade.*
                                                    (*Gammer Gvrtons Nedle*)

(11.29) Ford.:   Were they his men?
         Page.:   *Marry*, were they.
         Ford.:   I like it never the better for that. Does he lie at the Garter?
         Page.:   Ay, *marry*, does he. If he should intend this voyage toward my wife, I would turn her loose to him; and what he gets more of her than sharp words, let it lie on my head.
                                                    (MWW II.i.177–184)

(11.30) What is the next, William? sayes the king. *Marry*, this is the next: what is the cleanliest trade in the world? *Marry*, sayes the king, I think a comfit-maker, for hee deales with # nothing but pure ware, and is attired cleane in white linen when hee sels it. No, Harry, sayes [{he to}] the king; you are wide. # What say you, then? quoth the king. *Marry*, sayes Will, I say a # durtdauber.

(Nest of Ninnies)

Extract 11.28 is particularly interesting because one of the two speakers uses both the religious invocation *by S. Mary* and the abbreviated form *mary*. In all the examples, *marry* occurs at the beginning of an answer. It seems to suggest that in the opinion of the respondent the answer is rather obvious and the questioner might have known it himself.

In Present Day English the discourse marker *marry* has become obsolete. It dropped out of favour after the middle of the seventeenth century, and in the nineteenth century it must have been archaic and dialectal (Fischer 1998: 39). In Early Modern English, it co-existed with the propositional use of *marry*. As a discourse marker it was fully pragmaticalised and it performed both textual and interpersonal, i.e. subjectified functions.

Conclusion

Discourse markers are a very rich area of investigation for historical linguists, even if they are still ignored by most traditional histories of the English language. I have chosen the markers *oh*, *why*, *well*, *pray/prithee* and *marry* because they are the most frequent ones in my data and because they are very different from each other. *Oh* is a discourse marker that could also be analysed as an interjection. The discourse marker *why*, on the other hand, must be distinguished from the question particle or conjunction *why*. *Well* is the most prototypical discourse marker. It has both text-structuring and interpersonal functions. *Pray* and *prithee* are pragmaticalised forms of the parenthetical phrase *I pray you/thee* and serve as markers of deference. *Marry*, finally, is a pragmaticalised form of the religious invocation *by the Virgin Mary*. *Oh* and *well* still exist in Present Day English, *why* is restricted to American English, and *pray/prithee* and *marry* are only used as archaisms or humorously – if at all – in Present Day English.

The analysis has focused on three issues. First, the distribution of discourse markers is genre specific and linked to orality. In Early Modern English they are more or less restricted to the genres play, fiction and trial records. In all other genres of this period they are either rare or they do not occur at all. The individual markers also have different preferences to associate with specific speech acts, and to the extent that these speech acts have different frequencies in different genres, they are responsible for genre-specific variation of the frequency of individual markers.

Second, the frequency of discourse markers varies in time. Some markers increase in popularity and become more frequent, while other markers drop out of use and become obsolete. I have briefly mentioned *hwæt* and *wella*, which both did not survive beyond Old English. *Marry* and *pray* became popular in Late Middle English and Early Modern English but have dropped out of use since then. *Oh* and *well*, on the other hand have had a very long history as discourse markers and they are still pervasive in Present Day English.

And finally, several of the discourse markers analysed above could be shown to be the result of a pragmaticalisation process. Linguistic expressions with propositional uses were recruited to perform increasingly textual and interpersonal functions. In many cases these pragmaticalised forms co-existed for a period of time with the propositional function of the original expression. In addition, for many markers a subjectification process can be observed, that is to say they are used with increasingly interpersonal functions that express the speaker's emotions and attitudes towards the addressee.

Appendix: Sources

12A1i: Conversation between two California students. Private collection.

3H6: Shakespeare, William. *The Third Part of King Henry the Sixth*. Extract 11.3 gives the First Folio spelling, quoted after Blake (1996: 124)

Alice Lisle: The Trial of Lady Alice Lisle. A Complete Collection of State-Trials and Proceedings for High-Treason, and Other Crimes and Misdemeanours; From the Reign of King Richard II. to the End of the Reign of King George I. Second Edition, Vol. IV. Ed. F. Hargrave. London: Printed For J. Walthoe Sen. Etc., 1730. Quoted after Helsinki Corpus file CETRI3B.

Chaste Maid in Cheapside: Middleton, Thomas. *A Chaste Maid in Cheapside*, 1630. Ed. R. B. Parker. London: Methuen, 1969.

Gammer Gvrtons Nedle. By Mr. S[tevenson, William]. Mr. of Art. The Percy Reprints, 2. Ed. H. F. B. Brett-Smith. Oxford: Basil Blackwell, 1920. Quoted after Helsinki Corpus file CEPLAY1B.

MancPro: Chaucer, Geoffrey. *Canterbury Tales, The Manciple's Prologue*. The Riverside Chaucer, 3rd edition. Ed. Larry D. Benson. Boston: Houghton Mifflin, 1987.

Morte Darthur: Malory, Thomas. *Morte Darthur. The Works of Sir Thomas Malory*. Ed. E. Vinaver. London: Oxford University Press, 1954. Quoted after Helsinki Corpus file CMMALORY.

MWW: Shakespeare, William. *The Merry Wives of Windsor*. The Riverside Shakespeare. Ed. G. Blakemore Evans. Boston: Houghton Mifflin, 1974.

Nest of Ninnies. Fools and Jesters: With a Reprint of Robert Armin's Nest of Ninnies, 1608. London: The Shakespeare Society, 1842. Quoted after Helsinki Corpus file CEFICT2A.

Penny Merriments. Samuel Pepys' Penny Merriments. Ed. R. Thompson. London: Constable and Company Limited, 1976. Quoted after Helsinki Corpus file CEFICT3A.

Titus Oates: The Trial of Titus Oates. A Complete Collection of State-Trials and Proceedings for High-Treason, and Other Crimes and Misdemeanours; From The Reign of King Richard II. to the End of the Reign of King George I. Second Edition, Vol. IV. Ed. F. Hargrave. London: Printed for J. Walthoe Sen. Etc., 1730. Quoted after Helsinki Corpus file CETRI3A.

Notes

1 My thanks go to Rosemary Bock and Irma Taavitsainen, who read an earlier draft of this chapter. Their comments led to substantial improvements. The usual disclaimer applies.
2 The bibliographic details of all data sources are given in the Appendix (above).
3 I quote the extracts given by Taavitsainen with more context and from the editions mentioned in the Appendix (above).

Epilogue

12 Broadcasting the nonstandard message

David Crystal

In 1986 BBC television presented a nine-part series on the English language – *The Story of English* – which was the first major attempt by that medium to deal seriously with this topic.[1] The following year, I was approached, in a collaboration with Tom McArthur, to produce an eighteen-part radio version for the BBC World Service. I thought this would be an easy job. We were given access to the television scripts and footage, from which I assumed it would be a straightforward matter to select and rewrite. The assumption proved to be wildly wrong. I was underestimating the crucial difference between programmes made for radio and those made for television. The 'talking head' – the *sine qua non* of radio – proved to be so ancillary to the striking visual image that, when we came to listen to the recordings, there proved to be little that could be adapted directly. The TV dialogue and voiceovers routinely depended on the visual context in ways that made the audio tape ambiguous or unintelligible. Discourse was disrupted, from an auditory point of view, by visual sequences, some of which wandered away from the linguistic focus – for example, in the programme dealing with Shakespeare's influence on English, the viewer was taken on an interesting (but not wholly linguistically relevant) tour around Anne Hathaway's cottage! It made excellent television, but impossible radio. We had to begin from scratch, and found ourselves constructing our own 'story of English' anew.

This anecdote illustrates how easy it is to be taken in by the metaphor of the 'story' of a language. No language, as the opening chapter of this book stresses (Milroy, Chapter 1), has a single story. There are plainly many 'stories' of English, intricately and unpredictably interacting as they unfold through time. The character of each story will be affected by all kinds of constraints. One constraint is evidently the nature of the medium: the radio story cannot be the same as the television story. To illustrate further: the presentation of the written language (through manuscripts, inscriptions, handwriting styles, scribal idiosyncrasies, and so on) can be handled explicitly by television and only very indirectly by radio; conversely, radio greatly privileges the spoken word, allowing extended monologue of a kind that television eschews. But if we conflate radio and television, under the heading of *broadcasting*, a further contrast appears – between the story that this medium is able to tell and the story as told by conventional publishing. Textbooks on the post-medieval history of English, as the Introduction to this volume makes clear, tend to ignore dialect richness, concentrating 'on Standard English in England, with an occasional nod in the direction of the USA' and lacking 'consideration of the rich diversity and variety of the language'. Broadcast accounts of the history of English, however, have done exactly the reverse.

The Story of English begins with a series of introductory shots covering (*inter alia*) air-traffic control, magazines in India, newspapers abroad, American movies, popular music, and the Scottish Hebrides. We see a castle on the isle of Barra, and hear the voiceover telling us that it is 'the ancestral home of an old Scottish family, the Clan MacNeil'. Then we see the presenter of the series, Robert MacNeil, who introduces himself to the viewers in this way:

> My name is also MacNeil, Robert MacNeil. My branch of the clan left Scotland four generations ago and settled in the United States and Canada. I was brought up in Halifax, Nova Scotia, and educated in Canadian schools. The way I speak English is a product of that background, modified by 30 years as a journalist in Britain and the United States.

The voiceover continues:

> Like the people of Barra, people throughout the British Isles, in North America and around the world, we all speak varieties of English determined by our backgrounds.

And MacNeil then says to camera:

> Our story is not about the correct way to speak English but about all the different varieties and how they came to be. Why a MacNeil in Nova Scotia sounds different from a MacNeil here in Scotland, or one in North Carolina, or in New Zealand. Varieties of English are as old as the language itself ...

There could hardly be a stronger variationist perspective for a history of English. And a similar emphasis is found in the radio series, with its statement in the opening programme:

> We'll be illustrating the many varieties of English, especially those which are in the process of developing around the world ... .

Every programme stresses variety, dialect, and change, as these opening lines from programmes 6–10 illustrate:

6   [Tape of a range of US accents] That's just a tiny sample of the

range of variations in the way English is pronounced within the USA ...

7   [Tape of Gullah dialogue] That's the sound of Gullah, a variety of Black English spoken by about a quarter of a million people ... .

8   [Tape of Canadian speaker] To most British ears that sounds just like another piece of American English, but it isn't from the United States at all. It's Canadian. One thing that gives the game away is ...

9   [Tape of Liberian news] That was a broadcaster reading the news in Freetown, Sierra Leone. He was reading it in Krio, a creolised form of English spoken by ...

10   [Tape of Scots] That's Stanley Robertson of Aberdeenshire, speaking the traditional dialect that is still strong in the north-east of Scotland. It's a variety of Lowland Scots ...

The opening of programme 15 could have been a publicity manifesto for the present book:

15   [Tape of four regional accents] It's easy to give the impression, when you write an outline history of a language, that it's a single homogenous entity. The history of English, in many books, comes across as the history of its most prestigious variety, standard English. But it only takes a brief acquaintance with a living language to see that homogeneity is a myth.

Some readers might see in this scenario a Celtic plot. After all, we find television presenter Robert MacNeil accompanied by writer Robert McCrum, and radio presenter Tom McArthur accompanied by the patronymically more opaque (but nonetheless Welsh/Irish) David Crystal. But it is not so. The BBC's millennial approach, Radio 4's *The Routes of English*, produced by (Bristol-born) Simon Elmes, continues the emphasis, as can be seen in (Westmorland-born) presenter Melvyn Bragg's foreword to the printed version of the series (Elmes 1999: 3):

Spoken English drives the language and this series, *The Routes of English*, goes down that road. Written English has nailed and enhanced spoken English time and again, but the tongue has always had its say. In shade of expression and idiosyncratic precision, the spoken word can often out-fox the scripted version – as I know from local experience with the Wigton dialect of Cumbria. It may be lost to the national stock of words but is full of depth and charge to those few in the know ...

And the six programmes in the series express the production's regional emphasis, with the titles: Wigton, Winchester, Hastings, Canterbury, Edinburgh, and Liverpool.

It seems to be the nature of broadcasting to privilege linguistic variety, and the nature of conventional publishing to privilege the standard, with its roots in the written – and especially printed – language. Certainly, the contrast between the broadcasting treatments of the 'story' of English in recent decades and the published accounts – as summarised in the Introduction to this volume – are very different. This perhaps suggests that the 'sense of variety' which Trudgill and Watts wish to make available to their 2525 readership is much more likely to be achieved through mediums of communication other than the printed book. Indeed, I can see no way of convincing a prescriptively brainwashed and puristically sceptical world about the nature and importance of linguistic variety other than by employing the ever-increasing resources of multimedia. Without this, the gospel of this book is at risk of being read, but not heard. The quotations, illustrations, and phonetic transcriptions of earlier chapters, impressive as they are in their cumulative persuasiveness and academic accuracy, keep nonstandard varieties on the printed page – which is where they do not belong. There is more hope for a fairer-minded account of the history of English in an era characterised by the Internet, digital video discs, and interactive radio or television, than one in which the book reigns supreme.

Linguistic stereotypes and realities

The use of books to convey information loads the dice against the appreciation of nonstandard domains. Everything we know intuitively about regional dialects suggests that they routinely illustrate a level of expressiveness which is a source of admiration to those who operate only in standard English. We recall the narrative power of rural story-tellers, the energy and humour of city repartee (such as in Liverpool or Glasgow), and the memorability of nonstandard figurative expressions and idiom in 'new Englishes' from around the world. But it is so difficult to convey these features in printed form, and phonetic transcription is at its weakest when it tries to capture the full range of expressiveness of the voice or the dynamic properties of discourse. These are problems which have constrained the study of the standard language for decades, of course; but our lack of knowledge of the features which define linguistic expressiveness poses a particular difficulty to those trying to understand and convey the character of nonstandard variation. Especially critical is the role of prosody and paralanguage – with particular reference to the communicative role of intonation, rhythm, and tone of voice. As Wales puts it (Chapter 3), the lack of information about this area is the 'most striking omission'. It is true that some features of intonation have been described and have received considerable discussion – such as the New Zealand-derived high-rising sentence terminal – but these are only a small part of the picture.

Millar (Chapter 9, pp. 188–189) also draws proper attention to the way intonation is sometimes referred to, as part of her general concern about the neglect of eloquence as a subject in mainline studies – to which I would add other notions of oracy, highly valued in classical tradition, but virtually ignored today, such as elocution, spoken rhetoric, and everything that goes under the heading of the 'speech arts' (performance poetry, drama, etc.).[2] But these references are sporadic, impressionistic, and usually low-level in their focus, identifying individual tones or tunes. Discourse prosody is much more germane, in all areas of nonstandard oracy, and this has received very little attention. We are in the ironic position of wishing to raise the nonstandard flag, but unable to provide persuasive descriptions of some of the linguistic features which play a central role in its design. The illustrative power of multimedia is bound to facilitate the linguist's task, in this respect.

Technological developments in sound recording have already begun to free historians of nonstandard English from the most serious limitation of the past – the need to work through the written language. Several of the contributors to this book have drawn attention to the ways in which the inevitable reliance on writing limits our ability to perceive linguistic reality. Insofar as writers represented nonstandard English at all, the result has been a somewhat sanitised version. Indeed, as Millar illustrates (Chapter 9, pp. 174–175), conflicting 'reports' of a speech show how untrustworthy the written language can be as a guide to what was spoken. The point is even more strongly made when nonstandard language in literature is taken into account. Blake (1981) provides an extensive discussion and range of illustrations, with regional and social examples ranging from Chaucer through Shakespeare and Swift to the nineteenth-century novel (Bronte, Scott, Dickens, Hardy) and from there to Shaw, Lawrence, Wesker, and beyond; Phillips (1984) provides further instances. Sometimes the spellings are genuine attempts to reflect a phonetic reality, as in much of the writing of Twain or Dickens; but often the forms employed are no more than eye-dialects, in which a nonstandard spelling evokes a regional image, with no phonetic difference involved, as in *yu* for *you*. Even in the best examples of the attempts to render regional or social Englishes there is an uncertainty – and usually serious inconsistency – about what they were intended to convey, as we would expect from any amateur attempt at speech transcription. Vowel variation is particularly susceptible to difficulties of interpretation; prosodic features are given little expression, other than through the occasional piece of impressionistic verbal description. The distinction between idiosyncratic and group usage remains unclear: how far would all members of a character's speech community speak in the same way?

In cases where the influence of another language is involved (as in African, North American, Indian, or Celtic literature), often we simply cannot be sure whether a particular rendition is a genuine feature of the local dialect or an invention introduced by the author for literary effect. When Shakespeare makes Fluellen say 'look you', in *Henry V*, is this because he had heard local

Welsh speakers say this or because he shared the widespread but erroneous belief (still current today) that this is what Welsh-influenced speakers of English say? Regional stereotypes – that all Scots say 'Hoots mon' and all Irish say 'Begorrah' – characterise a great deal of the literary canon, and are no sure guide to regional reality. The need for even greater caution has to be advocated in such cases as the non-native domains illustrated by Mesthrie (Chapter 6), where the skill of an author from an unfamiliar language background may lead us to believe that an English expression is a genuine regional form, whereas in fact it is a purely literary creation. For example, imagine I am writing a novel which contained a character of an old Welshman, and at one point I put in his mouth, as he looks out of the window: 'What a storm! It's raining old women and sticks today!' What would be your reaction, as a reader? You would be likely to conclude that this rather curious expression is a vivid example of the regional English spoken in Wales. In fact it is a word-for-word translation of the Welsh equivalent of 'It's raining cats and dogs' (*Mae hi'n bwrw hen wragedd a ffyn*), and has nothing to do with the way English is spoken in Wales. When Welsh people speak English, and want to talk about heavy rain, they say 'It's raining cats and dogs'. No one says 'It's raining old women and sticks', except perhaps in jest. This does not ruin the literary brilliance of my novel, but it does make a nonsense of relying on my novel as a source for regional dialectology. We have to face up to this problem for all of the meagre set of written sources on the history of nonstandard English.

We cannot, it seems, very often trust the data, as represented in the writing of authors. Nor can we trust them when they become metalinguistic, and talk about the language themselves. A remarkable number of authors have in fact reflected on the nature of the language they use and hear around them,[3] but few of these observations are capable of being interpreted in terms which would satisfy a linguist. A good example is Dickens' fine descriptions of his characters' tones of voice, which have auditory plausibility while nonetheless defying phonetic interpretation. In *Nicholas Nickleby* (Ch. 10), Ralph is described thus:

> If an iron door could be supposed to quarrel with its hinges, and to make a firm resolution to open with slow obstinacy, and grind them to powder in the process, it would emit a pleasanter sound in so doing than did these words in the rough and bitter voice in which they were uttered by Ralph.

And in *Bleak House* (Ch. 8), we find Mrs Pardiggle:

> Always speaking in the same demonstrative, loud, hard tone, so that her voice impressed my fancy as if it had a sort of spectacles on too.

Often, an author's views present a stereotype which bears little relationship to contemporary reality. A good example is Wales' comment (Chapter 3, pp. 55–57) on the Lake Poets, some of whom wrote at length on the kind of language they were using. A very famous quotation from Wordsworth, in the Preface to the second edition of the *Lyrical Ballads* (1800), emphasises his effort to use 'a selection of language really used by men'. Insofar as this is a naturalistic reaction against the studied style of eighteenth-century poetry, the point is uncontentious. But when people make the assumption that Wordsworth was reflecting in his poetry the kind of speech which would have been current in the Cumbria of his day, they are far from the truth.

A further dimension of difficulty arises when we find we have to explore a writer's mindset or world view, or even the climate of the time, in order to make sense of a usage, or an observation about language. It is a point which applies just as much to grammarians, lexicographers, and stylists, as to novelists, dramatists, and poets. The telling of a (piece of the) story of English will be greatly influenced by the point of view of the teller, who will (consciously or unconsciously) select events and examples, and interpret what is and is not noteworthy or significant, from a particular agenda. Several cases have been illustrated in this book where social, political, historical, and other agendas must be taken into account when trying to evaluate the emphasis and orientation of linguistic texts. A political perspective is evident in the attitudes to language expressed by eighteenth-century writers (Watts, Chapter 8); a particular historicism inevitably conditions our views on the nature of the continuity between Old English (or Anglo-Saxon) and Middle English (Milroy, Chapter 1); a religious perspective is needed in Early Modern English, where we need to recognise the impact of Puritanism in order to understand the way in which oaths (and their euphemisms) are used variably in plays throughout the period (Jucker, Chapter 11).

The study of language always needs to take place within the perspective of its commentators' sociopolitical background. The point is a truism in non-linguistic domains. It is routine to allow our awareness of the political background of contemporary literary authors and social commentators to influence our interpretation of what they are saying; and any investigator who failed to take this background into account would (rightly) be considered naive. But this is precisely what histories of English generally fail to do, when giving an account of the older writers on language, many of whom have been influenced by political or social ideologies (Milroy, Chapter 1). Only in occasional cases are linguistic observations related to (and thus explained by) a writer's personal background. An example would be Dr Johnson, where the occasionally idiosyncratic definitions in the *Dictionary* have often been discussed with reference to his own background and beliefs. Which political party did Johnson support? *Tory* is defined as 'One who adheres to the antient constitution of the state, and the apostolical hierarchy of the church of England, opposed to a *whig*.' And *Whig*? 'The name of a faction'. But how many of us, interested in English linguistic history, would be able to say what the political, religious, moral, or other views were of the grammarians, lexicographers, and others whose linguistic observations we are attempting to evaluate?

Sometimes these views pervade a whole work, and make it extremely difficult to assess the representativeness of the linguistic observations it contains. This is especially true of the mindset permeating the study of English from the mid-eighteenth century, which was so profoundly influenced by Latin models and prescriptivism that it was routine to hear people reason that even 'our best Authors for want of some rudiments of this kind have sometimes fallen into mistakes, and been guilty of palpable errors in point of Grammar' (Watts, Chapter 8, p. 159). The arrival of major works of great influence on prescriptive attitudes – Johnson's dictionary, Lowth's grammar, Walker's pronunciation dictionary, all written within a few years of each other – mark a turning point, neatly demonstrated in the changing attitudes to variation shown in the grammars of the period (Poplack *et al.*, Chapter 5). By the middle of the following century, this orientation had developed, in some writers, into a whole social, moral, or political philosophy. William Cobbett, for example, makes his position clear in the dedication to Queen Caroline of his *Grammar of the English Language* (1829):

> A work, having for its objects, to lay the solid foundation of literary knowledge amongst the Labouring Classes of the community; to give practical effect to the natural genius found in the Soldier, the Sailor, the Apprentice, and the Plough-boy; and to make that genius a perennial source of wealth, strength, and safety to the kingdom.

The book is written as a series of letters to his son, 14-year-old James Paul Cobbett, who can have been left in no doubt about the role of grammar in indicating the general incompetence of those in power, some of whom had at one time forced Cobbett to flee the country to avoid imprisonment. This is one of the stronger parts of Letter XXII:

> How destitute of judgment and of practical talent these persons have been, in the capacity of Statesmen and of legislators, the present miserable and perilous state of England amply demonstrates; and I am not about to show you, that they are equally destitute in the capacity of writers.

And from Lesson 4 in Letter XXIV, Cobbett concludes an analysis of the errors in Castlereagh's grammar with:

> What do you say, what can you say, of such a man, but that nature might have made him for a valet, for a strolling player, and possibly for an auctioneer; but never for a Secretary of State. Yet this man was *educated* at the *University of Cambridge*!

When a grammar becomes such an index of (lack of) character and expertise, it needs careful evaluation, before its observations can be taken as a guide to the language it purports to describe.

Towards the telling of new stories

If there is one thing we can learn from the traditional way in which the 'story of English' has been presented, it is this: that the next period in English linguistic history should not be treated in such an unbalanced way. There are several factors which lead me to think that a more inclusive and representative historical linguistics will be the outcome. Awareness that there is a problem (as illustrated by the present volume) is already a step towards the solution of the problem, and reference to nonstandard domains, and to their linguistic characteristics, are today being increasingly included in 'standard' historical accounts [e.g. Hogg and Denison 2002; Mugglestone (forthcoming)]. The availability of recorded sound means that the dependence on written material, with all its disadvantages, can in future be avoided. But, most important of all, there is bound to be a change in the marginal status of nonstandard domains, simply because there are going to be more of them to take into account.

The growth in diversity is noticeable at both national and international levels. Nationally, urban dialects are adapting to meet the identity needs of immigrant groups, such as the currently evolving Caribbean Scouse in Liverpool. With over 300 languages now spoken within London, for example, it would be surprising indeed if several did not produce fresh varieties as they interact with English, even if some will doubtless be short-lived and transitional in character. The linguistic consequences of immigrant diversity have long been noted in cities in the USA, but are now a major feature of contemporary life in the urban centres of most other countries where English is a mother-tongue, notably Australia. At an international level, the evidence is overwhelming of the emergence of a new generation of nonstandard Englishes, as the global reach of English extends. While standard English continues to perform its traditional role in fostering a shared medium of global intelligibility, the adoption of English by international communities has led to immediate adaptation in the interests of expressing identity. Several authors in this book have drawn attention to the 'new Englishes' which have developed among mother-tongue speakers in recent centuries (Trudgill, Gordon and Sudbury, Mesthrie); but these are going to be a small group by comparison with the varieties which have yet to emerge as a consequence of the adoption of English by non-native-speaking communities. The proportion of native speakers of English to the total of world speakers of English has been steadily falling for some time (Graddol 1999): for every one native speaker there are now three non-native speakers.

Because no language has ever been spoken by so many people in so many places, it is difficult to predict what will happen to English, as a consequence of its global expansion; but increasing variation, extending to the point of mutual unintelligibility, is already apparent in the colloquial speech of local communities. The range of domains identified by Mesthrie (Chapter 6) illustrates one set of possibilities, but there are still other nonstandard varieties to be taken into account, such as the code-mixed varieties now found all over the world, and identified by such names as Singlish, Taglish, and Chinglish (McArthur 1998). Nor do current models yet allow for what is going to happen to English in communities where new types of social relationship have linguistic consequences – such as the thousands of children being born to parents who have only English as a foreign language in common, and who find themselves growing up with this kind of English as the norm at home. In such cases, non-native English (presumably including features which would be traditionally considered as learner errors) is being learned as a mother-tongue, and new kinds of nonstandard English must surely be the outcome.

At the very least, the gap between standard and nonstandard Englishes is likely to widen, with both domains expressing distinct and complementary functions of intelligibility and identity respectively. There are undoubtedly similarities with diglossic situations. It is, as Wales points out (Chapter 3), too soon to provide detail about what is happening in parts of the world where the language is changing very rapidly. On the other hand, published studies indicate that regional distinctiveness is a significant and steadily increasing presence. In vocabulary, coverage in regional dictionaries [such as Cassidy and Le Page (1967) or Branford and Branford (1991)] routinely reaches between 10,000 and 20,000 entries. In pronunciation, contact effects of both a segmental and non-segmental character can be heard: the former illustrated by the retroflexion of consonants in the Indian subcontinent; the latter by the use of syllable-timed speech (as noted for South Africa by Mesthrie) in most of these new varieties (Crystal 1996b). Even in grammar, regional distinctiveness is growing. Although a work such as *The Longman Grammar of Spoken and Written English* can say 'dialect differences [in grammar] are not as pervasive as we might imagine' and 'the core grammatical structures are relatively uniform across dialects' (Biber *et al.*, 1999: 20–1), this judgement is likely to be premature once further work on spoken grammar is undertaken (Wales, Chapter 3). And even in the Longman grammar, a detailed examination of the points of regional (lexico-)grammatical variation instantiated in that work shows that virtually all areas of English grammar are affected (Crystal 2002).

A comparative perspective

Any approach to nonstandard English needs to adopt two universalist axioms from general linguistics: one synchronic, the other diachronic. The view that all languages are 'equal', in the sense that they display a comparable range of structural properties and social functions, must be extended synchronically to all regional and social domains. The need to state this principle explicitly today is aimed at the popular mentality which views regional dialects as structurally or expressively inferior to the standard language; but it is a view which, as this book repeatedly illustrates, has had a dominant influence in the past. There also needs to be a diachronic extension: all language states (*états de langue*) of the past need to be conceived within the same structural and functional frame of reference as those available to present-day investigation. This is no more than a linguistic application of the geological principle of *uniformitarianism* – the notion that geological processes controlling the evolution of the Earth's crust were of the same kind throughout geological time as they are today. Although this frame of reference is uncontentious within linguistics, it is a long way from being routinely operationalised in relation to nonstandard domains. Thus, for example, the range of language functions which have been widely explored in standard English, such as the use of language to express identity, solidarity, and power (Mesthrie, p. 112), has rarely been explored in nonstandard English. There has been a tendency in traditional accounts to view nonstandard domains as stylistically or sociolinguistically uniform, by comparison with the standard language, which is manifested in many varieties. Certainly, one of the features of a standard language is its ability to accrete new varieties in a way that nonstandard domains do not: for example, the range of written varieties, or the range of varieties which identify broadcasting, are never going to be matched in a nonstandard domain. But this is not to say that nonstandard domains have no variation at all. On the contrary, the kind of variation illustrated by Mesthrie's lectal approach to South African Indian English is illustrative, and doubtless typical.

To demonstrate the case that there is genuine equivalence between standard and nonstandard domains, comprehensive structural and functional perspectives need to be adopted. We are, however, a long way from this goal. This book is a start, in the way it illustrates points of structural parity within nonstandard domains, especially in segmental phonology, morphology, and the lexicon, and to a lesser extent in syntax. Yet it is the product of its time. To a considerable extent, it is a reaction to a point of view (within prescriptivism) which itself focused on low-level points of language, such as *ain't*, double negation, regional vocabulary, and the use of glottal stops. This reaction is needed, in that such features of nonstandard English still attract more than their fair share of public attention (in the UK National Curriculum, for example, one would be forgiven for thinking that such matters are all that English grammar should be concerned with), and the need to explain their linguistic role in nonstandard varieties remains important. The book's emphasis is also understandable, in that these levels of language are those about which linguistics traditionally has had most to say. It remains easiest to demonstrate nonstandard structural complexity with reference to phonology and morphology, and this is what most people do. When it comes to other 'levels' of linguistic structure, such as nonsegmental phonology, semantics, discourse structure, and pragmatics – even syntax – all we can do is concur with Trudgill and Watts (Introduction, pp. 1–3) and Wales (Chapter 3) that we know very little about the way in which sensible comparisons between standard and nonstandard domains might be made. Even in standard English, the amount of descriptive work in some of these areas is limited and highly selective; for nonstandard English it is often no more than impressionistic and anecdotal. I believe that the harnessing of multimedia technology will soon begin to correct this imbalance. We shall not have to wait until 2525.

Notes

1 The book of the series was McCrum *et al.* (1986).
2 It is a welcome sign to see organisations (such as the English Speaking Union) in recent years engaging in debating competitions, public-speaking competitions, and the like; but the focus of these events is national or international, and is thus exclusively on standard English.
3 For a selection, see Crystal and Crystal (2000).

Bibliography

Adamson, S. (1998) 'Literary language', in Romaine, S. (ed.) *The Cambridge History of the English Language 1776–1997*, vol. 4, Cambridge: Cambridge University Press, 589–692.

Aickin, J. (1693) *The English Grammar*, Menston, UK: Scolar Press.

Aijmer, K. (1997) ' "I think" – an English modal particle', in Swan, T. and Westvik, O.J. (eds) *Modality in Germanic Languages: Historical and Comparative Perspectives*, Berlin: Mouton de Gruyter, 1–47.

Akenson, D.H. (1990) *Half the World from Home: Perspectives on the Irish in New Zealand 1860–1950*, Wellington: Victoria University Press.

Al-Banyan, A. and Preston, D.R. (1998) 'What is Standard American English?', *Studia Anglica Posnaniensia* 33: 29–46 (Festschrift for Kari Sajavaara).

Albury, P. (1975) *The Story of the Bahamas*, London: Macmillan.

Allan, S. (1990) 'The rise of New Zealand intonation', in Bell, A. and Holmes, J. (eds) *New Zealand Ways of Speaking English*, Clevedon: Multilingual Matters, 115–28.

Alston, R.C. (1965) *English Grammars Written in English and English Grammars Written in Latin by Native Speakers*, Leeds: E. J. Arnold.

Aly, B. and Tanquary, G. (1943) 'The early national period: 1788–1860', in Brigance, W. (ed.) *A History and Criticism of American Public Address*, vol. 1, New York: McGraw-Hill, 55–110.

Ammon, U., Dittmar, N., Mattheier, K. and Trudgill, P. (eds) (forthcoming) *Sociolinguistics: An International Handbook of the Science of Language and Society*, 2nd edn, Berlin: de Gruyter.

Andersen, R. (ed.) (1983) *Pidginization and Creolization as Language Acquisition*, Rowley, MA: Newbury House.

Anderson, R. (1805) *Cumberland Ballads*, Carlisle: T. W. Arthur.

Andersson, L. and Trudgill, P. (1990) *Bad Language*, Oxford: Blackwell.

Anonymous (1696) *An Essay in Defence of the Female Sex*. Written by a lady [i.e. Mary Astell? or Judith Drake? or H. Wyatt?], London: R. Clavel for A. Roper and E. Wilkinson.

Armitage, S. (1998) *All Points North*, London: Penguin.

Arthur, J. (1996) *Aboriginal English*, Melbourne: Oxford University Press.

Atwell, B. (1868) *Principles of Elocution and Vocal Culture*, Providence: Banys Williams News Co.

Axon, W.E. (1883) *English Dialect Words of the Eighteenth Century, as Shown in the Universal Dictionary of Nathaniel Bailey*, London: Trübner and Co.

Ayres H.M. (1933) 'Bermudian English', *American Speech* 8: 3–10.

Bækken, B. (1998) *Word Order Patterns in Early Modern English, with Special Reference to the Position of the Subject and the Finite Verb*, Oslo: Novus Press.

Bailey, C.-J.N. (1996) *Essays on Time-based Linguistic Analysis*, Oxford: Clarendon Press.

Bailey, G. and Smith, C. (1992) 'Southern American English in Brazil', *SECOL Review*: 71–89.

Bailey, R.W. (1991) *Images of English*, Ann Arbor, MI: University of Michigan Press.

—— (1996) *Nineteenth-century English*, Ann Arbor, MI: University of Michigan Press.

Baker, R. (1770) *Reflections on the English Language, in the Nature of Vaugelas's Reflections on the French; Being a Detection of Many Improper Expressions Used in Conversation, and of Many Others to be Found in Authors*, Menston, UK: Scolar Press.

Baker, S. (1966) *The Australian Language*, Sydney: Currawong.

Barbé, P. (1995) 'Guernsey English: a syntax exile?', *English World-Wide* 16: 1–36.

Barber, C.L. (1976) *Early Modern English*, London: Deutsch.

Barnes, W. (1859) *The Song of Solomon in the Dorset Dialect*, London.

—— (1878) *An Outline of English Speech-Craft*, London.

Baron, N. (2000) *Alphabet to email. How Written English Evolved and Where it's Heading*, London: Routledge.

Barrell, J. (1983) *English Literature in History, 1730–80*, London: Hutchinson.

Bartlett, C. (1992) 'Regional variation in New Zealand English: the case of Southland', *New Zealand English Newsletter* 6: 5–15.

Basler, R. (1969) *Abraham Lincoln: His Speeches and Writings*, New York: Kraus Reprint Co.

Bauer, L. (1979) 'The second great vowel shift?', *Journal of the International Phonetic Association* 9: 57–66.

—— (1986) 'Notes on New Zealand English phonetics and phonology', *English World Wide* 7: 225–58.

—— (1992) 'The second Great Vowel Shift revisited', *English World Wide* 13: 253–68.

—— (1994a) *Watching English Change: An Introduction to the Study of Linguistic Change in Standard Englishes in the Twentieth Century*, London: Longman.

—— (1994b) 'English in New Zealand', in Burchfield, R. (ed.) *The Cambridge History of the English Language. Volume V: English in Britain and Overseas*, Cambridge: Cambridge University Press, 382–429.

Bayard, D. (1990) 'Minder, mork and mindy? (-t) glottalisation and post-vocalic (r) in younger New Zealand speakers', in Bell, A. and Holmes, J. (eds) *New Zealand Ways of Speaking English*, Clevedon: Multilingual Matters, 149–64.

—— (1995) *Kiwitalk: Sociolinguistics and New Zealand Society*, Palmerston North: Dunmore Press.

—— (2000) 'New Zealand English: Origins, relationships and prospects', *Moderna Språk* 94: 8–14.

Bayly, A. (1772/1969) *A Plain and Complete Grammar with the English Accidence*, Menston, UK: Scolar Press.

Beal, J. (1993) 'The grammar of Tyneside and Northumbrian English', in Milroy, J. and Milroy, L. (eds) *Real English: The Grammar of Dialects in the British Isles*, London: Longman, 187–213.

—— (1996) 'The Jocks and the Geordies: Modified standards in the eighteenth-century pronouncing dictionaries', in Britton, D. (ed.) *English Historical Linguistics 1994*, Amsterdam: Benjamins, 363–82.

—— (2000) 'From Geordie Ridley to *Viz*: popular literature in Tyneside English', *Language and Literature* 9: 359–75.

Beattie, J. (1788/1968) *The Theory of Language*, Menston, UK: Scolar Press.

Becker, M. (1994) *The Emergence of Civil Society in the Eighteenth Century. A Privileged Moment in the History of England, Scotland and France*, Bloomington, IN: Indiana University Press.

Belich, J. (1996) *Making Peoples: A History of the New Zealanders*, Auckland: The Penguin Press.

Bell, A. (1984) 'Language style as audience design', *Language in Society* 13:145–204.

—— (1997) 'The phonetics of fish and chips in New Zealand', *English World Wide* 18: 243–90.

—— (2000) 'Maori and Pakeha English: a case study', in Bell, A. and Kuiper, K. (eds) *New Zealand English*, Amsterdam: Benjamins, 221–48.

Bell, A.M. (1887) *The Principles of Elocution*, 5th edn, Washington, DC: John C. Parker.

Bell, Jr, J. (ed.) (1812) *Rhymes of the Northern Bards*, Newcastle: M. Angus and Son.

Bell, A. and Holmes, J. (eds) (1990) *New Zealand Ways of Speaking English*, Clevedon: Multilingual Matters.

Bell, A. and Kuiper, K. (eds) (2000) *New Zealand English*, Amsterdam: Benjamins.

Bell, R. and Crawford, P. (1985) 'Appendix 2: Statistical analysis of women's printed writings 1600–1700', in Prior, M. (ed.) *Women in English Society 1500–1800*, London and New York: Methuen, 265–74.

Bennett, A. (1994) *Writing Home*, London: Faber.

Bennett, J. and Smithers, G. (1966) *Early Middle English Verse and Prose*, Oxford: Clarendon Press.

Benzie, W. (1972) *The Dublin Orator. Thomas Sheridan's Influence on Eighteenth-Century Rhetoric and Belles Lettres*, Leeds: School of English, University of Leeds.

Berger, D. (1994) 'Maxims of conduct into literature: Jonathan Swift and polite conversation', in Carré, J. (ed.) *The Crisis of Courtesy. Studies in the Conduct Book in Britain 1600–1900*, Leiden: E. J. Brill, 81–91.

Bergvall, V.L., Bing, J.M. and Freed, A.F. (eds) (1996) *Rethinking Language and Gender Research: Theory and Practice*, London: Longman.

Bernard, J. (1969) 'On the uniformity of Australian English', *Orbis* 18: 62–73.

Bertram, E. and Sharpe, K. (2000) 'Capitalism, work, and character', *American Prospect* 11, 20 (September 11): 44–8.

Bex, T. (1999) 'Representations of English in twentieth-century Britain: Fowler, Gowers and Partridge', in Bex, T. and Watts, R.J. (eds) *Standard English: The Widening Debate*, London: Routledge, 89–109.

Bex, T. and Watts, R.J. (eds) (1999) *Standard English: The Widening Debate*, London: Routledge.

Biber, D. (1995) *Dimensions of Register Variation*, Cambridge: Cambridge University Press.

Biber, D., Johansson, S., Conrad, S. and Finegan, E. (1999) *Longman Grammar of Spoken and Written English*, London: Longman.

Bickerton, D. (1975) *Dynamics of a Creole System*, New York: Cambridge University Press.

Blair, D. (1975) 'On the origins of Australian pronunciation', *Working Papers of the Speech and Language Research Centre*, Sydney: Macquarie University.

—— (1989) 'The development and current state of Australian English: a survey', in Collins, P. and Blair, D. (eds) *Australian English: The Language of a New Society*, St Lucia: University of Queensland Press.

Blake, N.F. (1981) *Non-standard Language in English Literature*, London: Deutsch.

—— (1996) *Essays on Shakespeare's Language*, 1st Series, Misterton: The Language Press.

Blake, R.A. (1997) *'All o' we is one?* Race, class, and language in a Barbados community', unpublished Ph.D. dissertation, Stanford University.

Blank, P. (1996) *Broken English Dialects and the Politics of Language in Renaissance Writings*, London: Routledge.

Bohman, G. (1943) 'The colonial period', in Brigance, W. (ed.) *A History and Criticism of American Public Address*, vol. 1, New York: McGraw-Hill, 3–54.

Borsay, P. (1989) *The English Urban Renaissance. Culture and Society in the Provincial Town 1660–1770*, Oxford: Clarendon Press.

Bourdieu, P. (1991) *Language and Symbolic Power*, Cambridge, MA: Harvard University Press.

Bradley, D. (1989) 'Regional dialects in Australian English phonology', in Collins, P. and Blair, D. (eds) *Australian English: the Language of a New Society*, St Lucia: University of Queensland Press, 260–70.

—— (1991) '/æ/ and /a:/ in Australian English', in Cheshire, J. (ed.) *English around the World: Sociolinguistic Perspectives*. Cambridge: Cambridge University Press, 227–34.

Bragg, M. (ed.) (1984) *Cumbria in Verse*, London: Secker and Warburg.

Brain, J.B. (1983) *Christian Indians in Natal*, Cape Town: Oxford University Press.

Brainerd, B. (1989) 'The contractions of *not*: A historical note', *Journal of English Linguistics* 22: 176–96.

Branford, W. (1994) 'English in South Africa', in Burchfield, R. (ed.) *The Cambridge History of the English Language. Volume V: English in Britain and Overseas*, Cambridge: Cambridge University Press, 430–96.

—— (1996) 'English in South African society: A preliminary overview', in DeKlerk, V. (ed.) *Focus on South Africa*, Amsterdam: John Benjamins, 35–53.

Branford, J. and Branford, W. (1991) *A Dictionary of South African English*, Cape Town: Oxford University Press.

Bredvold, L.I., Root, R.K. and Sherburn, G. (eds) (1935) *Eighteenth Century Prose*, New York: Nelson and Sons.

Brewer, E.C. (1877) *Errors of Speech and Spelling*, London: William Tegg.

Brewer, J. (1986) 'Durative marker or hypercorrection? The case of *-s* in the WPA ex-slave narratives', in Montgomery, M.B. and Bailey, G. (eds) *Language Variety in the South. Perspectives in Black and White*, Tuscaloosa, AL: University of Alabama Press, 131–48.

Brigance, W. (ed.) (1943) *A History and Criticism of American Public Address*, vols 1 and 2, New York: McGraw-Hill.

Brinton, L.J. (1996) *Pragmatic Markers in English. Grammaticalization and Discourse Functions*, Berlin: Mouton de Gruyter.

Britain, D. (1992) 'Linguistic change in intonation: the use of High Rising Terminals in New Zealand English', *Language Variation and Change* 4: 77–104.

—— (2000) 'A little goes a long way, as far as analysing grammatical variation and change in New Zealand English is concerned', in Bell, A. and Kuiper, K. (eds) *New Zealand English*, Amsterdam: Benjamins, 198–220.

Britain, D. and Sudbury, A. (in press) 'There's sheep and there's penguins: convergence, "drift" and "slant" in New Zealand and Falkland Islands English', in Jones, M. and Esch, E. (eds) *Contact Induced Language Change: An Examination of Internal, External and Non-Linguistic Factors*, Berlin: Mouton.

Brook, G.L. (1958) *History of the English Language*, London: Deutsch.

Brown, P. and Levinson, S. (1987) *Politeness: Some Universals of Language Use*, Cambridge: Cambridge University Press.

Brown, R. and Gilman, A. (1989) 'Politeness theory and Shakespeare's four major tragedies', *Language in Society* 18: 159–212.

Brunner, K. (1963) *An Outline of Middle English Grammar*, Oxford: Blackwell Publishers.

Bughwan, D. (1970) 'An investigation into the use of English by the Indians in South Africa, with special reference to Natal', unpublished Ph.D. thesis, University of South Africa.

Bullions, P. (1869) *The Principles of English Grammar: Comprising the Substance of the Most Approved English Grammar Extant*, New York, NY: Sheldon and Company.

Burchfield, R. (ed.) (1994) *The Cambridge History of the English Language. Volume V: English in Britain and Overseas*, Cambridge: Cambridge University Press.

Burgh, J. (1781) *The Art of Speaking*, 5th edn, London: Longman and Buckland.

Burke, P. (1993) *The Art of Conversation*, Cambridge: Polity Press.

Burles, E. (1652) *Grammatica Burles*, Menston, UK: Scolar Press.

Burn, J. (1786/1805) *A Practical Grammar of the English Language, in Which the Several Parts of Speech are Clearly and Methodically Explained; Their Concord and Government Reduced to Grammatical Rules, and Illustrated by a Variety of Examples*, Glasgow: James and Andrew Duncan.

Burnley, D. (1992) *The History of the English Language: A Source Book*, London: Longman.

Busse, U. (2000) 'The function of linguistic variation in the Shakespeare Corpus. A study of the morpho-syntactic variability of the address pronouns and their socio-historical and pragmatic implications', Habilitationsschrift, Universität Osnabrück.

Butler, S. (1863)(facsimile edition 1995) *A First Year in Canterbury Settlement*. Christchurch: Kiwi Publishers.

Campbell, G. (1776) 'The Philosophy of Rhetoric', in Golden, J. and Corbett, E. (1968) (eds) *The Rhetoric of Blair, Campbell and Whatley*, New York: Holt, Rineholt & Winston.

Carré, J. (1994) 'Introduction', Carré, J. (ed.) *The Crisis of Courtesy. Studies in the Conduct Book in Britain 1600–1900*, Leiden: E. J. Brill.

Carrington, L. (forthcoming). 'The anglophone Caribbean', in U. Ammon *et al.* (eds.).

Casperson, D. (1999) *Power Etiquette*, New York: Amacom.

Cassidy, F.G. and Le Page, R.B. (1967) *Dictionary of Jamaican English*, Cambridge: Cambridge University Press.

CEEC (The Corpus of Early English Correspondence) (1998) Helsinki: Department of English, University of Helsinki (©Sociolinguistics and Language History Project).

Chadwick, H.M. (1907) *The Origin of the English Nation*, Cambridge: Cambridge University Press.

Chambers, J.K. (ed.) (1975) *Canadian English: Origins and Structures*, Toronto: Methuen.

Chambers, J.K. (1995) *Sociolinguistic Theory*, Oxford: Blackwell.

Chambers, J. and Trudgill, P. (1980) *Dialectology*, Cambridge: Cambridge University Press.

Chambers, R.W. (1932) 'On the continuity of English prose from Ælfred to Thomas More and his school', in Hitchcock, E.V. (ed.) *Harpsfield's Life of More* (EETS OS 186), London: Oxford University Press, xlv–clxxiv.

Cheshire, J. (1982) *Variation in an English Dialect: A Sociolinguistic Study*, Cambridge: Cambridge University Press.

Cheshire, J. and Stein, D. (eds) (1997) *Taming the Vernacular: From Dialect to Written Standard Language*, London: Longman.

Christian, D., Wolfram, W. and Dube, N. (1988) *Variation and Change in Geographically Isolated Communities: Appalachian English and Ozark English*, Tuscaloosa, AL: American Dialect Society.

Claiborne, R. (1983) *Our Marvelous Native Tongue: the Life and Times of the English Language*, New York: Times Books.

Clark, P. and Souden, D. (1988) 'Introduction', in Clark, P. and Souden, D. (eds) *Migration and Society in Early Modern England*, Totowa, NJ: Barnes and Noble, 11–48.

Clarke, S. (1997) 'On establishing historical relationships between New and Old World varieties: habitual aspect and Newfoundland vernacular English', in Schneider, E. (ed.) *Englishes around the World*, vol. 1, Amsterdam: Benjamins, 277–93.

—— (1999) 'The search for origins: habitual aspect and Newfoundland vernacular English', *Journal of English Linguistics* 27: 328–40.

Cmiel, K. (1990) *Democratic Eloquence. The Fight over Popular Speech in Nineteenth-Century America*, New York: William Morrow and Company.

Coates, J. (ed.) (1998) *Language and Gender*, Oxford: Blackwell.

Cobbett, W. (1829) *Grammar of the English Language*, London: for the author.

Cochrane, G.R. (1989) 'Origin and development of the Australian accent', in Collins, P. and Blair, D. (eds) *Australian English: the Language of a New Society*, St Lucia: University of Queensland Press, 176–86.

Coleridge, S.T. (1817) *Biographia Literaria* (reprinted 1975/1991 in Watson, G. (ed.) London: J. M. Dent and Sons.

Collier, John of Urmston (1775) *The Miscellaneous Works of Tim Bobbin, Esq. Containing his View of the Lancashire Dialect*, Manchester: for the author and Mr Haslingden.

Collier, J. (1778) *An Alphabet for the Grown-up Grammarians of Great Britain*, Newcastle: T. Robson.

Collins, H.E. (1975) 'The sources of Australian pronunciation', Macquarie University, Speech and Language Research Centre, *Working Papers* 1: 115–28.

Collins, P. and Blair, D. (eds) (1989) *Australian English: the Language of a New Society*, St Lucia: University of Queensland Press.

Collyer, J. (1735/1968) *The General Principles of Grammar*, Menston, UK: Scolar Press.

Conway, K. (1995) 'Woman suffrage and the history of rhetoric at the Seven Sisters Colleges, 1865–1919', in Lunsford, A. (ed.) *Reclaiming Rhetorica. Women in the Rhetorical Tradition*, Pittsburgh: University of Pittsburgh Press, 203–26.

Cooper, C. (1685) *Grammatica Linguae Anglicanae*, Menston, UK: Scolar Press.

Coupland, N. (1988) *Dialect in Use: Sociolinguistic Variation in Cardiff English*, Cardiff: University of Wales Press.

Crawford, P. (1985) 'Women's published writings 1600–1700', in Prior, M. (ed.) *Women in English Society 1500–1800*, London: Methuen, 211–82.

Cressy, D. (1980) *Literacy and Social Order: Reading and Writing in Tudor and Stuart England*, Cambridge: Cambridge University Press.

Crowley, F. (1951) 'British immigration to Australia 1860–1914', unpublished Ph.D. thesis, Oxford University.

Crowley, F. (1974) *A New History of Australia*, Melbourne: Heinemann.

Crowley, T. (1989a) *Standard English and the Politics of Language*, Urbana: University of Illinois Press.

—— (1989b) *The Politics of Discourse: The Standard Language Question and British Cultural Debates*, London: Macmillan.

—— (1990) 'That obscure object of desire: A science of language', in Joseph, J.E. and Taylor, T.J. (eds) *Ideologies of Language*, London: Routledge, 27–50.

—— (ed.) (1991) *Proper English: Readings in Language, History and Cultural Identity*, London: Routledge.

—— (1999) 'Curiouser and curiouser: Falling standards in the Standard English debate', in Bex, T. and Watts, R.J. (eds) *Standard English: The Widening Debate*, London: Routledge, 271–82.

Cruttenden, A. (1997) *Intonation*, 2nd edn, Cambridge: Cambridge University Press.

Crystal, D. (1992) *An Encyclopedic Dictionary of Language and Languages*, Oxford: Blackwell.

—— (1996a) *Encyclopedia of the English Language*, Cambridge: Cambridge University Press.

—— (1996b) 'The past, present and future of English rhythm', in Vaughan-Rees, M. (ed.) *Changes in Pronunciation* (special issue of *Speak Out!*, International Association of Teachers of English as a Foreign Language), 8–13.

—— (1997) *English as a Global Language*, Cambridge: Cambridge University Press.

—— (2002) 'English world-wide', in Hogg, R. and Denison, D. (eds) *A History of the English Language*, Cambridge: Cambridge University Press.

Crystal, D. and Crystal, H. (2000) *Words on Words: Quotations about Language and Languages*, Harmondsworth: Penguin.

Culpeper, J. and Kytö, M. (1999) 'Modifying pragmatic force: Hedges in a corpus of Early Modern English dialogues', in Jucker, A.H., Fritz, G. and Lebsanft, F. (eds) *Historical Dialogue Analysis*, Amsterdam: Benjamins, 293–312.

—— (2000) 'Data in historical pragmatics: spoken interaction (re)cast as writing', *Journal of Historical Pragmatics* 1/2: 175–99.

Curme, G.O. (1977) *A Grammar of the English Language*, Essex, CT: Verbatim.

Cutler, C., Hackert, S. and Seymour, C. (forthcoming) 'Bermuda and the Bahamas area', in Ammon, U., Dittmar, N., Mattheier, K. and Trudgill, P. (eds) *Sociolinguistics: An International Handbook of the Science of Language and Society*, 2nd edn, Berlin: de Gruyter.

Danchev, A. (1992) 'Analytic and synthetic developments in English', in Rissanen, M., Ihalainen, O., Nevalainen, T. and Taavitsainen, I. (eds) *History of Englishes; New Methods and Interpretations in Historical Linguistics*, Berlin: Mouton de Gruyter, 25–41.

Davenport, M., Hansen, E. and Nielsen, H.F. (1983) *Current Topics in English Historical Linguistics*, Odense: Odense University Press.

Davidsen, M. (1974) *Life in America*, vol. II, Boston: Houghton Mifflin Company.

Davidson, W.V. (1974) *Historical Geography of the Bay Islands, Honduras: Anglo-hispanic Conflict in the Western Caribbean*, Birmingham, AL: Southern University Press.

Davis, H. (1999) 'Typography, lexicography and the development of the idea of "standard English" ', in Bex, T. and Watts, R.J. (eds) *Standard English: The Widening Debate*, London: Routledge, 69–88.

Defoe, D. (1698) *An Essay on Projects*, London.

—— (1724–26) *A Tour through the Whole Island of Great Britain*, 3 vols, 1927 edn, London: Peter Davies.

DeKlerk, V. (ed.) (1996) *Focus on South Africa*, Amsterdam: John Benjamins.

Dobson, E.J. (1968) *English Pronunciation 1500–1700*, 2nd edn, Oxford: Clarendon Press.

Dobson, S. (1969) *Larn Yersel Geordie*, Newcastle: Frank Graham.

Docherty, G.J., Foulkes, P., Milroy, J., Milroy, L. and Walshaw, D. (1997) 'Descriptive adequacy in phonology: a variationist perspective', *Journal of Linguistics* 33: 275–310.

Drake, G. (1977) *The Role of Prescriptivism in American Linguistics, 1820–1970*, Amsterdam: John Benjamins.

Duffey, E. (1877) *The Ladies' and Gentlemen's Etiquette: A Complete Manual of the Manners and Dress of American Society*, Philadelphia: Porter and Coates.

Duncan, G. (1870/1942) *How to Talk Correctly: A Pocket Manual to Promote Polite and Accurate Conversation, Writing and Reading ... With More Than 500 Errors in Speaking and Writing Corrected*, Toronto: Musson.

Dyson, B.T. (1997) 'Notes on the West Riding dialect almanacs', in Kellett, A. and Dewhirst, I. (eds) *A Century of Yorkshire Dialect*, Otley: Smith Settle, 164–77.

Eagleson, R. (1982) 'English in Australia and New Zealand', in Bailey, R. and Görlach, M. (eds) *English as a World Language*, Cambridge: Cambridge University Press, 415–38.

Easson, A. (1985) 'Elizabeth Gaskell and the novel of local pride', *Bulletin of the John Rowlands Library, University of Manchester* 67: 688–709.

Easther, A. (1883) *A Glossary of the Dialect of Almondbury and Huddersfield*, London: Trübner and Co.

Ehrhart-Kneher, S. (1996) 'Palmerston English', in Wurm, S.A., Mühlhäusler, P. and Tryon, D.T. (eds) *Atlas of Languages of Intercultural Communication in the Pacific, Asia, and the Americas*, Berlin: Mouton de Gruyter, 523–31.

Eisikovits, E. (1981) 'Inner Sydney-English: An investigation of grammatical variation in adolescent speech', unpublished Ph.D. thesis, University of Sydney, Sydney.

—— (1987) 'Variation in the lexical verb in inner-Sydney English', *Australian Journal of Linguistics* 9: 3–20.

—— (1989) 'Variation in the perfective in inner-Sydney English', *Australian Journal of Linguistics* 7: 1–24.

Elias, N. (1994) *The Civilizing Process*, Oxford: Blackwell.

Ellis, A.J. (1869–89) *On Early English Pronunciation*, 5 vols, London: Trübner.

—— (1890) *English Dialects – Their Sounds and Homes*, London: Kegan Paul, Trench, Trübner and Co.

Elmes, S. (1999) *The Routes of English*, London: BBC.

Emeneau, M.B. (1935) 'The dialect of Lunenburg, Nova Scotia', *Language* 11: 140–47. Republished in Chambers, J.K. (ed.) (1975) *Canadian English: Origins and Structures*, Toronto: Methuen.

Emrich, RS. (1962) 'New dictionary cheap, corrupt', *The Detroit News*, 10 February (cited in Sledd, J. and Ebbitt, W. (eds) (1962) *Dictionaries and that Dictionary*, Chicago: Scott, Foresman, 128–29).

Etiquette for Gentlemen with Hints on the Art of Conversation (1841) 14th edn, London: Tilt and Bogue.

Evans, B. (1962) 'Noah Webster had the same troubles', *The New York Times Magazine*, 13 May, pp. 11, 77, 79–80.

Fairclough, N. (1992) 'The appropriacy of "appropriateness"', in Fairclough, N. (ed.) *Critical Language Awareness*, London: Longman, 33–56.

Fanego, T. (1996) 'The development of gerunds as objects of subject-control verbs in English (1400–1760)', *Diachronica* 13: 29–62.

Farnaby, T. (1641/1969) *Systema Grammaticum*, Menston, UK: Scolar Press.

Farrar, K., Grabe, E. and Nolan, F. (1999) 'English intonation in the British Isles', in Upton, C. and Wales, K. (eds) *Dialectal Variation in English: Proceedings of the Harold Orton Centenary Conference 1998*, Leeds Studies in English, n.s. 30, 243–56.

Fasold, R. (1972) *Tense Marking in Black English: A Linguistic and Social Analysis*, Washington, DC: Center for Applied Linguistics.

Feagin, C. (1979) *Variation and Change in Alabama English: A Sociolinguistic Study of the White Community*, Washington, DC: Georgetown University Press.

Fehrenbacher, D. (1964) *Abraham Lincoln: A Documentary Portrait through his Speeches and Writings*, New York: The New American Library.

Fenning, D. (1771/1967) *A New Grammar of the English Language*, Menston, UK: Scolar Press.

Ferguson, C. and Brice Heath, S. (eds) (1981) *Language in the USA*, Cambridge: Cambridge University Press.

Finegan, E. (1980) *Attitudes toward English Usage*, New York: Teachers College Press.

Fischer, A. (1998) '*Marry*. From religious invocation to discourse marker', in Borgmeier, R., Grabes, H. and Jucker, A.H. (eds) *Anglistentag 1997 Giessen. Proceedings*, Trier: Wissenschaftlicher Verlag, 35–46.

Fisher, A. (1750/1968) *A New Grammar*, Newcastle: I. Thompson and Co.

Fisiak, J. and Krygier, M. (eds) (1998) *Advances in English Historical Linguistics (1996)*, Berlin: Mouton de Gruyter.

Fitzmaurice, S. (2000) '*The Spectator*, the politics of social networks, and language standardisation in eighteenth century England', in Wright, L. (ed.) *The Development of Standard English 1300–1800: Theories, Descriptions, Conflicts*, Cambridge: Cambridge University Press, 195–218.

Flint, E. (1964) 'The language of Norfolk Island', in Ross, A.S.C. and Moverley, A.W. *The Pitcairnese Language*, London: Deutsch.

Fogg, P.W. (1792/1970) *Elementa Anglicana*, Menston, UK: Scolar Press.

Foyster, E.A. (1999) *Manhood in Early Modern England: Honour, Sex and Marriage*, London: Longman.

Frazer, T.C., Murray, T.E. and Lee Simon, B. (1996) '*Need* + past participle in American English', *American Speech* 77,3: 255–71.

French, W.M. (1964) *America's Educational Tradition. An Interpretative History*, Lexington, MA: D. C. Heath and Company.

Fries, C.C. (1925) 'The periphrastic future with "shall" and "will" in modern English', *Publications of the Modern Linguistic Association of America* 40: 963ff.

—— (1940) *American English Grammar*, New York: Appleton-Century-Crofts.

Fuami, S. (1997) *Essays on Shakespeare's Language. Language, Discourse and Text*, Kyoto: Apollon-sha.

Gildon, C. and Brightland, J. (1711) *A Grammar of the English Tongue*, Menston, UK: Scolar Press.

Gill, A. (1619/1972) *Logonomia Anglica*, Stockholm: Almqvist and Wiksell.

Gimson, A.C. (1970) *Introduction to the Pronunciation of English*, 2nd edn, London: Edward Arnold.

Gladstone, J. (1893) *Elocution as an Art*, New Orleans: Dominican Academy.

Gordon, E. (1983) 'New Zealand English pronunciation: an investigation into some early written records', *Te Reo* 26: 29–42.

Gordon, E. and Deverson, T. (1998) *New Zealand English and English in New Zealand*, Auckland: New House.

Gordon, E. and Maclagan, M. (1990) 'A longitudinal study of the "ear/air" contrast in New Zealand speech', in Bell, A. and Holmes, J. (eds) *New Zealand Ways of Speaking English*, Clevedon: Multilingual Matters, 129–48.

Görlach, M. (1998) *An Annotated Bibliography of 19th-Century Grammars of English*, Amsterdam: John Benjamins.

Goswami, U. and Bryant, P. (1990) *Phonological Skills and Learning to Read*. Hove: Lawrence Erlbaum Associates.

Gough, D. (1995) 'English in South Africa', in Silva, P. (ed.) *A Dictionary of South African English on Historical Principles*, Oxford: Oxford University Press, xvii–xix.

—— (1996) 'Black English in South Africa', in DeKlerk, V. (ed.) *Focus on South Africa*, Amsterdam: John Benjamins, 52–77.

Gowing, L. (1996) *Domestic Dangers: Women, Words, and Sex in Early Modern London*, Oxford: Clarendon Press.

Graddol, D. (1999) 'The decline of the native speaker', in Graddol, D. and Meinhof, U.H. (eds) *English in a Changing World. AILA (l'Association Internationale de Linguistique Appliquée) Review* 13, Milton Keynes: Catchline.

Graddol, D., Leith, D. and Swann, J. (1996) *English: History, Diversity and Change*, London: Open University and Routledge.

Graham, G.F. (1869) *A Book About Words*, London.

Graham, J. (1992) 'Settler society', in Rice, G. (ed.) *The Oxford History of New Zealand*, 2nd edn, Auckland: Oxford University Press, 112–40.

—— (1996) 'The pioneers (1840–1870)', in Sinclair, K. (ed.) *The Oxford Illustrated History of New Zealand*, 2nd edn, Auckland: Oxford University Press, 49–74.

Gray, H. (1963) 'Renaissance humanism: The pursuit of eloquence', *Journal of the History of Ideas* 24: 497–514.

Great Orators, Statesmen and Divines (1881) Edinburgh: Nimmo and Co.

Greenwood, J. (1711/1968) *An Essay Towards a Practical English Grammar*, Menston, UK: Scolar Press.

Grose, F. (1787) *A Provincial Glossary*, Menston, UK: Scolar Press.

Guest, H. (1998) 'The deep romance of Manchester: Gaskell's *Mary Barton*', in Snell, K.D.M. (ed.) *The Regional Novel in Britain and Ireland 1800–1990*, Cambridge: Cambridge University Press, 78–98.

Guy, G. and Vonwiller, J. (1984) 'The meaning of an intonation in Australian English', *Australian Journal of Linguistics* 4: 1–17.

—— (1989) 'The high rising tone in Australian English', in Collins, P. and Blair, D. (eds) *Australian English: the Language of a New Society*, St Lucia: University of Queensland Press, 21–34.

Gwynne, P. (1855) *A Word to the Wise, or: Hints on the Current Improprieties of Expression in Writing and Speaking*, London: Griffith and Farran.

Hammerström, G. (1980) *Australian English: Its Origins and Status*, Hamburg: Helmut Buske.

Hancock, I. (1986) 'The domestic hypothesis, diffusion and componentiality: an account of Atlantic anglophone creole origins', in Smith, N. and Muysken, P. (eds) *Proceedings of the Workshop on Universals versus Substrata in Creole Genesis*, Amsterdam: Benjamins, 81–102.

Harris, G. (1752/1970) *Observations Upon the English Language*, New York: Garland.

Harrison, T. (1987) *Selected Poems*, 2nd. edn., London: Penguin.

Harrison, W. (1577, reproduced 1965) *The Description of England in Holinshed's Chronicles*, London: AMS Press.

Hartley, C. (1870) *Elocution Made Easy*, London: Groombridge and Sons.

Hatfield, J.T., Leopold, W. and Zieglschmid, A.J.F. (eds) (1930) *Curme Volume of Linguistic Studies*, Baltimore: Waverley Press.

Heal, F. and Holmes, C. (1994) *The Gentry in England and Wales 1500–1700*, London: Macmillan.

Heritage, J. (1984) 'A change-of-state token and aspects of its sequential placement', in Atkinson, J.M. and Heritage, J. (eds) *Structure of Social Action. Studies in Conversation Analysis*, Cambridge: Cambridge University Press, 299–345.

Heslop, O. (1892) *Northumberland Words: A Glossary of Words Used in the County of Northumberland and on Tyneside*, vol. 1, London: Kegan Paul, Trench, Trübner and Co.

Hewitt, M. and Poole, R. (2000) 'Samuel Bamford and northern identity', in Kirk, H. (ed.) *Northern Identities: Historical Interpretations of 'The North' and 'Northernness'*, Aldershot: Ashgate.

Hill, A.G. (ed.) (1984) *The Letters of William Wordsworth*, Oxford: Clarendon.

Hill, A.S. (1893) *The Foundations of Rhetoric*, New York, NY: American Book Co.

Hitchcock, E.V. (ed.) (1932) *Harpsfield's Life of More* (EETS OS 186), London: Oxford University Press.

Ho, M.L. and Platt, J.T. (1993) *Dynamics of a Dialect Continuum – Singapore English*, Oxford: Clarendon.

Hogg, R. and Denison, D. (eds) (2002) *A History of the English Language*, Cambridge: Cambridge University Press.

Hollingworth, B. (ed.) (1977) *Songs of the People: Lancashire Dialect Poetry of the Industrial Revolution*, Manchester: Manchester University Press.

Holm, J. (1978) 'The English creole of Nicaragua's Miskito Coast', unpublished Ph.D. thesis, University of London.

—— (1980) 'African features in White Bahamian English', *English World Wide* 1: 45–65.

—— (1983) 'Nicaragua's Miskito Coast Creole English', in Holm, J. (ed.) *Central American English*, Heidelberg: Julius Groos, 95–130.

—— (ed.) (1983) *Central American English*, Heidelberg: Julius Groos.

—— (1989) *Pidgins and Creoles*, Cambridge: Cambridge University Press.

—— (1994) 'English in the Caribbean', in Burchfield, R. (ed.) *The Cambridge History of the English Language. Volume V: English in Britain and Overseas*, Cambridge: Cambridge University Press, 328–81.

Holm, J. and Hackert, S. (1996) 'Southern Bahamian: Transported AAVE or transported Gullah?', in Lipski, J. (ed.) *African-American English and its Congeners*, Amsterdam: Benjamins.

Holm, J. and Shilling, A.W. (1982) *Dictionary of Bahamian English*, Cold Spring Harbor, NY: Lexik House.

Holme, S. (1898) *Elocution: A Manual for Classes and Students*, London: John Heywood.

Holmes, J. (1994) 'New Zealand Flappers: An analysis of *t* voicing in New Zealand English', *English World Wide* 15: 195–224.

—— (1995a) 'Glottal stops in New Zealand English: an analysis of variants of word final *t*', *Linguistics* 33: 433–63.

—— (1995b) *Women, Men and Politeness*, London: Longman.

—— (1997) 'Setting new standards: sound changes and gender in New Zealand English', *English World Wide* 18: 107–42.

—— (1998) 'Women's talk: the question of sociolinguistic universals', in Coates, J. (ed.) *Language and Gender*, Oxford: Blackwell, 461–83.

Holmes, J. and Bell, A. (1992) 'On shear markets and sharing sheep: The merger of EAR and AIR diphthongs in New Zealand English', *Language Variation and Change* 4: 251–73.

Holmes, J., Bell, A. and Boyce, M. (1991) *Variation and change in New Zealand English: a social dialect investigation (Project report to the Foundation for Research, Science & Technology)*, Wellington: Victoria University Linguistics Department.

Holmqvist, E. (1922) *On the History of the English Present Inflections Particularly -th and -s*, Heidelberg: Carl Winter.

Honey, J. (1988) 'Talking proper: schooling and the establishment of English "RP"', in Nixon, G. and Honey, J. (eds) *An Historic Tongue: Studies in English Linguistics in Honour of Barbara Strang*, London: Routledge, 209–27.

—— (1989) *Does Accent Matter? The Pygmalion Factor*, London: Faber and Faber.

—— (1997) *Language is Power: The Story of Standard English and its Enemies*, London: Faber and Faber.

Horvath, B. (1985) *Variation in Australian English*, Cambridge: Cambridge University Press.

Horvath, B. and Horvath, R. (1997) 'The geolinguistics of a sound change in progress: /l/ vocalisation in Australia', *University of Pennsylvania Working Papers in Linguistics* 4: 109–24.

—— (1999) 'Geolinguistics of /l/ vocalisation in Australian and New Zealand Englishes. A multilocality approach', Lecture given at the University of Essex, Colchester, November 1999.

Howe, D.M. and Walker, J.A. (2000) 'Negation in Early African American English: A creole diagnostic?', in Poplack, S. (ed.) *The English History of African American English*, Oxford: Blackwell Publishers, 109–40.

How to Shine in Society (1867) *How to Shine in Society; or the Art of Conversation Containing its Principles, Laws and General Usage in Modern Polite Society*, Glasgow: George Watson.

Hudson, R. (1996) *Sociolinguistics*, 2nd edn, Cambridge: Cambridge University Press.

Hudson, R. and Holmes, J. (1995) *Children's Use of Spoken Standard English*, London: School Curriculum and Assessment Authority.

Hume, A. (1617) *Of the Orthographie and Congruitie of the Britan Tongue: A Treates noe Shorter Than Necessarie, for the Schooles*, London: Trübner and Co.

Hume, D. (1825) *Of Eloquence*. In *Essays and Treatises on Several Subjects*, Edinburgh.

Hundt, M. (1998) *New Zealand English Grammar, Fact or Fiction: A Corpus-based Study in Morphosyntactic Variation*, Amsterdam: John Benjamins.

Ihalainen, O. (1994) 'The dialects of England since 1776', in Burchfield, R. (ed.) *The Cambridge History of the English Language. Volume V: English in Britain and Overseas*, Cambridge: Cambridge University Press, 197–270.

Inglis, K. (1974) *The Australian Colonists*, Melbourne: Melbourne University Press.

Irvine, J. (1975) 'Wolof speech styles and social status', working papers in sociolinguistics no. 23, Austin, TX: Southwest Educational Development Laboratory.

Iyeiri, Y. (1999) 'Multiple negation in Middle English verse', in Tieken-Boon van Ostade, I., Tottie, G. and van der Wurff, W. (eds) *Negation in the History of English*, Berlin: Mouton de Gruyter, 121–46

Jackson, G. (1830) *Popular Errors in English Grammar, Particularly in Pronunciation, Familiarly Pointed Out: For the Use of Those Persons Who Want Either Opportunity or Inclination to Study This Science*, London: Effingham Wilson.

James, D. (1996) 'Women, men and prestige speech forms: a critical review', in Bergvall, V.L., Bing, J.M. and Freed, A.F. (eds) *Rethinking Language and Gender Research: Theory and Practice*, London: Longman, 98–125.

Jamieson, K. (1988) *Eloquence in an Electronic Age. The Transformation of Political Speechmaking*, New York: Oxford University Press.

Jeremiah, M.A. (1977) 'The linguistic relatedness of Black English and Antiguan Creole: Evidence from the eighteenth and nineteenth centuries', unpublished Ph.D. dissertation, Brown University.

Jespersen, O. (1909/1949) *A Modern English Grammar. Part VI: Morphology*, London: George Allen and Unwin Ltd.

—— (1922) *Language: its Nature, Development and Origin*, London: George Allen and Unwin.

—— (1962) *Growth and Structure of the English Language*, 9th edn, Oxford: Blackwell.

Jewell, H. (1994) *The North–South Divide*, Manchester: Manchester University Press.

Johnson, N. (1993) 'The popularization of nineteenth-century rhetoric. Elocution and the private learner', in Clark, G. and Halloran, M. (eds) *Oratorical Culture in Nineteenth-Century America. Transformations in the Theory and Practice of Rhetoric*, Carbondale/Edwardsville: Southern Illinois University Press.

Johnson, S. (1752) *The Rambler*, no. 208 in *The Works of Samuel Johnson*, London 1796.

Johnson, S. (1779–81) *Lives of the Poets*, London.

Jones, C. (1993) 'Scottish Standard English in the late eighteenth century', *Transactions of the Philological Society* 91: 95–131.

Jones, H. (1724) *An Accidence to the English Tongue*, London: John Clarke.

Jonson, B. (1640/1972) *The English Grammar*, Menston, UK: Scolar Press.

Joseph, J.E. (1987) *Eloquence and Power: The Rise of Language Standards and Standard Languages*, London: Frances Pinter.

Joseph, J.E. and Taylor, T.J. (eds) (1990) *Ideologies of Language*, London: Routledge.

Jucker, A.H. (1997) 'The discourse marker *well* in the history of English', *English Language and Linguistics* 1: 91–110.

Jucker, A.H. and Smith, S.W. (1998) '*And people just you know like 'wow'*: Discourse markers as negotiating strategies', in Jucker, A.H. and Ziv, Y. (eds) *Discourse Markers: Descriptions and Theory*, Amsterdam: Benjamins, 171–201.

Jucker, A.H. and Ziv, Y. (1998) 'Discourse markers: Introduction', in Jucker, A.H. and Ziv, Y. (eds) *Discourse Markers: Descriptions and Theory*, Amsterdam: Benjamins, 1–12.

Kachru, B.B. (1983) *The Indianization of English*, Delhi: Oxford University Press.

Källgård, A. (1993) 'Present-day Pitcairnese', *English World Wide* 14: 71–114.

Keegan, T. (1996) *Colonial South Africa and the Origins of the Racial Order*, Charlottesville, VA: University of Virginia.

Kennedy, G. (1980) *Classical Rhetoric and its Christian and Secular Tradition from Ancient to Modern Times*, Chapel Hill, NC: University of North Carolina Press.

Kenyon, J.S. (1948) 'Cultural levels and functional varieties of English', *College English* 10: 31–6.

Kerswill, P. and Williams, A. (1999) 'Dialect recognition and speech community focusing in new and old towns in England', in Upton, C. and Wales, K. (eds) *Dialectal Variation in English: Proceedings of the Harold Orton Centenary Conference 1998*, Leeds Studies in English, n.s. 30, 205–37.

King, J. (1993) 'Maori English: a phonological study', *New Zealand English Newsletter* 7: 33–47.

Klein, L.E. (1986) 'Berkeley, Shaftesbury, and the meaning of politeness', *Studies in Eighteenth Century Culture* 16: 57–68.

—— (1989) 'Liberty, manners, and politeness in early eighteenth-century England', *The Historical Journal* 32: 583–605.

—— (1994) *Shaftesbury and the Culture of Politeness: Moral Discourse and Cultural Politics in Early Eighteenth-century England*, Cambridge: Cambridge University Press.

—— (1995) 'Politeness for plebes: Consumption and social identity in early eighteenth century England', in Bermingham, A. and Brewer, J. (eds) *The Consumption of Culture, 1600–1800: Image, Object, Text*, New York, NY: Routledge, 362–82.

Klemola, K.J. (1996) 'Non-standard periphrastic *do*: A study of variation and change', unpublished Ph.D. dissertation, Essex.

Knowles, G. (1997) *A Cultural History of the English Language*, London: Arnold.

Knowles, J. (1883) *The Elocutionist*, 28th edn, London: Gall and Inglis.

Krygier, M. (1994) *The Disintegration of the English Strong Verb System*, Frankfurt: Lang.

Kryk-Kastovsky, B. (1998) 'Pragmatic particles in Early Modern English tracts', in Borgmeier, R., Grabes, H. and Jucker, A.H. (eds) *Anglistentag 1997 Giessen. Proceedings*, Trier: Wissenschaftlicher Verlag, 47–56.

Kuiper, K. and Bell, A. (2000) 'New Zealand and New Zealand English', in Bell, A. and Kuiper, K. (eds) *New Zealand English*, Amsterdam: Benjamins, 11–22.

Kytö, M. (1993) 'Third-person present singular verb inflection in Early British and American English', *Language Variation and Change* 5: 113–39.

Labov, W. (1972) *Sociolinguistic Patterns*, Philadelphia: University of Philadelphia Press.

—— (1990) 'The intersection of sex and social class in the course of linguistic change', *Language Variation and Change* 2: 205–54.

—— (1994) *Principles of Linguistic Change, Vol. 1: Internal factors*, Oxford: Blackwell.

—— (2001) *Principles of Linguistic Change, Vol. 2: Social Factors*, Oxford: Blackwell.

Labov, W., Cohen, P., Robins, C. and Lewis, J. (1968) *A Study of the Non-Standard English of Negro and Puerto Rican Speakers in New York City*, Philadelphia: US Regional Survey.

Laird, C. (1970) *Language in America*, New York: World.

Langford, P. (1989) *A Polite and Commercial People. England 1727–1783*, Oxford: Oxford University Press.

Lanham, L. (1978) 'South African English', in Lanham, L. and Prinsloo, K.P. (eds) *Language and Communication Studies in South Africa: Current Issues and Directions in Research and Inquiry*, Cape Town: Oxford University Press, 138–66.

—— (1982) 'English in South Africa', in Bailey, R. and Görlach, M. (eds) *English as a World Language*, Cambridge: Cambridge University Press, 324–52.

—— (1995) 'The pronunciation of English in South Africa', in Silva, P. (ed.) *A Dictionary of South African English on Historical Principles*, Oxford: Oxford University Press, xxi–xxiv.

—— (1996) 'A history of English in South Africa', in DeKlerk, V. (ed.) *Focus on South Africa*, Amsterdam: John Benjamins, 18–34.

Lasch, C. (1978) *The Culture of Narcissism*, New York: W. W. Norton.

Lass, R. (1987) *The Shape of English*, London: Dent and Sons.

—— (1997) *Historical Linguistics and Language Change*, Cambridge: Cambridge University Press.

Lastra, Y. (forthcoming) 'Mexico and Central America', in Ammon, U., Dittmar, N., Mattheier, K. and Trudgill, P. (eds) *Sociolinguistics: An International Handbook of the Science of Language and Society*, 2nd edn, Berlin: de Gruyter.

Laycock, D. (1989) 'The status of Pitcairn–Norfolk: creole dialect or cant', in Ammon, U. (ed.) *Status and Function of Languages and Language Varieties*, Berlin: de Gruyter, 608–29.

Leith, D. (1983) *A Social History of English*, London: Routledge and Kegan Paul.

—— (1996) 'The origins of English', in Graddol, D., Leith, D. and Swann, J. (eds) *English: History, Diversity and Change*, London: Open University and Routledge, 95–132.

Leith, D. and Graddol, D. (1996) 'Modernity and English as a national language', in Graddol, D., Leith, D. and Swann, J. (eds) *English: History, Diversity and Change*, London: Open University and Routledge, 136–79.

Lester, A. (1998) '"Otherness" and the frontiers of empire: the Eastern Cape Colony, 1806–c.1850', *Journal of Historical Geography* 24: 2–19.

Lewis, G. (1996) 'The origins of New Zealand English: a report on work in progress', *New Zealand English Journal* 10: 25–30.

Lippi-Green, R. (1997) *English with an Accent*, London: Routledge.

Little Female Orators (1770) London.

Lodge, R.A. (1993) *French: from Dialect to Standard*, London: Routledge.

Lodowyck, F. (1652/1968) *The Ground-Work of a New Perfect Language*, Menston, UK: Scolar Press.

Long, D. (ed.) (1998) 'The linguistic culture of the Ogasawara Islands', *Japanese Language Centre Research Reports* 6. Osaka: Shoin Women's College.

—— (2000) 'Evidence of an English contact language in the 19th century Bonin Islands', *English World Wide* 20: 251–86.

—— (forthcoming) 'Examining the Bonin (Ogasawara) Islands within the contexts of Pacific language contact', in Fischer, S. and Sperlich, W.B. (eds) *Leo Pasifika: Proceedings of the Fourth International Conference on Oceanic Linguistics*.

Lowe, S. (1723–38/1971) *Four Tracts on Grammar*, Menston, UK: Scolar Press.

Lowth, R. (1761/1967) *A Short Introduction to English Grammar*, Menston, UK: Scolar Press.

Lucas, D. (1987) *The Welsh, Irish, Scots and English in Australia*, Australia: Australian National University Printing Service.

Lucas, J. (1990) *Ideas of Nationhood in English Poetry 1791–1819*, London: Hogarth Press.

Lunsford, A. (ed.) (1995) *Reclaiming Rhetorica. Women in the Rhetorical Tradition*, Pittsburgh: University of Pittsburgh Press.

Lutz, A. (1998) 'The interplay of external and internal factors in morphological restructuring: the case of *you*', in Fisiak, J. and Krygier, M. (eds) *Advances in English Historical Linguistics (1996)*, Berlin: Mouton de Gruyter 189–210.

MacArthur, B. (1995) *The Penguin Book of Historical Speeches*, London: Viking.

McArthur, T. (1985) 'The superior, inferior and barbarous Britains', *English Today*: 24.

—— (1992) *The Oxford Companion to the English Language*, Oxford: Oxford University Press.

—— (1998) *The English Languages*, Cambridge: Cambridge University Press.

McCrum, R., Cran, W. and MacNeil, R. (1986) *The Story of English*, London: BBC Publications/Faber and Faber.

McIntosh, C. (1986) *Common and Courtly Language. The Stylistics of Social Class in 18th-century English Literature*, Philadelphia: University of Pennsylvania Press.

—— (1998) *The Evolution of English Prose, 1700–1800: Style, Politeness, and Print Culture*, Cambridge: Cambridge University Press.

Macintyre, S. (1999) *A Concise History of Australia*, Australia: Cambridge University Press.

Maclagan, M. and Gordon, E. (1996) 'Out of the AIR and into the EAR: Another view of the New Zealand diphthong merger', *Language Variation and Change* 8: 125–47.

MacMahon, M. (1998) 'Phonology', in Romaine, S. (ed.) *The Cambridge History of the English Language. Vol. IV: 1776–1997*, Cambridge: Cambridge University Press, 373–535.

Malan, K. (1996) 'Cape Flats English', in DeKlerk, V. (ed.) *Focus on South Africa*, Amsterdam: John Benjamins, 125–48.

Malone, K. (1930). 'When did Middle English begin?', in Hatfield, J.T., Leopold, W. and Zieglschmid, A.J.F. (eds) *Curme Volume of Linguistic Studies*, Baltimore: Waverley Press, 110–17.

Marsh, G.P. (1865) *Lectures on the English Language*, edited by W. Smith, London: John Murray.

Mason, G. (1633) *Grammaire Angloise*, Menston, UK: Scolar Press.

Melchers, G. (1978) 'Mrs Gaskell and dialect', *Studies in English Philology, Linguistics and Literature (Stockholm Studies in English)* 46: 112–24.

Mendelson, S.H. (1985) 'Stuart women's diaries and occasional memoirs', in Prior, M. (ed.) *Women in English Society 1500–1800*, London: Methuen, 181–210.

Mendelson, S. and Crawford, P. (1998) *Women in Early Modern England 1550–1720*, Oxford: Clarendon Press.

Meriton, G. (1683) *A Yorkshire Dialogue*, edited by A.C. Cawley (1959), *Yorkshire Dialect Society*, reprint no. 2, Otley: Smith Settle.

Mesthrie, R. (1990) '"Did the Butler do it?": on an analogue of Butler English in Natal', *World Englishes* 9: 281–8.

—— (1992a) *English in Language Shift: The History, Structure and Sociolinguistics of South African Indian English*, Cambridge: Cambridge University Press.

—— (1992b) *A Lexicon of South African Indian English*, Leeds: Peepal Tree Press.

—— (1995) 'South African Indian English: from L2 to L1', in Mesthrie, R. (ed.) *Language and Social History: Studies in South African Sociolinguistics*, Cape Town: David Philip, 251–64.

—— (1996a) 'Language contact, transmission, shift: South African Indian English', in DeKlerk, V. (ed.) *Focus on South Africa*, Amsterdam: John Benjamins, 79–98.

—— (1996b) 'Imagint excusations: Missionary English in the nineteenth-century Cape colony, South Africa', *World Englishes* 15:139–57.

—— (1998) 'Words across worlds: aspects of language contact and language learning in the eastern Cape, 1800–1850', *African Studies* 57: 5–26.

—— (1999) 'The study of new varieties of English', Inaugural Lecture, University of Cape Town, 6 October 1999. University of Cape Town pamphlet: New Series No. 214.

Miège, G. (1688) *The English Grammar*, Menston, UK: Scolar Press.

Millar, S. (1998) 'Language prescription: a success in failure's clothing?', in Hogg, R. and van Bergen, L. (eds) *Historical Linguistics 1995*, Vol. 2, *Germanic*, Amsterdam: John Benjamin.

Milroy, J. (1977) *The Language of Gerard Manley Hopkins*, London: Deutsch.

—— (1983) 'On the sociolinguistic history of /h/ dropping in English', in Davenport, M., Hansen, E. and Nielsen, H.F. (eds) *Current Topics in English Historical Linguistics*, Odense: Odense University Press, 37–53.

—— (1992) *Linguistic Variation and Change: On the Historical Sociolinguistics of English*, Oxford: Blackwell.

—— (1999) 'The consequences of standardisation in descriptive linguistics', in Bex, T. and Watts, R.J. (eds) *Standard English: The Widening Debate*, London: Routledge, 16–39.

—— (2000) 'Historical description and the ideology of the standard language', in Wright, L. (ed.) *The Development of Standard English 1300–1800: Theories, Descriptions, Conflicts*, Cambridge: Cambridge University Press, 11–28.

Milroy, L. (1999a) 'Standard English and language ideology in Britain and the United States', in Bex, T. and Watts, R.J. (eds) *Standard English: The Widening Debate*, London: Routledge, 173–206.

—— (1999b) 'Women as innovators and norm-creators: the sociolinguistics of dialect leveling in a northern English city', in Wertheim, S., Bailey, A.C. and Corston-Oliver, M. (eds) *Engendering Communication: Proceedings of the Fifth Berkeley Women and Language Conference*, Berkeley, CA: BWLG, 361–76.

Milroy, J. and Milroy, L. (1985) *Authority in Language*, London: Routledge.

—— (eds) (1993a) *Real Language: The Grammar of Dialects in the British Isles*, London: Longman.

—— (1993b) 'Mechanisms of change in urban dialects: the role of class, social network and gender', *International Journal of Applied Linguistics* 3: 57–77.

—— (1999) *Authority in Language*, 3rd edn, London: Routledge.

Minkova, D. and Stockwell, R. (1990) 'The Early Modern English vowels: More O' Lass', *Diachronica* 7 (2): 199–214.

Mitchell, A.G. and Delbridge, A. (1965) *The Pronunciation of English in Australia*, Sydney: Angus and Robertson.

Mobärg, M. (1989) *English 'Standard' Pronunciations: A Study of Attitudes*, Göteborg: Acta Universitatis Gothoburgensis.

Mohrmann, G.P. (1983) 'Oratorical delivery and other problems in current scholarship on English Renaissance rhetoric', in Murphy, J. (ed.) *Renaissance Eloquence. Studies in the Theory and Practice of Renaissance Rhetoric*, Berkeley, CA: University of California Press.

Montgomery, M. and Melo, C.A. (1990) 'The phonology of the lost cause', *English World Wide* 10: 195–216.

—— (1995) 'The language: the preservation of southern speech among the colonists', in Dawsey, C.B. and Dawsey, J.M. (eds) *The Confederados: Old South Immigrants in Brazil*, Tuscaloosa, AL: University of Alabama Press, 176–90.

Moorhouse, G. (1973) *The Missionaries*, London: Eyre Methuen.

Morse-Jones, E. (1971) *Role of the British Settlers in South Africa*, Cape Town: A. A. Balkema.

Mufwene, S. (1996) 'The Founder Principle in creole genesis', *Diachronica* 13: 83–134.

Mugglestone, L. (1995) *'Talking Proper': The Rise of Accent as a Social Symbol*, Oxford: Clarendon Press.

—— (ed.) (forthcoming) *The Oxford History of the English Language*, Oxford: Oxford University Press.

Mühlhäusler, P. (1998) 'How creoloid can you get?', *Journal of Pidgin and Creole Languages* 13: 355–71.

Murray, J.A.H. (1873) *The Dialect of the Southern Counties of Scotland: Its Pronunciation, Grammar and Historical Relations*, London: Philological Society.

Murray, L. (1795/1968) *English Grammar*, Menston, UK: Scolar Press.

Mustanoja, T.F. (1960) *A Middle English Syntax*, Part 1 (Mémoires de la Société Néophilologique 23), Helsinki: Société Néophilologique.

Myers-Scotton, C. (1993) *Social Motivations for Codeswitching – Evidence from Africa*, Oxford: Clarendon.

Myhill, J. and Harris, W.A. (1986) 'The use of verbal -*s* inflection in BEV', in Sankoff, D. (ed.) *Diversity and Diachrony*, Amsterdam: John Benjamins, 25–32.

Narratives of a Late Expedition against the Indians (1783) The Garland Library of Narratives of North American Indian Captivities, vol. 12, 1978, New York: Garland Publishing.

Nesfield, J.C. (1898) *English Grammar, Past and Present*, New York: Macmillan.

Nevalainen, T. (1996) 'Gender difference', in Nevalainen, T. and Raumolin-Brunberg, H. (eds) *Sociolinguistics and Language History: Studies based on The Corpus of Early English Correspondence*, Amsterdam: Rodopi, 77–91.

—— (1997) 'Recycling inversion: the case of initial adverbs and negators in Early Modern English', *Studia Anglica Posnaniensia* 31: 203–14.

—— (1998) 'Social mobility and the decline of multiple negation in Early Modern English', in Fisiak, J. and Krygier, M. (eds) *Advances in English Historical Linguistics (1996)*, Berlin: Mouton de Gruyter, 263–91.

—— (2000) 'Gender differences in the evolution of Standard English: evidence from the *Corpus of Early English Correspondence*', *Journal of English Linguistics* 28: 38–59.

Nevalainen, T. and Raumolin-Brunberg, H. (1994) '*Its* strength and the beauty *of it*: the standardization of the third person neuter possessive in Early Modern English', in Stein, D. and Tieken-Boon van Ostade, I. (eds) *Towards a Standard English 1600–1800*, Berlin: Mouton de Gruyter, 171–216.

—— (1996a) '*The Corpus of Early English Correspondence*', in Nevalainen, T. and Raumolin-Brunberg, H. (eds) *Sociolinguistics and Language History: Studies based on The Corpus of Early English Correspondence*, Amsterdam: Rodopi, 39–54.

—— (eds) (1996b) *Sociolinguistics and Language History: Studies based on The Corpus of Early English Correspondence*, Amsterdam: Rodopi.

—— (forthcoming) *Historical Sociolinguistics*, London: Longman.

Nevalainen, T., Raumolin-Brunberg, H. and Trudgill, P. (2000) 'Chapters in the social history of East Anglian English: the case of the third-person singular', in Fisiak, J. and Trudgill, P. (eds) *History of East Anglian English*, Cambridge: Boydell and Brewer, 187–204.

Newbrook, M. (1999) 'West Wirral: Norms, self-reports and usage', in Foulkes, P. and Doherty, G. (eds) *Urban Voices: Accent Studies in the British Isles*, London: Arnold, 90–106.

Niedzielski, N. and Preston, D.R. (1999) *Folk Linguistics*, Berlin: Mouton de Gruyter.

Nielsen, H.F. (1981) *Old English and the Continental Germanic Languages*, Innsbruck: Innsbrucker Beiträge zur Sprachwissenschaft.

Nihalani, P., Tongue, R.K. and Hosali, P. (1978) *Indian and British English: a Handbook of Usage and Pronunciation*, Delhi: Oxford University Press.

Nurmi, A. (1999) *A Social History of Periphrastic DO* (Mémoires de la Société Néophilologique de Helsinki 56), Helsinki: Société Néophilologique.

Oasa, H. (1989) 'Phonology of current Adelaide English', in Collins, P. and Blair, D. (eds) *Australian English: the Language of a New Society*, St Lucia: University of Queensland Press, 271–87.

O'Connor, L. (1954) *Pioneer Women Orators*, New York: Columbia University Press.

Okulska, U. (1999) 'Stereotypes and language stigma: the causes of prejudice against the weaker sex in Early Modern England', *Studia Anglica Poznaniensia* 34: 171–90.

O'Mara, V.M. (1996) 'Female scribal activity in Late Medieval England: the evidence?' *Leeds Studies in English* N.S. 27: 87–130.

O'Neil, W. (1993) 'Nicaraguan English in history', in Jones, C. (ed.) *Historical Linguistics*, London: Longman, 279–318.

On Public Speaking (1904) *On Public Speaking. What eloquence is and how to acquire it*, by a public speaker. Dublin: James Duffy and Co.

Orsman, H. (ed.) (1997) *The Dictionary of New Zealand English*, Auckland: Oxford University Press.

Orton, H. (1933) *The Phonology of a South Durham Dialect*, London: Kegan Paul, Trench and Trübner.

Orton, H. and Barry, M.V. (1963) *The Survey of English Dialects*, vol. 1: *The Six Northern Counties and the Isle of Man*, Leeds: Edward Arnold.

Orton, H. and Wright, N. (1974) *A Word Geography of England*, London: Seminar Press.

Paddock, H. (1975) 'The folk grammar of Carbonair, Newfoundland', in Chambers, J.K. (ed.) *Canadian English: Origins and Structures*, Toronto: Methuen, 25–32.

Padley, G. (1985) *Grammatical Theory in Western Europe, 1500–1700*, Trends in Vernacular Grammar I, Cambridge: Cambridge University Press.

Palander-Collin, M. (1999) *Grammaticalization and Social Embedding; I THINK and METHINKS in Middle and Early Modern English* (Mémoires de la Société Néophilologique 55), Helsinki: Société Néophilologique.

Palmer, R. (ed.) (1979) *Everyman's Book of English Country Songs*, London: J. M. Dent.

Patrick, P.L. (1999) *Urban Jamaican Creole: Variation in the Mesolect*, Amsterdam: John Benjamins.

Peacham, H. (1577/1971) *The Garden of Eloquence*, Menston, UK: Scolar Press.

Peacock, R.B. (1863) *On Some Leading Characteristics of the Dialects Spoken in the Six Northern Counties of England (or Ancient Northumbria): And on the Variations in their Grammar From That of Standard English: With Their Probable Etymological Sources*, n.p.

Pedersen, L.A. (1967) 'Middle class Negro speech in Minneapolis', *Orbis* 16: 347–53.

Pegge, S. (1803/1814) *Anecdotes of the English Language: Dialect of London*, London: J. Nichols, Son and Bentley.

Percy, T. (1765) *Reliques of Ancient English Poetry*, London: J. Dodsley.

Perley, D. (1834) *A Grammar of the English Language*, Andover, MA: Gould and Newman.

Phillipps, K.C. (1984) *Language and Class in Victorian England*, Oxford: Blackwell.

Phillippson, R. (1992) *Linguistic Imperialism*, Oxford: Oxford University Press.

Pitts, W. (1981) 'Beyond hypercorrection: The use of emphatic -*z* in BEV', *Chicago Linguistic Society* 17: 303–10.

Poplack, S. (ed.) (2000a) *The English History of African American English*, Malden: Blackwell Publishers.

Poplack, S. (2000b) 'Variation, prescription and praxis: Stages of prescriptive grief', paper presented at *Sociolinguistic Symposium 2000*, Bristol, UK.

Poplack, S. and Sankoff, D. (1987) 'The Philadelphia story in the Spanish Caribbean', *American Speech* 62: 291–314.

Poplack, S. and Tagliamonte, S. (1991) 'African American English in the diaspora: The case of old-line Nova Scotians', *Language Variation and Change* 3: 301–39.

—— (1996) 'Nothing in context: Variation, grammaticization and past time marking in Nigerian Pidgin English', in Baker, P. (ed.) *Changing Meanings, Changing Functions: Papers Relating to Grammaticalization in Contact Languages*, Westminster, UK: University of Westminster Press, 71–94.

—— (2001) *African American English in the Diaspora*, Oxford: Blackwell.

Porter, E. (1827) *Analysis of the Principles of Rhetorical Delivery as Applied in Reading and Speaking*, Andover: Mark Newman.

Porter, F. and Macdonald, C. (eds) (1996) *My Hand Will Write What My Heart Dictates*, Auckland: Auckland University Press and Bridget Williams Books.

Potkay, A. (1994) *The Fate of Eloquence in the Age of Hume*, Ithaca: Cornell University Press.

Pratt, T.K. (1988) *Dictionary of Prince Edward Island English*, Toronto: University of Toronto Press.

Prentis, M. (1983) *The Scots In Australia*, Sydney: Sydney University Press.

Preston, D.R. (1989) *Perceptual Dialectology: Nonlinguists' Views of Areal Linguistics*, Dordrecht: Foris.

—— (1996) 'Where the worst English is spoken', in Schneider, E. (ed.) *Focus on the USA*, Amsterdam: Benjamins, 297–360.

Prevost, E.W. (1905) *A Supplement to the Glossary of the Dialect of Cumberland*, London: Henry Frowde.

Priestley, J. (1761/1969) *The Rudiments of English Grammar*, Menston, UK: Scolar Press.

Priestley, J.B. (1934) *English Journey*, London: Heinemann.

Prior, M. (ed.) (1985) *Women in English Society 1500–1800*, London: Methuen.

Puttenham, G. (1589) *The Arte of English Poesie*, edited by E. Arber (1869), London: Alex Murray and Son; reprinted Cambridge: Cambridge University Press, 1936.

Quinn, H. (2000) 'Variation in New Zealand English syntax and morphology', in Bell, A. and Kuiper, K. (eds) *New Zealand English*, Amsterdam: Benjamins, 173–97.

Radcliffe, Mrs (1799) *Description of the Scenry of Skiddaw, 1794*, Appx. XI in T. West (1799, 7th edn).

Ramisch, H. (1989) *The Variation of English in Guernsey, Channel Islands*, Frankfurt: Peter Lang.

Ramsay, A. (1740) *The Tea-table Miscellany*, Glasgow: R. Duncan.

Ramson, W. (ed.) (1970) *English Transported: Essays on Australian English*, Canberra: Australian National University Press.

—— (ed.) (1988) *The Australian National Dictionary*, Melbourne: Oxford University Press.

Raumolin-Brunberg, H. (2000) 'WHICH and THE WHICH in Late Middle English: Free variants?', in Taavitsainen, I., Nevalainen, T., Pahta, P. and Rissanen, M. (eds) *Placing Middle English in Context* (Topics in English Linguistics 35), Berlin: Mouton de Gruyter, 209–25.

Rawnsley, S. (2000) 'Constructing "The North": Space and a sense of place', in Kirk, N. (ed.) *Northern Identities*, Aldershot: Ashgate, 3–22.

Ray, J. (1670) *A Collection of English Proverbs* (2nd edn, 1678), London: J. Hayes for W. Mordern.

—— (1674) *A Collection of English Words*, Menston, UK: Scolar Press.

Reed, A. and Kellogg, B. (1886) *Higher Lessons in English*, Delmar, NY: Scholars' Facsimiles and Reprints.

Rickert, W. (1978) 'Commercializing elocution: "Parlor books" for home entertainments', *The Southern Speech Communication Journal* 43: 384–94.

Rickford, J. (1986) 'Some principles for the study of Black and White speech in the south', in Montgomery, M.B. and Bailey, G. (eds) *Language Variety in the South*, Tuscaloosa, AL: University of Alabama Press, 38–62.

Rissanen, M. (1997) 'The pronominalization of *one*', in Rissanen, M., Kytö, M. and Heikkonen, K. (eds) *Grammaticalization at Work: Studies of Long-term Developments in English*, Berlin: Mouton de Gruyter, 87–143.

—— (2000) 'Standardisation and the language of early statutes', in Wright, L. (ed.) *The Development of Standard English 1300–1800: Theories, Descriptions, Conflicts*, Cambridge: Cambridge University Press, 117–30.

Ritson, J. (1810) *The Northern Garlands* [*The Bishopric Garland* (1784), *The Yorkshire Garland* (1788), *The Northumberland Garland* (1793), *The North-Country Chorister* (1802)], Darby, PA: Norwood 1973.

Robinson, O.W. (1992) *Old English and its Closest Relatives*, Stanford, CA: Stanford University Press.

Robson, L. (1965) *The Convict Settlers of Australia*, Melbourne: Melbourne University Press.

Romaine, S. (1989) *Bilingualism*, Oxford: Basil Blackwell.

Ross, A.S.C. and Moverley, A.W. (1964) *The Pitcairnese Language*, London: Deutsch.

Rudé, G. (1964) *The Crowd in History: A Study of Popular Disturbances in France and England 1730–1848*, New York: John Wiley.

Rumsey, A. (1992) 'Wording, meaning, and linguistic ideology', *American Anthropologist* 92: 346–61.

Russell, W. (1851) *The American Elocutionist*, 5th edn, Boston: Jenks, Palmer and Co.

Ryan, J. (1973) 'Blayk is white on the Bay Islands', *Michigan Papers in Linguistics* 1: 129–39.

Rydland, R. (1999) 'Front rounded vowels in Northumberland English: The evidence of the Orton corpus', in Upton, C. and Wales, K. (eds) *Dialectal Variation in English: Proceedings of the Harold Orton Centenary Conference 1998*, Leeds Studies in English, n.s. 30, 1–15.

Saussure, F. de (1983), *Course in General Linguistics*, trans. R. Harris, London: Duckworth.

Schendl, H. (1994) 'The 3rd plural present indicative in Early Modern English – variation and linguistic contact', in Britton, B. (ed.) *English Historical Linguistics 1994: Papers from the 8th International Conference on English Historical Linguistics*, Amsterdam: John Benjamins, 143–60.

Schenkein, J. (1978) 'Explanation of transcript notation', in Schenkein, J. (ed.) *Studies in the Organization of Conversational Interaction*, New York: Academic, xi–xvi.

Schiffrin, D. (1987) *Discourse Markers*, Cambridge: Cambridge University Press.

Schreier, D. (forthcoming a) 'Third-person singular zero in Tristan da Cunha English'.

—— (forthcoming b) 'The English of Tristan da Cunha', unpublished Ph.D. thesis, Fribourg University.

Schreier, D., Sudbury, A. and Wilson, S. (forthcoming) 'English in the South Atlantic', in Ammon, U., Dittmar, N., Mattheier, K. and Trudgill, P. (eds) *Sociolinguistics: An International Handbook of the Science of Language and Society*, 2nd edn, Berlin: de Gruyter.

Scott, D. (1980) 'The popular lecture and the creation of a public in mid-nineteenth-century America', *The Journal of American History* 66: 791–809.

Sey, K.A. (1973) *Ghanaian English*, London: Macmillan.

Shaftesbury, Anthony Ashley Cooper, the 3rd Earl of (1711) *Characteristicks of Men, Manners, Opinions, Times: An Inquiry Concerning Virtue or Merit*, London.

Sheridan, T. (1762) *A Course of Lectures on Elocution*, London: Millar, Dodsley *et al.*

—— (1780) *A General Dictionary of the English Language*, facsimile reprint, 1967, Menston, UK: Scolar Press.

Shilling, A. (1982) 'Bahamian English – a non-continuum?', in Day, R. (ed.) *Issues in English Creoles*, Heidelberg: Julius Groos, 133–46.

Shivachi, C. (1999) 'A case study in language contact: English, KiSwahili and Luhyia amongst the Luhyia People of Kenya', unpublished Ph.D. thesis, University of Cape Town.

Shnukal, A. (1982) 'You're getting' somethink for nothing: two phonological variables of Australian English', *Australian Journal of Linguistics* 2: 197–212.

Shorrocks, G. (1996) 'Non-standard dialect literature and popular culture', in Klemola, J., Kytö, M. and Rissanen, M. (eds) *Speech Past and Present*, Frankfurt: Peter Lang, 385–411.

—— (1997) 'Field methods and non-standard grammar', in Ramish, H. and Wynne, K. (eds) *Language in Time and Space*, Stuttgart: Franz Steiner, 212–22.

Shortland, M. (1987) 'Moving speeches: Language and elocution in eighteenth-century Britain', *History of European Ideas* 8: 639–53.

Sichel, W. (1909) *Sheridan*, vol. I, London: Constable and Company.

Sigley, R. (1997) 'Choosing your relatives: relative clauses in New Zealand English', unpublished Ph.D. thesis, Victoria University, Wellington.

Silva, P. (1996) *A Dictionary of South African English on Historical Principles*, Oxford: Oxford University Press.

Simpson, T. (1997) *The Immigrants: the Great Migration from Britain to New Zealand, 1830–1890*, Auckland: Godwit.

Sivertsen, E. (1960) *Cockney Phonology*, Oslo: Oslo University Press.

Skeat, W. (1873) *Questions for Examination in English Literature*, Cambridge: Cambridge University Press.

—— (1897) 'The Proverbs of Alfred', *Transactions of the Philological Society*.

—— (ed.) (1911) *Nine Specimens of English Dialects*, London: Oxford University Press.

Sledd, J. and Ebbitt, W. (eds) (1962) *Dictionaries and that Dictionary*, Chicago: Scott, Foresman.

Slobin, D. (1973) 'Cognitive prerequisites for the development of grammar', in Ferguson, C.A. and Slobin, D.I. (eds) *Studies of Child Language Development*, New York: Holt, Rinehart and Wilson, 175–208.

Smith, C.W. (1855) *Common Blunders Made in Speaking and Writing, Corrected on the Authority of the Best Grammarians*, n.p.

Smith, J. (1996) *An Historical Study of English*, London: Routledge.

Smith, O. (1984) *The Politics of Language 1791–1819*, Oxford: Oxford University Press.

Smollett, T. (1771) *Humphry Clinker*, Signet edition (1960), New York.

Sparks, A. (1990) *The Mind of South Africa*, London: Heinemann.

Spectator, The (1803) *The British Classics*, 8 vols, London: Sharpe.

Steele, R. (1709) 'The Gentleman; The Pretty Fellow', *The Tatler*, No. 21, Saturday May 28th, in *The Norton Anthology of English Literature*, 6th edn, vol. 1.

—— (1711) *The Spectator*, No. 147, August 18th, in Bond, D. (ed.) (1965) *The Spectator*, vol. II, 78–81, Oxford: Clarendon Press.

Strang, B.M.H. (1970) *A History of English*, London: Methuen and Co. Ltd.

Sudbury, A. (2000) 'Dialect contact and koineisation in the Falkland Islands: the development of a Southern Hemisphere English?', unpublished Ph.D. thesis, University of Essex.

Sundby, B., Bjørge, A.K. and Haugland, K.E. (1991) *A Dictionary of English Normative Grammar 1700–1800*, Amsterdam: John Benjamins.

Swann, J. (1996) 'Stye shifting, code switching', in Graddol, D., Leith, D. and Swann, J. (eds) *English History, Diversity and Change*, London: Routledge, 301–37.

Sweet, H. (1877), 'Dialects and prehistoric forms of Old English', *Transactions of the Philological Society 1875–6* (London, 1877): 543–69.

—— (1890) *A Primer of Spoken English*, Oxford.

—— (1967) *Anglo-Saxon Reader*, revised by Dorothy Whitelock, Oxford: Clarendon Press.

—— (1971) *The Indispensable Foundation*, edited by E. Henderson, Oxford: Oxford University Press.

Swift, J. (1712) *A Proposal for Correcting, Improving and Ascertaining the English Tongue in a Letter to the Most Honourable Robert Earl of Oxford and Mortimer, Lord High Treasurer of Great Britain*, London: Benjamin Tooke.

—— (1738/1963) *Polite Conversation*, with 'Introduction, Notes and Extensive Commentary' by E. Partridge, London: Andre Deutsch.

Taavitsainen, I. (1995) 'Interjections in Early Modern English: From imitation of spoken to conventions of written language', in Jucker, A.H. (ed.) *Historical Pragmatics: Pragmatic Developments in the History of English*, Amsterdam: Benjamins, 439–65.

Tagliamonte, S. (1991) 'A matter of time: Past temporal reference verbal structures in Samaná English and the Ex-slave Recordings', unpublished Ph.D. dissertation, University of Ottawa.

—— (1999) '*Come/came* variation in English: Where did it come from and which way is it going?', paper presented at *American Dialect Society*, Los Angeles, CA.

Tagliamonte, S. and Poplack, S. (1993) 'The zero-marked verb: Testing the creole hypothesis', *Journal of Pidgin and Creole Languages* 8: 171–206.

Tagliamonte, S. and Smith, J. (2000) 'Old *was*; new ecology: Viewing English through the sociolinguistic filter', in Poplack, S. (ed.) *The English History of African American English*, Oxford: Blackwell Publishers, 141–71.

Tatler, The (1803) *The British Classics*, 4 vols, London: Sharpe.

Taylor, J. (1991) 'Remarks on the KIN-PIN vowels in South African English', *English World Wide* 12: 75–85.

Thomason, S.G. and Kaufman, T. (1988) *Language Contact, Creolization and Genetic Linguistics*, Berkeley, CA: University of California Press.

Thompson, L. (1990) *A History of South Africa*, Newhaven: Yale University Press.

Thompson, S.A. and Mulac, A. (1991) 'A quantitative perspective on the grammaticization of epistemic parentheticals in English', in Traugott, E.C. and Heine, B. (eds) *Approaches to Grammaticalization*, 2 vols, Amsterdam: Benjamins, 313–29.

Tidholm, H. (1979) *The Dialect of Egton in North Yorkshire*, Göteborg: Bokmaskine.

Tottie, G. and Harvie, D. (2000) 'It's all relative: Relativization strategies in early African American English', in Poplack, S. (ed.) *The English History of African American English*, Oxford: Blackwell Publishers, 198–230.

Traugott, E.C. (1989) 'On the rise of epistemic meanings in English: An example of subjectification in semantic change', *Language* 65: 31–55.

—— (1995) 'Subjectification in grammaticalisation', in Stein, D. and Wright, S. (eds) *Subjectivity and Subjectivisation: Linguistic Perspectives*, Cambridge: Cambridge University Press, 31–54.

Troup, F. (1972) *South Africa: An Historical Introduction*, Methuen: London.

Trudgill, P. (1972) 'Sex, covert prestige, and linguistic change in the urban British English of Norwich', *Language in Society* 1: 179–95.

—— (1986) *Dialects in Contact*, Oxford: Blackwell.

—— (1990) *The Dialects of England*, Oxford: Blackwell.

—— (1996) 'Dual source pidgins and reverse creoles: northern perspectives on language contact', in Broch, I. and Jahr, E.H. (eds) *Language Contact in the Arctic: Northern Pidgins and Contact Languages*, Berlin: Mouton de Gruyter, 5–14.

—— (1999) 'Standard English: What it isn't', in Bex, T. and Watts, R.J. (eds) *Standard English: The Widening Debate*, London: Routledge, 117–28.

—— (2000) 'Sociohistorical linguistics and dialect survival: a note on another Nova Scotian exclave', in Ljung, M. (ed.) *Linguistic Structure and Variation*, Stockholm: Stockholm University Press.

Trudgill, P. and Chambers, J.K. (eds) (1991) *Dialects of English: Studies in Grammatical Variation*, London: Longman.

Trudgill, P. and Hannah, J. (1994) *International English: An Introduction to Varieties of Standard English*, 3rd edn, London: Edward Arnold.

Trudgill, P., Gordon, E. and Lewis, G. (1998) 'New dialect formation and Southern Hemisphere English: The New Zealand short front vowels', *Journal of Sociolinguistics* 2: 35–51.

Trudgill, P., Gordon, E., Lewis, G. and Maclagan, M. (2000) 'The role of drift in the formation of native-speaker southern hemisphere Englishes. Some New Zealand evidence', *Diachronica* XVII, 1.111–38.

Trudgill, P., Long, D., Schreier D. and Williams, J.P. (forthcoming) 'On the reversibility of mergers: /w/, /v/ and evidence from lesser-known Englishes'.

Turner, G. (1966) (1972, 2nd edition) *The English Language in Australia and New Zealand*, London: Longman.

—— (1967) 'Samuel McBurney's newspaper article on colonial pronunciation', *AUMLA (Australasian Universities Modern Languages Association)* 27: 81–5.

—— (1994) 'English in Australia', in Burchfield, R. (ed.) *The Cambridge History of the English Language. Volume V: English in Britain and Overseas*, Cambridge: Cambridge University Press, 551–68.

Valdman, A. (1977) 'Creolization: elaboration in the development of creole French dialects', in Valdman, A. (ed.) *Pidgin and Creole Linguistics*, Bloomington, IN: Indiana University Press.

Vanbrugh, J. (1697) *The Relapse; or Virtue in Danger*. London: Printed for Samuel Briscoe. Reproduced in *English Prose Drama Full-text Database*, 1996: Cambridge: Chadwyck-Healey.

Vandenhoff, G. (1845) *A Plain System of Elocution or Logical and Musical Reading and Declamation*, 2nd edn, New York: C. Shepard.

Van Herk, G. (1999) 'The ain't complaint: Negation that isn't in Early African-American English letters', paper presented at Methods X, Memorial University of Newfoundland.

—— (2000) 'Inversion in Early African American English questions', in Poplack, S. (ed.) *The English History of African American English*, Oxford: Blackwell Publishers, 175–97.

Vorlat, E. (1975) *The Development of English Grammatical Theory 1586–1737 with Special Reference to the Theory of Parts of Speech*, Leuven: Leuven University Press.

Wakelin, M.F. (1972) *English Dialects: An Introduction* (revised edition 1977), London: Athlone Press.

Wales, K. (2000) 'North and south: An English linguistic divide?', *English Today* 16(1), 4–15.

Walker, J. (1781) *Elements of Elocution*, vols I and II, Facsimile reprint 1969, Menston, UK: Scolar Press.

—— (1791) *A Critical Pronouncing Dictionary*, Menston, UK: Scolar Press.

Walker, J.A. (2000) 'Rephrasing the copula: Contracted and zero copula in Early African American English', in Poplack, S. (ed.) *The English History of African American English*, Oxford: Blackwell Publishers, 35–72.

Wall, A. (1958) '"The way I have come". Broadcast talk'. Christchurch: Radio New Zealand Sound Archives.

Wallis, J. (1653/1969) *Grammatica Linguae Anglicanae*, Menston, UK: Scolar Press.

Warantz, E. (1983) 'The Bay Islands English of Honduras', in Holm, J. (ed.) *Central American English*, Heidelberg: Julius Groos, 71–94.

Warren, P. and Britain, D. (2000) 'Intonation and prosody in New Zealand English', in Bell, A. and Kuiper, K. (eds) *New Zealand English*, Amsterdam: Benjamins, 146–172.

Washabaugh, W. (1977) 'Constraining variation in decreolization', *Language* 53: 329–52.

—— (1983) 'Creoles of the off-shore islands', in Holm, J. (ed.) *Central American English*, Heidelberg: Julius Groos, 157–80.

Waswo, R. (1987) *Language and Meaning in the Renaissance*, Princeton: Princeton University Press.

Watermeyer, S. (1996) 'Afrikaans English', in DeKlerk, V. (ed.) *Focus on South Africa*, Amsterdam: John Benjamins, 99–124.

Watt, D. and Milroy, L. (1999) 'Patterns of variation and change in three Newcastle vowels: Is this dialect levelling?', in Foulkes, P. and Doherty, G. (eds) *Urban Voices*, London: Arnold, 25–46.

Watts, R.J. (1999a) 'Language and politeness in early eighteenth century Britain', *Pragmatics* 9: 5–20.

—— (1999b) 'The social construction of standard English: Grammar writers as a "discourse community"', in Bex, T. and Watts, R.J. (eds) *Standard English: The Widening Debate*, London: Routledge, 40–68.

—— (2000) 'Mythical strands in the ideology of prescriptivism', in Wright, L. (ed.) *The Development of Standard English 1300–1800: Theories, Descriptions, Conflicts*, Cambridge: Cambridge University Press, 29–48.

Webster, N. (1789/1967) *Dissertations on the English Language*, Menston, UK: Scolar Press.

Wells, J.C. (1982) *Accents of English*, Cambridge: Cambridge University Press.

—— (1984) 'English accents in England', in Trudgill, P. (ed.) *Language in the British Isles*, Cambridge: Cambridge University Press, 55–69.

West, T. (1778; 2nd edn 1779) *A Guide to the Lakes*, 2nd edn, London: W. J. and J. Richardson.

Wheeler, M. (1994 [1995]) '"Politeness", sociolinguistic theory and language change', *Folia Linguistica Historica* 15: 149–74.

Williams, A. and Kerswill, P. (1999) 'Dialect levelling: Change and continuity in Milton Keynes, Reading and Hull', in Foulkes, P. and Doherty, G. (eds) *Urban Voices*, London: Arnold, 141–61.

Williams, J. (1987) 'Non-native varieties of English: a special case of language acquisition', *English World Wide* 8: 161–99.

Williams, J.P. (1987) 'Anglo-Caribbean English: a study of its sociolinguistic history and the development of its aspectual markers', unpublished Ph.D. thesis, University of Texas, Austin.

—— (1988) 'The development of aspectual markers in Anglo-Caribbean English', *Journal of Pidgin and Creole Languages* 3, 245–63.

Wilson, H.R. (1975) 'Lunenburg Dutch: fact and folklore', in Chambers, J.K. (ed.) *Canadian English: Origins and Structures*, Toronto: Methuen.

Wilson, T. (1553) *The Arte of Rhetorique*, London: R. Graftonus.

Winford, D. (1992) 'Back to the past: The BEV/Creole connection revisited', *Language Variation and Change* 4: 311–57.

Wolfram, W. and Fasold, R. (1974) *Social Dialects and American English*, Englewood Cliffs, NJ: Prentice-Hall.

Woods, N. (1997) 'The formation and development of New Zealand English: Interaction of gender-related variation and linguistic change', *Journal of Sociolinguistics* 1: 95–125.

Wordsworth, W. (1798) *Advertisement* and *Preface* to *Lyrical Ballads* (2nd edn 1800), London.

Wright, J. (1892) *Grammar of the Dialect of Windhill in the West Riding of Yorkshire*, London: Kegan Paul, Trench and Trübner.

—— (1898–1905) *The English Dialect Grammar*, Oxford: Clarendon Press.

Wright, L. (ed.) (2000) *The Development of Standard English 1300–1800: Theories, Descriptions, Conflicts*, Cambridge: Cambridge University Press.

Wright, S. (1996) 'Accents of English', in Graddol, D., Leith, D. and Swann, J. (eds) *English History, Diversity and Change*, London: Routledge, 259–300.

Wyld, H.C. (1927) *Short History of English*, 3rd edn, London: John Murray.

—— (1936) *A History of Modern Colloquial English*, 3rd edn, Oxford: Basil Blackwell.

Yeager, W. (1943) 'Wendell Phillips', in Brigance, W. (ed.) *A History and Criticism of American Public Address*, vol. 1, New York: McGraw-Hill, 329–62.

Young Man's Own Book (1838) *Young Man's Own Book: A Manual of Politeness, Intellectual Improvement and Moral Deportment*, London.

Zettersten, A. (1969) *Lund Studies in English*, Lund: Gleerup.

Zuill, W.S. (1973) *The Story of Bermuda and her People*, London: Macmillan.

Index

Vanbrugh, Sir John 191
Vandenhoff, G. 177, 185
Vanuatu 30
variance and legitimisation 10
variation: conditioning of 98–100;
  gender consistency in 206;
  inferences from the OGREVE 95–7;
  mining in the OGREVE for 93–100
verb-class membership in AAVE 102–5
verbal -*s* function: in AAVE 105–6; in
  third-person plural in Early AAV 108
Victorian: 'corruptions' 12, 14;
  perspective on historicity 17
Virgin Islands 29
'vulgarisms' and legitimisation 11

Wales 29, 238
Walker, John 54–5, 178, 188, 240
Wandesford, Christopher 198
Wash–Severn linguistic divide 48–9
Washington, DC 141
Watford Gap 47, 51
Webster, Noah 148
*Webster's Third New International
  Dictionary* 149
Wentworth, Sir Thomas 198–9, 201, 202
Wesley, John 176
West, Thomas 56
Wilson, Joe 58
Wilson, Thomas 53

Wolof culture 135
women's writings: CEEC *(Corpus of Early
  English Correspondence)* 193, 194–5,
  197–9, 201–5; discourse style 195–6,
  197–200; *An Essay in the Defence of the
  Female Sex* (anon., 1696) 207; gender
  advantage in language change 204–
  5; gender variation, consistency in
  206; historical gender differences
  207; language change 196–7, 200–5;
  linguistic change 197–205; markers
  of involvement 197–200; private
  writings 193–4; published writings
  193; sociolinguistics 195–7; spelling
  206–7; supralocal language change
  200–5; textual resources 193–5;
  written registers 206
Wordsworth, William 56, 57, 239
working-class solidarity, dialect as
  marker 61–2
world status of Standard English 15
Wright, Joseph 62
written registers, women's 206
Wyld, Henry Cecil 10, 11, 14, 191–2,
  205–6

Yorkshire Dialogues 58–9
Young Man's Own Book (London, 1838)
  184

Zimbabwe 30, 43